Standard Grade PHYSICS

McCormick and Baillie

Hodder & Stoughton

A MEMBER OF THE HODDER HEADLINE GROUP

Preface

This book covers both the general and credit level material for the Standard Grade Physics course. Credit material has been set in tinted boxes. Questions are given at the end of each chapter and answers are available as a separate edition of the book (ISBN 0-340-66414-2).

Physics has many applications in everyday life and this is the central theme of the course. We have attempted to develop these ideas in all aspects of the book. Hopefully, this book will encourage you to see Physics as part of your future.

We would like to thank many people for their help and support in making this book possible. To Rothwell Glen for his help, advice and for his care and attention to editorial work. Any errors or omissions are our own. At Hodder and Stoughton we would like to thank Catherine Boulton for encouraging us to write the book and Sarah Kilvington for putting the manuscript into an acceptable editorial form. Many thanks, also, to SEB for permission to reproduce past exam questions.

Our thanks to colleagues and pupils who have often unwittingly given us insights into issues in physics education.

Finally our thanks to our families who have had forbearance for this task.

British Library Cataloguing in Publication Data

McCormick, Andrew K.
   Standard Grade Physics. – (Standard Grade science)
     1.Physics 2.Physics – Examinations – Study guides 3.Physics – Problems, exercises, etc.
   I.Title II.Baillie, Arthur E.
   530

ISBN 0–340–65854–1

First published 1997
Impression number   10 9 8 7 6 5 4 3 2 1
Year   2002 2001 2000 1999 1998 1997

Copyright © 1997 Andrew McCormick and Arthur Baillie

All rights reserved. No part of this publication may be reproduced or transmitted in any form or by any means, electronic or mechanical, including photocopy, recording, or any information storage and retrieval system, without permission in writing from the publisher or under licence from the Copyright Licensing Agency Limited. Further details of such licences (for reprographic reproduction) may be obtained from the Copyright Licensing Agency Limited, of 90 Tottenham Court Road, London W1P 9HE.

Typeset by Wearset, Boldon, Tyne and Wear.
Printed in Great Britain for Hodder & Stoughton Educational, a division of Hodder Headline Plc, 338 Euston Road, London NW1 3BH by Scotprint Ltd, Musselburgh, Scotland.

Contents

1 Telecommunication — 2
1.1 Communication through the air and wires — 3
1.2 Waves and wave patterns — 5
1.3 Radio, television and mobile phones — 7
1.4 Sending signals by light (fibre optics — 14
1.5 Dish aerials and satellites — 17
1.6 Modern communications — 20
Study questions — 23

2 Using electricity — 25
2.1 From the wall socket — 25
2.2 Alternating and direct current — 28
2.3 Resistance — 30
2.4 Useful circuits — 34
2.5 Behind the wall — 41
2.6 Movement from electricity — 44
Study questions — 50

3 Health physics — 52
3.1 Using thermometers — 52
3.2 Using sound — 55
3.3 Light and sight — 59
3.4 Using the spectrum — 64
3.5 The atom and radiation — 70
Study questions — 81

4 Electronics — 85
4.1 Overview — 85
4.2 Output devices — 86
4.3 Input devices — 90
4.4 Digital processes — 96
4.5 Analogue processes — 104
Study questions — 109

5 Transport — 112
5.1 Speed — 112
5.2 May the force be with you — 116
5.3 Movement means energy — 123
Study questions — 133

6 Energy matters — 137
6.1 Supply and demand — 137
6.2 Generation of electricity — 142
6.3 Source to consumer — 146
6.4 Heat in the home — 153
Study questions — 162

7 Space physics — 164
7.1 Space: the final frontier — 164
7.2 Jets and rockets — 170
Study questions — 183

8 Data sheet — 186

9 Electrical and electronic graphical symbols — 187

Index — 188

Acknowledgements — 190

1 Telecommunication

Brian and some friends had decided to go climbing. They were well equipped with a map, compass, suitable clothing and had left a note of their climb and the time that they expected to be home. However, Duncan fell halfway through the climb and hurt his ankle which began to swell, so he couldn't walk. They shouted to some people they saw but the sound was carried away in the wind. They signalled with their hands but nobody noticed them because they were too far away. Eventually one of the group thought of using her mobile phone and called the emergency services. The police contacted the rescue service and the helicopter pilot called back on the short waveband of the radio. Finally help arrived and Duncan was helped to safety before the mist and the air temperature dropped on the mountain.

Communication is when information (a message) is successfully transmitted or sent and received. We live at a time when communication is an important part of everyday life. We use faxes and the telephone in many businesses. Many people use mobile phones and the Internet. In 200 years we have gone from talking and writing, to telephoning, to browsing the Web. This chapter explains the ideas behind various forms of modern communications and examines how Physics is important to communication in five different ways:

1. Communication through the air and wires.
2. The properties and uses of waves.
3. Radio, television and mobile phones.
4. Fibre optics.
5. Dish aerials and satellites.

Here are some important events in communications:

Event	Date
Samuel Morse uses his code to send a message	1835
Cooke and Wheatstone use the electric telegraph on the railways	1837
James Clerk Maxwell from Edinburgh shows mathematically that electricity can be sent as waves	1864
Alexander Graham Bell develops the telephone	1876
Heinrich Hertz shows that electricity can be sent as waves	1888
Marconi sends the first wireless message across the English Channel	1899
First radio broadcast in the UK and USA	1920
John Logie Baird demonstrates television	1926
First video recorder	1958
Communications satellite launched called 'Telstar'	1962

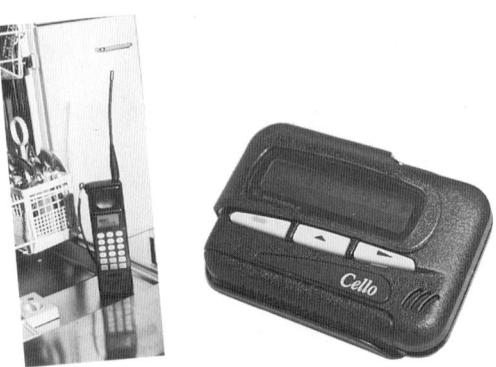

FIGURE 1.1 *Modern communications. How many have you seen being used?*

3 a) A *species* is a group of living things that are so similar to one another genetically that they are able to interbreed and produce fertile offspring. *Speciation* is the process by which new species are formed. (2)
   b) If a population of organisms becomes *isolated* from the other members of its species, it may undergo *speciation* and eventually become a new species. This happens if *natural selection* follows a different path in this new environment and some *mutations* that would have been neutral or disadvantageous before now confer an *advantage* on the organisms. (4)

4 a) F – mutation (1)
   b) F – a disadvantage (1)
   c) T (1)
   d) F – adaptation (1)
   e) T (1)

Applying Your Knowledge and Skills Answers

Chapters 1–6

1. a) Row 2 (1)
   b) Row 3 (1)
   c) Row 5 (1)
2. a) 10 μm (1)
   b) 0.007 mm (1)
   c) 8 μm (1)
3. a) 1 = C, 2 = A, 3 = B (3)
   b) Cylinder 1 is firm and larger because it has taken in water by osmosis from a region of HWC (water). Cylinder 2 is rubbery and smaller because it has lost water by osmosis from a region of HWC (cell contents) to a region of LWC (very concentrated sugar solution). Cylinder 3 is unchanged because it has neither gained nor lost water by osmosis since the dilute sugar solution is equal in water concentration to the contents of the turnip cells. (3)
4. a) i) X = diffusion, Y = active transport
      ii) Y
      iii) X (4)
   b) i) It will decrease.
      ii) The process of active transport requires energy from respiration but respiration decreases at lower temperatures. (2)
5. a) Box P = 22.7, box Q = 29.8 (2)
   b) i) In a DNA molecule, the number of A bases equals the number of T bases and the number of G bases equals the number of C bases.
      ii) Yes
      iii) In each species, %A = %T and %G = %C. (3)
6. a) See Figure An KS1.1. (3)

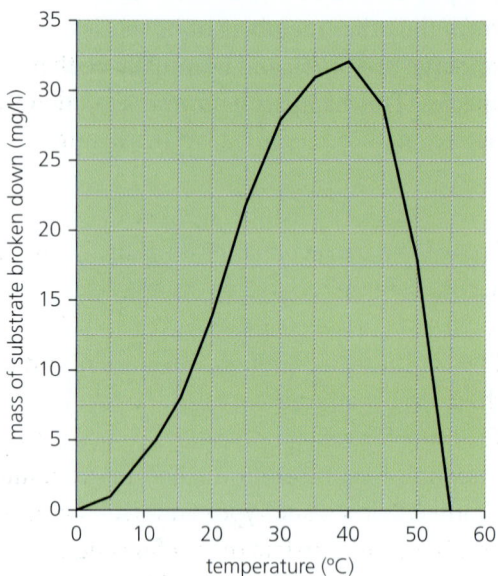

Figure An KS1.1

   b) i) Optimum temperature means the temperature at which an enzyme works best.
      ii) 40 °C (2)
   c) i) 2 times
      ii) As temperature increases from 20 °C to 30 °C, the rate of molecular movements and the frequency of collisions between enzyme and substrate molecules increase. A greater number of enzyme-substrate complexes are formed at the higher temperature, resulting in a doubling of the reaction rate. (3)
   d) 20 to 25 °C (1)
   e) The enzyme molecules have become denatured and their active sites have been permanently destroyed. (1)
   f) 0 g (1)

Applying Your Knowledge and Skills Answers

7   a) X = 0.5–4.5, Y = 5–9, Z = 8–12 (3)
    b) i) It is equal for each of these enzymes.
       ii) There is no part of the pH working range that they all share. (2)
    c) X = 2.5, Y = 7, Z = 10 (3)
    d) i) Y
       ii) X (2)

8   a) Ethics means the rules and principles that ought to govern human behaviour so that the right thing is done instead of the wrong thing. (2)
    b) For: **A, C, D, H**. Against: **B, E, F, G**. (2)
    c) There is no correct answer for **i)** or **ii)** since it depends on the person's own opinion.

9   a) A chemical that acts as a weedkiller. (1)
    b) The plant cannot photosynthesise without chloroplasts so it dies of starvation. (1)
    c) The gene for resistance to herbicide is extracted from one type of bacterium and inserted into another. The second type can infect plants with its DNA so it transfers the useful gene to some plants on infecting them. By this means one or more GM plants resistant to herbicide are produced. (3)
    d) 90% (1)
    e) A gene that deactivates glufosinate was found to occur in species of *Streptomyces* bacteria. (1)

10 a) A valid comparison between two set-ups can only be made if they differ by the one factor being investigated (in this case, type of food) and by no other.
       i)   A and B fail because they have the same food and differ from one another in two ways – needle or spoon and volume of water.
       ii) A and C fail because they have the same food and differ from one another in two ways – mass of food and volume of water.
       iii) Although A and E have different foods, they fail because they also differ from one another in two other ways – needle or spoon and mass of food. (6)
    b) C's volume of water would need to be reduced to 50 cm³, its mass of food reduced to 1 g and its mounted needle exchanged for a spoon. (3)
    c) i) Peanut = 9.24 kJ, glucose = 5.04 kJ
       ii) Heat lost to the surroundings is greatly reduced by the burning food being enclosed in the food calorimeter and by the presence of a coiled chimney. Both of these promote maximum transfer of heat energy to the water. Burning the food in air enriched with oxygen (instead of normal atmospheric air) ensures that the food is burned to ashes and that all of its energy has been released. (4)

11 a) As carbon dioxide concentration increases, pH decreases. (1)
    b) A has turned purple because most of the CO_2 originally dissolved in the liquid has been used by the plants during photosynthesis in bright light. B has turned yellow because no photosynthesis occurred in darkness but the plants have continued to respire and give out CO_2. C has remained red because the quantity of CO_2 taken in for photosynthesis in dim light is equal to the quantity of CO_2 given out by respiration. (6)
    c) i) The time would decrease.
       ii) A larger surface area of plant material would be exposed to the light, making the rate of photosynthesis increase. (2)

Chapters 7–13

1   a) C (1)
    b) 13 hours (1)
    c) 65% (1)
2   a) i) 300
       ii) 3 (2)
    b) C (1)
    c) 16 hours (1)
    d) They had run out of both food and oxygen. (2)
3   Its small size and concave shape enable it to present a relatively large surface area for uptake of oxygen. (2)
4   See Table KS 2.1. (9)

System	Organ(s)	Function
digestive	stomach, intestines	digestion
excretory	kidneys, bladder	elimination of wastes
respiratory	lungs, trachea	exchange of gases
reproductive	ovaries, testes	production of sex cells
nervous	brain	co-ordination of body
circulatory	heart and blood vessels	transport of blood

Table An KS2.1

Applying Your Knowledge and Skills Answers

5 a) B, C, F, G (1)
   b) A, D, E, H (1)
6 a) 1 = D, 2 = F, 3 = B, 4 = E, 5 = C, 6 = A (1)
   b) It makes the leg move away from the danger quickly without needing time to think about it. (1)
   c) The *stimulus* that triggers this reflex action is the piece of dirt and the *receptor* is the surface of the eye. An impulse is sent via the sensory, inter and motor neurons to the *effector*, which is the tear gland. The *response* it makes is the secretion of tears. This is of *protective value* because the dirt is washed out of the eye. (5)
7 a) See Figure An KS2.1. (4)

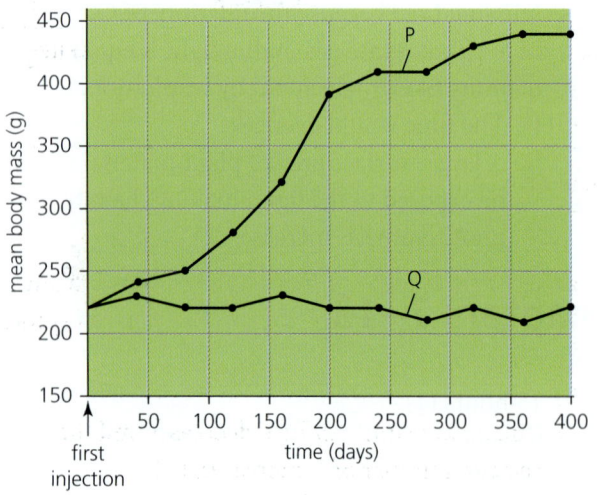

Figure An KS2.1

   b) It remained unchanged. (1)
   c) It promotes increase in body mass. (1)
   d) i) To prevent a second variable factor being included in the experiment.
      ii) Temperature and food supply (other answers also possible) (3)
   e) The experiment could be repeated several times and a much larger number of rats could be used. (2)
8 a) C (1)
   b) A (1)
   c) C (1)
9 a) 1, 2, 3 and 4 are diploid; 5 and 7 are haploid. (2)
   b) Gamete formation (1)
   c) Fertilisation (1)
   d) Growth/cell division (1)

10 a) B (1)
   b) A (1)
   c) i) Arch = 10%, compound = 5%, loop = 70%, whorl = 15%
      ii) See Figure An KS2.2. (4)

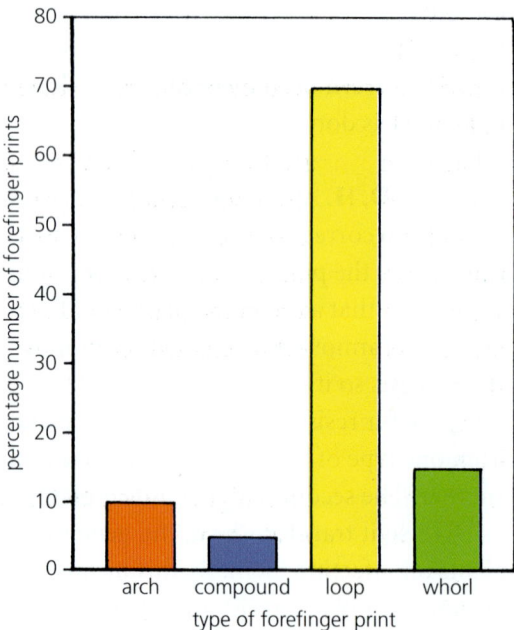

Figure An KS2.2

   d) See Table An KS2.2 (other answers also possible). (4)

Discrete variation	Continuous variation
i) would definitely be exactly alike	ii) could differ from one another
blood group	height
tongue rolling ability/ inability	body mass

Table An KS2.2

11 a) Black and red (2)
   b) Black (1)
   c) BB × bb
       ↓
      all Bb (2)
   d) i) No
      ii) Because they will produce both black and red offspring. (2)

Applying Your Knowledge and Skills Answers

12 a) i) Increase in temperature reduces time taken.
　　 ii) Increase in wind speed reduces time taken.
　　 iii) Darkness increases time taken. (3)
　 b) There were two variable factors involved at the same time. (1)
　 c) 9 (1)
　 d) 4 and 8 (1)
　 e) 5 and 6 (1)
13 a) It had been produced by photosynthesis. (1)
　 b) Phloem (1)
　 c) It had been changed to sugar and transported from leaf B down to other parts of the plant. (1)
　 d) No phloem was present at the region where the ring of tissue had been removed so transport of sugar from leaf A down the plant could not take place. Therefore leaf A retained most of its starch. (2)
14 a) i) C
　　 ii) A
　　 iii) Blood at site C has higher concentration of CO_2 than blood at site A. (3)
　 b) i) C
　　 ii) A
　　 iii) B (2)
　 c) X = pulmonary vein, Y = pulmonary artery (2)
　 d) 3, 5, 4, 2, 1 (1)

Chapters 14–19

1 a) T (1)
　 b) F – smaller (1)
　 c) T (1)
　 d) F – rabbits (1)
　 e) F – more (1)
　 f) F – primary (1)
2 a) 7.1 ppm (1)
　 b) 4 (1)
　 c) H (1)
　 d) 3 (1)
　 e) 6 (1)
　 f) i) The higher the concentration of calcium, the greater the number of species of snail present.
　　 ii) Snails need calcium to make their shells so if plenty of calcium is available this will create ideal conditions for many species of snail to thrive without having to compete fiercely with one another for calcium. (2)

3 a) See Table An KS3.1. (4)

Feature of experimental design	Reason
equal mass of cotton wool and equal volume of water added to each carton	to ensure that the cartons differ only by the one variable factor under investigation
yoghurt cartons are encased in black paper or painted black	to create competitive conditions where light is available from above only
only recently purchased cress seeds are used	to ensure that seeds are viable and capable of growth
experiment is repeated many times and results are pooled	to improve the reliability of the results

Table An KS3.1

　 b) Add a transparent lid to each carton. (1)
4 a) An inverse relationship – as the distance from the ground increases, the total number of spiders decreases. (1)
　 b) Y (1)
　 c) The relative number of Y decreases and the relative number of X increases. (1)
　 d) i) Y will gather at A and X will gather at B.
　　 ii) End A of the tube is damp like the dense vegetation on damp soil where Y normally gathers. End B is dry like high up on sparse vegetation exposed to air, which is where X normally gathers. (2)
5 a) W = perch, X = catfish (2)
　 b) Tiny scales and two or more barbels around the mouth. (2)
　 c) Large scales and two dorsal fins, the first with spiny rays. (2)
　 d) i) Y = miller's thumb
　　 ii) Z = shad (2)
　 e) A pike has large scales and one dorsal fin whereas a miller's thumb has small scales and two dorsal fins. (2)
6　1 = B, 2 = E, 3 = C, 4 = A, 5 = D (1)
7 a) i) Light intensity
　　 ii) CO_2 concentration (2)

Applying Your Knowledge and Skills Answers

b) The apparatus containing the water plant was immersed in a thermostatically controlled water bath. (1)
c) Light intensity (1)
d) 5 units (1)
e) i) Light intensity
   ii) Temperature (2)

8 a) 1% (1)
   b) 90% (1)
   c) 5600 (1)

9 a) plant plankton → animal plankton → minnow → grebe (1)
   b) See Table An KS3.2. (2)

Organism	Concentration of DDT (ppm)
plant plankton	0.04
animal plankton	0.16
minnow	0.96
grebe	6.00

Table An KS3.2

   c) i) 800 times
      ii) Between animal plankton and minnow. (2)
   d) i) Grebe
      ii) It had the highest concentration of the poison in its cells as a result of bioaccumulation of pesticide. (2)
   e) Because it builds up along food chains and seriously affects the final consumers. (1)

10 a) Dosage of X-rays (1)
   b) 4 (1)
   c) Type of fruit fly and temperature of culture tubes (other answers also possible) (2)
   d) The percentage of X chromosomes showing a lethal mutation increases with increased dosage of X-rays. (1)
   e) Infrequent exposure to X-rays is harmless but frequent exposure runs the risk of mutations occurring in the person's cells. (1)

11 a) 51–5 mm (1)
   b) i) 1
      ii) 2
      iii) 2
      iv) 1 (4)
   c) A direct relationship – as one increases so does the other. (1)
   d) Sea water (1)
   e) They could allow them to interbreed and see if the subspecies when crossed can produce fertile offspring or not. (1)

telecommunication 1

Telecommunications describes communication which takes place between people who can't see or hear each other directly. The word 'tele' comes from the Greek word meaning 'at a distance'.

1.1 Communication through the air and wires

Which is faster – sound or light?

Early communications used sound and light signals to send messages. Let's compare the speed of sound with the speed of light.

Imagine a car is standing a few hundred metres away from you, and the driver sounds the horn. At the same instant, the car's headlights are switched on by a passenger. You can see the lights before the sound of the horn is heard. What does this tell us? It tells us that light travels faster than sound. But how fast does sound travel?

To answer this question we need to measure the speed of sound.

Speed is the distance travelled in one second by a moving object.

Example

June runs a distance of 200 m in 40 seconds.

$$\text{Therefore June travels } \frac{200}{40} \text{ m in 1 s}$$

$$\text{June's speed} = \frac{200}{40} = 5 \text{ m/s}$$

In our example 200 m was the distance travelled and 40 s was the time taken:

$$\text{speed} = \frac{\text{distance travelled}}{\text{time taken}}$$

Another way of saying this is:

$$v = \frac{d}{t}$$

where v = speed in metres per second

d = distance travelled in metres

t = time taken in seconds.

How can you measure the speed of sound? To do this, you will need to do the following:

- A pupil with a source of sound (e.g. two metal plates) and a pupil with an arm raised stand side by side at the end of a field.
- At the other end of the field is a pupil with a stop-watch.
- Measure the length of the field in metres.
- Get the pupil at the source to drop the arm when the sound is produced and the timekeeper to start the watch.
- When the timekeeper hears the sound, the watch is stopped and the time noted. The experiment is repeated (say, four times) and an average time calculated. There will be some uncertainty in the measurement of the time due to the timekeeper's reaction on seeing

the event happen. So it is better to repeat the measurements of the times and calculate an average for the time taken.

Typical results might be:

$$\text{Times noted} = 0.63 \text{ s}, 0.55 \text{ s}, 0.58 \text{ s}, 0.61 \text{ s}$$

$$\text{Average time} = \frac{0.63 + 0.55 + 0.58 + 0.61}{4} \text{ s} = 0.59 \text{ s}$$

$$\text{Length of field} = 200 \text{ m} = \text{distance travelled}$$

$$\text{Speed of sound} = \frac{\text{distance travelled}}{\text{average time taken}} = \frac{200}{0.59} = 339 \text{ m/s}$$

Another more accurate method is to use a computer to obtain the measurements of the time interval (figure 1.2). This eliminates the reaction time problem which exists with the previous method.

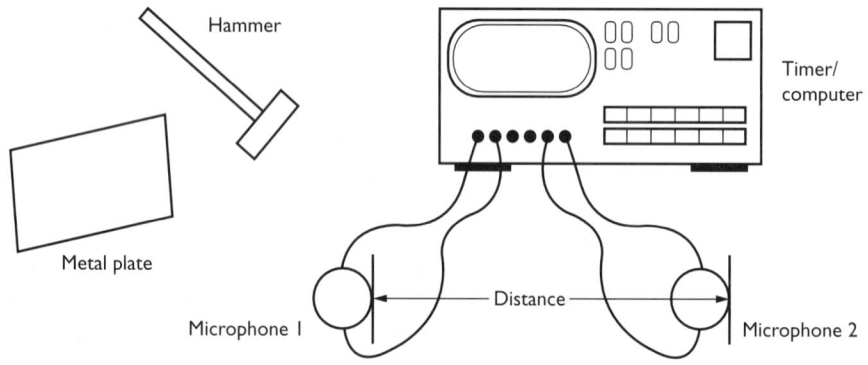

FIGURE 1.2 *Measuring the speed of sound using a timer*

- Place the microphones at least 1 m apart. The distance (d) will have to be measured precisely.
- Switch on the timer. Make a loud sound by hitting the metal plate with the hammer. When the sound reaches microphone 1, the timer starts timing. When the sound reaches microphone 2, the timer stops timing.

Distance between the microphones = 1.0 m

$$\text{Time on the timer} = 3 \text{ ms} = \frac{3}{1000} = 0.003 \text{ s} \quad (\text{ms} = \text{millisecond which is } 1/1000 \text{ s})$$

$$\text{Speed of sound} = \frac{\text{distance travelled}}{\text{time taken}} = \frac{1}{0.003} \text{ m/s}$$

$$= 333 \text{ m/s}$$

Communication

While we can send signals by sound they are very slow and we normally send large amounts of information using wires or waves. There are advantages of using communication with wires or waves:

- The volume of information that can be sent can be very large.
- Information can be sent over long distances.
- The information can be sent very quickly at almost the speed of light.

telecommunication 1

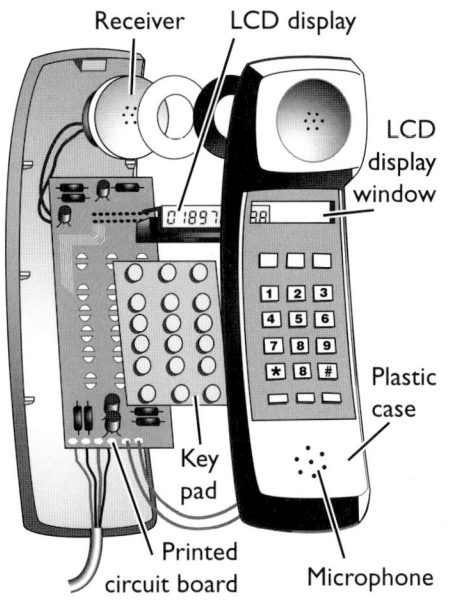

FIGURE 1.3 *Telephone handset*

The telephone

In 1876, Alexander Graham Bell, a Scotsman, sent the first spoken sentence by telephone. He was a teacher for the deaf and had been trying to help people hear messages. When working on his transmitter, he spilled some acid on his clothes. He shouted to his friend, 'Mr Watson, come here – I want you'. Mr Watson was the first person in the world to hear a message on the telephone. Bell's original machine was a transmitter and receiver. It worked well as a receiver but not as a transmitter.

Any communication system needs a transmitter and a receiver and the most common is the telephone. This consists of a microphone which acts as a transmitter (figure 1.3). There is also a loudspeaker which acts as a receiver. In addition there will be a buzzer or bell to tell us when we receive a call.

The key parts and the energy changes are shown in the table below:

Part of telephone	Transmitter or receiver	Name of electrical device inside	Energy changes that take place inside
Earpiece	receiver	loudspeaker	electrical to sound
Mouthpiece	transmitter	microphone	sound to electrical

During a telephone conversation, electrical signals are sent along the communicating wire and these can be examined using an oscilloscope. The oscilloscope shows the electrical signals on a screen.

1.2 Waves and wave patterns

Waves send energy from one part of a system to another. The water waves that roll on to a beach are sending movement energy. All waves have certain properties. A typical wave pattern is shown in figure 1.4.

- The top part of the wave is called the *crest* and the bottom part is the *trough*.
- The line running through the middle of the wave pattern is called the *axis*.
- The distance from the axis to the top of the crest or the bottom of the trough is called the *amplitude*.
- The *wavelength* is the distance after which the pattern repeats itself. It is given the symbol λ (lambda).
- All distances are measured in metres or occasionally centimetres.
- The *frequency* of the wave is the number of waves per second and is measured in hertz (Hz).

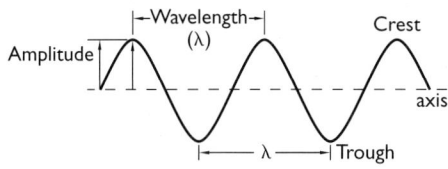

FIGURE 1.4 *Wave characteristics*

5

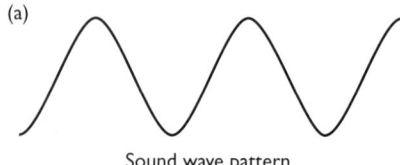
(a) Sound wave pattern

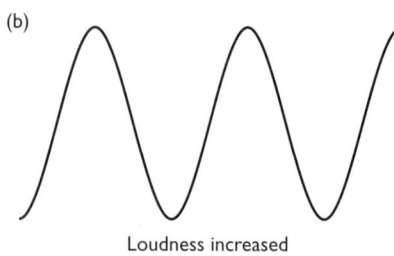
(b) Loudness increased

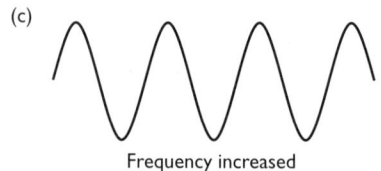
(c) Frequency increased

FIGURE 1.5 *Wave patterns on an oscilloscope*

The speed of the wave can be found from the equation we saw previously:

$$\text{speed} = \frac{\text{distance travelled}}{\text{time taken}}$$

However, the speed of the wave can also be found from:

$$\text{speed} = \text{frequency} \times \text{wavelength}$$
$$v = f \times \lambda$$
$$\text{m/s} = \text{hertz} \times \text{metres}$$

Patterns on the oscilloscope

It is possible to display wave patterns for sound signals on an oscilloscope and to see the effect of changes.

An oscilloscope displays an electrical trace of sound signals, as shown in figure 1.5 (a). If the loudness of the sound is increased, the pattern on the oscilloscope changes to that shown in figure 1.5 (b). If the frequency of the note is increased, the pattern changes to that shown in figure 1.5 (c).

These changes show us that:
- When the amplitude of a sound changes, the loudness changes but the frequency is unchanged.
- When the frequency of a sound changes, the note we hear changes but the loudness is unchanged. The term 'pitch' is used to describe how a noise or musical note sounds to us.
- The higher the pitch, the higher the frequency.

Octave

Octave is a term often used in music and is linked with frequency. If the frequency of a wave is doubled, then the sound will go up one octave.

Example: A sound is made at a frequency of 440 Hz. This sound is then increased by one octave. What is the new frequency?
Solution: The frequency is doubled so it becomes 880 Hz.

Did you know?

Graphic equalisers are used in amplifiers to increase the amplitude of the signals at different frequencies. Find out what frequencies are used and if you can hear any differences as you alter the controls.

> ### Wave calculations
> We can use the wave equations to find out about some of the features of waves.
>
> **Example:** Water waves travel from one side of a pond to the other, a distance of 8 m in 2 s. The distance between successive crests is 8 cm. Calculate the frequency of the waves.

Solution: The speed can be found from

$$v = \frac{d}{t} \text{ where } d = 8 \text{ m and } t = 2 \text{ s.}$$

This gives $v = 4$ m/s
The distance between successive crests gives
$\lambda = 8$ cm $= 0.08$ m
From $v = f \times \lambda$
$4 = f \times 0.08$

$$f = \frac{4}{0.08} = 50 \text{ Hz}$$

1.3 Radio, television and mobile phones

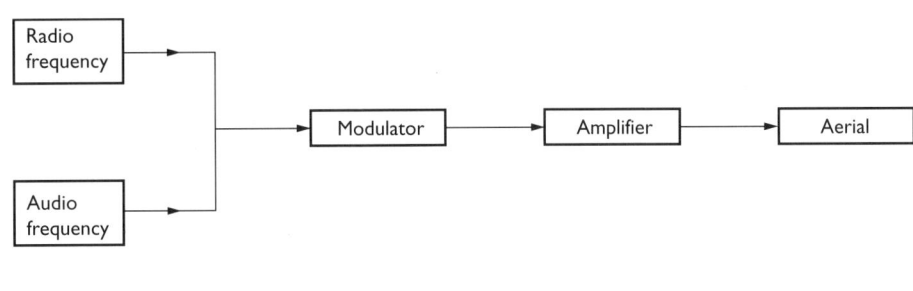

FIGURE 1.6 *Radio transmitter*

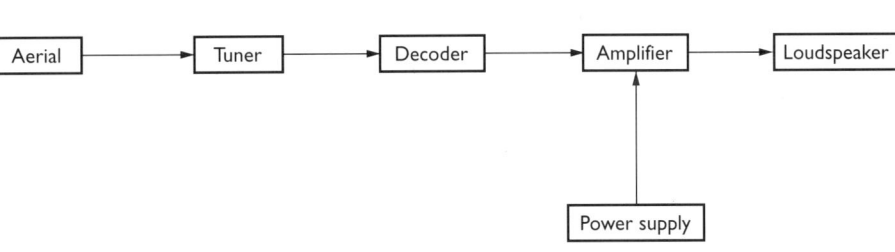

FIGURE 1.7 *A radio receiver*

All communication systems use a transmitter and receiver (figures 1.6 and 1.7). Radio and television are examples of very long-range communication which do not need wires between the transmitter and the receiver. These signals travel as waves and so carry energy. They also travel very quickly – their speed in air is 3×10^8 m/s (300 000 000 m/s).

Altering the amplitude

Sounds are transmitted by waves which have a relatively low frequency. The range of the frequencies that humans can hear is from about 20 Hz to 20 000 Hz. It is not practical to convert these low frequencies into radio waves and transmit them as they will only travel short distances. Radio waves must have frequencies of hundreds or thousands of kHz, so the radio wave must be adapted to carry the lower frequency sound wave information by altering it in some way.

standard grade physics

FIGURE 1.8 *Electrical signals carrying voice information. Audio frequency*

FIGURE 1.9 *Carrier signal. Radio frequency*

FIGURE 1.10 *Amplitude modulated radio signal*

FIGURE 1.11 *Frequency modulation*

- The sound wave is called the **audio frequency** or a.f. wave (figure 1.8). This wave is produced by the source of the sound (record player, microphone, etc.). It is produced electronically in the transmitter.
- The radio wave is also called the **radio frequency** or r.f. wave (figure 1.9). The r.f. wave can be made to carry the a.f. wave by altering its size or amplitude. For this reason it is sometimes called a 'carrier wave'.

- The r.f. amplitude is modulated by the a.f. wave – **amplitude modulation** (AM) radio. Amplitude modulation is a way of varying the amplitude of a high frequency radio wave so that it carries a low frequency audio wave. This is shown in figure 1.10.
- In a similar way, the signal can be altered by changing the frequency of the carrier wave. This is shown in figure 1.11. This is called **frequency modulation** (FM). It is often used by many radio stations. The stations can be heard with no interference but the signals do not travel as far as AM signals and more transmitters are needed.

Radio transmission

The parts of a radio transmission system are shown in figure 1.6.

- The high frequency radio and the lower frequency audio signals are electrical signals.
- The modulator combines the radio signal and the audio signal.
- This combined electrical signal is passed on to the amplifier which makes the electrical signal stronger.
- The transmitting aerial now changes the electrical signal into a radio wave and sends them out in all directions.

Radio reception

The different parts of the radio receiver are shown in figure 1.7.

The aerial
When radio waves arrive at the aerial of a radio receiver, they cause the electric charges inside the aerial to move backwards and forwards, i.e. to oscillate or vibrate. This movement of electric charges makes a small electric current. The aerial receives all of the radio signals and changes them into electrical signals.

Tuning
A radio is able to receive radio waves from many different stations. To keep the signals separate, each station transmits on a different wavelength (and therefore different frequency). The tuner selects the particular radio station you want to receive.

The decoder
When a radio signal is picked up by a receiver it has to be decoded so that it can be changed into speech or music. This separates the higher frequency carrier wave from the lower frequency audio wave which we wish to hear.

The amplifier
The signal received by the radio aerial has a very small amplitude and has

to be amplified. The amplifier increases the received signal, i.e. it makes the amplitude larger.

- The amplifier has made the signal bigger and so it now has more energy. This extra energy is supplied from the battery or electrical supply connected to the amplifier.
- The amplitude of the output signal is controlled by the variable resistor on the amplifier unit. On a radio this is called the 'volume control'.

Listening

The decoded and amplified signal must now be turned into sound energy so you can hear it. This requires a loudspeaker. The loudspeaker changes electrical energy into sound energy.

- When the frequency is increased, the diaphragm vibrates rapidly and a high pitched note is produced.
- When the output control is increased, the current through the coil is increased and the vibrations of the diaphragm are much larger, and a louder sound is produced.

The radio spectrum

This table illustrates the radio frequency bands in the UK:

Radio waveband	Frequency range	Wavelength range	Use and example(s)
Low frequency (long wave)	30 kHz–300 kHz	10 km–1 km	Medium to long distance. Radio 4 (200 kHz/1500 m)
Medium frequency (medium wave)	300 kHz–3 MHz	1 km–100 m	Both local and distant sound broadcasts. Ship–shore links. Radio Scotland (810 m); Radio Forth (194 m)
High frequency (short wave)	3 MHz–30 MHz	100 m–10 m	Long distance communication, ship–shore links, navigation, radio beacons, amateur radio, C.B. Citizen's Band (27 MHz, FM)
Very high frequency (VHF)	30 MHz–300 MHz	10 m–1 m	Short distance communication, FM sound broadcasts often in stereo. Local radio station Radio Clyde (102.5 MHz)
Ultra high frequency (UHF)	300 MHz–3000 MHz (3 GHz)	1 m–10 cm	Air–air, air–ground, short distance communication, colour TV 625 lines BBC 1 and 2, ITV and Channel 4
Super high frequency (SHF)	3 GHz–30 GHz	10 cm–1 cm	Microwave, point–point communication. Radar, satellites

1 GHz = 1 gigahertz = 1 000 000 000 Hz   1 MHz = 1 megahertz = 1 000 000 Hz

Example: From the table, what is the wavelength and frequency of Radio Scotland and in which waveband is it?
Solution: Wavelength = 810 m.
To calculate the frequency we need to use the equation

$$v = f \times \lambda \text{ with } v = 3 \times 10^8 \text{ m/s}$$
$$3 \times 10^8 = f \times 810$$
$$f = \frac{3 \times 10^8}{810}$$
$$= 3.7 \times 10^5 \text{ Hz}$$
$$= 370 \text{ kHz}$$

This frequency is in the medium waveband.

Television transmission

The block diagram shows the parts of a TV transmission system (figure 1.12).

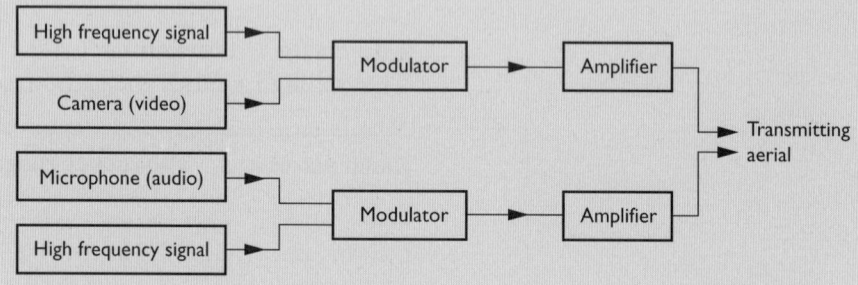

FIGURE 1.12 *TV transmission*

- The high frequency, video and audio signals are electrical signals.
- The modulator combines the high frequency signals with the video and audio signals.
- The modulated signals are sent to amplifiers which make the electrical signals stronger.
- The aerial changes these electrical signals into radio and TV waves which are transmitted in all directions.

The television receiver

The main parts of a TV are:

- Aerial – picks up wave energy with many different frequencies.
- Tuner – picks out the frequency of the TV station you want.
- Decoder (vision) – selects the picture signal from the waves.
- Amplifier (vision) – makes the picture signal stronger.
- Decoder (audio) – selects the sound signal from the waves.
- Amplifier (audio) – makes the sound signal stronger.
- TV tube – turns the electrical signal into a picture.
- Loudspeaker – turns the electrical signal into sound.

The audio and visual signals are sent out separately by the transmitter. This sometimes means that although we can see a programme, we cannot hear the sound due to a fault in the transmission (figure 1.13).

telecommunication

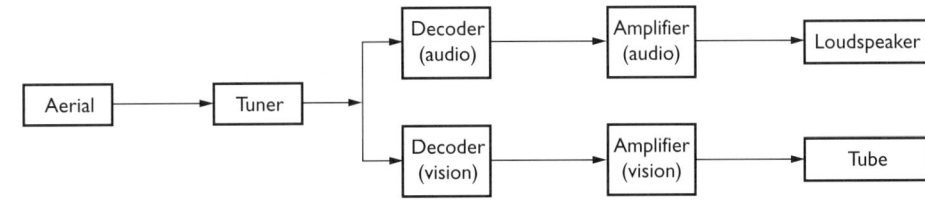

FIGURE 1.13 *Reception*

Batteries or mains electricity are required to make the television receiver operate.

- The energy changes in the loudspeaker are electrical to sound.
- The energy changes that take place on the TV screen are electrical to light.

The picture tube

The electron gun, which is at the narrow end of the tube, produces negative charges (electrons) and 'fires' them as an invisible beam. As they cannot travel very far in air, there is a vacuum (i.e. there is no air) inside the tube to allow them to reach the screen.

A special substance called a fluorescent coating on the screen produces a tiny spot of light when hit by the electrons (figure 1.14). This spot can be moved around the screen by deflecting the electron beam. In a TV picture tube, electromagnets are used. These are magnets powered by electricity and are coils of wire carrying a current. One pair of coils is arranged to move the beam up and down (vertically) and another pair arranged to move it from side to side (nearly horizontally). Because the electrons in these tubes come from a part of the electron gun called the cathode, the tubes are sometimes called **cathode ray tubes**.

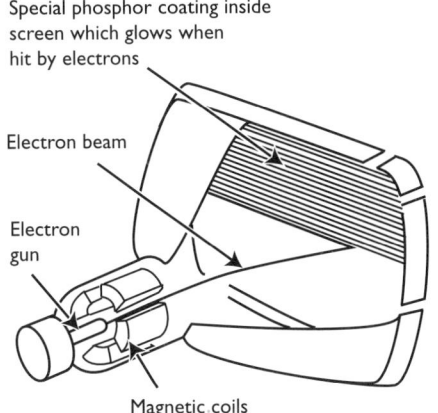

FIGURE 1.14 *Inside a TV tube*

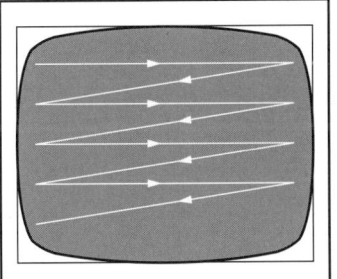

FIGURE 1.15 *The time taken for the beam to travel from the top to the bottom of the screen is 0.025 seconds*

How a television picture is formed

A British television picture is built up from 625 horizontal lines across the screen, but in the USA it is 525 lines. The more lines, the better the definition or clarity of the picture. The electron beam begins at the top left corner and moves across the screen at a speed of about 7000 m/s. On completing the line, the beam is switched off and moves to the left side, before starting the next one. The lines which build up the picture are not built up in sequence but as lines 1, 3, 5, etc. followed by 2, 4, 6, etc. (a technique called 'interlacing'). This continues until all 625 lines are completed so forming one picture. The beam then returns to the top left corner to start on the next picture (figure 1.15).

Image retention or persistence of vision

The eye takes about 1/10th of a second (0.1 s) to become aware of an object suddenly placed in front of it, and this vision persists for about 1/10th of a second after the object has disappeared. When the brain receives pictures quickly one after another it holds each picture for a short time. If the next picture appears before the previous one disappears, the brain processes the pictures together and is not aware of a space in between. This is what happens at the cinema or on a TV screen.

In a TV, there are 25 pictures every second (one picture every 0.04 s) and, in the cinema, 24, each one slightly different from the one before – the effect of the persistence of vision is of continuous movement rather than a set of still pictures.

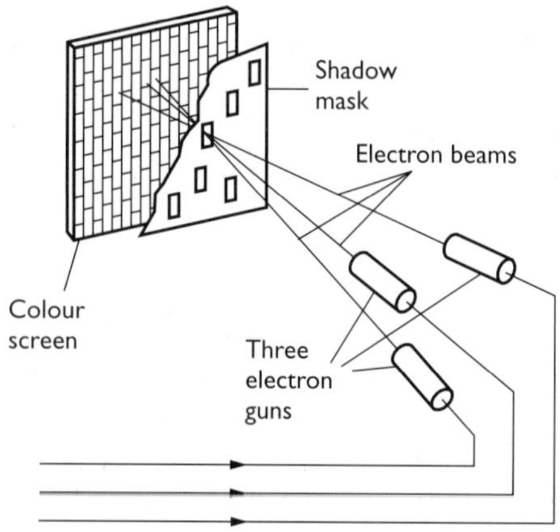

Black-and-white TV

A black-and-white TV is really just a picture tube with two main circuits. One sweeps the electrons (the spot) across the screen, while the other deflects the electrons down the screen. In this way the screen is lit up with nearly horizontal lines.

The TV signal from the aerial controls the brightness of the spot, by altering the number of electrons which travel from the electron gun to the screen. The greater the number of electrons, the brighter the spot. The brightness can vary from white through grey to black as it sweeps across the screen.

The electron gun fires an invisible beam of electrons. Magnetic coils move it up or down while other coils move it across so that the electrons can be aimed at any point on the screen.

The colour TV tube

A colour TV has three electron guns and a screen coated with about one million tiny dots arranged in triangles. When these dots are hit by electrons, one dot in each triangle gives out red light, another green light and the third blue light. It is the material of the dots which gives out the colour. *There are no coloured electrons.*

As the three electron beams sweep or scan the screen, an accurately placed 'shadow mask' consisting of a metal plate with about one-third of a million holes on it makes sure that each beam strikes only dots of one colour, e.g. electrons from the 'red' gun only hit 'red' dots. When a triangle is struck it may be that the red and green electron beams are very strong (intense) but not the blue. The triangle will give out red and green light strongly and appear yellowish. The triangles are struck in turn and since the dots are so small and the sweeping so fast, we see a continuous colour picture (figure 1.16). With each separate picture, the colour pattern may change, creating the effect of a moving picture.

FIGURE 1.16 *Shadow mask (colour television)*

The mixing of the three different colours can produce other colours.

- Red light and blue light give magenta light.
- Blue light and green light give cyan light.
- Green light and red light give yellow light.
- Red, blue and green lights give white light (figure 1.17).

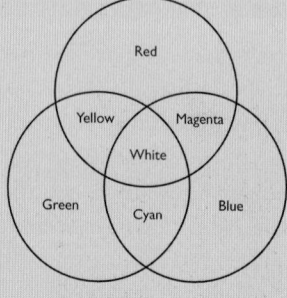

FIGURE 1.17 *Colour mixing in TV pictures*

Diffraction of waves

Diffraction is a bending of waves and occurs when waves go through a very narrow gap or round an obstacle. You can observe this effect as water waves enter a harbour. A typical effect is shown in figure 1.18.

FIGURE 1.18 *The greater the wavelength, the greater the diffraction*

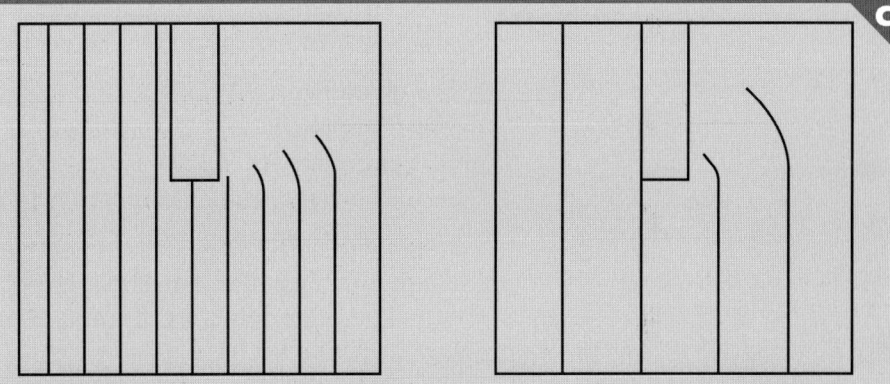

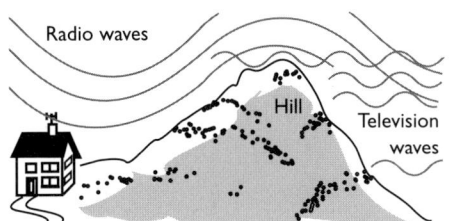

FIGURE 1.19 *Long and medium wavelength radio waves bend around hills much better than short wavelength TV waves. Therefore, this house will have poor TV reception*

The amount of diffraction of a wave depends on the wavelength. The larger the wavelength (the smaller the frequency), the more the diffraction. This also applies to radio and TV waves, i.e. long wavelengths (low frequencies) are diffracted more than short wavelengths (high frequencies).

Diffraction of radio and TV waves
TV waves, having a shorter wavelength than radio waves, are diffracted less, therefore are more difficult to pick up in certain areas such as in a glen (figure 1.19). This is because there is lower strength of signal received by the television receiver due to less diffraction.

Mobile phones

Look around you or in TV programmes and you will see the growth in the use of personal phones that we can take anywhere. Each phone is a miniature radio transmitter and receiver which operates by batteries. The idea is not new but the problem was to have a large number of users within a limited amount of frequencies. To avoid interference, each call must be made on its own frequency but each user cannot be given their own frequency since this would use up large amounts of the frequency range.

The solution is to divide the country into a number of areas called 'cells'. Within each cell, one precise group of frequencies called 'channels' is used to both transmit and receive calls. The same set cannot be used in a neighbouring cell since calls would interfere with each other, but can be used in a cell that is further away (figure 1.20).

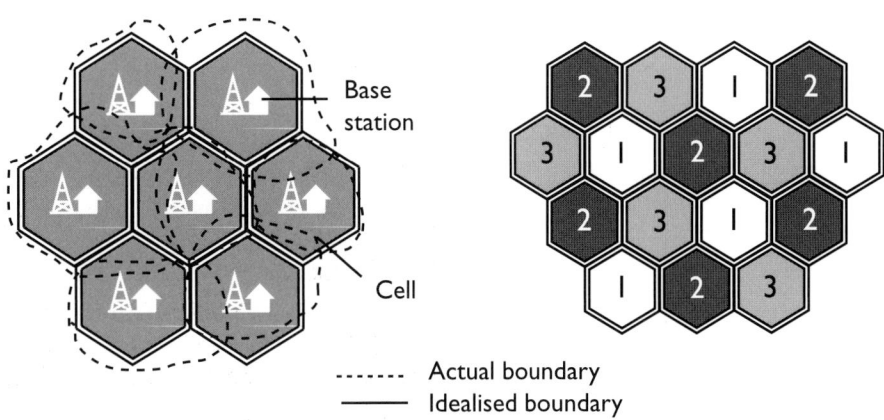

FIGURE 1.20 *Cells for mobile phones*

standard grade physics

The frequencies used are UHF, i.e. above 300 MHz. These have suitable transmission characteristics:

- A short useful range.
- They work best when there is clear line of sight between the transmitter and receiver.
- The waves can be directed very precisely and need only small aerials.

To help with the growth in the use of these phones, the cells in a city area are much smaller than those in country areas.

There are some disadvantages of mobile phones:

- They cannot pick up signals in some hilly areas.
- They cannot receive signals inside metal places like a lift.
- They may be a health danger. There is evidence that the microwaves used can cause some brain damage if they are used for long periods of time, since they generate heat.

1.4 Sending signals by light (fibre optics)

Originally, any signals that were sent down cables were electrical ones. The signals were sent down thick copper cables. With the growth of communication systems, this meant more cables would have to be used. However if signals can be sent as pulses of light, then fewer and thinner cables could be used. This would allow systems to expand rapidly. These special cables are called optical fibres.

To understand how fibre optics operate we must look at the reflection of light.

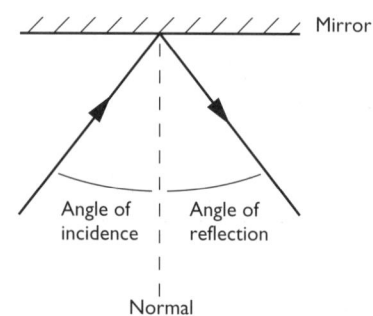

FIGURE 1.21 *Reflection of light*

Law of reflection

A ray of light is shone from a ray box at a mirror. The angle of the ray is measured from a line drawn at right angles to the surface called a **normal**. This is the **angle of incidence**. The angle of the reflected ray is measured. This is the angle of **reflection**. This can be repeated for other angles of incidence.

It is found that the angle of incidence equals the angle of reflection (figure 1.21).

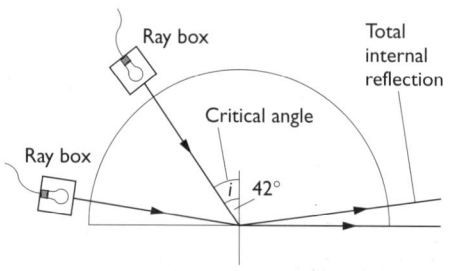

FIGURE 1.22 *Total internal reflection of light*

Total internal reflection

A ray of light is shone into a semi-circular block. As the angle of incidence is increased, then at a certain angle no light will pass from the semi-circular block through the flat face of the block (figure 1.22). When no light passes from glass to air we have what is called **total internal reflection**. The smallest angle of incidence at which total internal reflection takes place is called the **critical angle**. The critical angle for glass is about 42°. One use of total internal reflection is in fibre optics.

telecommunication 1

FIGURE 1.23 *An optical fibre is as fine as a human hair!*

Optical fibres

Optical fibres comprise thin flexible glass threads about one-eighth of a millimetre in diameter. Most of the glass thread is an outer layer of glass called cladding glass. In the middle of the thread is a different kind of glass which is less than one-hundredth of a millimetre in thickness. The fibres are made of extremely pure glass to cut down light loss and have a protective surface coating which reflects the light – keeping it inside the fibre.

An optical fibre is formed from glass so pure that a block 36 km thick would be as clear as an ordinary window pane. This means that we could see down to the bottom of the sea! One fibre is no thicker than a strand of hair (figure 1.23).

- Optical fibres are *lighter, carry more information* (up to 1000 telephone calls per fibre) and give better quality communications than normal telephone wires.
- The signal that passes along the fibre is not electrical, so it is less likely to be affected by other people's telephone calls or by other forms of electrical interference like mains hum.
- They are cheaper to make than copper wires since glass is mainly composed of silica.
- The disadvantage is that it is more difficult to join fibres together than copper wires.

Many modern telecommunication systems use optical fibres instead of copper wires. One single hair-like fibre can carry all the information needed to bring telephone messages, cable TV, videotext and computer services into your home.

Optical fibres operate by the light being reflected down the fibre, since no light can leave the outside of the fibre due to the angle of incidence being greater than the critical angle (figure 1.24). It has been estimated that one optical fibre cable could take all the telephone calls being made at any one time anywhere in the world.

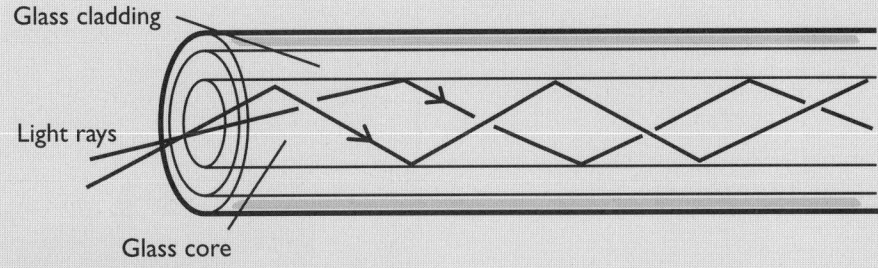

FIGURE 1.24 *Light being sent down a fibre*

Transmission and detection

To send speech information along glass fibres, it is first necessary to change sound signals into suitable pulses of electrical energy. The microphone (transmitter) in a telephone handset and some microelectronics do this. These pulses of electricity control a small laser (a narrow, very powerful beam of light; see Chapter 3) which then produces pulses of light which are transmitted through the optical fibre (figure 1.25).

15

standard grade physics

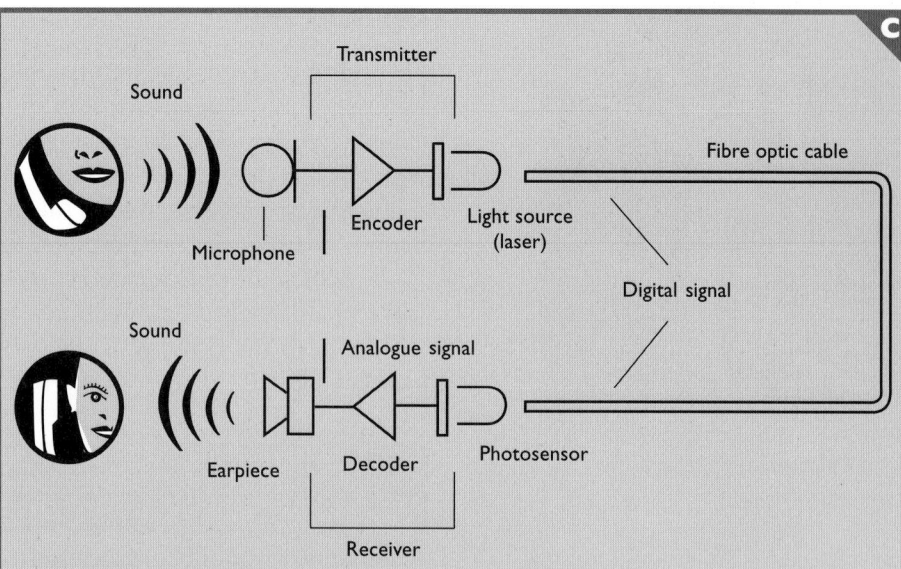

FIGURE 1.25 *Use of fibre optics in a simple system*

At the receiving end, the light pulses are changed back into pulses of electricity by a small device called a 'photodiode'. The electrical signal is fed to the earpiece (receiver) which then reproduces the original sound. In 1926, John Logie Baird invented a television system which used optical fibres, but it was not until some 40 years later that Charles Kao and George Hockham suggested that optical fibres might replace copper wires for telecommunications. In 1977 the world's first optical fibre telephone system became operational in America and in 1978 they were used in a town in Manitoba, Canada, to carry telephone, television, radio and computer information.

In 1980, the first trial lengths of submarine optical cables were laid in Loch Fyne and in 1982 an optical fibre link came into operation between London and Birmingham. All of Britain's major cities are now linked by the major fibre link trunk system. A transatlantic optical fibre link is now available (figure 1.26).

FIGURE 1.26

Modern optical fibres transmit light signals with very little signal loss and can be used over distances of about 100 km without amplification. With conventional copper cables, there is so much loss (or 'attenuation') of the signal that repeater amplifiers have to be installed every 4 km.

1.5 Dish aerials and satellites

Nowadays, we can send and receive both television and telephone signals from nearly any part of the world. To do this we need a transmitting aerial dish and a receiving dish. These then send and receive signals from a satellite orbiting the earth.

Dish aerials

If a transmitting aerial is placed at the focus of a curved reflector (or dish), the reflected signal from the dish has the shape of a narrow beam (just like the light from a torch). This allows a strong (concentrated) signal to be sent in a particular direction from the transmitting dish aerial (figure 1.27a).

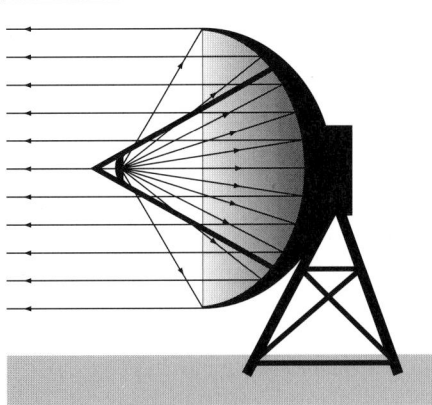

FIGURE 1.27a *A transmitting dish aerial*

Using dish aerials (curved reflectors)

When radio broadcasting began in 1920, the medium frequency (MF) radio signals then used could travel about 1600 km. Soon after, high frequency (HF) radio bands were discovered and these were used for world-wide communication. Very high frequencies (VHF) soon followed, but these were unable to travel round the curvature of the Earth (the higher the frequency, the smaller the wavelength and the smaller the diffraction). Today, VHF is used mainly for mobile communication, e.g. between aircraft and ground stations. As more and more information was transmitted, the available frequencies became overcrowded and even higher frequencies had to be found. This led to the use of microwaves whose frequency is about 10^9 Hz (1 GHz). Microwaves were useful since large amounts of information could be sent with little power and it was also found that they were easily focused using dish aerials.

Receiving dishes gather in most of the signal and reflect it to one point called the 'focus'. The receiving aerial is placed at the focus to receive the strongest signal (figure 1.27b).

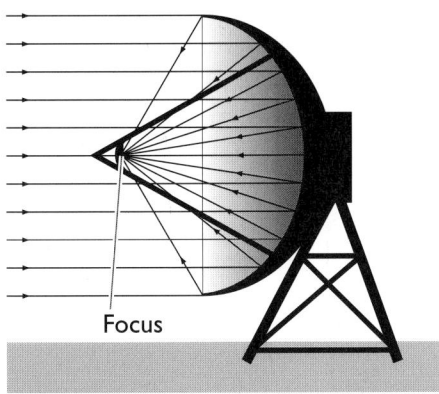

FIGURE 1.27b *A receiving dish aerial*

> Microwaves are unable to diffract (bend) round obstacles because of their small wavelength. This means that the transmitting and receiving dish aerials must be in line of sight and are often located on towers, e.g. the British Telecom Tower in London. Since microwaves have a fairly short range, a series of repeater (relay) stations are needed every 40 km. The incoming microwaves are focused on to the receiving dish aerial. Then after being amplified they are passed to the aerial at the focus of the transmitting dish to produce a parallel narrow beam which is sent to the next repeater station. Using microwaves for round-the-world communication would require several hundred relay stations at ground level. However, only three satellite relay stations can cover the whole Earth if they are in the correct positions. This was predicted by Arthur C. Clarke in 1945. He is the author of many science-fiction books. See if you can find out about any books that he has written.

standard grade physics

Satellites

A satellite has a very sensitive receiver as microwaves have to travel about 36 000 km to reach it. The signal, when received and focused, is amplified and transmitted back to Earth. Very large dish aerials on the Earth are required to pick up the weak signals coming from satellites and also to send signals accurately to them. The dish to receive the signals is the same design as the transmission one but the signals are received in a parallel beam and the rays are then brought to a focus. The diagram is the same but the direction of the arrows is reversed.

History of communication satellites

In 1962, 'Telstar' was launched from Cape Canaveral. Travelling at 15 000 mph, at heights varying from 1000 to 6000 km, it orbited the Earth in about two hours (the time taken for one orbit is called the 'period'). In Britain and America, ground stations had been built, having giant dish aerials. For 20 minutes of each orbit while 'Telstar' was visible above the horizon, they tracked it and for the first time clear television pictures and telephone conversations were transmitted across the Atlantic via satellite. Some satellites and the number of TV channels and telephone circuits they transmit are shown below. Not all members of the Intelsat series are shown.

Name of satellite	Launch year	Number of TV channels	Number of telephone circuits
Intelsat 1	1965	0	240
Intelsat 3	1968	0	1 500
Intelsat 4	1971	2	4 000
Intelsat 5	1980	2	12 000
Intelsat 6	1989	3	120 000

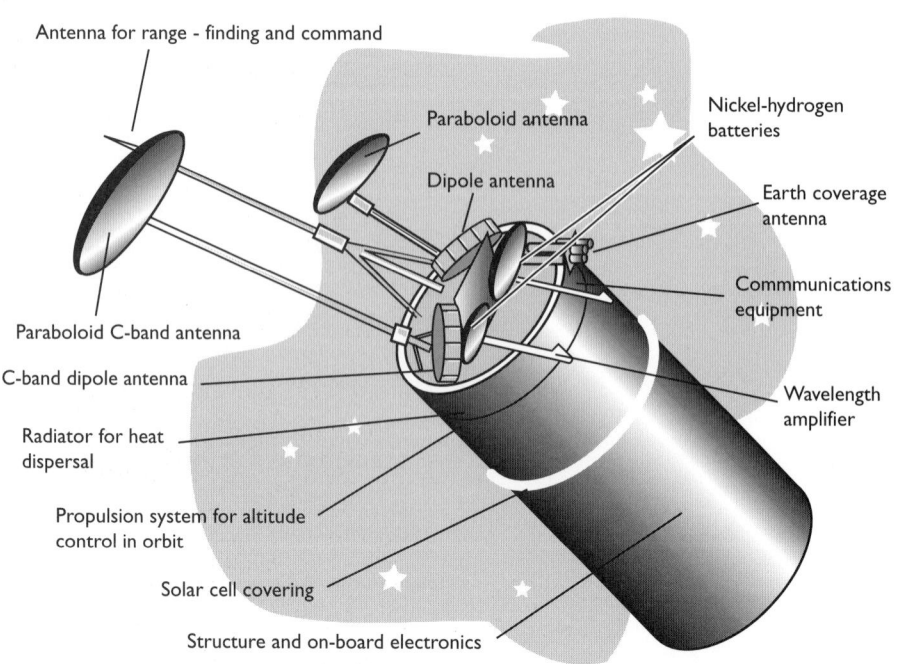

FIGURE 1.28 *Intelsat satellite*

By comparison, the latest TV satellites can carry up to 40 TV channels. The power received decreases as the transmission pattern changes across the country. Suggest a reason why you will need a different size of dish in Scotland from that in the south of England.

Geostationary satellites

The period of a satellite depends on its height above the Earth's surface. The further the satellite is from the Earth, the slower it appears to move. It has been calculated that a satellite in orbit 36 000 km above the equator would complete one orbit in the same time as the Earth revolves, i.e. 24 hours. This is called the geostationary satellite, i.e. it appears to be stationary above the Earth. Satellites in geostationary orbit must be in orbit above the equator. Some satellites are placed in higher orbits.

In 1965, 'Early Bird' was placed in a geostationary orbit. With its receiving dish aerial, it picked up microwave signals, and focused, amplified and transmitted them as a narrow parallel beam back to Earth. Panels of solar cells provided the energy to do this.

The satellite communication system has expanded rapidly. In 1971 there were 13 satellites in geostationary orbit and over 200 Earth satellites. Each new satellite is an improvement on the previous ones. 'Early Bird' could relay 240 telephone calls at once.

Sending a signal

When you pick up the telephone and use it to call America, a complex sequence of events takes place. This is shown in figure 1.29, and it is important to note that the satellite does not act as a mirror but is a combined receiver and transmitter.

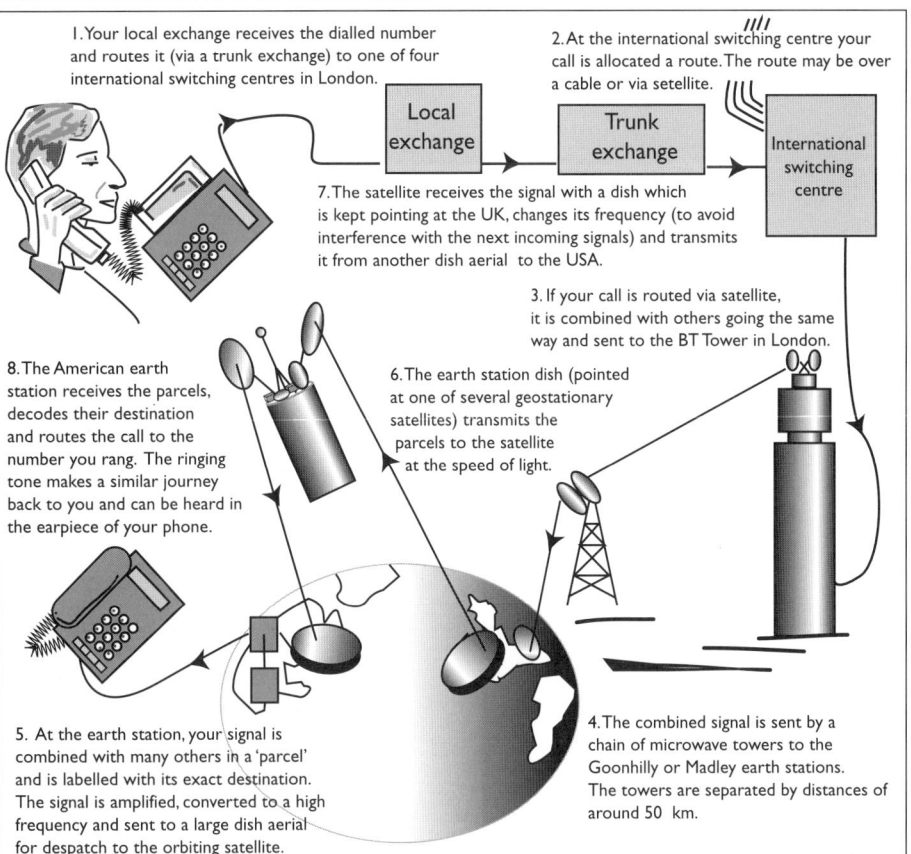

FIGURE 1.29 *You can see what happens in the time between dialling the first digit and hearing the ringing tone in New York*

1.6 Modern communications

Over the last few years, the communications industry has changed rapidly. It is impossible to cover all the possible developments or to know what will happen next. Here are a few examples:

Browsing the Web

Perhaps you have used the Internet to find a Web site like NASA which will give you the latest on the space shuttle. The Internet is a computer-linked system which connects through the telephone system to other computers world-wide. To do this you need a **modem** (a **mod**ulator **dem**odulator). This is a device which changes the computer signals into an electrical form which can be sent down a phone link and can do the reverse task for the incoming signals. The different parts of the information system are called 'Web sites'. See if you can visit a few Web sites.

Sky phones

The latest system of communication allows you to telephone from an aircraft to a ground station using a satellite. Alexander Graham Bell could not have predicted this when he invented the telephone.

Cable television

With the growth in television channels, some companies are now offering a cable to bring these channels into your home. This means that there is no need for a satellite dish and you can receive more channels. The cables are laid underground (figure 1.30). Large satellite dishes receive the programmes and then distribute them down a cable system using fibre optics to maintain the signal. The advantage is that, with more channels, there is an extra capacity in the system which would be difficult to obtain with a small dish.

FIGURE 1.30

LEARNING OUTCOMES

After studying this chapter you should be able to:

Section 1.1

1. Give an example which illustrates that the speed of sound in air is less than the speed of light in air, e.g. a car.
2. Describe a method of measuring the speed of sound in air (using the relationship between distance, time and speed).
3. Carry out calculations involving the relationship between distance, time and speed in problems on sound transmission.
4. Describe a method of sending a message using code (Morse or similar).
5. State that coded messages or signals are sent out by a transmitter and are replayed by a receiver.
6. State that the telephone is an example of long-range communication using wires between transmitter and receiver.
7. State the energy changes (a) in a microphone (sound to electrical) and (b) in a loudspeaker (electrical to sound).
8. State that the mouthpiece of a telephone (transmitter) contains a microphone and the earpiece (receiver) contains an earphone (loudspeaker).
9. State that electrical signals are transmitted along the communicating wires during a telephone communication.
10. Describe the effect on the signal pattern displayed in an oscilloscope due to a change in (a) loudness in sound and (b) frequency of sound.
11. Describe, with examples, how the following terms relate to sound: frequency and amplitude.
12. State that a telephone signal is transmitted very quickly (at a speed much greater than the speed of sound in air).
13. State that a telephone signal is transmitted at a speed of (almost) 300 000 000 m/s.
14. Explain the electrical signal pattern in telephone wires in terms of loudness and frequency changes in the sound signal. **Credit**

Section 1.2

1. State that waves are one way of transmitting signals.
2. Use the following terms correctly in context: wave, frequency, wavelength, speed, energy (transfer), amplitude.
3. Carry out calculations involving the relationship between distance, time and speed in problems on water waves.
4. Carry out calculations involving the relationship between speed, wavelength and frequency for water and sound waves.
5. Explain the equivalence of $f \times \lambda$ and $\dfrac{d}{t}$. **Credit**

Section 1.3

1. State that mobile phones, radio and television are examples of long-range communication which do not need wires (between transmitter and receiver).
2. State that microwaves, radio and television signals are waves which transfer energy.
3. State that microwaves, radio and television signals are transmitted at very high speed.
4. State that microwaves, radio and television signals are transmitted through air at 300 000 000 m/s.
5. State that the main parts of a radio receiver are: aerial, tuner, decoder, amplifier, loudspeaker, electricity supply. Be able to identify these parts on a block diagram of a radio receiver.
6. Describe in a radio receiver the function of the aerial, tuner, decoder, amplifier, loudspeaker and electricity supply.
7. State that a radio transmitter can be identified by wavelength or frequency values.
8. State that the main parts of a television receiver are: aerial, tuner, decoders, amplifiers, tube, loudspeaker, electricity supply. Be able to identify these parts on a block diagram of a television receiver.
9. Describe in a television receiver the function of: aerial, tuner, decoder, amplifier, tube, loudspeaker, electricity supply.
10. Describe how a picture is produced on a TV screen in terms of line build-up.

learning outcomes

11 State that mixing red, green and blue lights produces all colours seen on a colour television screen.

12 Carry out calculations involving the relationship between distance, time and speed in problems on radio and television waves. `Credit`

13 Describe the general principle of radio transmission in terms of transmitter, carrier wave amplitude modulation, receiver. `Credit`

14 Carry out calculations involving the relationship between speed, wavelength and frequency for radio waves. `Credit`

15 Explain in terms of diffraction how wavelength affects radio and television reception. `Credit`

16 Explain some of the differences in properties of radio bands in terms of source strength, reflection, etc. `Credit`

17 Describe the general principle of television transmission in terms of transmitter, carrier wave, modulation, video and audio receivers. `Credit`

18 Describe how a moving picture is seen on a television screen in terms of: line build-up; image retention; brightness variation. `Credit`

19 Describe the effect of colour mixing lights (red, green and blue). `Credit`

Section 1.4

1 State what is meant by an optical fibre.

2 Describe one practical example of telecommunication which uses optical fibres.

3 State that electrical cables and optical fibres are used in some telecommunication systems.

4 State that light can be reflected.

5 Describe the direction of the reflected light ray from a plane 'mirror'.

6 State that light variations at one end of an optical fibre are transmitted quickly to the other end of the fibre.

7 State that signal transmission along an optical fibre takes place at very high speed.

8 Compare some of the properties of electrical cables and optical fibres, e.g. size, cost, weight, signal speed, signal capacity, signal quality, signal reduction per kilometre. `Credit`

9 State the principle of reversibility of ray paths. `Credit`

10 Describe the principle of operation of an optical fibre transmission system. `Credit`

11 Carry out calculations involving the relationship between distance, time and speed in problems on light transmission. `Credit`

Section 1.5

1 State that the period of satellite orbit depends on its height above the Earth.

2 State that a geostationary satellite stays above the same point on the Earth's surface.

3 Describe the principle of intercontinental telecommunication using a geostationary satellite and ground stations.

4 State that curved reflectors on certain aerials or receivers make the received signal stronger.

5 Explain why curved reflectors on certain aerials or receivers make the received signal stronger.

6 Describe an application of curved reflectors used in telecommunication, e.g. TV link, boosters, repeaters or satellite communication.

7 Explain the action of curved reflectors on certain transmitters. `Credit`

STUDY QUESTIONS

1 In an experiment to measure the speed of sound, a starting pistol is fired and at the same time a stopclock is started. When the sound is heard at the end of a 200 m racetrack, the stopclock is stopped. If the speed of sound is 340 m/s, calculate the time that the sound takes to travel to the end of the track.

2 Give three reasons why communication with wires is better than other forms of communication.

3 (a) Light is often used to communicate rather than sound. What is the advantage of using light rather than sound?

(b) State another advantage of using fibre optics.

(c) The length of a fibre optics section is 800 km and the time for light to travel from one end to the other is 5 ms. Calculate the speed of light in the fibre.

4 The trace of a note from a musical instrument is displayed on an oscilloscope (below). The note has a frequency of 440 Hz.

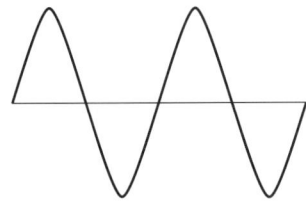

(a) Another note is played which is quieter than the first. Draw the new trace seen on the oscilloscope.

(b) Another note is played. This has a frequency which is one octave up from the original frequency. What is the frequency of this new note?

(c) If the speed of sound is 340 m/s, calculate the wavelength of the 440 Hz note.

5 The telephone is the most used form of communication in the world today.

(a) Which electrical component is used in the mouthpiece and what is the energy change that takes place in this part?

(b) Telephone signals can be sent to America via a satellite. Explain why the signals cannot be sent straight across the Atlantic.

(c) The satellite used is described as geostationary.

(i) How long does this satellite take to orbit the Earth?

(ii) Early satellites orbited the Earth in a period of 90 minutes. Were these satellites in a lower or higher orbit than the geostationary one?

(d) The signal transmitted from a satellite to Earth is picked up by a curved dish. Explain clearly, using a diagram, how the curved dish will pick up the signals.

6 Local radio stations can operate within the medium waveband. One such station called Radio Fun operates at 1152 kHz.

(a) Calculate the wavelength of this station.

(b) Another station, Radio Serious, can be received in a valley between two hills but Radio Fun cannot be picked up. Which station has the greater wavelength?

(c) Explain the reason for this effect.

7 In a radio station transmitter, the audio signal cannot be sent out directly. The audio signal has to be combined with a high frequency signal.

(a) What name is given to this process in the wave?

   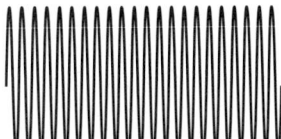

Audio signal   High frequency signal

(b) The diagram above shows two possible parts in this process. Complete the third part to show clearly the wave pattern.

(c) When the signal is received in a radio, it has to be received by the radio and the station selected. Name the two different parts that are needed for this to take place.

study questions

8 A radio uses an amplifier.

(a) State the purpose of this component.

(b) Illustrate your answer with a diagram which shows the effect of an amplifier on the input trace.

9 British television screens use 625 lines to show a picture.

(a) Explain clearly how the electrons from the tube create a picture.

(b) Explain how three electron guns can create different colours on the screen.

(c) What colour can be seen if red and blue are mixed?

10 In a black-and-white television:

(a) Explain how parts of the picture appear brighter than others.

(b) If the picture lasts 0.04 s on the screen, how many pictures are needed for an advert that lasts 20 s?

11 (a) A telephone handset has an earpiece and a mouthpiece as shown.

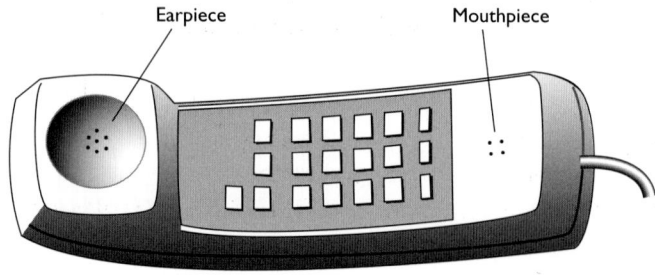

Make a list of the missing words.

The earpiece contains a loudspeaker which changes ① energy to sound energy. In the mouthpiece there is a ② which changes ③ energy to ④ energy. The signal from the mouthpiece is transmitted along the wires at a speed of almost 300 000 000 metres per second which is the speed at which ⑤ travels.
SEB   **GENERAL** KU

(b) A telephone cable between Scotland and America is 4800 kilometres long.

(i) How long will it take a signal to travel along the cable from Scotland to America?
GENERAL PS

(ii) Why will it take longer for the signal to reach America if it is transmitted by satellite link rather than along the cable?
SEB   **GENERAL** PS

12 Two timekeepers Smith and Jones are timing a 100 m sprint. Smith starts her stopwatch when she sees the smoke from the starter's gun. Jones starts his watch when he hears the bang from the gun. Both stop their watches at the instant the winner reaches the finishing line. Both timekeepers are 100 m from the starter.

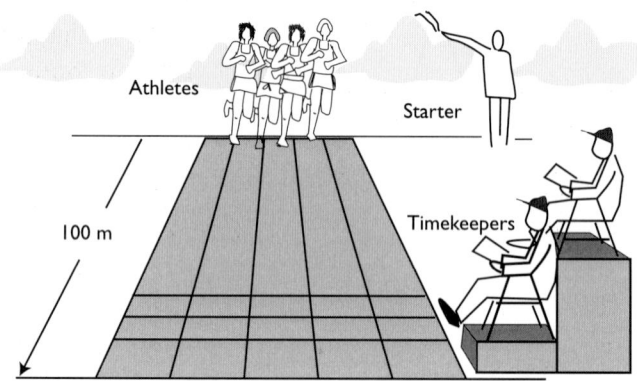

(a) Which timekeeper records the shorter time for the winner? Explain your answer.   **CREDIT** PS

(b) The reading on Jones' watch is 11.3 s. What is the reading on Smith's watch?

(Data you require will be found in the Data sheet on page 186).
SEB   **CREDIT** PS

Using electricity

2.1 From the wall socket

Introducing electricity

It is not very often that we have a 'blackout' but when it does happen, as a result of the mains electricity failing, what a disruption and inconvenience it causes – yet the convenience of having mains electricity in our homes only became normal to the majority of people in this country during the 1920s and 1930s.

We are now used to so many electrical appliances at home for cooking, cleaning, heating and entertainment, it's hard to imagine life without them. However, before the pressing of a switch can activate an appliance, the electricity has to be produced and transmitted to our homes – this is explained in Chapter 6.

An understanding of what electricity is, and how it can be safely used, are important elements of this chapter. Always remember:

> **mains electricity can kill!**

The electrical appliances which we use in our homes, industry and schools use **electrical energy** from the mains supply or from batteries. They change electrical energy into a form which is useful to what we are doing (and in many cases into other forms of energy which are not so useful). For instance, a lamp changes electrical energy into light energy and heat energy. The most useful, and main, energy change for a lamp is the change from electrical energy into light energy.

The list below shows the main energy change for a number of household appliances:

- A kettle changes electrical energy into **heat energy**.
- A radio changes electrical energy into **sound energy**.
- A lamp changes electrical energy into **light energy**.
- A washing machine changes electrical energy into **kinetic** (movement) **energy**.

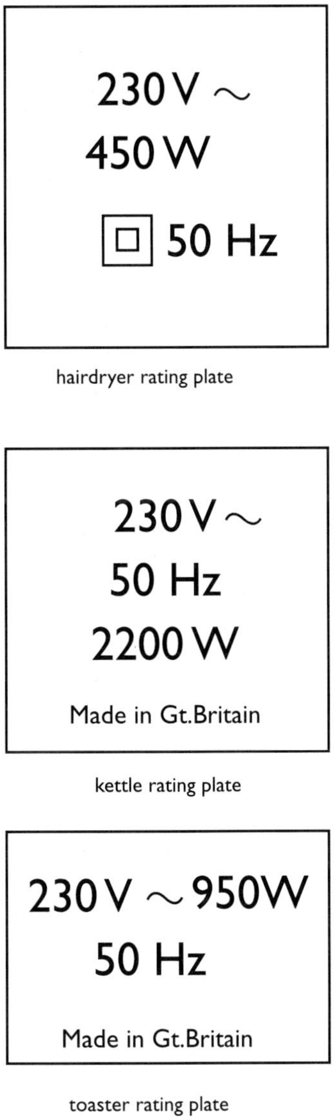

Flexes, plugs and fuses

Let's look at three common household appliances – a hairdryer, a kettle and a toaster. They are fitted, like most electrical appliances, with **rating plates** and these are shown in figure 2.1. The rating plate gives information about the appliance – the voltage (the figure with the letter 'V' after it) and frequency (the figure with the letters 'Hz' after it) required to operate it safely, its power rating (the figure with the letter

FIGURE 2.1 *Typical rating plates for a hairdryer, kettle and a toaster*

hairdryer rating plate:
230 V ~
450 W
□ 50 Hz

kettle rating plate:
230 V ~
50 Hz
2200 W
Made in Gt.Britain

toaster rating plate:
230 V ~ 950 W
50 Hz
Made in Gt.Britain

2 standard grade physics

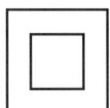

FIGURE 2.2 *Double insulation symbol*

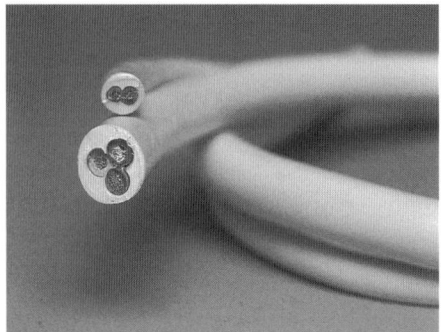

FIGURE 2.3 *Three-core and two-core flexes*

'W' after it), and the symbol shown in Figure 2.2 if it is double insulated.

The electric kettle has the highest power rating at 2200 **watts** (**W**) and because of this the flexible cord, or flex, which connects it to the mains wall socket will, generally, be the thickest. A flex consists of two or three cores of thin, stranded, copper insulated wire within an outer insulating sheath as shown in figure 2.3. The brown covered core is the **live** wire, the blue covered core is the **neutral** wire and, in three-core flexes, the green and yellow striped covered core is the **earth** wire.

The cores in a flex during normal use heat up when a current passes through them. However, if they carry too high a current they will become too hot and overheat, and this could cause a fire. To protect the flex from too high a current, the three-pin plug connected to the flex is fitted with a fuse. A **fuse** is, simply, a thin piece of wire. When an electric current passes through it, it heats up. If the current gets too high, then the fuse wire will become so hot that it melts or 'blows', breaking the electrical circuit and so protecting the flex.

Fuses for three-pin plugs, known as **cartridge fuses**, are available in a number of sizes – the most common being 3 A (**amperes**) and 13 A.

There are a number of different types of flex available for different applications. They differ in the maximum safe current they can carry (which depends on the thickness of the conductors making up the core), the number of cores, the type of outer insulation and in their cost. Table 2.1 shows the minimum thickness of conductor required for appliances of different power ratings.

Power rating	Typical appliance	Thickness of conductor	Maximum current
up to 720 W	clock, food mixer	0.50 mm^2	3 A
720–1440 W	hairdryer, toaster	0.75 mm^2	6 A
1440–2400 W	kettle, fan heater	1.0 mm^2	10 A
2400–3000 W	3 kW heater	1.25 mm^2	13 A

TABLE 2.1

Choosing a fuse

To select the correct size of fuse the **power rating** or wattage (W) of the appliance, marked on the rating plate, must be known. Generally, if the power rating of the appliance is less than 720 W then a 3 A fuse should be fitted. For a power rating greater than or equal to 720 W a 13 A fuse should be fitted. (Some appliances such as refrigerators and freezers need a larger fuse than the wattage on the rating plate indicates, and in these cases the instructions given by the manufacturer must be followed!)

Table 2.2 shows the power ratings and cartridge fuse values for the three appliances given in figure 2.1.

Appliance	Power rating	Fuse
hairdryer	450 W	3 A
kettle	2200 W	13 A
toaster	950 W	13 A

TABLE 2.2

using electricity 2

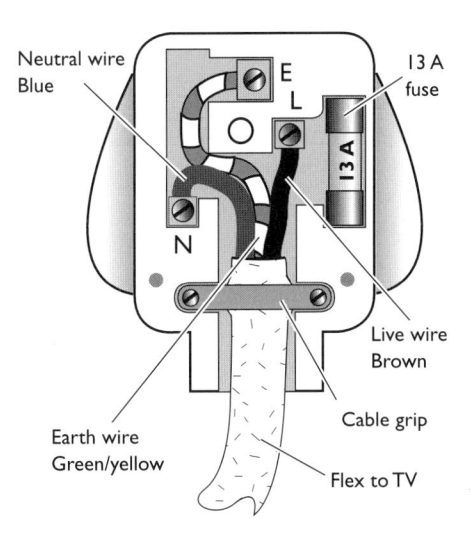

FIGURE 2.4 *A correctly wired three-pin plug*

Wiring a three-pin plug

For safety, it is very important that a three-pin plug is wired correctly (figure 2.4). Provided the appliance is working properly, then electrical current only passes through the live and neutral cores of the flex – no current passes through the earth wire. The earth wire is connected to the outer metal casing of the appliance and to the earth pin in the three-pin plug. Its purpose is to provide a very easy path for electrical current to pass to earth should a fault occur and it may be considered as a 'safety' wire.

Figures 2.5 (a) and (b) show what happens when an electrical fault develops so that the live wire comes into contact with the outer metal casing of a toaster.

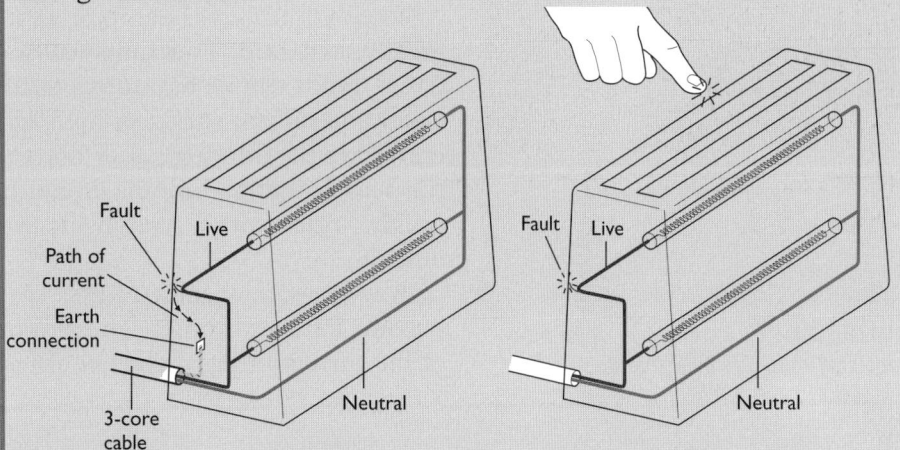

FIGURE 2.5 *(a) and (b) show a faulty toaster. In (a) the fuse 'blows' when the fault occurs and the toaster can be touched safely. In (b) the earth wire is disconnected and the person receives a shock.*

In (a) a large current will pass through the live and earth wires. This current will be much larger than the fuse value and so the fuse will 'blow', breaking the electrical circuit. The toaster is now safe for anyone touching it as the broken fuse has disconnected it from the live wire.

In (b) the earth wire is not connected and so the metal parts of the toaster are 'live'. Anyone touching the toaster will get a shock and could be killed – current will pass from the live wire through the person to earth. The danger is greatly increased if the person's body is wet, as the water helps to conduct the electricity.

As we have discovered, the plug fuse is fitted to protect the flex from overheating. It, however, must be connected to the live wire, because if the fuse 'blows' as a result of the live wire touching a metal part of the appliance then no part of the appliance or flex can remain live. Also, if the appliance has a switch it must be connected to the live wire so that when it is 'off', no part of the appliance can remain live. However, connecting the live and neutral wires the wrong way round would mean that the appliance, although not working, remains live even when the switch on the appliance is off!

Double insulation

Some appliances, such as hairdryers and electric drills, do not require an earth wire since there are two layers of insulation around their electrical parts. This makes the earth wire unnecessary and so a two-core flex is fitted. The **double insulation** symbol was shown in figure 2.2. Appliances which are double insulated have this symbol on their rating plate. Of the three rating plates shown in figure 2.1, the hairdryer is the only appliance that is double insulated.

Dangerous situations

The wall socket shown in figure 2.6 has too many appliances plugged into it. This could result in too much current being drawn from the wall socket, which could lead to the socket overheating.

When your body is damp or wet, its ability to conduct electricity is greatly increased. Touching wall sockets or light switches with wet or damp hands can be hazardous as the water can conduct electricity. If water entered the socket or light switch this could provide a path for current to pass through your body and you could be electrocuted. It is for this reason that bathrooms do not have wall sockets and the light switch is either fitted with a cord inside the bathroom or placed on a wall outside.

Frayed, worn or joined flexes are all dangerous, since the live core may become bare and someone may touch it. In these cases a replacement flex of the correct rating should be fitted.

FIGURE 2.6 *With too many appliances connected to it, the socket could overheat*

2.2 *Alternating and direct current*

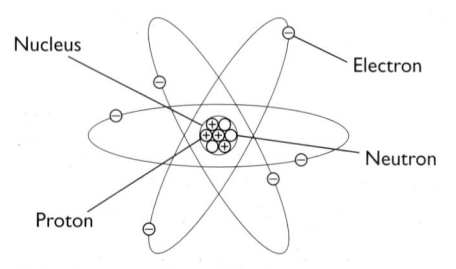

FIGURE 2.7 *A model of an atom*

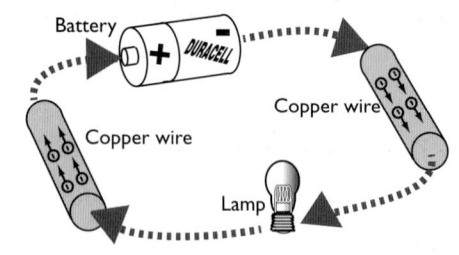

FIGURE 2.8 *An electric current is the movement of electrons from the negative to the positive terminals of an energy source or battery*

What is electricity?

All solids, liquids and gases are made up of **atoms**. An atom consists of a positively charged centre or **nucleus** surrounded by a 'cloud' of rapidly revolving negative charges called **electrons**. The nucleus is made of particles called **protons** (positively charged) and **neutrons** (uncharged).

Charge is measured in **coulombs** (**C**). The charge on a proton is equal in size to that of an electron. This value is 1.6×10^{-19} C.

Charge, current and time

Consider a simple electrical circuit – a lamp connected to a battery. The lamp lights because negative charges from the negative terminal of the battery move through the wires and lamp to the positive terminal of the battery. This movement of negative charges is called an **electric current** (or current for short). A current is a movement of electrons. Therefore, when current passes, (negative) charge is transferred.

28

The amount of charge transferred is given by:

charge transferred = current × time

$Q = It$

where Q = charge transferred, I = current and t = time.

Current is measured in amperes (A) and time in seconds (s) so 1 coulomb = 1 ampere second (1 C = 1 A s).

> **Example:** How many coulombs of charge are transferred in three minutes by a current of 0.1 ampere?
> *Solution:*
> $Q = It$
> $= 0.1 \times (3 \times 60)$
> $= 18\ C$

Conductors and insulators

Negative charges (i.e. electrons) can only move from the negative terminal to the positive terminal of a battery if there is an electrical path between them. Materials which allow negative charges to move through them easily, to form an electric current, are known as **conductors**. Conductors are mainly metals, such as copper, gold and silver. However, carbon is also a good conductor.

Materials which do not allow electrons to move through them easily are called **insulators**. Glass, plastic, wood and air are examples of insulators.

Voltage

Look again at figure 2.8. The battery changes chemical energy, from the substances inside it, into electrical energy. This electrical energy is carried by the charges (electrons) that move round the circuit and is given up as heat and light as they pass through the filament of the lamp.

> The electrical energy given to the negative charges by the battery is a measure of the voltage of the battery. To be exact, the **voltage** of a battery is the electrical energy given to one coulomb of charge passing through the battery. For example, a 9 volt battery gives six times as much energy to each coulomb of charge passing through it as a 1.5 volt battery.

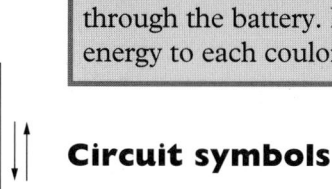

Circuit symbols

Some commonly used circuit symbols are shown in the list on page 187.

Direct and alternating current

Figure 2.9 (a) shows a battery connected to a lamp and figure 2.9 (b) shows a mains-supplied transformer (low-voltage power supply) connected to an identical lamp of equal brightness.

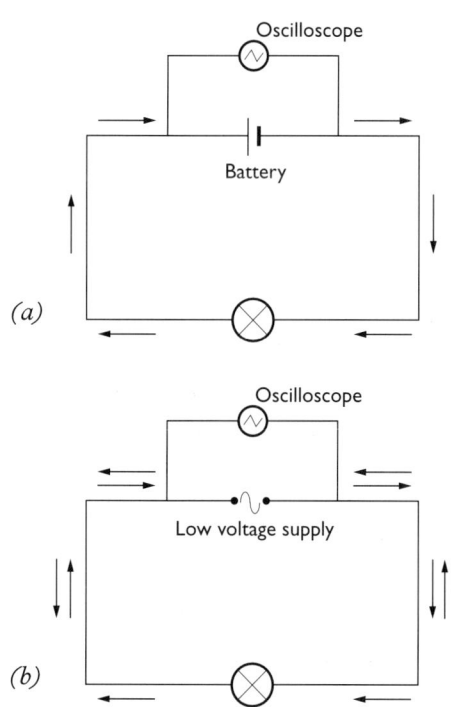

FIGURE 2.9 *(a) Electrons move in only one direction. This is known as direct current (d.c.). (b) Electron movement is to and fro. This is known as alternating current (a.c.)*

2 standard grade physics

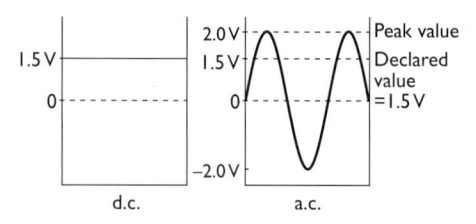

FIGURE 2.10 *Oscilloscope traces from Figure 2.9(a) and (b)*

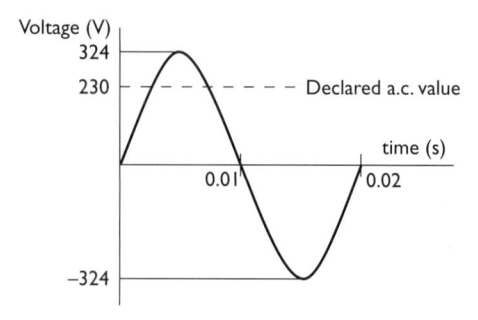

FIGURE 2.11 *Oscilloscope trace for mains electricity*

In figure 2.9 (a) electrons (negative charges) move from the negative terminal through the lamp and wires to the positive terminal of the battery. This means that the electrons move in only one direction – this is known as **direct current** or **d.c.** for short.

In figure 2.9 (b) electrons move in one direction, then in the other direction and back again, i.e. the electrons move to and fro. This alternating movement of the electrons is known as **alternating current** or **a.c.** for short. The to-and-fro movement of the electrons is very frequent. It occurs 50 times every second and so the frequency of mains electricity is 50 hertz (50 Hz).

The oscilloscope traces from the circuits in figure 2.9 are shown in figure 2.10. The d.c. trace has a constant value of 1.5 V (volts) while the a.c. trace alternates from about +2 V to −2 V.

> The **declared a.c. voltage** is always smaller than the **peak a.c. voltage**.

The alternating voltage of mains electricity in the UK is 230 volts – this is the declared value of the voltage (figure 2.11).

2.3 Resistance

Measuring current and voltage

Measuring current

Electric current is measured in amperes (A) and we use an **ammeter** to measure it. Figure 2.12 shows how an ammeter is connected in an electrical circuit.

Note: an ammeter measures the current *through* a component.

Step 1 Set up the electrical circuit and identify the position where the ammeter is to be placed

Step 2 Make a gap in the circuit into which the ammeter is placed. The positive terminal of the ammeter should be connected towards the positive terminal of the battery

Step 3 The ammeter reads the current flowing through the lamp

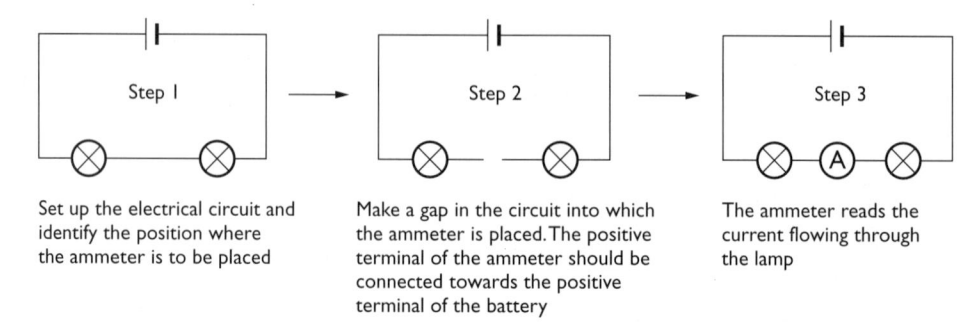

FIGURE 2.12 *Connecting an ammeter into an electrical circuit*

Measuring voltage

Voltage is measured in volts (V) and we use a **voltmeter** to measure it. Figure 2.13 shows how a voltmeter is connected to an electrical circuit.

Note: a voltmeter measures the voltage *across* a component.

using electricity 2

FIGURE 2.13 *Connecting a voltmeter into an electrical circuit*

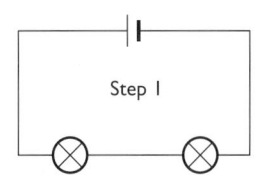

Step 1 — Set up the electrical circuit

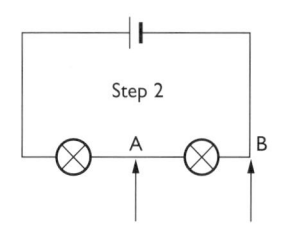

Step 2 — Identify the two points where the voltage is to be measured. The positive terminal of the voltmeter should be connected towards the positive terminal of the battery

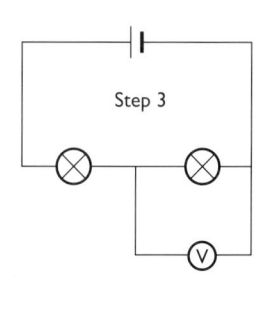

Step 3 — The voltmeter reads the voltage across the lamp

Ammeters and voltmeters can be connected to the same circuit using the instructions given above.

Resistance

All materials oppose current passing through them. This opposition to the current is called **resistance**. Resistance is measured in **ohms** (Ω).

For most materials resistance depends on the:

- type of material – the better the conductor the lower the resistance;
- length of the material – the longer the material the higher the resistance;
- thickness of the material – the thinner the material the higher the resistance;
- temperature of the material – the higher the temperature the higher the resistance.

For a resistor, the resistance value remains constant for different currents, provided the temperature of the resistor does not change.

An **ohmmeter** can be used to measure resistance. The circuit symbol for an ohmmeter is shown in figure 2.14 (a). Figure 2.14 (b) shows an ohmmeter being used to measure the resistance of a resistor.

The resistance of a resistor can also be measured using an ammeter and a voltmeter as shown in figure 2.15. In this method the voltage across, and the current through, the resistor have to be measured. The resistance of the resistor can then be calculated using:

$$\text{resistance} = \frac{\text{voltage across resistor}}{\text{current through resistor}}$$

i.e.
$$R = \frac{V}{I}$$

This is known as **Ohm's law**.

In units:
$$\text{ohms } (\Omega) = \frac{\text{volts (V)}}{\text{amperes (A)}}$$

Ohm's law is normally written as:

voltage across resistor = current through resistor × resistance of resistor

or
$$V = IR$$

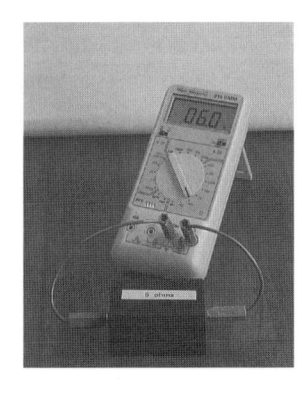

FIGURE 2.14 *(a) The symbol for an ohmmeter, (b) measuring resistance using an ohmmeter*

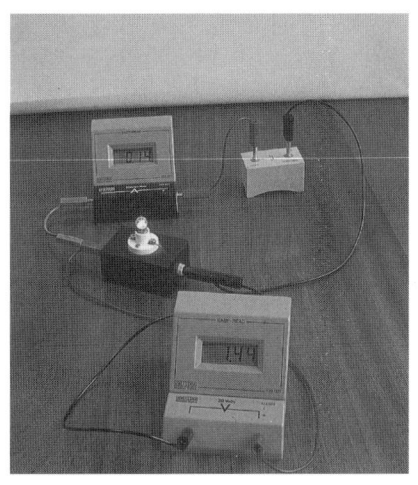

FIGURE 2.15 *The resistance of the resistor (in this case a lamp) can be calculated using the voltmeter and ammeter readings*

31

Example: A lamp has a voltage of 12 V across it and a current of 1.5 A passing through it. Calculate its resistance.
Solution:

$$V = IR \quad 12 = 1.5\,R \quad R = \frac{12}{1.5} = 8\,\Omega$$

A resistor whose resistance can be changed is known as a **variable resistor**. The resistance is changed by altering the length of the wire in the resistor (the longer the wire, the higher the resistance). Variable resistors are often used as volume or brightness controls in televisions, and in dimmer switches for lights.

Power

When an electric current passes through a wire, the electrons making up the current collide with the atoms of the wire. These collisions make the wire hotter and so some of the electrical energy is changed into heat in the wire. The amount of heat produced depends on the current and the resistance of the wire. Heating elements for electric fires and kettles change electrical energy into heat energy in the resistive wire inside the element.

A lamp transfers electrical energy into heat energy and light energy in a resistance wire called the **filament**. How quickly it does this is known as the **power rating** of the lamp.

Power is the energy transferred in one second:

$$\text{Power} = \frac{\text{energy transferred}}{\text{time taken}}$$

$$P = \frac{E}{t}$$

In units:

$$\text{watts (W)} = \text{joules per second (J/s)}$$
$$1\,W = 1\,J/s$$

Example: A lamp uses 216 000 joules of energy in a time of six minutes. What is the power of the lamp?
Solution:

$$P = \frac{E}{t} = \frac{216\,000}{6 \times 60} = 60\,W$$

using electricity 2

Power rating of lamp	Voltage	Current
6 W	12 V	0.5 A
24 W	12 V	2.0 A
36 W	12 V	3.0 A
48 W	12 V	4.0 A

TABLE 2.3

Power, current and voltage

Four different lamps of known power ratings were connected to an electrical supply; the recordings of the voltage across and the current through the lamps are shown in table 2.3.

Calculate the value of current × voltage for each lamp, and compare it with the power rating of the lamp. You should see that the power rating of the lamp is equal to the current multiplied by the voltage. From this we have:

$$\text{power} = \text{current} \times \text{voltage}$$
$$P = IV$$
but from Ohm's law $V = IR$
$$P = I(IR)$$
$$P = I^2R$$

Alternatively:
$$P = IV$$
but from Ohm's law $I = \dfrac{V}{R}$
$$P = \dfrac{(V)}{R}V$$
$$P = \dfrac{V^2}{R}$$

The equations $P = IV$, $P = I^2R$ and $P = V^2/R$ are used to find the power rating of appliances. Use Ohm's law to calculate the resistance of each of the lamps in the table and then check that the above equations can be used to calculate the power rating of the lamps.

> **Example:** A lamp has a resistance of 4 Ω and a current of 3 A passes through it. Calculate the power rating of the lamp.
> *Solution:* $P = I^2R = 3^2 \times 4 = 36$ W

Filament lamps

An electric lamp consists of a filament (usually of thin tungsten wire) housed in a glass container. As an electric current passes through the resistance wire (**filament**), so much electrical energy is changed into heat energy that the filament glows white hot. Filament lamps produce both heat and light. Electrical energy is changed into heat energy and light energy in the filament (resistance wire) of the lamp. Filament lamps are normally classified in terms of their power rating. The most common household lamps are 100 W (watt), 60 W and 40 W. They will work for approximately 1000 hours before the filament breaks.

2 standard grade physics

FIGURE 2.16 *A 100 W filament lamp (left) and four 20 W compact fluorescent lamps. Each fluorescent lamp gives out about the same amount of light as the filament lamp*

Gas discharge lamps

Gas discharge lamps depend on an electric current passing through a gas or vapour. They are cooler in operation as more of the electrical energy is converted into light energy. Discharge lamps are therefore much more efficient than filament lamps. There are a number of different types of discharge lamps such as neon, argon, mercury and sodium vapour lamps. Fluorescent lamps are filled with mercury vapour at low pressure. When an electric current is passed through the gas it produces invisible ultraviolet light. As this would not be seen by the human eye, the lamps are coated on the inside with a special chemical which absorbs ultraviolet light and produces visible light. This process is called **fluorescence**. Compact fluorescent light lamps are available which provide the same amount of light as the filament lamps mentioned above, but which only consume about one quarter of the electricity. They also last about eight times as long as filament lamps but are more expensive to buy – although their whole-life cost is much lower than that of a filament lamp.

IN *summary*

The following equations can be used to calculate the power rating of an appliance:

$$\text{Power} = \frac{\text{energy transferred}}{\text{time taken}} \qquad \text{i.e. } P = \frac{E}{t}$$

$$\text{Power} = \text{current} \times \text{voltage} \qquad \text{i.e. } P = IV$$

$$\text{Power} = \text{current}^2 \times \text{resistance} \qquad \text{i.e. } P = I^2 R$$

$$\text{Power} = \frac{\text{voltage}^2}{\text{resistance}} \qquad \text{i.e. } P = \frac{V^2}{R}$$

2.4 *Useful circuits*

Types of circuit

Electrical components, such as lamps and resistors, can be connected in series, in parallel, or a mixture of series and parallel. A **series circuit** has only one electrical path from the negative terminal of the battery to the positive terminal. A **parallel circuit** has more than one electrical path from the negative terminal of the battery to the positive terminal. Figure 2.17 (a) shows three lamps connected in series while figure 2.17 (b) shows three lamps connected in parallel. Figure 2.17 (c) shows a mixed series and parallel circuit in which a lamp is connected in series with two resistors which are connected in parallel.

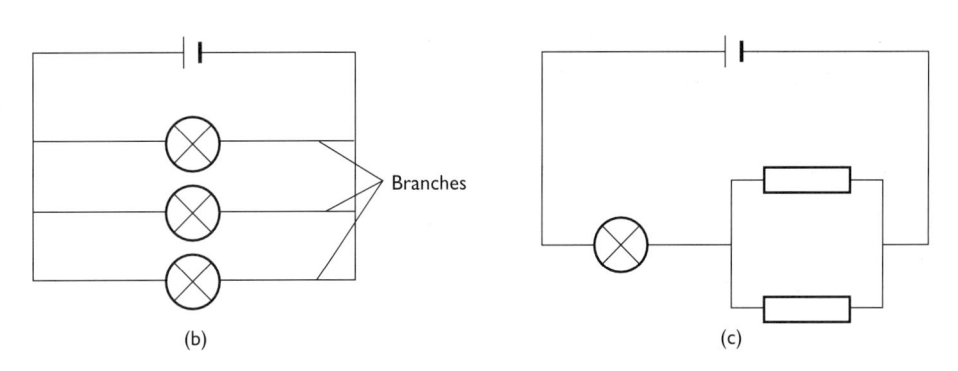

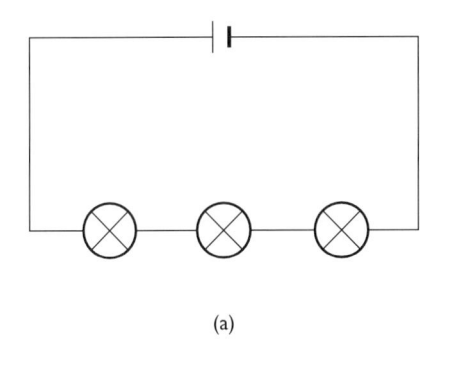

FIGURE 2.17 (a) A series circuit, (b) a parallel circuit, (c) a mixed series and parallel circuit

A series circuit

Three resistors of resistance 3 Ω, 4 Ω and 1 Ω are connected in series. Their combined (or total) resistance is measured by an ohmmeter as 8 Ω, as shown in figure 2.18.

Figure 2.19 (a) shows the same three resistors in series but with ammeters connected to measure the current at various positions. Voltmeters have also been connected to measure the voltage across each resistor. Table 2.4 shows the readings on the meters. Use Ohm's law to confirm the value of each resistor.

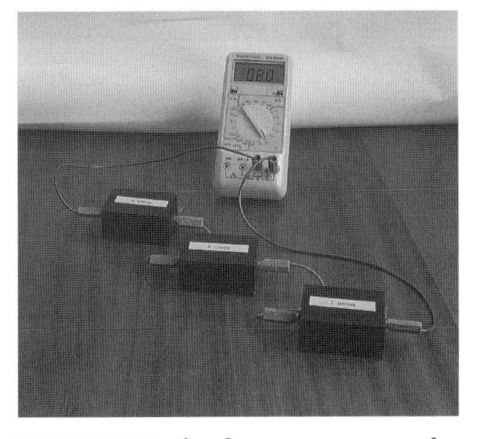

FIGURE 2.18 An ohmmeter measures the combined resistance of three resistors connected in series

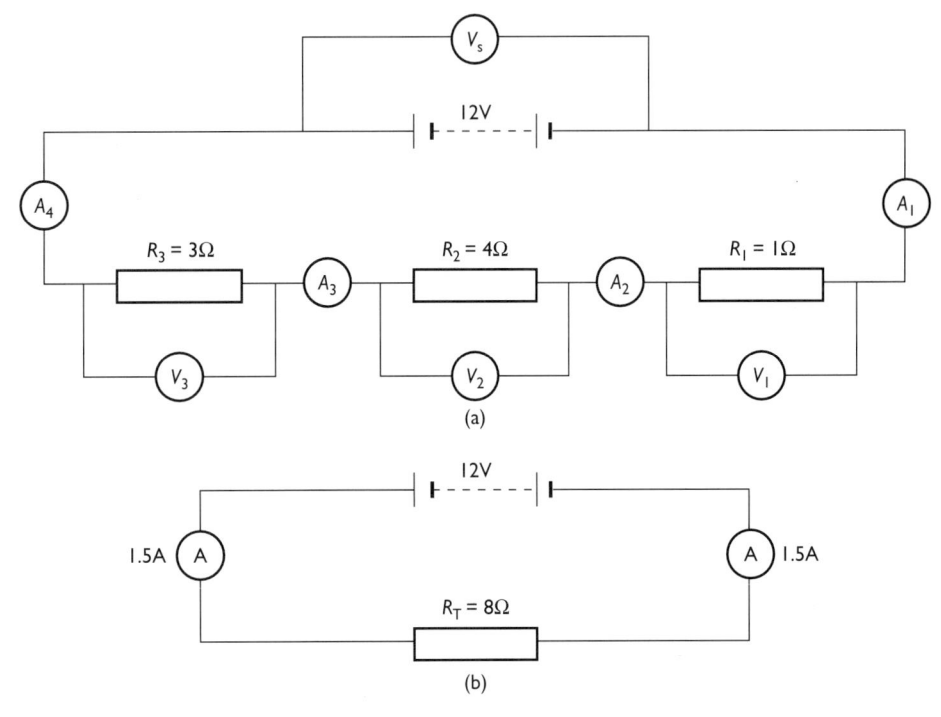

FIGURE 2.19 (a) Measuring the current through and the voltage across resistors in series, (b) the equivalent circuit to that shown in figure (a)

TABLE 2.4

Current	Voltage	Resistance
$A_1 = 1.5$ A	$V_1 = 1.5$ V	$R_1 = 1\ \Omega$
$A_2 = 1.5$ A	$V_2 = 6.0$ V	$R_2 = 4\ \Omega$
$A_3 = 1.5$ A	$V_3 = 4.5$ V	$R_3 = 3\ \Omega$
$A_4 = 1.5$ A	$V_S = 12$ V	$R_T = 8\ \Omega$

2 standard grade physics

- What do you notice about the current at different positions in a series circuit?
- What do you notice about the voltages V_1, V_2, V_3 and V_S for a series circuit?
- What do you notice about the resistances R_1, R_2, R_3 and R_T for a series circuit?

FIGURE 2.20 (a) Current and voltage in a series circuit, (b) the equivalent circuit to (a) provided $R_T = R_1 + R_2 + R_3$

The circuit in figure 2.19 (b) is equivalent to that in (a), i.e. the two circuits are the same, as both have the same supply voltage and current.

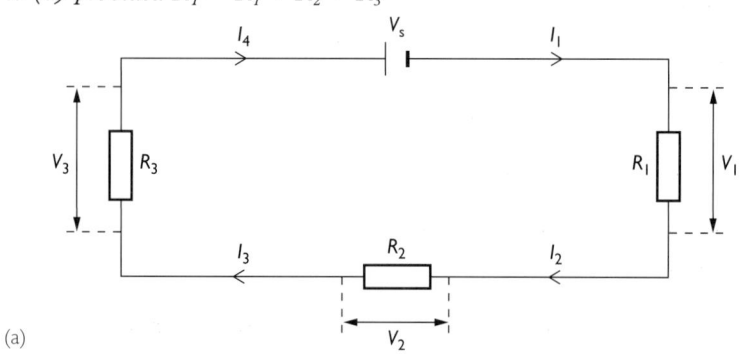

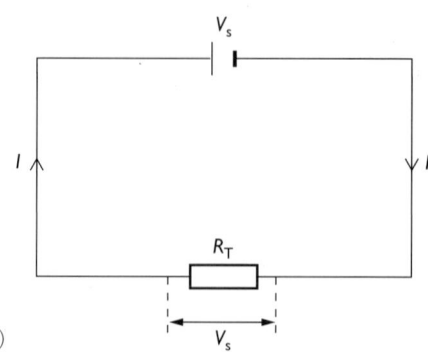

In the series circuit shown in figure 2.20 (a):

- The current is the same at all positions – the current does not split up, i.e. $I_1 = I_2 = I_3 = I_4$.
- The supply voltage is equal to the sum of the voltages round the circuit, i.e. $V_S = V_1 + V_2 + V_3$.
- The total resistance (R_T) of the circuit is equal to the sum of the individual resistance's: $R_T = R_1 + R_2 + R_3$.

Example: For the circuit shown (figure 2.21) calculate the readings on the ammeters A_1 and A_2, and the voltage across each of the resistors.

Solution: Total resistance of circuit:
$$R_T = R_1 + R_2 + R_3 + R_4 = 4 + 8 + 10 + 2 = 24 \, \Omega$$

From Ohm's law:
$$\text{circuit current } I = \frac{V_S}{R_T} = \frac{12}{24} = 0.5 \text{ A}$$

So ammeter $A_1 = A_2 = 0.5$ A (since the current in a series circuit is the same at all points). The voltages across each resistor are calculated using Ohm's law:

voltage across resistor = current through resistor × resistance of resistor
$$V_{4\Omega} = I \times R_{4\Omega} = 0.5 \times 4 = 2 \text{ V}$$
$$V_{8\Omega} = I \times R_{8\Omega} = 0.5 \times 8 = 4 \text{ V}$$
$$V_{10\Omega} = I \times R_{10\Omega} = 0.5 \times 10 = 5 \text{ V}$$
$$V_{2\Omega} = I \times R_{2\Omega} = 0.5 \times 2 = 1 \text{ V}$$

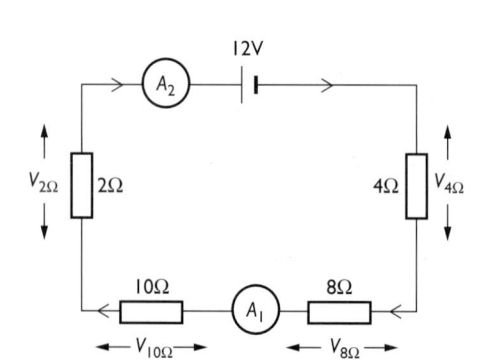

FIGURE 2.21 *Example for a series circuit*

A parallel circuit

Two resistors of value 6 Ω and 12 Ω are connected in parallel. Their combined (or total) resistance is measured by an ohmmeter as 4 Ω, as shown in figure 2.22.

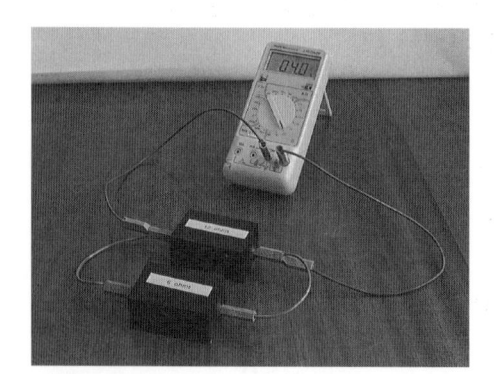

FIGURE 2.22 *An ohmmeter measures the combined resistance of two resistors connected in parallel*

using electricity 2

Figure 2.23 (a) shows these resistors connected in parallel with ammeters connected to measure the current at various positions. Voltmeters have also been connected to measure the voltage across each resistor. Table 2.5 shows the readings on the meters. Use Ohm's law to confirm the value of each resistor.

Current	Voltage	Resistance
$A_1 = 2$ A	$V_1 = 12$ V	6 Ω
$A_2 = 1$ A	$V_2 = 12$ V	12 Ω
$A_3 = 3$ A	–	–
$A_4 = 3$ A	–	–
–	$V_S = 12$ V	4 Ω

TABLE 2.5

- What do you notice about the voltages across resistors connected in parallel?
- What do you notice about the ammeter readings A_1, A_2, A_3 and A_4 for a parallel circuit?
- What do you notice about the sizes of the resistances R_1 and R_2 compared with R_T?

The circuit in figure 2.23 (b) is equivalent to that in (a), i.e. the two circuits are the same, as both have the same supply voltage and current from the supply.

The combined resistance of 4 Ω is obtained from the two resistors as follows:

$$\frac{1}{R_T} = \frac{1}{R_1} + \frac{1}{R_2} = \frac{1}{6} + \frac{1}{12} = 0.167 + 0.083 = 0.25$$

$$\frac{1}{R_T} = 0.25$$

$$R_T = \frac{1}{0.25} = 4\ \Omega$$

Notice that this can also be obtained from Ohm's law using the equivalent circuit shown in figure 2.23 (b).

$$V_S = IR$$
$$12 = 3R$$
$$R = \frac{12}{3} = 4\ \Omega$$

For the parallel circuit shown in figure 2.24:

- The current splits up so the circuit current equals the sum of the currents in the branches, i.e. $I = I_1 + I_2$.
- The voltage across resistors connected in parallel is the same, i.e. $V_1 = V_2$ and in this case $V_S = V_1 = V_2$.

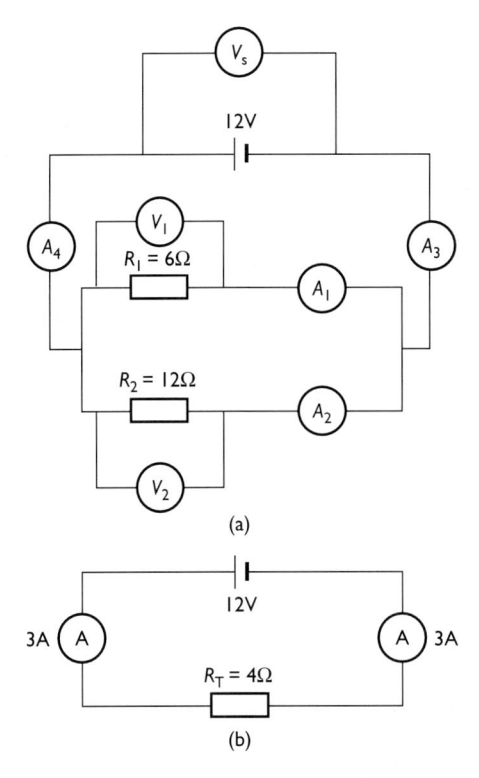

FIGURE 2.23 *(a) Measuring the current through and the voltage across resistors in parallel, (b) the equivalent circuit to that shown in figure (a)*

37

standard grade physics

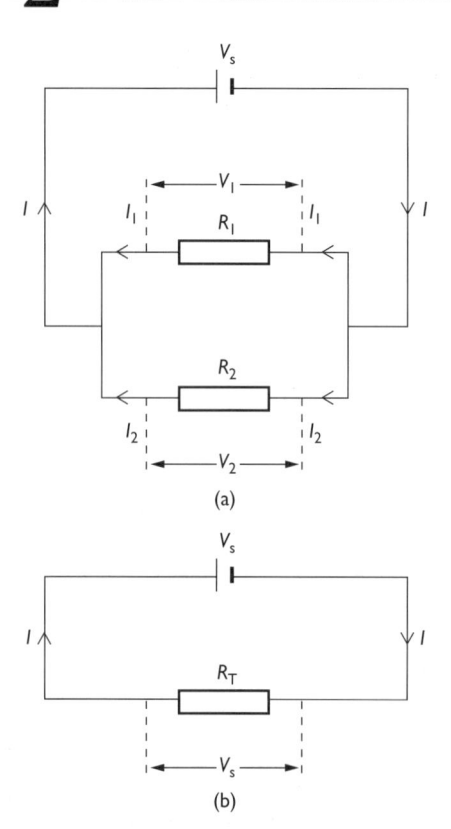

FIGURE 2.24 (a) Current and voltage in a parallel circuit, (b) the equivalent circuit to (a) provided

$$\frac{1}{R_T} = \frac{1}{R_1} + \frac{1}{R_2}$$

FIGURE 2.26 Example for a mixed series and parallel circuit

- The total resistance of the circuit is found using:

$$\frac{1}{R_T} = \frac{1}{R_1} + \frac{1}{R_2}$$

Note: For a parallel circuit, the total resistance is less than the value of the smallest resistance.

Example: Three resistors of resistance 100 Ω, 200 Ω and 100 Ω are connected in parallel. Calculate the total resistance of the circuit.
Solution:

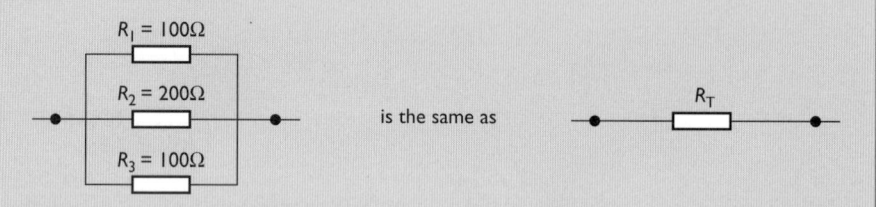

FIGURE 2.25 Example for a parallel circuit

$$\frac{1}{R_T} = \frac{1}{R_1} + \frac{1}{R_2} + \frac{1}{R_3} = \frac{1}{100} + \frac{1}{200} + \frac{1}{100} = 0.01 + 0.005 + 0.01 = 0.025$$

$$\frac{1}{R_T} = 0.025$$

$$R_T = \frac{1}{0.025} = 40 \; \Omega$$

As a check on our answer we would expect it to be smaller than 100 Ω.

Example: Two resistors each of resistance 20 Ω are connected in parallel. Calculate the total resistance of the circuit.
Solution:

$$\frac{1}{R_T} = \frac{1}{R_1} + \frac{1}{R_2} = \frac{1}{20} + \frac{1}{20} = 0.05 + 0.05$$

$$\frac{1}{R_T} = 0.10$$

$$R_T = \frac{1}{0.10} = 10 \; \Omega$$

Note: that the total resistance of two identical resistors connected in parallel is half that of one of the resistors.

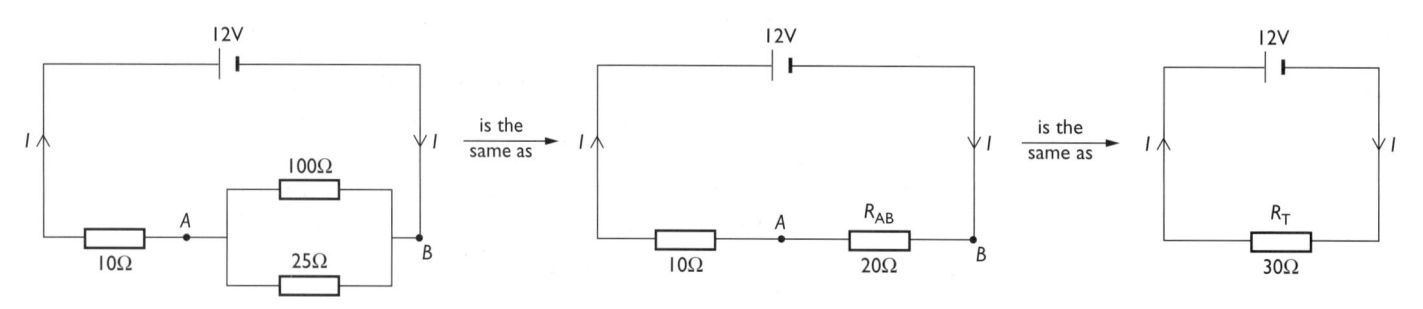

Example: In the circuit shown in figure 2.26, calculate (a) the total resistance, (b) the current in the circuit, (c) the voltage across the 10 Ω resistor.

Solution:

(a) $\dfrac{1}{R_{AB}} = \dfrac{1}{R_1} + \dfrac{1}{R_2} = \dfrac{1}{100} + \dfrac{1}{25} = 0.01 + 0.04 = 0.05$

$R_{AB} = \dfrac{1}{0.05} = 20\ \Omega$

Total resistance $R_T = 10 + R_{AB} = 10 + 20 = 30\ \Omega$.

(b) $V_S = IR_T$ gives $12 = I \times 30$. Hence $I = 12/30 = 0.4$ A.

(c) Voltage across 10 Ω resistor = current through resistor × resistance of resistor
$V = IR = 0.4 \times 10 = 4$ V.

IN *summary*

For three resistors, connected either in series or parallel:

	Current	Voltage	Total resistance
Series	Same at all points	Adds up	$R_T = R_1 + R_2 + R_3$
Parallel	Adds up	Same at all points	$\dfrac{1}{R_T} = \dfrac{1}{R_1} + \dfrac{1}{R_2} + \dfrac{1}{R_3}$

A practical parallel circuit – car wiring

Figure 2.27 shows how the side lights and headlights in a car are wired.
When S_1 is closed, the sidelights come on. When S_1 and S_2 are both closed, the headlights and the sidelights are both on.
The lights are wired in parallel so that (a) all lamps get the same voltage and (b) if one lamp breaks then the others continue to light.

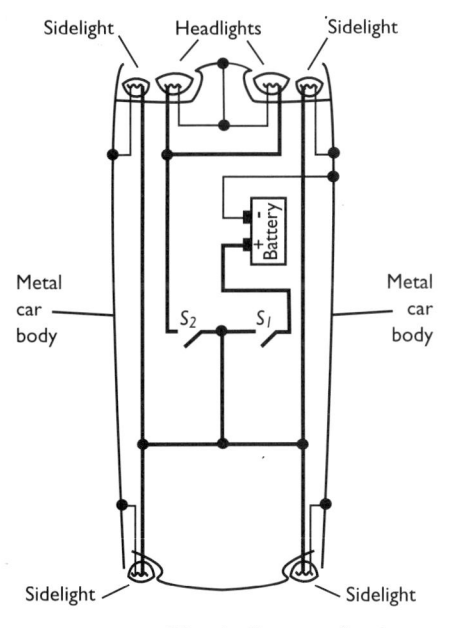

FIGURE 2.27 *Circuit diagram for the wiring of the lights in a car*

Fault finding

There are two types of fault that can occur in an electrical circuit – a short circuit and an open circuit. An ohmmeter can be used to test for these faults.

Figure 2.28 (a) shows a wire connected to an ohmmeter. The ohmmeter reads zero (or very close to zero, the resistance of the wire), i.e. 0 Ω. This is known as a **short circuit**. Short circuits can only occur with an electrical component, not with a wire.

Figure 2.28 (b) shows a wire with an electrical break connected to the ohmmeter. The ohmmeter reads the largest value the meter can indicate (on most models of ohmmeter this is shown by the number '1'), i.e. infinity. This is known as an **open circuit**. Open circuits can occur with both electrical components and wires.

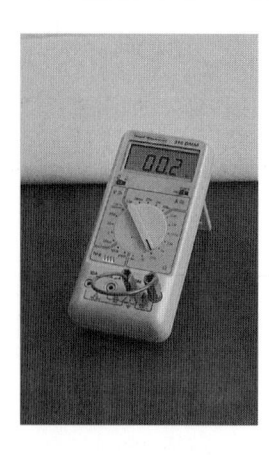

Consider a circuit in which a lamp does not light. This could be due to:

- the filament of the lamp being broken, i.e. an open circuit lamp (a likely possibility);
- a piece of wire being connected in parallel with the lamp, i.e. a short circuited lamp;
- a broken wire between the battery and the lamp;
- the battery being 'flat'.

Using the ohmmeter, the fault in this circuit may be found by:

(a) Testing the lamp. When the ohmmeter is connected across the lamp, it will show:

- a reading which is the same as the resistance of a working lamp;
- a very, very high reading, i.e. an open circuit, indicating that the lamp filament is broken (fault found);
- zero resistance, i.e. a short circuit (in this case a wire is connected in parallel with the lamp) (fault found).

(b) Testing the wires in the circuit. Each wire is connected to the ohmmeter as shown in figure 2.28 (a). It will show:

- zero resistance, i.e. a short circuit, the wire provides an electrical path;
- a very, very high reading, i.e. an open circuit, indicating that the wire is broken (fault found).

If none of the above has detected a fault then the battery should be replaced.

(a)

(b)

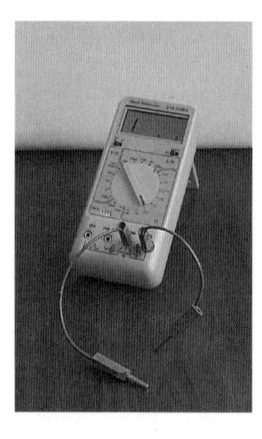

FIGURE 2.28 *(a) A short circuit, (b) an open circuit*

A simple circuit tester

An ohmmeter can be an expensive piece of equipment. A cheaper and simpler circuit tester is shown in figure 2.29.

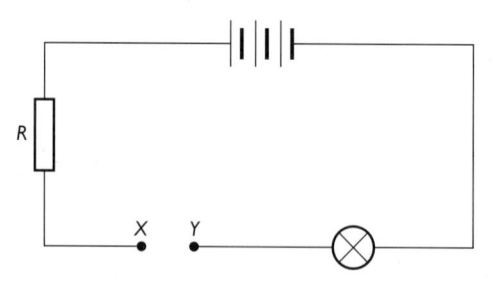

FIGURE 2.29 *A simple circuit tester*

The resistor R is present so that when wires X and Y are joined, the lamp is as bright as it safely can be – it is called a **protective resistance** and prevents too much current passing through the lamp and 'blowing' it. Any other piece of electrical equipment, e.g. a resistor or a lamp, joined between X and Y will increase the resistance of the circuit so there will be less current and the lamp will be less bright.

Before using the tester to look for a fault, X and Y are joined together to check that the lamp lights. If it does not light, the lamp or battery should be replaced – after having checked for a loose connection.

2.5 Behind the wall

Electricity and house wiring

Electricity is conveyed from power stations to our homes by the National Grid system. It arrives in our homes by a cable called the **service cable**. Figure 2.30 shows the various connections that are made to it when it enters your house.

Electricity board fuse box – this contains a fuse which cuts off the house supply from the service cable should a serious fault develop in the house

Electricity meter – this measures the electrical energy used in the house

Earth terminal – there is often a terminal near the service cable which is connected to earth and to which all the earth wires in the house are linked

Domestic circuit cables – these leave the consumer unit and distribute electricity throughout the house

Consumer unit – this contains a main switch which isolates the house wiring from the service cable, and fuses for the various domestic circuits

FIGURE 2.30 *Service cable – electricity is brought into the house by an underground 230 V service cable (live and neutral wires)*

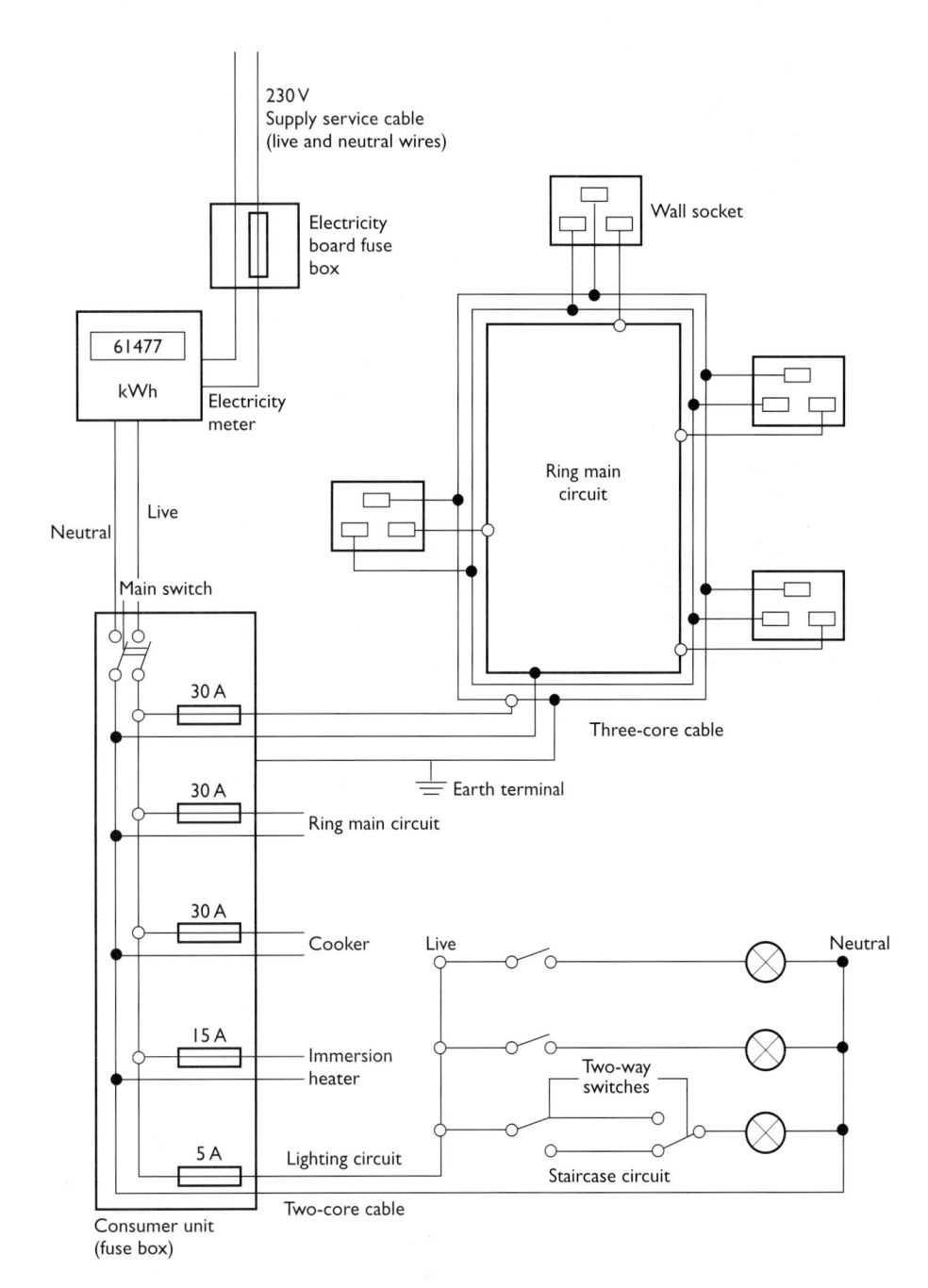

Look at the lighting and ring main circuits shown in figure 2.30.

The **lighting circuit** – the house lights are connected in parallel with each other. Normally there are two lighting circuits (one for downstairs, the other for upstairs), each having a 5 A fuse in the **consumer unit** (or fuse box).

41

> The **ring main circuit** – the electrical sockets are connected in parallel to the live, neutral and earth wires which loop round the house.

There are normally two ring circuits (again one for downstairs, the other for upstairs), each having a 30 A fuse in the consumer unit. Notice that the ring main circuit is different from the lighting circuit in that the live, neutral and earth wires form a 'ring'.

> The difference between these two circuits can be demonstrated through the 'conventional' parallel and ring circuits shown in figure 2.31. Both circuits have identical lamps of equal brightness and ammeters have been positioned in the circuits. The ammeter readings are shown in table 2.6. 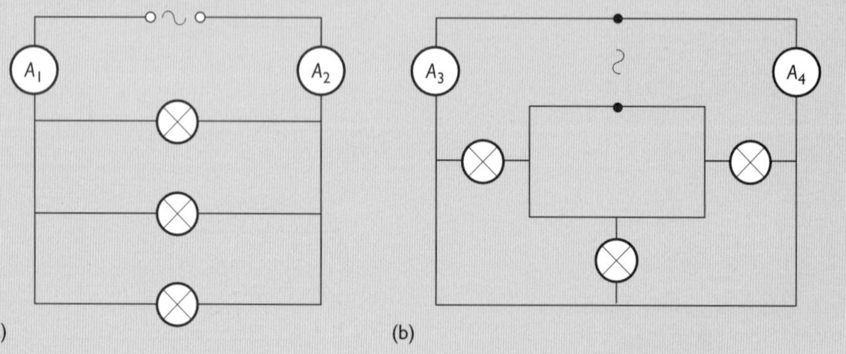
>
> **FIGURE 2.31** *(a) A 'conventional' parallel circuit, (b) a ring circuit*
>
> Notice that the current in the ring circuit is half that in the parallel circuit. This is due to the current in a ring having two possible routes round the circuit. This means that although the power delivered to the lamps is the same for both circuits, the cables in the ring circuit carry a smaller current than those in the parallel circuit. Since the ring main cable carries less current, it will produce less heat. It is a safer arrangement and the cable can be made thinner. Thinner cable is less costly since it contains less conductor (usually copper).
>
> A ring main is used where the power requirement can be high. The much lower power requirements of a lighting circuit already allow thin cables to be used and so a ring circuit in this case is not justified.

Circuit	Ammeter	Readings
parallel	A_1 = 1.8 A	A_2 = 1.8 A
ring	A_3 = 0.9 A	A_4 = 0.9 A

TABLE 2.6

Mains fuses and circuit breakers

Domestic wiring circuits are protected by fuses in the consumer unit. These are in addition to the fuse in each three-pin plug. They are used to protect the hidden cables (behind the walls) from overheating. A fuse will melt and break the electrical circuit if the current becomes too high.

Mains fuses will 'blow' if the circuit is overloaded or if the fuse wire is of too low a rating. Typical values for consumer unit fuses are shown in table 2.7. Most modern houses are now fitted with circuit breakers instead of fuses.

Circuit/Appliance	Fuse
lighting circuit	5 A
ring circuit	30 A
immersion heater	15 A
cooker	30 A

TABLE 2.7

using electricity 2

Circuit breakers

Figure 2.32 shows a consumer unit fitted with circuit breakers. **Circuit breakers** are used in some consumer units instead of fuses. They automatically switch themselves off (trip) if the circuit is overloaded. When the fault has been corrected, the circuit can be reconnected simply by resetting the circuit breaker. A fuse, however, could be replaced with a higher value of fuse wire, allowing a faulty circuit to work. This very dangerous situation (the cables could overheat and catch fire!) cannot arise with a circuit breaker, as it will continue to trip until the fault has been corrected. Before replacing a fuse or resetting a circuit breaker, the fault should always be found and corrected.

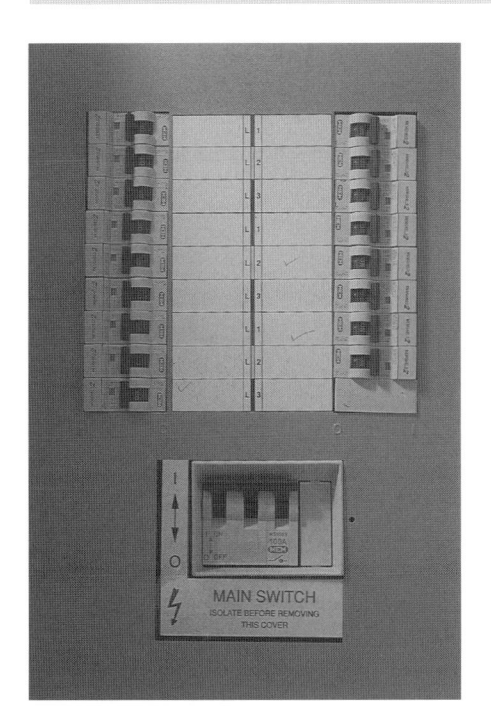

FIGURE 2.32 *Most modern house consumer units are fitted with circuit breakers*

Calculating your electricity bill

The electricity meter measures the electrical energy used by the appliances in your house. It does this in **kilowatt hours** (**kWh**) or '**units**' of electricity.

---

1 kWh represents the energy used by a 1 kW heater for one hour.

$$\begin{aligned}
\text{Energy used} &= \text{power} \times \text{time} \\
&= 1 \text{ kW} \times 1 \text{ hour} \\
&= 1000 \text{ W} \times (60 \times 60) \text{ seconds} \\
&= 3\,600\,000 \text{ joules} \\
&= 3.6 \text{ MJ}
\end{aligned}$$

i.e. 1 kWh = 3.6 MJ.

Number of kWh = number of kilowatts × number of hours
Cost = number of kWh used × price of 1 kWh

Example: A 100 W lamp is left switched on for eight hours. Calculate the energy used in kWh.
Solution:

$$P = \frac{E}{t}$$

$$0.1 = \frac{E}{t}$$

Therefore, $E = 0.1 \times 8 = 0.8$ kWh.

Example: A cooker element has a power rating of 1.5 kW and is used for 20 minutes. If the cost of one unit of electricity is 8p, calculate the cost of the energy used.

Solution:
$$\text{Energy used} = \text{power} \times \text{time} = 1.5 \times \frac{20}{60} = 0.5 \text{ kWh.}$$

$$\begin{aligned}\text{Cost} &= \text{number of kWh} \times \text{price of 1 kWh} \\ &= 0.5 \times 8 \\ &= 4\text{p.}\end{aligned}$$

2.6 Movement from electricity

Permanent magnets

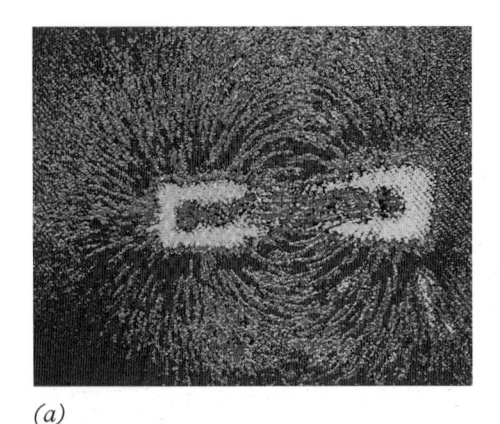

A **permanent magnet**, as its name implies, has a magnetic field surrounding it which cannot be switched off. The opposite ends, or **poles**, of a magnet are called **north** and **south** (a north pole means a north-seeking pole, i.e. it always wants to point north). The shape of the magnetic field surrounding a magnet can be shown by scattering iron filings on a piece of paper placed on top of it. The direction of the magnetic field can be found using a compass (figure 2.33).

When two permanent magnets are placed close together, their magnetic fields produce forces in such a way that:

- a north pole repels a north pole;
- a south pole repels a south pole;
- and a north pole attracts a south pole;

i.e. **like poles repel and unlike poles attract**.

Some metals such as iron and steel are attracted to magnets.

Electromagnetism

FIGURE 2.33 (a) Iron filings show the magnetic field lines, (b) direction of magnetic field lines for a permanent magnet

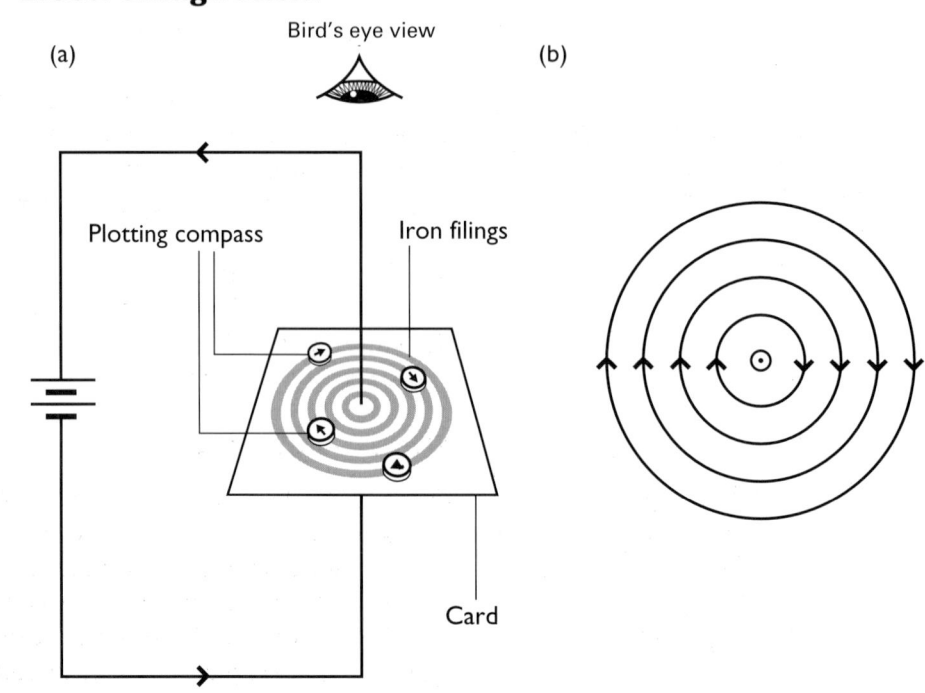

FIGURE 2.34 (a) The magnetic field surrounding a current carrying wire, (b) the magnetic field lines as seen from above

using electricity 2

Figure 2.34 (a) shows a long straight wire passing vertically through a piece of card. A magnetic field surrounds the wire when it carries an electrical current. Increasing the current through the wire increases the strength of magnetic field surrounding the wire. Reversing the direction of the current through the wire reverses the direction of the magnetic field around the wire. Figure 2.34 (b) shows the pattern of magnetic field lines surrounding the wire when looking from above. Figure 2.35 (a) shows the symbol which is used to indicate current passing out of the paper (towards you) and figure 2.35 (b) shows the symbol for current passing into the paper (away from you).

FIGURE 2.35 *(a) Current passing out of paper, (b) current passing into paper*

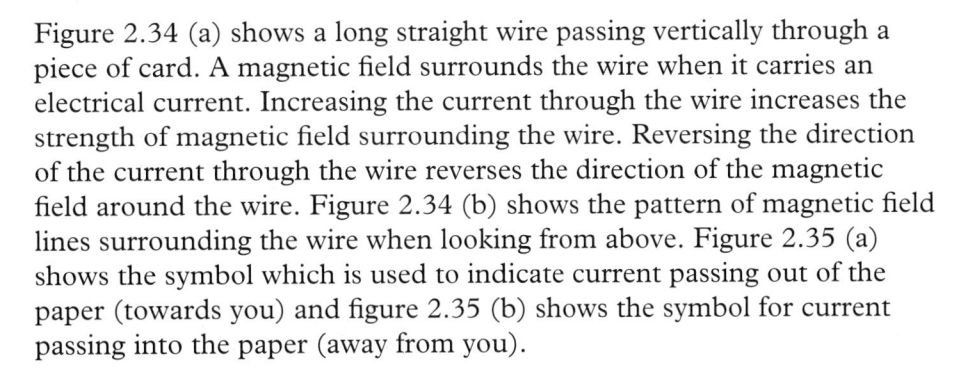

Electromagnets

When an electric current passes through a wire which is coiled around an iron core, the core becomes magnetised and an **electromagnet** is produced, as shown in figure 2.36. However, the electromagnet has little strength without the iron core. The iron core is able to concentrate the magnetic field within itself so giving a stronger magnetic effect.

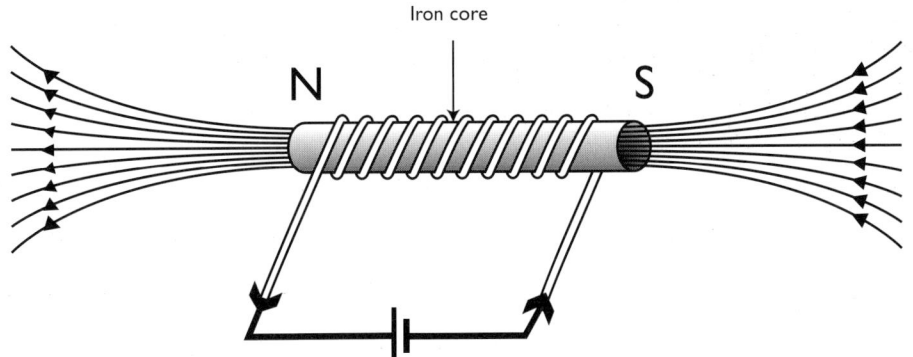

FIGURE 2.36 *An electromagnet*

The magnetic field of an electromagnet can be made stronger by (a) increasing the current through the coils of wire; (b) increasing the number of turns of wire on the core. When an a.c. supply is used, the electromagnet still produces a magnetic field – but one which alternates each time the current changes direction. There is no magnetic field when the electric current is switched off. This on–off nature of the magnetic field can be used in various ways, such as to lift and release scrap iron as shown in figure 2.37.

Electromagnets are essential parts of many electrical devices.

FIGURE 2.37 *Electromagnets can lift heavy magnetic objects*

The electric bell

Figure 2.38 shows an electric bell. When the door bell is pressed, switch S closes and completes the electrical circuit. A current passes through the electromagnet which becomes magnetised and attracts the iron bar or armature. However, when the striker moves to hit the bell, the electrical circuit is broken at T and the electromagnet loses its magnetism. The springy metal strip is now able to pull the armature back, and in so doing the electrical circuit is re-made at T. This completes the circuit again and continuous ringing occurs as long as the door bell is pressed.

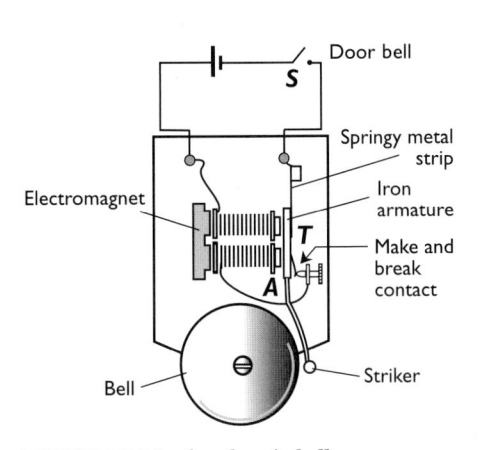

FIGURE 2.38 *An electric bell*

45

The magnetic relay

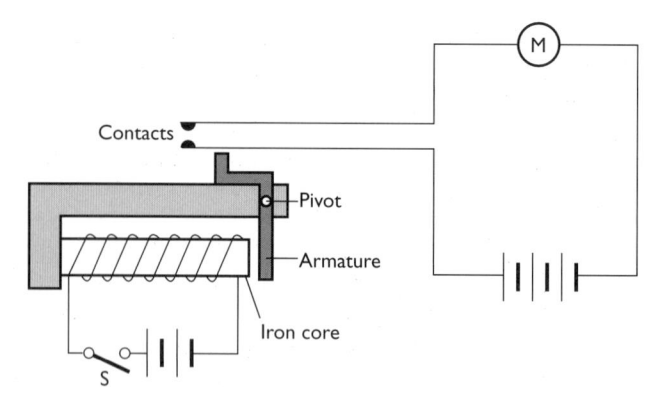

FIGURE 2.39 *The motor is switched via the relay when switch S is closed*

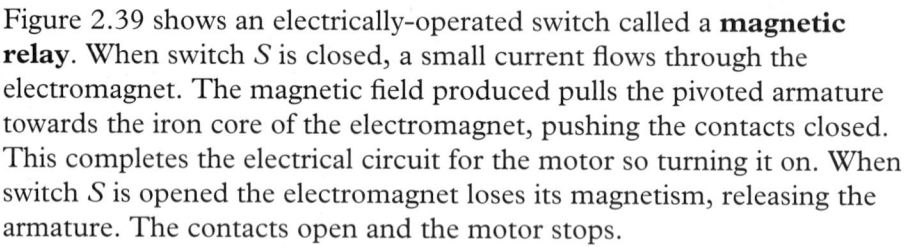

Figure 2.39 shows an electrically-operated switch called a **magnetic relay**. When switch S is closed, a small current flows through the electromagnet. The magnetic field produced pulls the pivoted armature towards the iron core of the electromagnet, pushing the contacts closed. This completes the electrical circuit for the motor so turning it on. When switch S is opened the electromagnet loses its magnetism, releasing the armature. The contacts open and the motor stops.

Relays are very useful devices. They are used when it is desirable for a small current in a control circuit to open or close a switch in a main circuit which will carry a large current.

FIGURE 2.40 *The current carrying foil is forced out of the magnetic field of the permanent magnet*

A current-carrying conductor in a magnetic field

Figure 2.40 shows a strip of aluminium foil which has been placed between the poles of a strong permanent magnet. When a current passes through the foil the magnetic field produced combines with the magnetic field of the permanent magnet to give a force on the aluminium foil which pushes it out of the field of the magnet. Figure 2.41 shows the same effect on current-carrying wires placed in the magnetic field of a permanent magnet. Notice that the force acting on the current-carrying wire is at right angles to the direction of the current and at right angles to the direction of the magnetic field.

> The direction of the force (or movement) on the wires can be reversed by either reversing the direction of the current, (i.e. reversing the terminals on the battery), or by reversing the direction of the magnetic field (i.e. reversing the poles of the permanent magnet).

The force between a permanent magnet and a current-carrying conductor is put to use in an electric motor.

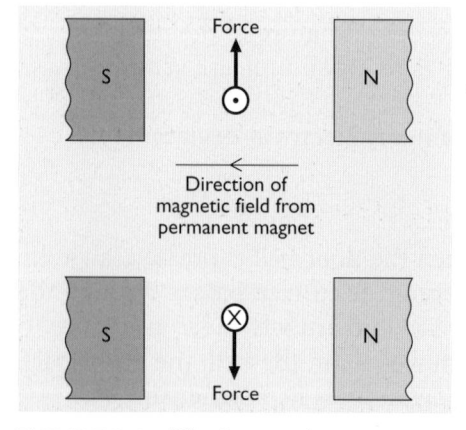

FIGURE 2.41 *The force acting on a current-carrying conductor, when placed in an external magnetic field*

using electricity

The electric motor

Figure 2.42 shows a simple model electric motor. The main parts of a motor are:

- a magnet;
- a few coils of wire;
- power supply.
- split-ring commutator;
- carbon brushes;

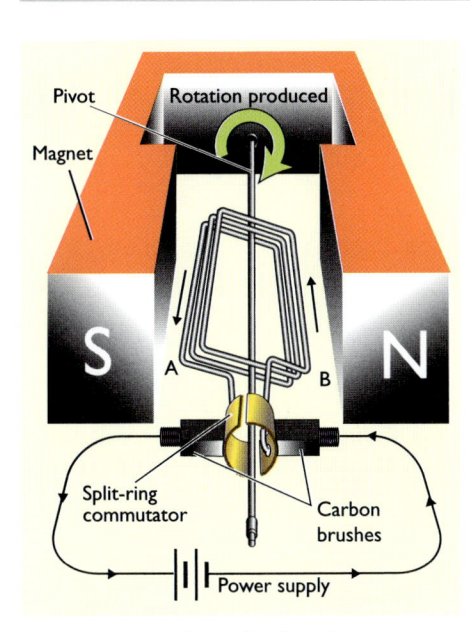

FIGURE 2.42 *A simple electric motor*

A strong magnetic field exists between the poles of the magnet. The coils of wire are connected to the **split-ring commutator**. This assembly is free to rotate about a central axis within the magnetic field of the magnet. **Carbon brushes** are pushed lightly against the split-ring commutator by springs. The current from the negative terminal of the supply passes through one brush, one half of the commutator, round the coils of wire, through the other half of the commutator, and on through the second brush to the positive terminal.

Due to the combined effect of the magnetic fields from the magnet and the current-carrying coils of wire, each side experiences a force, but in opposite directions as shown in figures 2.43 (a) and (b). These make the coils turn clockwise, until it reaches a point where no current passes through the coils of wire and so there are no forces on the coils (figure 2.43 (c)). However, in practice the coils are carried slightly past this position. The current through the coils is now reversed by the commutator. The forces again have a clockwise turning effect since the current has been reversed (figures 2.43 (d) and (e)). The coils have now completed half a revolution. This is exactly the same situation as shown in figure 2.43 (a) and so the process is repeated and the coils rotate, with the commutator automatically changing the direction of the current through the coils of wire every half revolution to give a continuous clockwise turning force.

This simple motor produces a low turning effect and a jerky action. Practical motors give a much improved performance because:

- Each coil consists of hundreds of turns of wire creating a greater turning force.
- Several coils are used, each set at a different angle and each connected to its own pair of commutator segments. This gives a greater turning force and smoother running.
- An electromagnet replaces the permanent magnet. An electromagnet is more compact and produces a stronger magnetic field than a permanent magnet of the same size.

In practical motors the brushes are made of carbon because it:

- gives good electrical contact;
- moulds itself to the shape of the commutator;
- withstands high temperature;
- reduces wear on the commutator.

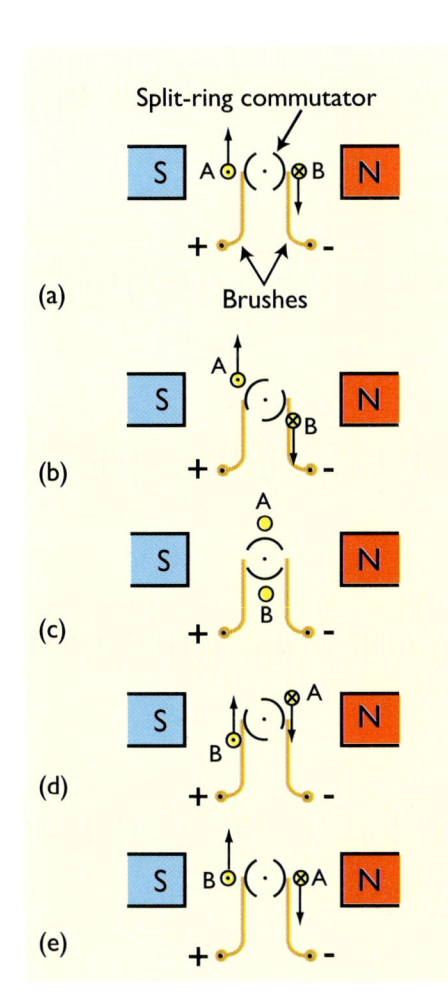

FIGURE 2.43 *Forces on a coil during rotation*

47

LEARNING OUTCOMES

After studying this chapter you should be able to:

Section 2.1

1. Describe the mains supply/battery as a supply of electrical energy and describe the main energy transformations occurring in household appliances.
2. State approximate power ratings of different household appliances.
3. Select an appropriate flex given the power rating of an appliance.
4. State that fuses in plugs are intended to protect flexes.
5. Select an appropriate fuse given the power rating of an appliance.
6. Identify the live, neutral and earth wire from the colour of their insulation.
7. State to which pin each wire must be connected for a plug, lampholder and extension socket.
8. State that the human body is a conductor of electricity and that moisture increases its ability to conduct.
9. State that the earth wire is a safety device.
10. State that electrical appliances which have the double insulation symbol do not require an earth wire.
11. Draw the double insulation symbol.
12. Explain why situations involving electricity could result in accidents (to include proximity of water, wrong fuses, wrong, frayed or badly connected flexes, short circuits and misuse of multiway adaptors).
13. Explain how the earth wire acts as a safety device. `Credit`
14. Explain why fuses and switches must be in the live lead. `Credit`

Section 2.2

1. State that the mains supply is a.c. and a battery is d.c.
2. Explain in terms of current the terms a.c. and d.c.
3. State that the frequency of the mains supply is 50 Hz.
4. State that the declared value of the mains voltage is quoted as 230 V.
5. Draw and identify the circuit symbol for a battery, fuse, lamp, switch, resistor, capacitor, diode and variable resistor.
6. State that electrons are free to move in a conductor.
7. Describe the electric current in terms of the movement of charges around a circuit.
8. Use correctly the units 'ampere' and 'volt'.
9. State that the declared value of an alternating voltage is less than its peak value. `Credit`
10. Carry out calculations involving the relationship between charge, current and time. `Credit`
11. Use correctly the unit 'coulomb'. `Credit`
12. State that the voltage of a supply is a measure of the energy given to the charges in a circuit. `Credit`

Section 2.3

1. Draw and identify the circuit symbols for an ammeter and voltmeter.
2. Draw circuit diagrams to show the correct positions of an ammeter and voltmeter in a circuit.
3. State that an increase in resistance of a circuit leads to a decrease in the current in that circuit.
4. Carry out calculations involving the relationship between resistance, current and voltage.
5. Use correctly the unit 'ohm'.
6. Give two practical uses of variable resistors.
7. State that when there is an electric current in a wire, there is an energy transformation.
8. Give three examples of resistive circuits in the home, in which electrical energy is transformed into heat.
9. State that the electrical energy transformed each second = IV.
10. State the relationship between energy and power.
11. Use correctly, in context, the terms energy, power, joule and watt.
12. Carry out calculations involving the relationship between power, current and voltage.

Learning outcomes

13 State that in a lamp, electrical energy is transformed into heat and light.

14 State that the energy transformation in an electric lamp occurs in resistance wire (filament lamp) or gas (discharge tube).

15 State that a discharge tube lamp is more efficient than a filament lamp (i.e. more of the energy is transformed into light and less into heat).

16 State that the energy transformation in an electric heater occurs in resistance wire (element).

17 State that V/I for a resistor remains approximately constant for different currents. `Credit`

18 Explain the equivalence of IV and I^2R. `Credit`

19 Carry out calculations using the relationship between power, current and resistance. `Credit`

Section 2.4

1 State a practical application in the home which requires two or more switches used in series.

2 State that in a series circuit, the current is the same at all points.

3 State that the sum of currents in parallel branches is equal to the current drawn from the supply.

4 Explain that connecting too many appliances to one socket is dangerous because a large current could be drawn from the supply.

5 State that the voltage across components in parallel is the same for each component.

6 State that the sum of voltages across components in series is equal to the voltage of the supply.

7 Describe how to make a simple continuity tester.

8 Describe how a continuity tester may be used for fault finding.

9 Draw circuit diagrams to describe how the various car lighting requirements are achieved. `Credit`

10 Carry out calculations involving the relationships $R_T = R_1 + R_2 + \ldots$ and $1/R_T = 1/R_1 + 1/R_2$ `Credit`

Section 2.5

1 State that household wiring connects appliances in parallel.

2 State that mains fuses protect the mains wiring.

3 State that a circuit breaker is an automatic switch which can be used instead of a fuse.

4 State that a kWh is a unit of energy.

5 Describe, using a circuit diagram, a ring circuit. `Credit`

6 State advantages of using the ring circuit as a preferred method of wiring in parallel. `Credit`

7 Give two differences between the lighting circuit and the power ring circuit. `Credit`

8 State one reason why a circuit breaker may be used in preference to a fuse. `Credit`

9 Explain the relationship between kilowatt hours and joules. `Credit`

Section 2.6

1 Identify on a simple diagram of an electric motor, the rotating coil, field coil (magnet) brushes and commutator.

2 State that a magnetic field exists around a current-carrying wire.

3 Give two examples of practical applications which make use of the magnetic effect of a current.

4 State that a current-carrying wire experiences a force when the wire is in a magnetic field.

5 State that the direction of force on a current-carrying wire depends upon the direction of current and of the field. `Credit`

6 Explain the operation of a d.c. electric motor in terms of forces acting on the coil and the purpose of the brushes and commutator. `Credit`

7 State the reasons for the use in commercial motors of carbon brushes, multi-section commutators and field coils. `Credit`

STUDY QUESTIONS

1 Name five electrical appliances in your home and give the main energy change for each.

2 (a) Cartridge fuses of values 3 A and 13 A are available to you. What value of fuse should you fit to the three-pin plug of a (i) 250 W television; (ii) 750 W electric drill; (iii) 300 W food mixer; (iv) 1100 W iron?

(b) What is the minimum safe thickness of conductor in a flex that would be required for (i) a table lamp with a power rating of 60 W; (ii) a washing machine with a power rating of 2950 W? (Use the table on page 26 to help you.)

3 (a) A fault develops which allows the outer metal casing of an electrical appliance to become live. Explain how the earth wire acts as a safety device when this happens.

(b) What is unsafe about the situations shown in the figures below?

4 (a) The current through a lamp is 0.5 A. How much charge flows through it in 15 seconds?

(b) A charge of 200 coulombs flows for 40 seconds. Calculate the current.

(c) 1000 C of charge are transferred by a current of 2 A. How long did it take for the charge to be transferred?

5 The diagram below shows the rating plate of a vacuum cleaner.

(a) What value of voltage does it require to work properly?

(b) What is the frequency of the electrical supply to the vacuum cleaner?

(c) What value of fuse will be required to be fitted to the three-pin plug?

(d) How many cores will there be in the flex? Explain your answer.

TYPE 3010 C
230V ~ 50 Hz 1000 W

6 (a) A current of 2 A flows through a lamp of resistance 12 Ω. What is the voltage across it?

(b) A current of 0.5 A flows through a resistor. What is the resistance of the resistor if the voltage across it is 5 V?

(c) A 10 Ω resistor is connected to a 12 V supply. What current passes through the resistor?

7 (a) The element of a 230 V mains cooker has a resistance of 50 Ω. What is the power rating of the element?

(b) A lamp is rated at 12 V, 24 W. Assuming the lamp is operating at its correct rating, calculate the current in the lamp.

(c) The power rating of a heating element of a hairdryer is 100 W when the current through the element is 0.5 A. What is the resistance of the hairdryer element?

8 A current of 4 A passes through a resistor for three minutes. If the voltage across the resistor is 20 V, find

(a) the power of the resistor;

(b) the energy dissipated (used up) by the resistor.

9 The ammeter shown in in the circuit below reads 0.5 A. Calculate the:

(a) total resistance of the circuit;

(b) voltage across each resistor;

(c) supply voltage.

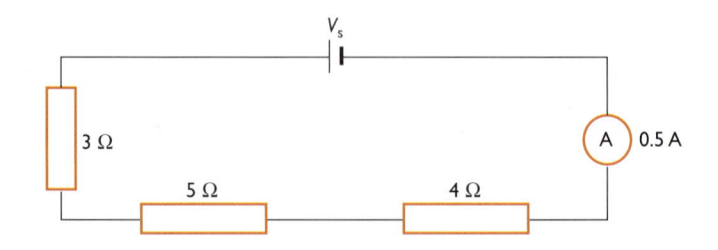

10 For the circuit shown below, calculate the:

(a) voltage across the 10 Ω resistor;

(b) voltage across R;

(c) resistance of R.

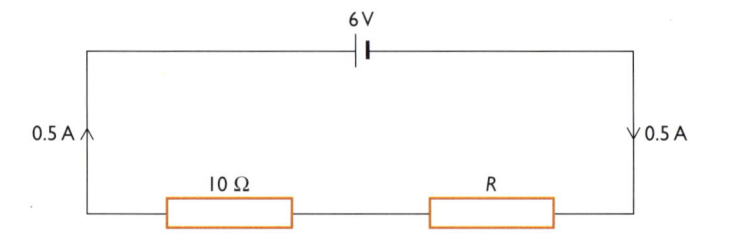

50

study questions

11 A circuit has three resistors of value 15 Ω, 30 Ω and 15 Ω connected in series. Calculate:

(a) the total resistance of the resistors;

(b) the current in the circuit when it is connected to the 230 V mains supply;

(c) the voltage across the 30 Ω resistor.

12 For the circuit shown below calculate the:

(a) total resistance of the circuit;

(b) current through each resistor.

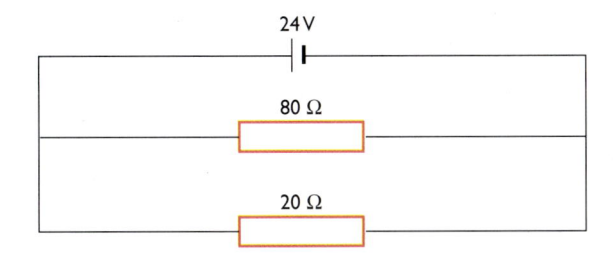

[Circuit diagram: 24 V supply with 80 Ω and 20 Ω resistors in parallel]

13 For the circuit shown below calculate the:

(a) total resistance of the circuit;

(b) ammeter reading.

[Circuit diagram: 10 V supply with ammeter A, two 50 Ω resistors in parallel, in series with 15 Ω]

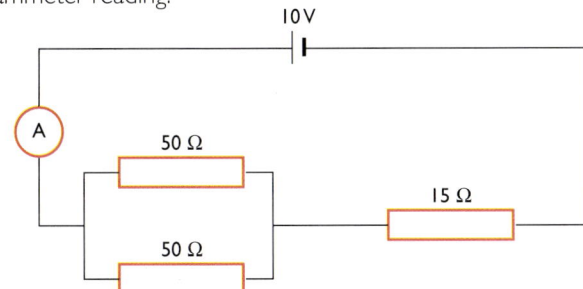

14 For the circuit shown below calculate the:

(a) total resistance of the circuit;

(b) ammeter reading.

[Circuit diagram: 18 V supply with ammeter A; 5 Ω parallel with 20 Ω, in series with 10 Ω parallel with 10 Ω]

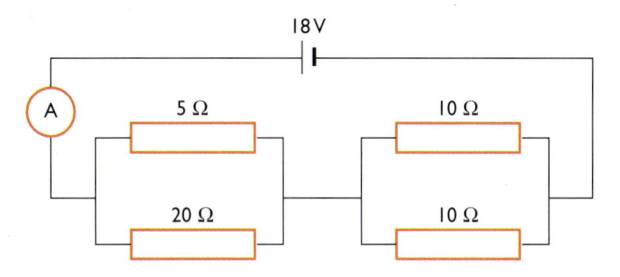

15 One of the lamps in the electrical circuit shown below is not working. Describe how you would use an ohmmeter to discover which of the lamps was not working. Would the ohmmeter indicate a short circuit or an open circuit when connected across the broken lamp?

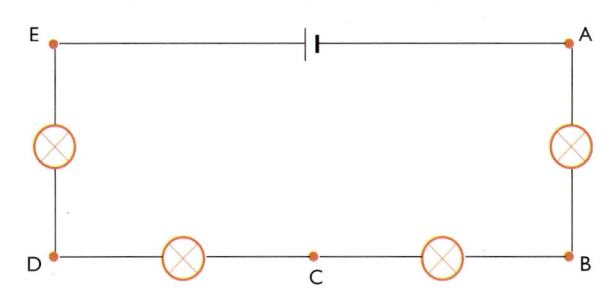

[Circuit diagram with lamps at corners E, A, D, B and along bottom at C]

16 The maximum current that a ring circuit can carry is greater than the maximum current a lighting circuit can carry. Which circuit, if any, uses thicker cable?

17 A kettle of power rating 2 kW is used ten times in a day. It is on for three minutes on each occasion. How many kWh of electricity are used in a day?

Health Physics

This chapter describes and explains how physics is used in the detection and treatment of different health problems. A large amount of work in health physics is concerned with looking inside the body without cutting it open.

3.1 Using thermometers

When you are ill, the doctor often takes your temperature to check how your body is responding to the illness and sometimes to find out how you are reacting to treatment.

Most people normally have a body temperature somewhere between 36°C and 38°C. Temperatures above or below this range can be dangerous and require medical attention.

Normal body temperature is 36.9°C. This is an average temperature and can vary by 0.5°C either way. It rises to a peak during the day with maximum activity and falls when we are asleep.

Thermometers

A thermometer is a device which measures temperature. Various kinds of thermometers work on different principles, e.g. a mercury thermometer uses the property of the expansion of a liquid.

Liquid-in-glass thermometer

This kind of thermometer uses the expansion of a liquid (e.g. mercury) to measure temperatures. The greater the temperature, the greater the expansion of the liquid. As the mercury gets warmer, it expands along the glass tube, where there is a scale of numbers marked in °C (degrees Celsius). There is no air above the mercury, so it can easily move along the tube.

The thermometer shows small changes in the temperature by producing a movement of mercury which can be easily seen. This means that the thermometer should be sensitive. A thermometer which is sensitive will have a narrow tube and a large bulb. To make the thermometer respond to rapid changes in temperature, it should have a bulb made of thin glass so that the heat can get through easily.

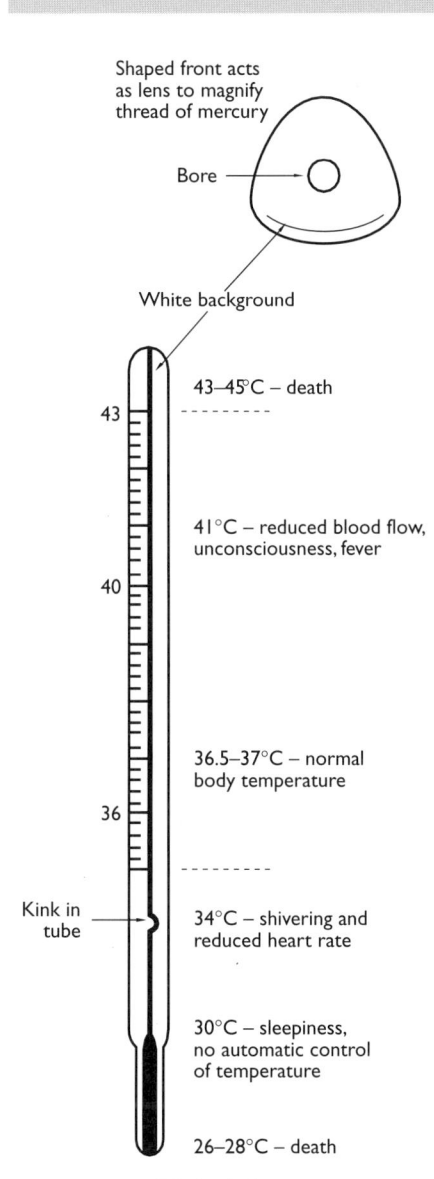

health physics 3

An ordinary liquid-in-glass thermometer cannot accurately measure body temperature since:

- The range is too large to measure small temperature changes of the human body.
- When the thermometer is removed from your mouth, the liquid in the tube starts to fall because the air temperature is cooler than your body, so the reading is changed.

Clinical thermometer

In the clinical thermometer, the scale is from 35 to 42°C. The bulb is thin at the front to allow heat to flow quickly into it, but it is thick at the back to make it difficult to break (figure 3.1).

A clinical thermometer is designed to indicate – and continue indicating – the maximum temperature of the body. It works on the principle that a liquid – usually mercury – expands when it is heated. Moreover, it expands more than the glass so that the column of mercury moves up the tube. The narrow tube gives a very fine mercury thread, which expands quickly over a large length for a small change in temperature. This makes the thermometer very sensitive.

To find a patient's temperature, the thermometer bulb is placed under the tongue and left for a minute or more. As the mercury expands in the tube, it forces its way past the bend or kink and eventually stops rising. The thermometer is then removed from the patient's mouth. Because the air temperature is cooler than your body, the mercury immediately starts to contract. But, because there is a narrow bend in the tube, the mercury thread breaks, leaving a short thread of mercury to indicate the maximum temperature recorded.

To reset a clinical thermometer so you can make a new reading, it has to be shaken fairly vigorously – but with care!

Changes in the state of your body can be shown by a change in your temperature. Some are shown in figure 3.1.

Sometimes clinical thermometers have a digital scale powered by a battery. A special sensor is used instead of the liquid in the glass bulb (figure 3.2a). Other thermometers use a special kind of chemical (liquid crystals), which changes colour when the temperature changes. These thermometers can be placed on the head to give the body temperature (figure 3.2b).

FIGURE 3.1 *Clinical thermometer*

FIGURE 3.2a *Digital thermometer*

3 standard grade physics

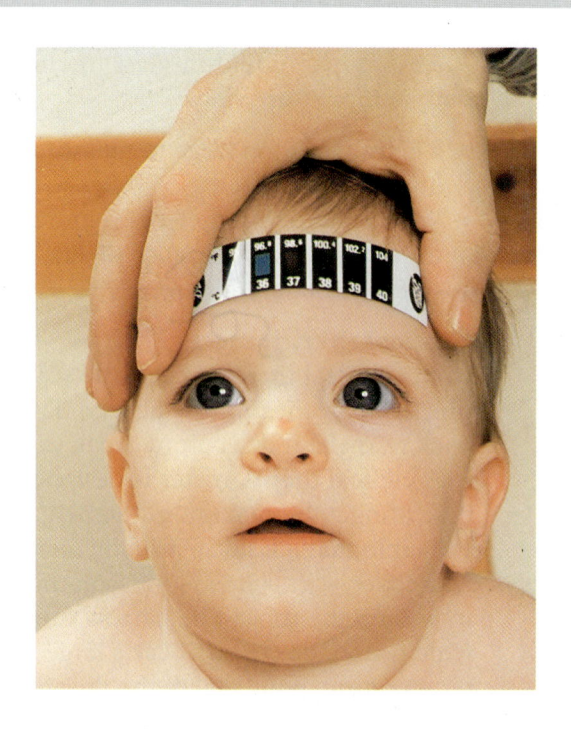

FIGURE 3.2b *Liquid crystal forehead thermometer*

Body temperature and changes

Under normal conditions, the body maintains the vital organs, such as the heart, lungs, abdominal organs and brain, at a fairly constant temperature of about 37°C, known as the 'core' or simply 'body temperature'. A lowering of body temperature is known as **hypothermia** and can happen by exposure to cold and damp conditions.

A more gradual deterioration in body function is observed during exposure to high temperatures caused, for example, by hot surroundings, heat therapy, fever or vigorous exercise. The condition, known as **hyperthermia**, is shown by the skin's blood vessels dilating, increased heart rate and reduced blood flow to the brain which may result in unconsciousness. At about 41°C, the central nervous system (i.e. the brain) starts to deteriorate, you may go into a fit, and finally death occurs between 43°C and 45°C.

Dr Findlay's casenotes

If you travel to certain tropical countries, you may get malaria. This means that you will sweat and may become unconscious. Your temperature could reach 39°C. There are medicines available to prevent you getting malaria.

Hypothermia and fever are two examples of your body temperature going very low or very high. But even small changes in temperature can have a big effect on your body. If your body temperature falls by as little as 1°C, you will begin to shiver. Shivering movements help to heat you up again.

In very warm weather, the human body cannot cope with overheating. This happened during a fun race in Australia in 1988 when a runner's body temperature rose to 42.8°C. The passage on the next page describes what happened to the athlete. From the passage, explain why the measurement of body temperature was very important in this case.

health physics 3

How a fun run meant meltdown for Mark Dorrity's body

By Sue-Ellen O'Grady

On February 27 this year, Mark Dorrity set off on what he expected to be an easy 8-kilometre fun run in Wagga, southern NSW. But near the finishing line, the fit 28-year-old collapsed, his body destroyed.

In less than an hour, his thigh muscles had overheated, liquefied and died. One leg has since had to be amputated at the buttock, because of gangrene.

Before Mark collapsed, his kidneys failed because the dying muscles had released toxic proteins into his blood, which thickened to a molasses-like consistency. Every organ in his body was affected.

He suffered brain damage. His lungs could not function unaided. His buttock and hamstring muscles also liquefied, but not as severely as his thigh muscles.

Mark's heart stopped at least once. When it started again, it hammered away at 150 beats a minute, compared to its normal 70. He was on a dialysis machine for eight weeks, and in a coma for three months. When he regained consciousness, he could not walk or talk.

Even now, five months later, Mark cannot turn over or get out of bed unaided. He faces months of intensive rehabilitation.

The devastating damage to Mark Dorrity's body was caused by heat exhaustion and dehydration resulting in a rare condition known as rhabdomyolysis, the extreme result of what every runner and athlete knows as muscle fatigue.

The director of research at the Sports Medicine Institute, Dr Tony Miller, says the condition usually affects runners taking on more than they are used to in training.

"In Mark's case it was caused by his body severely overheating – to 42.8 degrees. At the same time, he was extremely dehydrated. When someone has a temperature that high, they are delirious. They ignore the body's warnings to stop."

Mark Dorrity was no weekend jogger. When he graduated from the University of NSW with an honours degree in Science in 1974, he won a Blue for athletics. He moved to Melbourne to work as a wool exporter, and ran four kilometres through the Botanical Gardens every day. As well, he swam a kilometre three times a week. He had minimal body fat.

He travelled to Wagga in February with a group of friends, all planning to compete in a local event. When the temperature that day rose to 42 degrees, the locals cancelled their run.

But Mark and his friends, deceived by the dry heat, decided to hold their own race.

"It just didn't feel that hot," he remembers. "So we ran off."

He drank several glasses of water before beginning to run, but none during the race. That, say doctors, proved to be his near-fatal mistake.

When Mark collapsed, he was leading the race by a kilometre. Friends driving alongside rushed him to the local hospital, where he was packed in ice to lower his body temperature. He remained there for two weeks before being moved to St Vincent's for dialysis treatment.

Mark recalls nothing of this. "I don't recall collapsing. I remember waking up twice at Wagga Hospital, and then waking here."

"How do I feel? I'm very lucky to be alive. I know that. I'm a medical miracle. And it's a warning to other runners to be extremely careful."

The Sydney Morning Herald 3.8.1988

3.2 Using sound

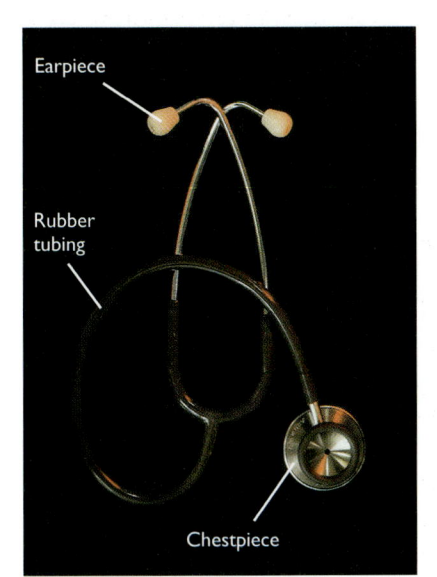

FIGURE 3.3
(Earpiece, Rubber tubing, Chestpiece)

The stethoscope

The stethoscope is a hearing aid which allows a doctor or nurse to listen to sounds made within the body. It is most often used to listen to the heart and the lungs. These sounds can be useful in the diagnosis of various diseases.

The main parts of a modern stethoscope are shown in figure 3.3.

- The chestpiece has two 'bells', one open and the other closed by a thin diaphragm (a semi-rigid disc). A valve can be turned to change from the open to the closed bell.
- The open bell is used to listen to sounds from the heart as it beats.
- The closed bell is used to listen to sounds which have a higher frequency than heart sounds, such as from the lungs.
- Sounds picked up by the open bell or the diaphragm are transmitted to the earpieces through the air in the tubing. The eardrum of the listener is also a pressure-sensitive diaphragm. To create sufficient pressure change at the ear for movements of the diaphragm, it is important to have a bell with as small a volume as possible. The volume of the tubes

should also be small and this requires short tubes with a small diameter. But we also need to have very little loss of sound due to friction and this requires large tube diameters!
- The earpieces have to be a good fit with the ears to avoid sound loss and to prevent background sounds from interfering with those coming from the heart and the lungs.

Ultrasound: sounds beyond your hearing

Young people can hear sounds with frequencies 20 to 20 000 Hz. This is the normal range of frequencies, but as we grow older the upper range of frequencies decreases. Above this frequency range, the vibrations are called ultrasound or ultrasonic vibrations. When these higher frequency ultrasonic waves are sent out by a transmitter and hit an object, some of the waves will pass through the object while some will be reflected. Bats use the echoes from such reflections to find their way about.

In medicine, the frequencies used are between 1 and 20 MHz (M = mega = 1 million). The waves are sent out from a transducer, which is a simple hand-held device which changes one form of energy into another form (e.g. force to electrical). The transducer also acts as a receiver which can pick up the reflected waves.

Very high frequencies of several megahertz are used in medicine. The speed of sound in soft biological tissue is about 1500 m/s and the distances being measured are of the order of 0.15 m, so the echo time is around 200 microseconds (200 × 10^{-6} s = 0.0002 s). Check this calculation yourself.

> Ultrasonic pulses are sent into the body from a transmitter placed in good contact with the skin. Reflections then come back from any boundary between materials of different sound properties. The more ultrasound that is reflected from the surface, the less detail that can be seen of structures in the body. These reflections happen where there is a large change in the structure, for example, from bone to muscle or from bone to soft tissue.

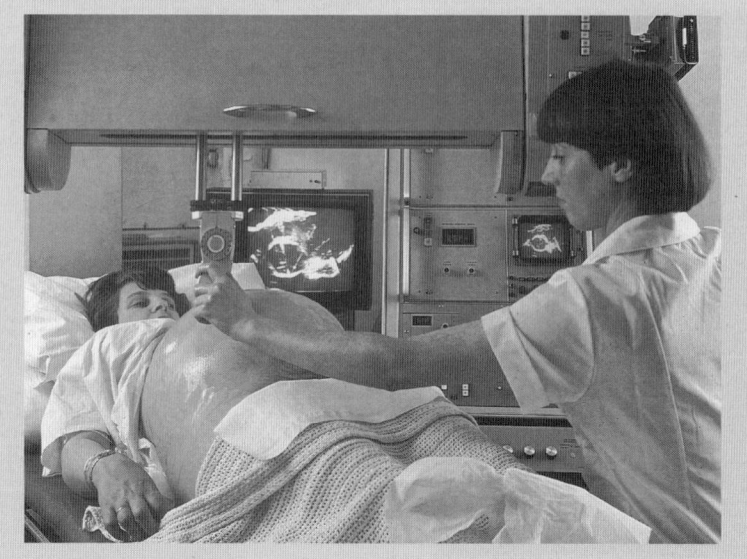

FIGURE 3.4 *Use of ultrasound*

health physics 3

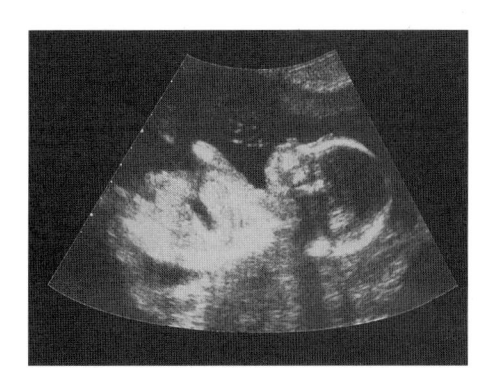

FIGURE 3.5 *Scan of a foetus*

Some waves must be transmitted into the body so good contact between the transmitter and the skin (body surface) is very important. This is to stop most of the ultrasound from being reflected at the boundary between the air and the skin, so little of the ultrasound would enter the body. To make good contact between the transmitter and the skin, and so allow most of the ultrasound into the body, a gel is smeared on the patient's skin. The pattern of reflected ultrasound can be used to build up a picture of the inside of the body (figure 3.4).

The greater the frequency, the smaller the wavelength and the greater the detail that can be seen. However, the greater the frequency, the more the waves are absorbed by body tissues. Different frequencies of ultrasound are used for different organs in the body. This allows the greatest amount of detail to be seen.

A typical ultrasound scan is shown in figure 3.5 which checks on the progress of a foetus (baby) in the womb. By measuring the diameter of the head, we can check the age of the foetus. Another use is to check the functioning of the valves in the heart.

The main advantages of ultrasound are:

- The body does not have to be cut open to see inside.
- No harmful effects on the body have been found and it is even safer than X-rays. This means that it can be safely used to check on the progress of a foetus.

Losing stones – in minutes!

Ultrasound has been used to treat patients with kidney stones. These are particles which may form in the kidneys. The stones block the flow of waste material and can cause excruciating pain. Instead of opening up the body to cut them out, the stones can be broken up by a lithotripter (figure 3.6). This uses several ultrasound beams focused on the stones so that shock waves are produced at a common point, shattering the stones but not the surrounding tissue. After the stone is broken into small pieces, it is then passed out in the normal waste from the body.

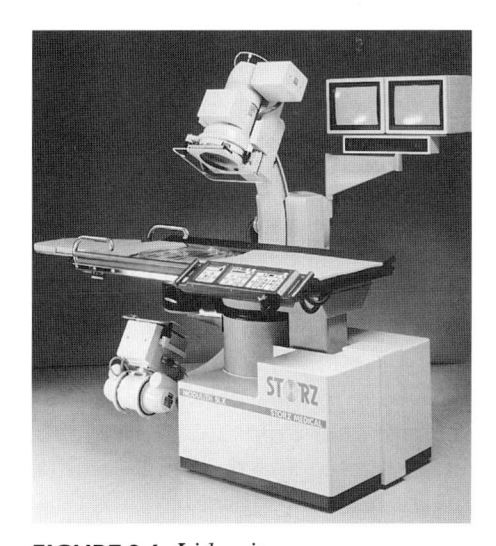

FIGURE 3.6 *Lithotripter*

Measuring sound level

The human ear is a sensitive detector of sound and can be damaged by very loud sounds. The loudness of sound is measured in **decibels (dB)** using a sound level meter (figure 3.7).

The decibel scale is not like the scale on a ruler. If one sound is ten times more powerful than another then it is said to be 10 dB greater. If it is 100 times greater, then it is 20 dB greater. The power produced by sound is actually very small. At a typical football or rugby game, the sound produced by the crowd shouting would only provide enough energy to heat a cup of coffee!

Noise pollution

Noise is unwanted sound. It may be sound from traffic, from a neighbour's TV or radio, from machinery at work, and so on. Because it is unwanted, noise is a kind of pollution.

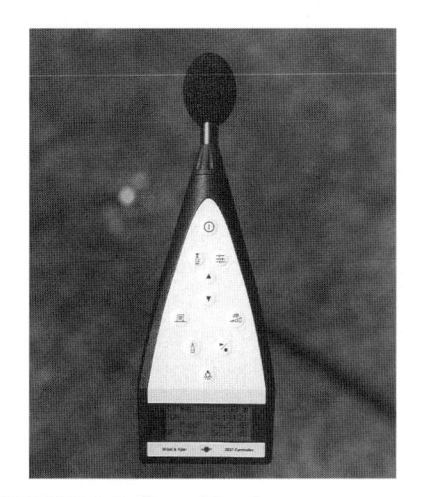

FIGURE 3.7 *Sound level meter*

Typical noise levels are shown in the table.

Source of sound	Sound level (dB)
Jet engine at 50 m	130
Disco, 1 m from loudspeaker	120
Pneumatic drill at 5 m	100
Heavy goods vehicle from pavement	90
Alarm clock 0.5 m from bedside	80
Telephone ringing at 2 m	70
Vacuum cleaner at 3 m	70
Normal conversation at 1 m	60
Boiling electric kettle at 2 m	50
Residential area at night	40
Quiet country lane	20
Silence (hearing threshold of humans)	0

Everyone agrees that excessively loud noises (that is above 90 dB) can be unpleasant and some can cause damage to the inner ear. There is, however, disagreement about the damage caused by certain kinds of sounds, e.g. disco music. In factories or noisy workplaces near pneumatic drills and aircraft, or in heavy vehicles or tractors, the noise level can be over 100 dB. This can cause permanent damage to the ears with a serious loss of hearing ability. A 'ringing' sound heard after exposure is a warning sign. Some people become irritable, short tempered and tired as a result of exposure to very loud noises. Ear protection – ear-plugs, ear-muffs or a helmet – can be used in many cases to reduce the level of noise heard. These devices work by filtering out the sound by using a thick material to reduce the sound level. Noise coming through a window can be reduced by about 20 dB if double glazing is fitted.

The silencer of a motor car exhaust system is designed to trap the sound. In particular, the high frequency sounds from the explosions in the engine are absorbed. A new silencer can reduce the sound level from 150 dB to 85 dB.

The small bones which transmit vibrations from the eardrum to the inner ear stiffen up and transmit the vibrations less effectively at sound levels above 80 dB. This, to some extent, protects the ear from loud sounds. However, the ear's reflex action takes time to operate and it is during this time (less than one second) that the short peaks of sound can pass into the inner ear and cause damage. The noise level and how long it lasts will affect your hearing. The law limits exposure to noise to no more than 90 dB for eight hours and 93 dB for four hours, 96 dB for two hours, etc.

health physics 3

Hearing loss

As we grow older, we all experience some deafness. One in four people over 65 years old have some hearing loss.

Hearing impairment varies from total deafness, usually caused by a defect at birth or by disease or accidental damage to the ear mechanism, to the slight impairment which often comes with age. Hearing aids can be used to correct some of these problems and restore almost normal hearing.

Hearing aids consist of a small microphone, amplifier, battery and earphone (figure 3.8). For many hearing-impaired people, hearing loss is greater at certain frequencies. High frequency deafness, for example, is quite common. In such cases the hearing aid has to amplify high frequencies more than low frequencies. The first frequencies to be lost are those above the speech frequencies, which is normally 4 kHz. Hearing loss is normally measured at 1, 2 and 3 kHz. Normal speech frequencies are in the range 400 to 4000 Hz.

High audio frequencies are needed for sounds such as 's', 'sh', 't' and 'f'. It is these high frequency sounds which make speech intelligible. The latest hearing aids can amplify the important frequencies which are used in speech but filter out background noise such as traffic and crowd noise.

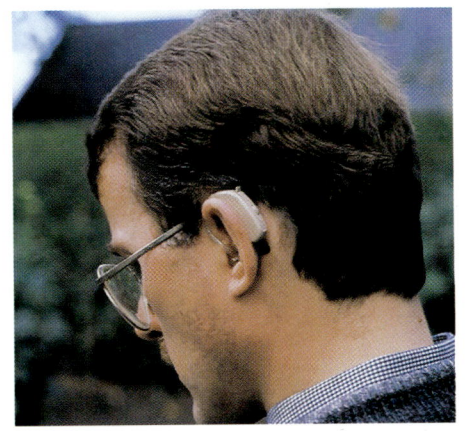

FIGURE 3.8

3.3 Light and sight

Many people need to wear spectacles or contact lenses and we will nearly all need to have some help with reading books like this one as we grow older. The changes made to light as it passes through spectacle lenses can explain how some eye defects such as long- and short-sightedness can be corrected. We will discuss this later.

Refraction of light

Light travels in a straight line. However, when light travels from one material (or 'medium') to another it may be bent as it enters the new material and its speed will change. This effect is called **refraction**. It is the principle on which spectacles work.

Rays of light can travel through various objects. The paths of the rays passing through and leaving the objects are shown in figure 3.9. The dotted line drawn at right angles (90°) to the surface is called the 'normal'.

Plane rectangular block

When the incident ray (figure 1.21 on page 14) travels parallel to the normal, there is no change in direction. When the incident ray is at an angle to a plane rectangular block, the ray coming out of the block is parallel to the incident ray (figure 3.10 on page 60).

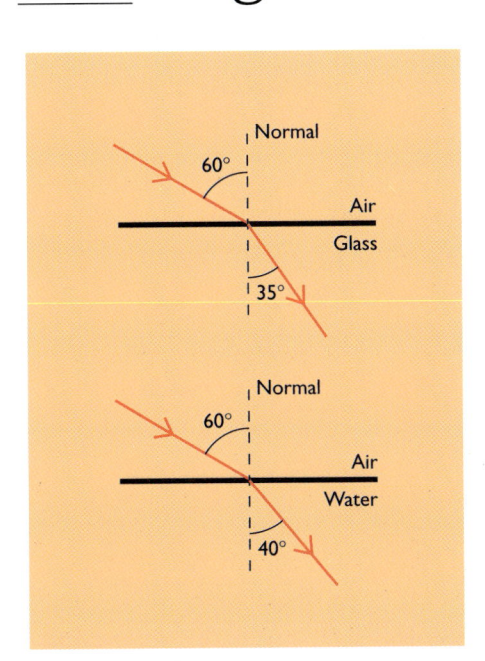

FIGURE 3.9 *Light travels more slowly in glass than it does in water. So a light ray bends more when it goes into glass*

59

FIGURE 3.10

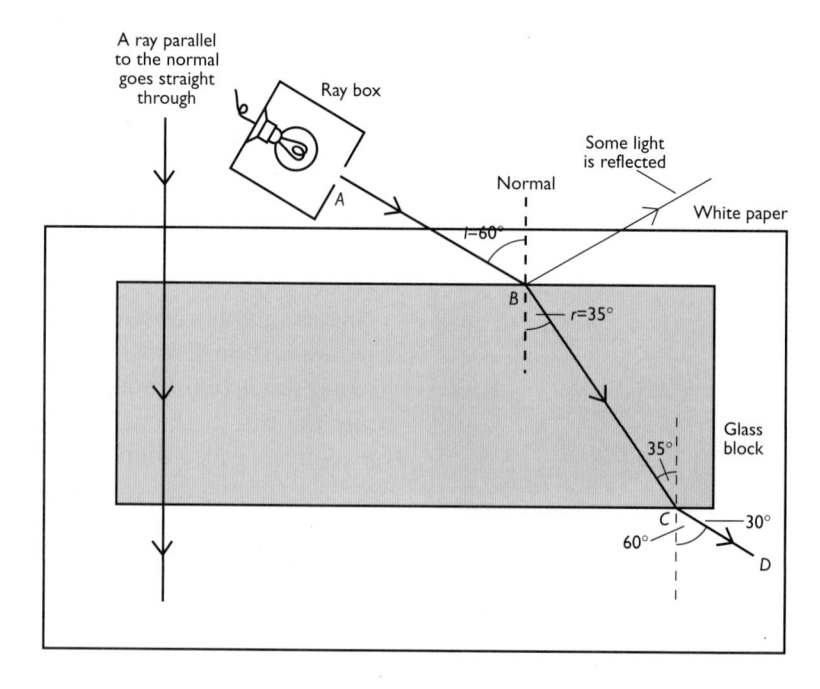

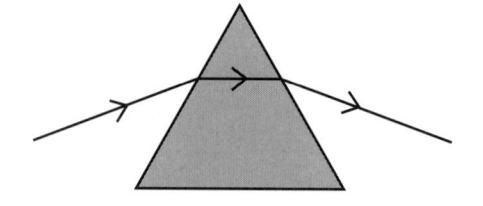

FIGURE 3.11

Triangular prism
The ray bends towards the normal as it goes into the prism and away as it comes out (figure 3.11).

Convex or converging lens
The middle ray goes straight on and the outer rays bend and meet on the middle line at a point called the **focus** (figure 3.12). If the lens is thick, the same effect occurs but the focus is nearer the lens (figure 3.13).

Concave or diverging lens
The rays spread out (figure 3.14).

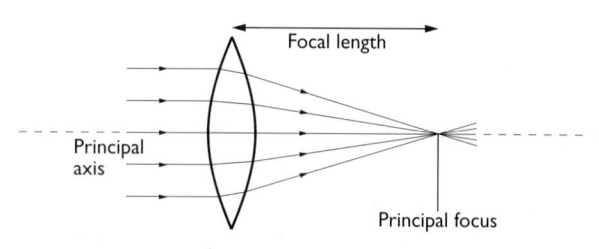

FIGURE 3.12 *A thin lens is a weak lens; it has a longer focal length than the strong lens*

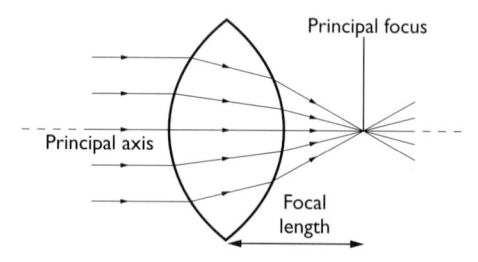

FIGURE 3.13 *A thick lens is a strong lens; it has a short focal length*

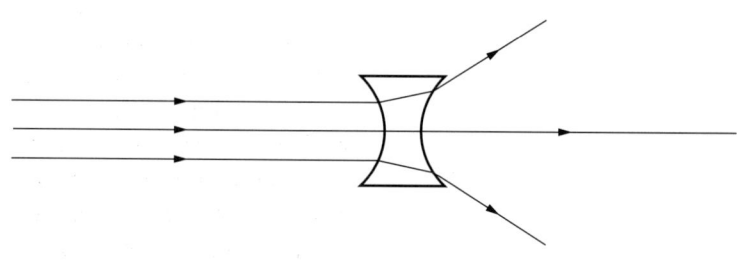

FIGURE 3.14 *A concave or diverging lens*

health physics 3

The eye

Our eyes tell us what's going on in the 'outside world'. They enable us to grasp, hit or touch objects 'out there' and, of course, to avoid being grasped, hit or touched by threatening objects. Our eyes tell us the shape, size and colour of objects. An outline of the eye is shown in figure 3.15.

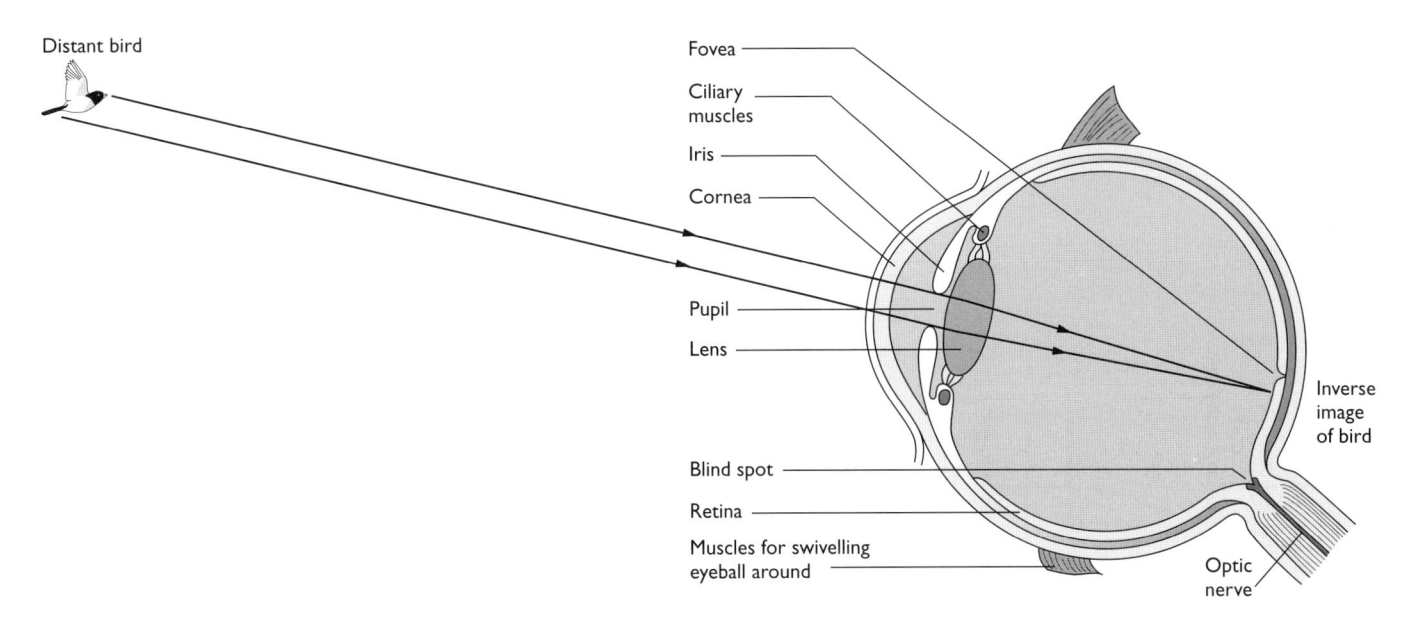

FIGURE 3.15 *The human eyeball*

The different parts of the eye and their functions are:

- Light enters the front of the eye at the **cornea**. This is transparent and it is here that most of the refraction or bending of light occurs.
- The light enters a **lens**, which is a jelly-like substance, and more refraction takes place.
- The lens is held by fibres which act like muscles. These can change the shape of the lens from thick to thin.
- The light then passes through a gel-like substance which makes the light spread out.
- The light reaches the **retina** at the back of the eye. This has special cells to receive the light. It has about 100 million tiny nerve endings (cells) called **rods** and **cones**. The rods are sensitive to small amounts of light and are used in night vision. The cones give us colour vision and help us to see detailed sharp images. In poor light, the cones do not function and we tend to see objects in shades of grey.
- The area of sharpest vision is called the **fovea** or **yellow spot**. It is packed with cones and therefore responds well to sharp, bright, coloured images.
- The iris controls the amount of light entering the eye by the **pupil**, which can alter in the size of the opening.
- Electrical signals pass along the nerve fibres to the brain. The part of the retina where the nerve fibres leave the retina contains no light-sensitive cells. It is called the **blind spot**.

3 standard grade physics

> The amount of refraction which takes place at the cornea does not change. However, in order to focus on near and on distant objects, an adjustable lens is needed. This is provided by the eye's lens. This lens is held by muscle-like fibres in the ciliary body which can change the shape of the lens from thick to thin. When the lens is thin, it can focus on distant objects. To view near objects, the muscles change the lens shape to thick. When light enters the eye, the image formed on the retina is upside down. The brain learns to turn this image the 'right way up'.

Lenses

Focal length

Some lenses bend light more than others, due to their thickness and the amount of curving of the lens. One way to indicate the amount of refraction is to measure the focal length of the lens. A convex or converging lens can make rays of light come together to a point after they have passed through the lens (the **focus**). The position of the focus depends on where the rays come from. When the rays come from a distant object which is so far away that the rays are parallel, the focus is closer to the lens. In this case, the focus is called the **principal focus**. The distance from the lens to the principal focus is called the **focal length** and is measured in metres.

Measuring the focal length of a lens
- A converging lens is held near a window frame and the image of an object outside is brought to a focus on a piece of card.
- The card is moved until the image is sharp.
- The distance between the lens and the card is measured with a ruler.
- This distance is the focal length (figure 3.16).

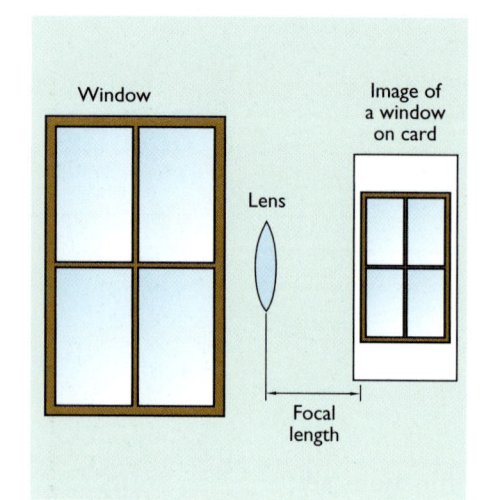

FIGURE 3.16

Typical values for the focal length of a school lens are in the range from 2 to 25 cm.

> ### Power of a lens
>
> People who have severe eye defects may need stronger (more powerful) lenses to correct their eyesight than those who have only slight defects. (A more powerful lens is one which causes more refraction.) An optician must therefore have a range of lenses to suit different people's needs. The powers of these lenses can be indicated by giving their focal lengths – the most powerful lenses having the shortest focal lengths. Another way to indicate the amount of refraction caused by a lens is to calculate its power from the equation
>
> $$\text{Power} = \frac{1}{\text{focal length}}$$
>
> where the focal length is measured in metres and the power is given in dioptres (D).
>
> - Converging (convex) lenses have positive powers (e.g. $+10\,\text{D}$, $+17\,\text{D}$).
> - Diverging (concave) lenses have negative powers (e.g. $-10\,\text{D}$, $-17\,\text{D}$).

Example: A convex lens has a focal length of 10 cm. Find the power of the lens.
Solution:

$$\text{Focal length} = 0.1 \text{ m}$$

$$\text{Power} = \frac{1}{\text{focal length}}$$

$$= \frac{1}{0.1}$$

$$= 10 \text{ D}$$

Example: A lens has power of −2 D. This tells us that this is a concave lens since there is a negative sign. Calculate its focal length.
Solution:

$$\text{Power} = -2 \text{ D}$$

$$\text{Power} = \frac{1}{\text{focal length}}$$

$$-2 = \frac{1}{\text{focal length}}$$

$$\text{Focal length} = \frac{1}{-2}$$

$$= -0.5 \text{ m}$$

Long- and short-sightedness

Long sight

A long-sighted person can see distant objects clearly. Objects quite close to the eye appear blurred. The eye lens brings the rays to a focus beyond the retina. This may happen if the person's eyeball is a shorter than normal distance from front to back. It may also be caused by ciliary muscles which cannot relax for the lens to be thick enough.

A converging (convex) lens corrects this fault since it will increase the bending of the light rays before they enter the eye lens and so will be focused on the retina and thus seen clearly (figure 3.17).

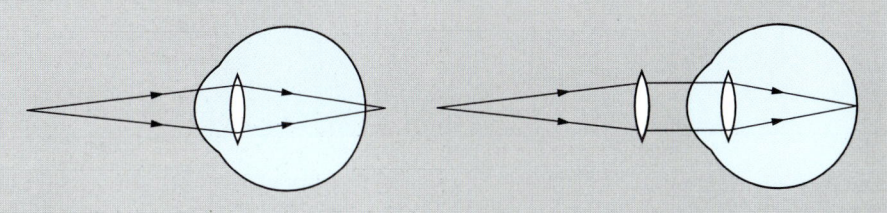

FIGURE 3.17 *(a) A long-sighted eye cannot see near objects clearly, (b) a converging lens corrects long sight*

3 standard grade physics

Short sight

A short-sighted person finds that distant objects are blurred but near objects are in focus. The eye lens brings light to a focus in front of the retina due to the lens having a large curvature. The muscles cannot make the lens thin enough. A diverging (concave) lens corrects this fault, since it will spread the light out more before it enters the eye lens and so will be focused on the retina (figure 3.18).

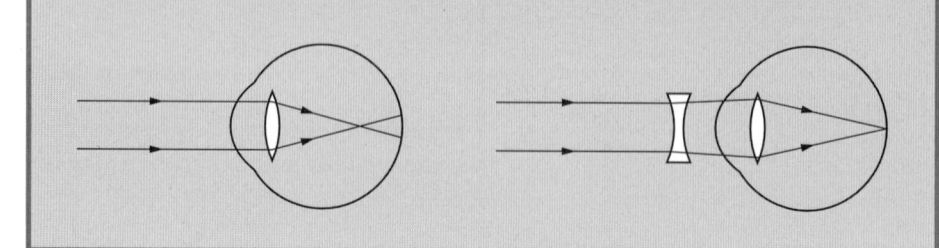

FIGURE 3.18 *(a) A short-sighted eye cannot see distant objects, (b) a diverging lens corrects short sight*

Did you know?

The first spectacle lenses were developed around about 1270 but there is a legend that the Emperor Nero had an emerald cut as a lens to enable him to see more clearly. Contact lenses were first suggested by Leonardo da Vinci, who noticed that he could see more clearly when he opened one of his eyes under a bowl of water. Different lens have been developed which allow oxygen to pass into the eye which helps to prevent some eye diseases (figure 3.19). Some lenses can be thrown away after use each day.

FIGURE 3.19 *Contact lenses*

3.4 Using the spectrum

The light that we can detect with our eyes is only a small part of all the wavelengths that exist. The range is called the electromagnetic spectrum. The complete spectrum is shown in figure 3.20. We will return to the topic of the different radiations in Chapter 7.

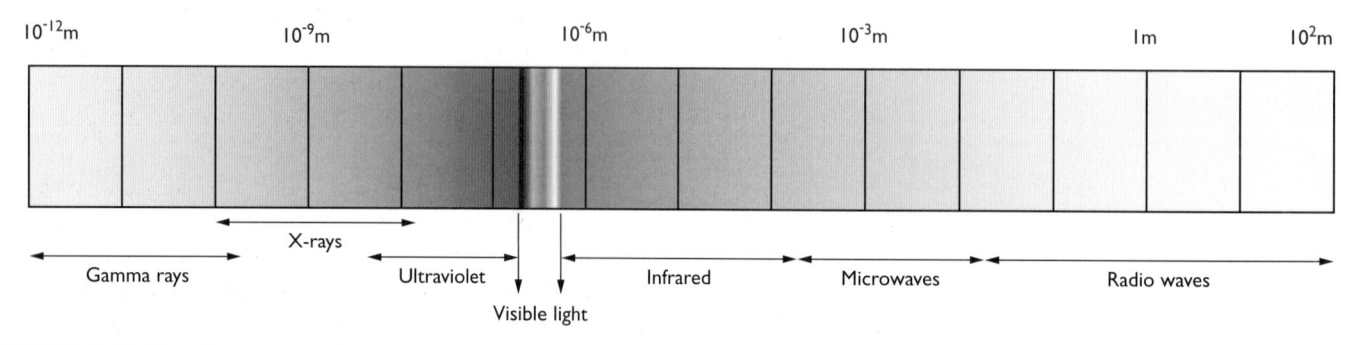

10^{-12}m 10^{-9}m 10^{-6}m 10^{-3}m   1m 10^{2}m

Gamma rays — X-rays — Ultraviolet — Visible light — Infrared — Microwaves — Radio waves

FIGURE 3.20 *The electromagnetic spectrum*

health physics 3

The parts of the spectrum all travel through space at a speed of 3×10^8 m/s (300 000 000 m/s). Each member of the electromagnetic spectrum has a different wavelength and frequency.

Infrared radiation in medicine

All hot objects give off invisible 'heat rays' called infrared radiation. Typical wavelengths are from 700 to 1500 nm (nm = nanometre = 10^{-9}m). Special infrared cameras can be used to take colour photographs called thermograms using this type of radiation instead of visible light. Infrared radiation allows us to measure small temperature changes inside the body. Thermograms of a patient's body show areas of different temperature. Doctors have found that malignant tumours are warmer than healthy tissue and show up clearly on thermograms. In a patient suffering from arthritis, the affected joint will show up as a different temperature from the normal joint (figure 3.21).

Another use of thermography is the heat-seeking cameras used to detect people who may be trapped in buildings (figure 3.22).

Infrared radiation is used in a different way by physiotherapists to treat people who have suffered a muscle injury. They use this radiation to penetrate the skin and heat muscles and tissues. Heat results in more rapid healing.

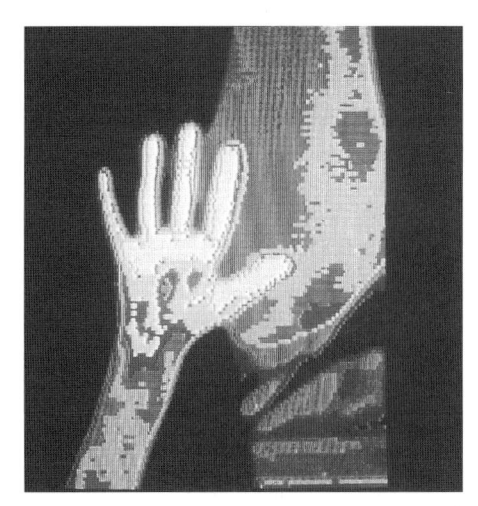

FIGURE 3.21 *Thermogram of arthritic joints*

Ultraviolet radiation

Ultraviolet is another type of invisible radiation. The wavelength of ultraviolet rays is in the range from 200 to 400 nm. This is shorter than the wavelength of infrared or visible light. There are two types of ultraviolet light: UVA and UVB.

UVA ranges from 315 to 400 nm and we receive it each day from the sun. We need it for healthy growth and to make vitamin D. UVA is mostly removed by the atmosphere around the Earth.

There is a risk from long exposure to ultraviolet light under sun-beds, and care should be taken to cover the eyes since they are especially sensitive to damage. Too much ultraviolet light on the skin produces sunburn and can cause the skin to turn red and be very painful. Suntan lotions absorb some of the ultraviolet rays which cause the burning, but they allow the lower frequency rays to reach the skin and produce a tan. The tan is due to a pigment called melanin being produced.

Excessive exposure to UVB may cause a melanoma, a form of skin cancer. Though it is rare, in the last few years skin cancer has increased more than any other type of cancer in the UK. Your skin can 'remember' the last amount of exposure to the sun that it received and over a period of time this may lead to skin cancer.

Ultraviolet radiation is used in the treatment of certain skin diseases such as acne. This involves the use of a drug called psoralin being taken and then the patient being exposed to a carefully controlled amount of radiation. This drug was also known to the ancient Egyptians, who found that chewing a certain leaf and sitting in the sun helped reduce the effect of skin disease.

FIGURE 3.22 *Heat-seeking camera mounted on the front of a rescue helicopter*

standard grade physics

Fibre optics in medicine

In fibre optics, the fibres are about the thickness of a human hair. Each fibre consists of a thin piece of glass coated with a thin layer or cladding of another glass. This cladding prevents the light, which enters the end of the fibre, from escaping or passing through the sides to another fibre in the bundle (see Chapter 1). Fibre bundles can be constructed so that each fibre has the same position at each end. **Coherent** fibres can transmit an image down the fibres. **Incoherent** fibres are arranged in a random way and only allow light to be sent down them.

Optical fibres in medicine are used in devices called endoscopes or bronchoscopes (figure 3.23). The key parts are:

- An incoherent bundle of fibres sends light down to the internal organs.
- Light is then reflected from the organs and an image sent up a coherent bundle of fibres.
- A channel cleans the lens.

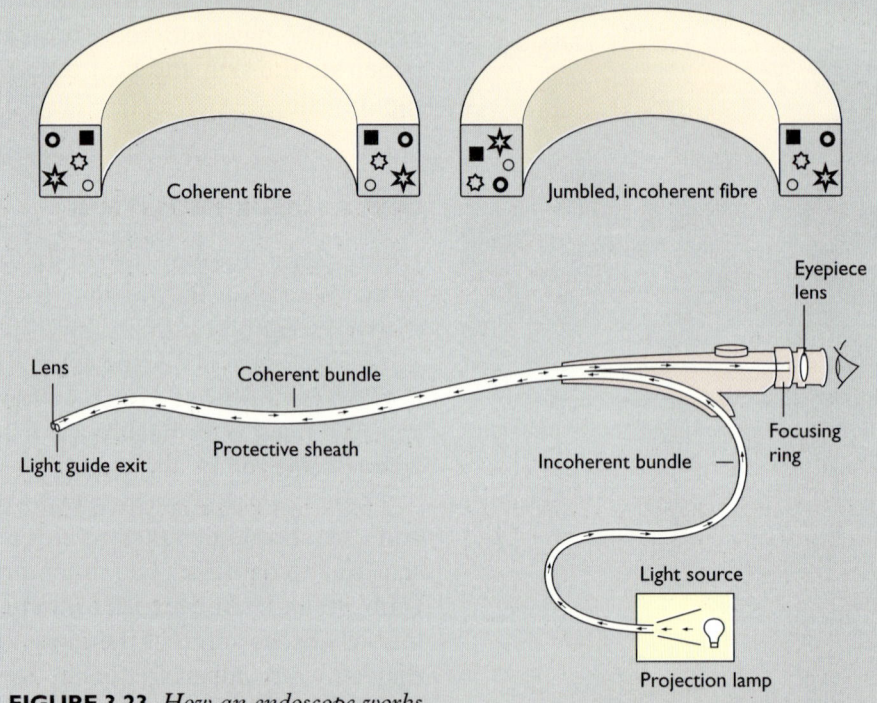

FIGURE 3.23 *How an endoscope works*

They have a bending section near the tip so the observer can direct the instrument during insertion.

The heat from the lamp does not pass down the fibres. This means that the other end of the guide is cold (called a 'cold light source'). This is one of the advantages of the endoscope.

Dr Findlay's casenotes

Endoscopes can be used to view a tumour which might occur in the lungs (figure 3.24). An X-ray can show possible areas of concern but the use of a bronchoscope will show up a tumour which may have been caused by smoking. A large part of the lung may have to be removed.

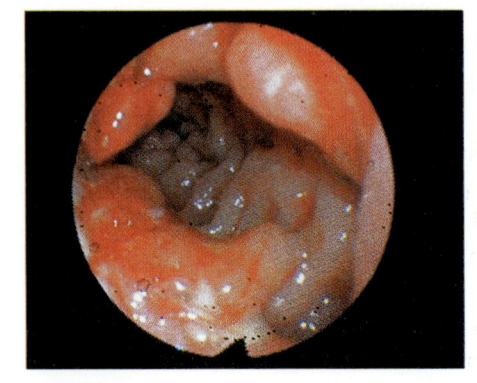

FIGURE 3.24

health physics 3

Lasers in medicine

A laser is a very concentrated form of light. The light is also of one particular wavelength. Soon after the first laser was made in 1960 by Theodore Maiman, it was described as a 'solution looking for a problem'! The areas in which lasers are now used include communication, surveying, nuclear physics, holography and entertainment. In medicine, the laser has proved itself invaluable for some types of surgery, yet it has not replaced the scalpel to the extent which was predicted.

In medicine, the laser is used to produce extreme heating in a very small piece of tissue. In one application, the laser beam is used to seal blood vessels by coagulating them. In another, the narrow beam is focused on a tumour, causing it to vaporise. The properties of different lasers are shown in the table.

Laser	Power	Wavelength (nm)
Carbon dioxide	20 W	10 600 (infrared)
Helium neon	5 mW	630 (red light)
Argon	1 W	500 (blue-green)
Neodymium-YAG	50 W	1064 (infrared)

nm = nanometre = 1/1 000 000 000 m.

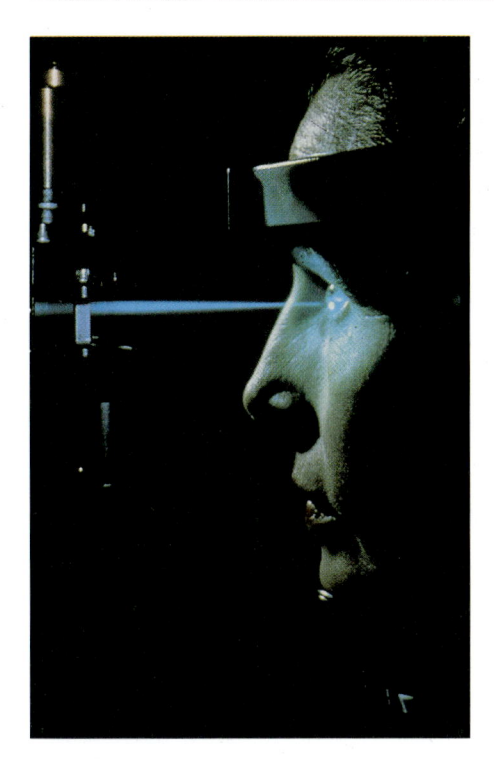

FIGURE 3.25

Doctors use the neodymium-YAG laser to vaporise tumours that obstruct the flow of air to the lungs. After laser treatment for a tumour that blocks the oesophagus, the patient can swallow more easily.

Laser as a scalpel

As the carbon dioxide laser beam is almost totally absorbed in the first tenth of a millimetre of tissue, it is particularly suited for use as a 'laser scalpel'. The shallow penetration makes it ideal for treating areas where it is important not to damage underlying structures. Certain malignant tumours can be vaporised using a carbon dioxide laser.

Eye problems

Eye surgery is the best known application of argon lasers. The retina of a diabetic person sometimes does not get enough oxygen from the blood vessels. To compensate for this lack of oxygen, abnormal vessels grow forwards and bleed into the eye. Vision at the edge is altered and the patient can eventually go blind.

The eye surgeon uses an argon laser to seal the less important areas of the retina. Although this reduces the patient's field of vision, the patient is much less likely to go blind. This technique can be used for repairing retinal tears and holes which develop prior to the retina coming away from the back of the eye (figures 3.25 and 3.26).

A further use of lasers is when a patient has had a lens inserted in the eye after a cataract operation. Strands of tissue grow behind the eye and do not allow the light to pass through the lens. A few pulses from a neodymium laser will split the tissue and restore the patient's sight immediately.

FIGURE 3.26

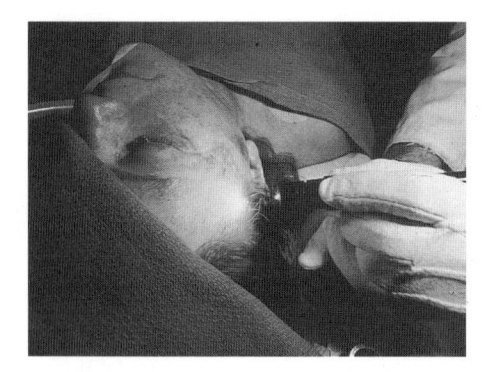

3 standard grade physics

FIGURE 3.27

Other uses of lasers

'Port wine' birthmarks are caused by blood vessels which have not sealed properly. The light from the argon laser is absorbed by the blood vessels causing them to seal (figure 3.27). A similar treatment can be used on some tattoos. In this case the argon laser breaks up the dye.

X-rays in medicine

X-rays are used either to see inside the body or to treat some diseases. They are made by putting a high voltage across a tube which has been evacuated (i.e. no air is present). One of the wires is heated to emit electrons and these are accelerated until they hit another piece of metal which gives off X-rays (figure 3.28). The greater the voltage across the two plates, the greater the energy of the X-rays. If the voltage is between 80 and 120 kV, then the X-rays can be used to produce pictures. Voltages of greater than 200 kV can produce X-rays for treating cancers.

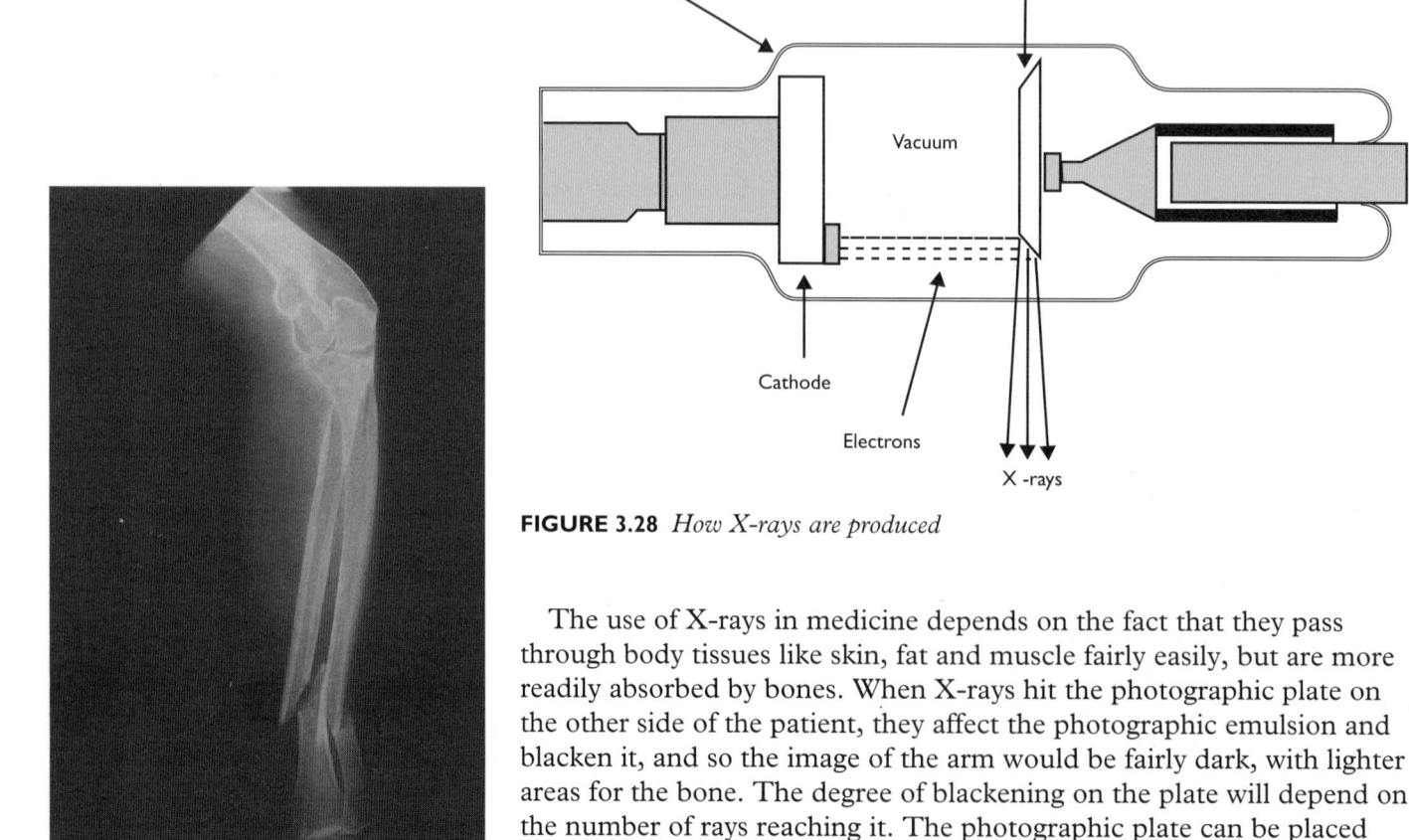

FIGURE 3.28 *How X-rays are produced*

The use of X-rays in medicine depends on the fact that they pass through body tissues like skin, fat and muscle fairly easily, but are more readily absorbed by bones. When X-rays hit the photographic plate on the other side of the patient, they affect the photographic emulsion and blacken it, and so the image of the arm would be fairly dark, with lighter areas for the bone. The degree of blackening on the plate will depend on the number of rays reaching it. The photographic plate can be placed between two other plates called intensifying screens which reduce the X-ray exposure required to produce a picture. Any break in a bone lets X-rays through and may show up as a dark crack (figure 3.29).

The boundary between organs, both made of similar tissue, may not be clear. A contrast agent is used, such as iodine or barium, which absorbs X-rays. Barium is drunk by the patient as a 'barium meal' to outline the stomach and iodine is used to outline the arteries and veins.

FIGURE 3.29

health physics 3

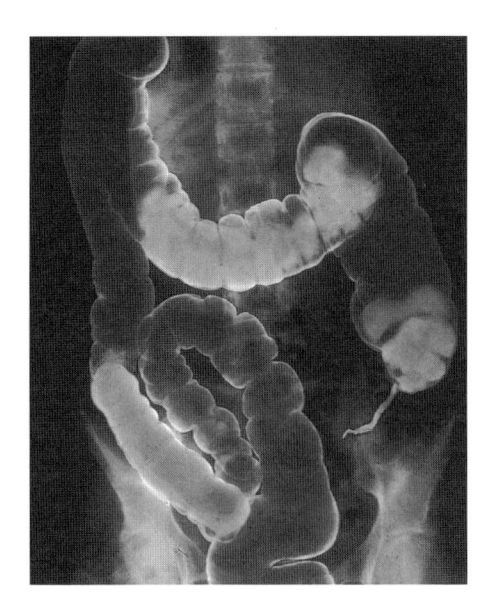

FIGURE 3.30

The organ which has the contrast agent will show up lighter on the photographic plate (figure 3.30). Some X-ray machines do not use film to record results but use special detector tubes called image intensifiers to receive the rays and convert them into electrical signals. These can be converted into digital signals and displayed on a monitor screen (figure 3.31).

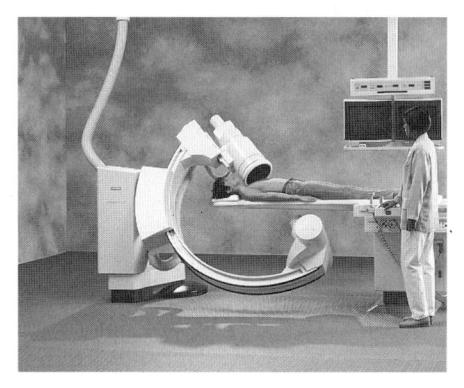

FIGURE 3.31 *X-ray machine with digital display*

Computed tomography

The problem
In a normal X-ray, the details of organs at different depths are laid on top of each other and any information on depth is lost. You can try to take X-rays at different angles but this means that the radiologist has to work out which parts of each image correspond to each organ. This is a very difficult task, particularly with some organs. Normal X-rays cannot show small differences in the density of tissue. This is quite important in detecting disease.

The solution
A team of scientists at EMI developed a technique called CAT (computerised axial tomography), also called computed tomography or CT. The machine uses an X-ray tube and a detector which are mounted on a gantry and can scan around the patient. The system takes a series of measurements in one position by scanning around the body. Then the patient is moved into a new position and a repeat series of measurements is taken. The process is then repeated for a series of 'slice' thicknesses which are about 10 mm. A kidney CT scan would have ten slices, while others which have greater depth will require more. The measurements are then used by a computer which can carry out 20 million operations. These will produce a slice image which is displayed on the screen (figure 3.32). Early CT scanners took up to 15 minutes to make measurements from a slice, but the latest scanners can take the measurements in one to two minutes (figure 3.33). They use a fan-shaped beam and a complete ring of 720 detectors. If the patient moves while the measurements are taken, then the image will be fuzzy.

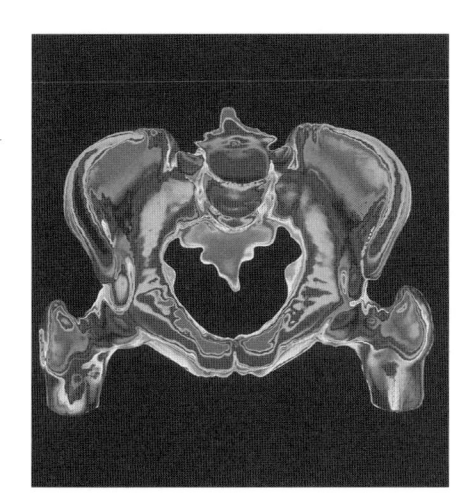

FIGURE 3.32

3 standard grade physics

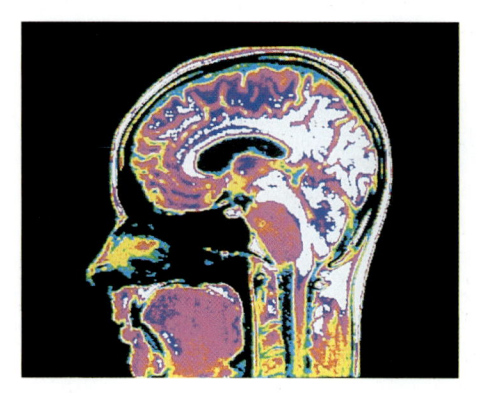

FIGURE 3.34

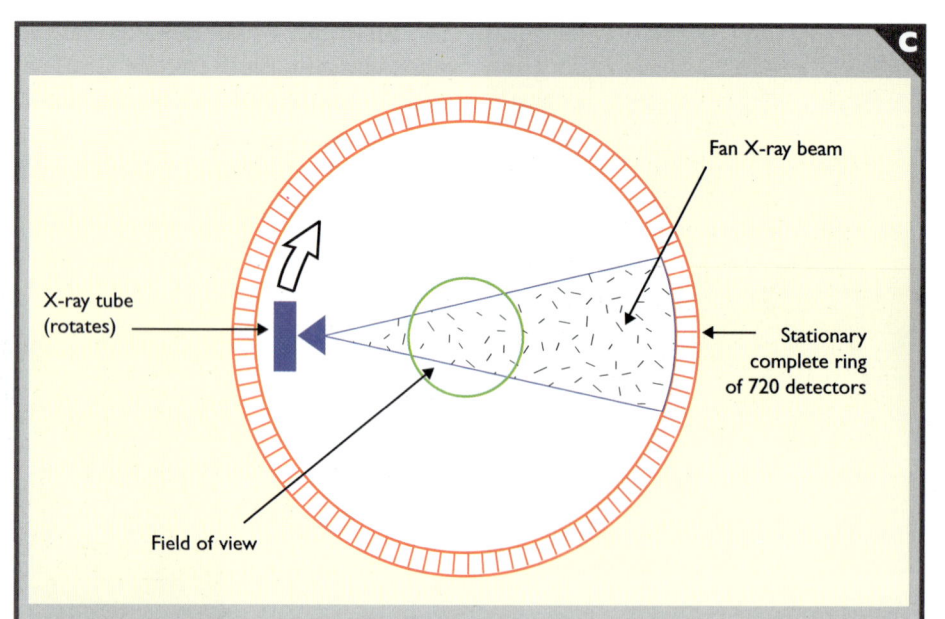

FIGURE 3.33 *How modern CT scanners work*

One main use of CT scanners is for diagnosis before brain surgery. The very small changes in tissue caused by cancer can be used to detect brain tumours (figure 3.34). Another use is for detecting internal bleeding as a result of car accidents.

Dr Findlay's casenotes
During a football match, a player sustained an injury to the head that resulted in dizziness and a feeling of sickness. A CT scan showed that internal bleeding had occurred, and knowing the exact location of the bleeding allowed the surgeon to operate and drain away the blood.

3.5 The atom and radiation

Atoms are the smallest possible particles of the elements which make up everything around us. All atoms of one element are identical to one another, but they are different from all other elements. This is because they are made up from different combinations of electrons, protons and neutrons – the three main particles which make up atoms (table 3.1). All atoms have a tiny central nucleus which has a positive charge. We can imagine the negatively-charged electrons to be circling around this, rather like planets around the Sun. The nucleus contains the positive protons and the neutrons, which are uncharged. Look back at figure 2.7 on page 28.

Particle	Charge
Proton	Positive
Neutron	Zero
Electron	Negative

TABLE 3.1 *Particles making up an atom*

70

health physics 3

The GM tube
A Geiger–Muller or GM tube consists of a hollow tube filled with a low pressure gas, with a very thin window at one end and two electrodes with a voltage connected across them. Radiation passing through the thin window causes ionisation (see below) of the gas and this results in electrical pulses which can be counted.

Radiation

There are three types of radiation:

- Alpha (α) particles
- Beta (β) particles
- Gamma (γ) rays

These can be identified by what happens as they reach different materials. Alpha radiation can be completely stopped by a sheet of paper. Beta radiation can be absorbed by a sheet of aluminium. Gamma radiation is part of the electromagnetic spectrum. Concrete, lead and other dense materials will absorb the radiations. The thicker the material, the more radiation will be absorbed.

When the alpha or beta or gamma radiation passes through a material, it loses energy by colliding with the atoms of that material. Eventually the radiations lose so much energy that they cannot get through the material and so are absorbed (figure 3.35).

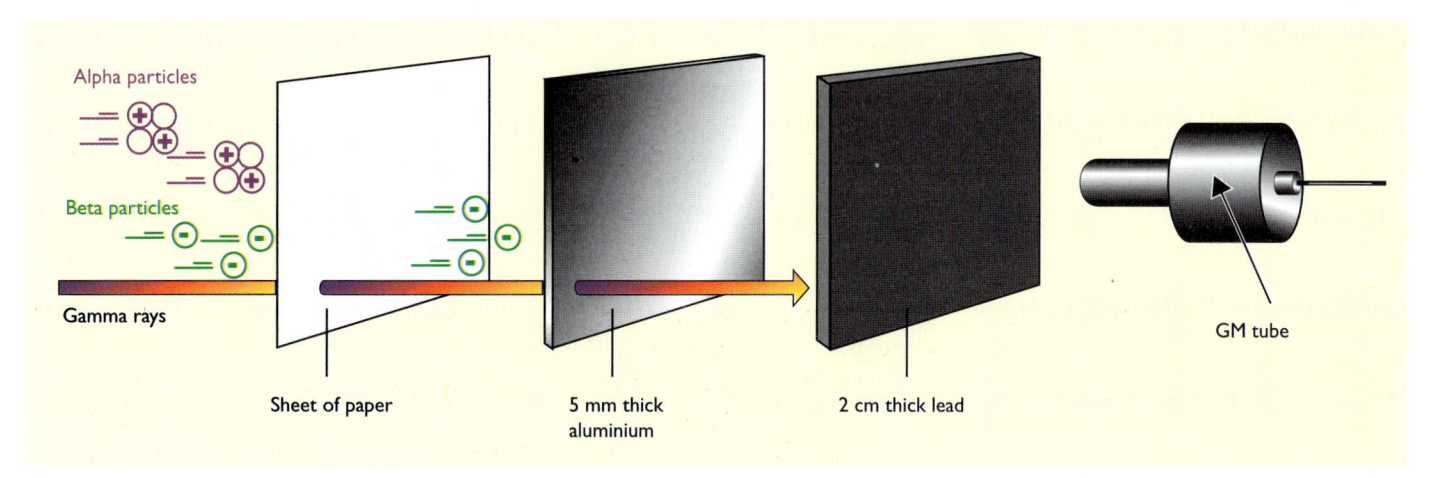

FIGURE 3.35

Ionisation

If an electron is added or removed from an atom, what is left is called an **ion**. The process is called **ionisation**. The removal of an electron creates a positive ion, and if an electron is added then a negative ion is formed.

The process of ionisation by an alpha particle is shown in figure 3.36. In (a) the alpha particle is approaching the neutral atom and in (b) it has passed by having, created an ion pair. This means that the alpha particle has caused the atom to break up into positive and negative parts, i.e. ions.

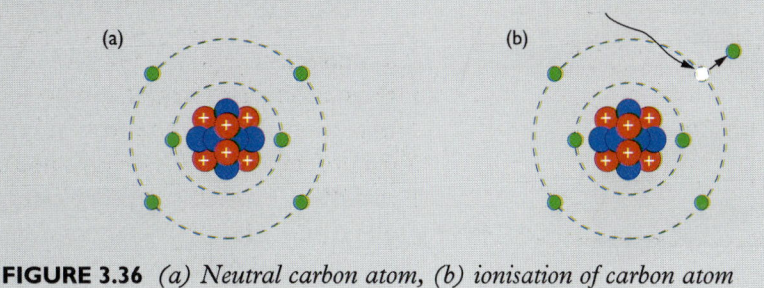

FIGURE 3.36 *(a) Neutral carbon atom, (b) ionisation of carbon atom*

Effect on the human body

- Alpha radiation will produce ionisation through a short distance of body tissue. This type of radiation outside the body is absorbed by the skin and little damage will occur. Swallowing the radiation will produce large amounts of ionisation and would be dangerous.
- Beta radiation will be absorbed in about 1 cm of tissue and any beta radiation outside the body will cause damage to that tissue, but a small amount can penetrate the body. If the radioactive source were to get into the body then internal organs could be damaged.
- Gamma rays and X-rays pass through the body and can damage tissue whether the source is inside or outside of the body.

Sterilisation

As radiation can be used to kill cells, it can also be used to kill bacteria or germs. In the past, medical instruments such as syringes had to be sterilised by heat or chemicals. Now cheap, plastic, throw-away syringes can be used – they are prepacked and then irradiated by an intense gamma ray source. This kills any bacteria but does not make the syringe radioactive.

Detecting radiation

Photographic fogging

Photographic film has a thin layer of silver-based chemical on the surface of the plastic or paper. Normally, this silver salt is affected by light falling on it – wherever it lands, it changes the chemical and blackens or fogs the film surface.

Alpha, beta or gamma have a similar effect on this photographic emulsion, and so photographic film can be used to detect them. In fact, radioactive substances were first discovered by accident, when Henri Becquerel left some uranium rocks near photographic paper. He discovered that the paper had been blackened, and when he went on to investigate why, he started the study of radioactivity.

Workers who use radioactive materials (e.g. health workers in hospitals) wear film badges throughout their working day so that a check can be made on the amount of radiation they have been exposed to. When the film is developed, the amount of fogging gives a measure of the radiation exposure (figure 3.37). Different windows on the badge are used to measure the amounts of the different types of radiation:

- A plastic window will absorb different energies of beta rays.
- Metal windows absorb different energies of gamma and X-rays.
- Aluminium will absorb low energy X-rays.
- Other metals will absorb high energy X-rays.

Scintillations

Some substances such as zinc sulphide are fluorescent. This means that they absorb radiation and give out energy again as a tiny burst of light. These flashes of light are called 'scintillations', and they may be observed by the naked eye or counted by a light detector and an electronic circuit. These scintillation counters are used in many modern instruments including the gamma camera.

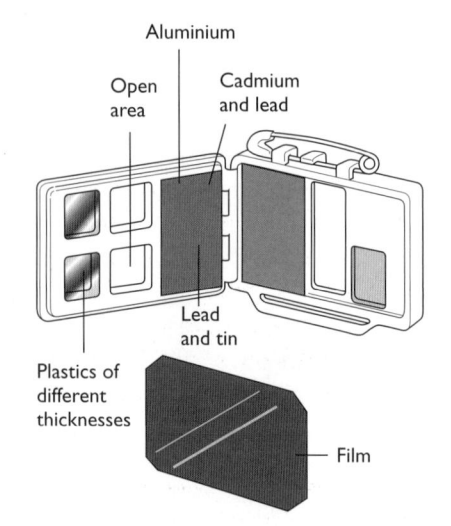

FIGURE 3.37 *Film badge*

health physics 3

Radioactive decay

Radiation from a source is caused by radioactive atoms breaking up. The activity of a radioactive source is a measure of how much radiation it is giving out. This depends on the number of radioactive atoms which break up every second and give out radiation. The unit of **activity** is the **becquerel (Bq)**. A source has an activity of 1 Bq if one of its atoms disintegrates each second and gives out a particle of radiation. The becquerel is a very small unit. Radioactive sources used in medicine have activities measured in megabecquerels (MBq).

$$\text{One million Bq} = 1 \text{ MBq} = 10^6 \text{ Bq}$$

Half-life

When a radioactive substance disintegrates the activity (number of disintegrations or count rate) depends only on the number of radioactive nuclei present, i.e. double the number, double the activity.

The half-life of a radioactive substance is the time taken for half the radioactive nuclei to disintegrate, i.e. the time taken for the activity to fall by one half.

Half-life is measured in units of time – seconds, minutes, days or years. Typical half-lives are:

- Uranium-238: 4.5×10^9 years
- Radium-226: 1600 years
- Cobalt-60: 5.3 years
- Sodium-24: 15 hours
- Copper-66: 5.2 minutes

After one half-life ($t_{\frac{1}{2}}$), the activity and the measured count rate drop to half the initial value. After a second half-life, the count rate halves again – it is now one-quarter of its original value. Three half-lives will see the activity and count rate reduce to 1/8th, and so on.

A graph of count rate against time is shown in figure 3.38. Taking the initial activity as 1, a table can be produced.

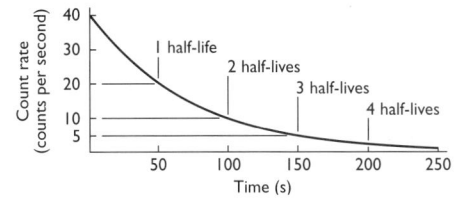

FIGURE 3.38

Number of half-lives	0	1	2	3	4
Activity	1	1/2	1/4	1/8	1/16

Total count rate and background count rate

In any radioactive experiment, a count rate will be obtained even if no radioactive source is present. This is due to background radiation, which comes from almost all natural sources. The background count rate can be found by measuring the number of background counts in a known time and working out an average count rate (counts per second or counts per minute) from this. Alternatively, when carrying out your experiment you could measure the total count rate with your measuring device where:

Total count rate = count rate from radioactive source + count rate due to background

Example 1: A radioactive source gives an initial count rate of 1600 Bq. After 120 minutes the count rate is found to be 100 Bq. Calculate the half-life of the source.

Solution:
>After 1 half-life the count rate is 800 Bq
>After 2 half-lives the count rate is 400 Bq
>After 3 half-lives the count rate is 200 Bq
>After 4 half-lives the count rate is 100 Bq
>4 half-lives = 120 minutes
>1 half-life = 30 minutes

Example 2: A radioactive source has a half-life of four days. At the start of an experiment, the total activity recorded is 990 counts per minute. Find the total recorded activity after 20 days, if the background count rate is 30 counts per minute.

Note:
1. Total count rate = count rate of source + background count rate.
2. The background rate is constant and does not decrease with time.

Solution:

$$\text{Count rate of source} = 990 - 30$$
$$= 960 \text{ counts per minute}$$
$$\text{Number of half lives} = \frac{20}{4}$$
$$= 5$$

After 1 half-life the count rate is 480 counts per minute
After 2 half-lives the count rate is 240 counts per minute
After 3 half-lives the count rate is 120 counts per minute
After 4 half-lives the count rate is 60 counts per minute
After 5 half-lives the count rate is 30 counts per minute
Total recorded count rate is 30 + 30 = 60 counts per minute

The biological effects of radiation

All living things, plant or animal, are made of cells. Ionising radiation may damage the cells they pass through. The damage caused may be severe and cause immediate effects, or it may be more subtle and have effects which are not seen for a long time. The effects depend on both:

- the type of radiation, and
- the part of the body the radiation is going through.

Short-term effects of radiation

On 26 April 1986, there was an accident at the Chernobyl nuclear power station near Kiev in Russia. A fire there caused a number of firemen to be exposed to very large amounts of radiation, and around 30 died as a result (figure 3.39). The explosion was caused by an experiment on the reactor going wrong. Over 30 fires were started and lives were lost due to the radioactive materials emitted from the core of the reactor. The damage to the immediate area was extensive but

FIGURE 3.39

the radiation effects over a wide area were considerable: 135 000 people were removed from an area within a radius of 30 km. The smoke and radioactive debris reached a height of 1200 m and travelled across Russia and Poland and then to Scandinavia. On 2 May 1986, the cloud of material reached Great Britain and, with heavy rain, there was material deposited on parts of north Wales, Cumbria and Scotland. This caused certain farm animals such as lambs to be banned from sale since they absorbed radiation from the grass.

Long-term effects of radiation
There are other effects of radiation which take much longer to show. In some ways these are more important to us because they can be caused by much lower levels of radiation. The most important long-term effect is to cause cancers in various parts of the body. There is much evidence for these effects. Uranium miners tended to get lung cancer due to breathing in gases which emitted alpha particles. People who used to paint the dials of clocks with luminous paint developed bone cancer from using their lips to make points on the brushes. Marie Curie and many other early workers with radioactivity died of cancer.

Genetic damage can be caused to cells by radiation, including the cells which are involved in reproduction. Plant and animal studies have shown small increases in the numbers of mutations in future generations. These mutations – changes to the structure or physiology of the plant or animal – are usually harmful. Although mutations do occur naturally anyway, the rate of mutation is greater after the irradiation. However, the science fiction mutations of animals with two heads or elephant-sized spiders are just fantasy!

> The total effect of the radiation is a combination of:
> - the type of the radiation;
> - the part of body tissue which absorbs it;
> - the total amount of energy absorbed.

Dose equivalent
The biological risk caused by the radiation is represented by a quantity called the **dose equivalent**. It is measured in a unit called the sievert (Sv), although we often talk of doses in millisieverts (mSv) or microsieverts (μSv). (A millisievert is a thousandth and a microsievert a millionth of a sievert.) A sievert is a very large dose of radiation, and could only happen as a result of a very serious accident or after a nuclear explosion.

How dangerous is a dose equivalent of 1 Sv? It is impossible to say for any one person. However, suppose that 100 people all receive a dose equivalent of 1 Sv spread over the whole body. It is estimated that, of the 100 people, on average four of them would eventually die as a result of the radiation. But precisely who would die, or when they would die, or what illness they would die of, cannot be predicted.

Background radiation
We have seen that there is radiation all around us – our detectors in the lab pick up radiation even when none of the lab sources is anywhere near. Tables 3.2 and 3.3 show the typical dose equivalent we get every year

from background radiation and other sources. They are average figures, and vary a lot depending on our job and where we live. The different percentages are shown in figure 3.40. You can see that natural radiation is far the biggest influence on us. The total annual dose equivalent in the UK averages about 2000 µSv (2 mSv). But there is a big variation from person to person. If you take several aeroplane trips across the Atlantic each year you are getting more than your fair share. If you live in Aberdeen or especially in Cornwall where the granite rocks are giving off radioactive radon gas, you are subjected to a much higher background rate.

FIGURE 3.40 *Average percentage sources of annual dose of radiation to the population of the UK*

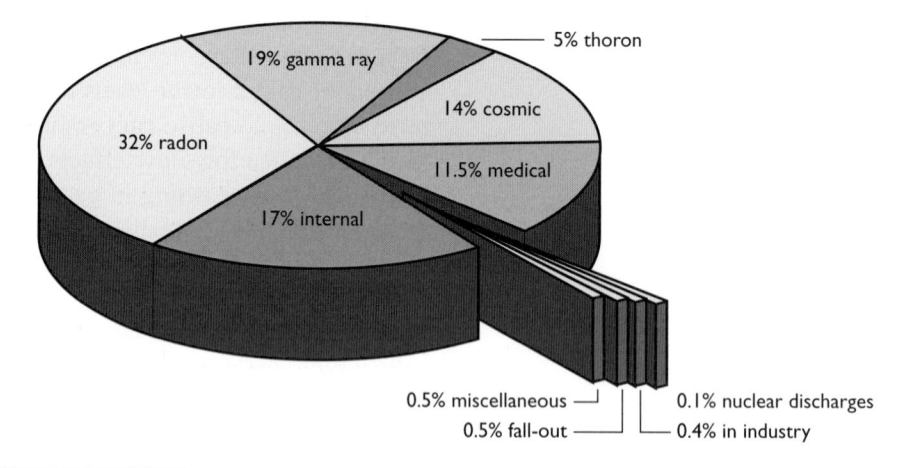

- 19% gamma ray
- 5% thoron
- 14% cosmic
- 32% radon
- 11.5% medical
- 17% internal
- 0.5% miscellaneous
- 0.5% fall-out
- 0.1% nuclear discharges
- 0.4% in industry

Source	Annual dose (µSv)
Radon and thoron gas from rocks and soil	800
Gamma rays from ground	400
Carbon and potassium in body	370
Cosmic rays at ground level	300
	Total = 1870

TABLE 3.2 *Natural sources of radiation*

Source	Annual dose (µSv)
Medical uses – X-rays, etc.	250
Chernobyl (first year)	50
Fall-out from weapons testing	10
Job (average)	5
Nuclear industry (e.g. waste)	2
Others (TV, aeroplane trips, etc.)	11
	Total = 328

TABLE 3.3 *Man-made sources of radiation*

Other risks

It is interesting to compare radiation risks with those of other types of risk. It is estimated that medical uses of radiation – while they can have great value and save many lives – will probably cause the death of one person out of every 240 000. Other risks we are exposed to are given in table 3.4 for comparison.

Death risk – cause	Death risk for a 40 year old
All causes	1 per 500
Smoker – 10 cigarettes per day	1 per 2000
Road accidents	1 per 5000
Home accidents	1 per 10 000
Work accidents	1 per 20 000
All radiations	1 per 27 500
Medical radiations	1 per 240 000

TABLE 3.4

health physics 3

There are people who, as a result of their work, are exposed to ionising radiations. These people include medical workers using X-rays in hospitals, dentists and vets, research workers using radiation sources in their experiments and people who work in the nuclear power industry. Shielding a source of radiation with an appropriate thickness of absorber can reduce the risk. For example, a radiographer wears a lead-lined apron.

Safety with radioactivity
1 Always use forceps or a lifting tool to remove a source. Never use bare hands.
2 Arrange a source so that its radiation window points away from the body.
3 Never bring a source close to your eyes for examination.
4 When in use, a source must always be attended by an authorised person and it must be returned to a locked and labelled store in its special shielded box immediately after use.
5 After any experiment with radioactive materials, wash your hands thoroughly before you eat.
6 In the UK, students under 16 years old may not normally handle radioactive sources.

The symbol for radiation sources being stored is

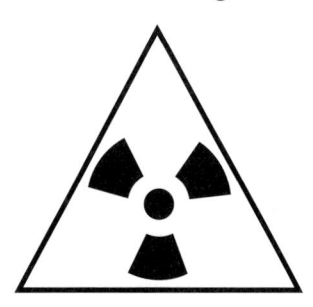

Using radiation in medicine
Treating cancer
Radiation not only causes cancer but can also be used to treat it. Radiotherapy is the treatment of cancers by radiation. Cancers are growths of cells which are out of control. These cells do not perform their intended function. Cancerous tumours (groups of cancerous cells) can be treated by drugs, surgery or radiation. The choice of treatment depends on the size and position of the tumour. The purpose of the radiation treatment is to cause damage to the cancer cells which then stop reproducing. The tumour then shrinks.

Unfortunately, healthy cells can also be damaged by radiation, and so the amount of radiation has to be very accurately calculated so that sufficient damage is done to cancer cells without overdoing the damage to other cells. The radiation must be aimed very accurately at the tumour. This can be done using a simulator. A series of X-ray photographs is taken at different angles and a computer can build up a picture of the tumour and measure the amount of radiation to be given. Some localised tumours (e.g. a bone tumour) can be treated by irradiation with high energy X-rays or gamma rays (figure 3.41).

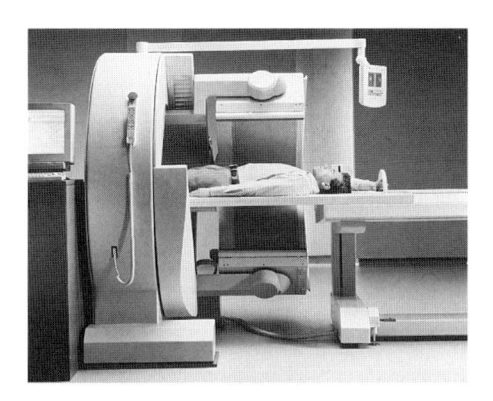

FIGURE 3.41

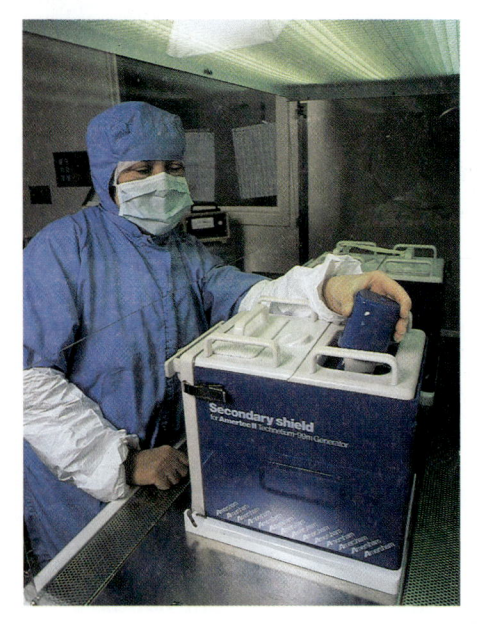

standard grade physics

FIGURE 3.42

- The gamma rays are emitted from a cobalt-60 source – a radioactive form of cobalt. The cobalt source is kept within a thick, heavy metal container (figure 3.42). This has a slit in it to allow a narrow beam of gamma rays to emerge.
- The X-rays are generated by a linear accelerator. This machine fires high energy electrons at a metal target and when the electrons strike the target, X-rays are produced. The X-rays are shaped into a narrow beam by movable metal shutters.

With either technique, the apparatus is arranged so that it can rotate around the couch on which the patient lies. This allows the patient to receive radiation from different directions. Therefore, the diseased tissue receives radiation all of the time but the healthy tissue receives only a small amount of radiation. Treatments are given as a series of small doses because tumour cells are killed more easily when they are dividing, and not all cells divide at the same time. This reduces side effects.

The gamma camera

It is important for scientists to be able to study internal organs without surgery. To see how the kidneys are working, a **radiopharmaceutical** is used which can act as a tracer. The radiopharmaceutical has two parts (figure 3.43):

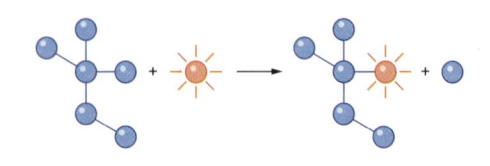

- A drug which is chosen for the particular organ that is being studied. (Different organs require different drugs.)
- A radioactive substance which is a gamma emitter.

Gamma is chosen since alpha or beta would be absorbed by tissues and would not be detected outside the body. A substance called technitium 99m (m = metastable) is normally used because it has a half-life of six hours. The half-life is important because:

Pharmaceutical and radioactive atom   Radiopharmaceutical

FIGURE 3.43

- A shorter time than six hours would be too difficult to make measurements.
- A longer time would increase the amount of radiation to the body.

The combined substance is then injected into the patient.

To detect the radiation a *gamma camera* is used. This device has special crystals which give off flashes of light when the radiation reaches them. Tubes called photomultipliers can change the light energy into electrical energy. The signals can then be displayed on a screen (figure 3.44).

Two types of studies are possible:

- A static study where there is a time delay between injecting the radioactive material and the build-up of radiation in the organ. This occurs in bone, lung or brain scans.
- A dynamic study where the amount of radioactivity in an organ is measured over time. This occurs in the examination of the operations of the kidneys.

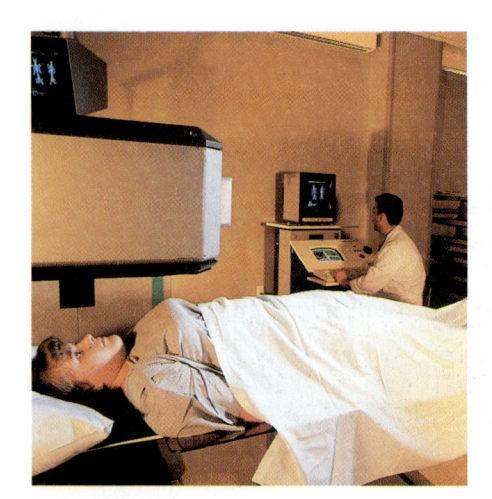

FIGURE 3.44 *Gamma camera*

health physics 3

Kidney examination or renogram

This technique examines the working of the kidneys. The radioactive material reaches the kidneys in the drug given to the patient. The radioactive material is removed from the bloodstream by the kidneys. Within a few minutes of the drug being injected, the radiation is concentrated in the kidneys. After ten to 15 minutes, almost all the radiation should be in the bladder. The gamma camera takes readings every few seconds for 20 minutes. The computer adds up the radioactivity in each kidney. This can be shown as a graph of activity against time (figure 3.45). The left kidney is not working correctly since the radioactivity is taken up by both kidneys but does not decrease as rapidly as with the other kidney.

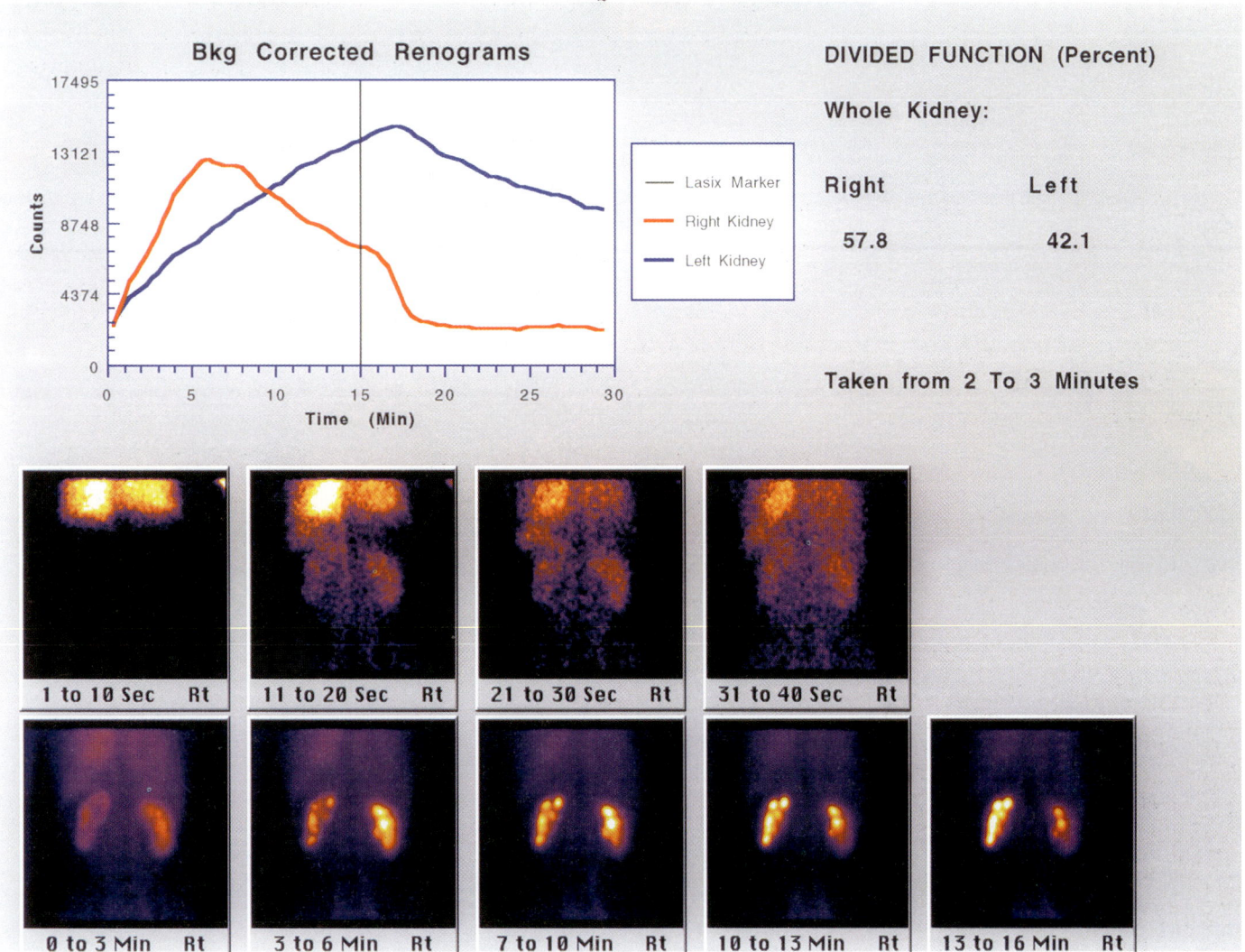

FIGURE 3.45

LEARNING OUTCOMES

After studying this chapter you should be able to:

Section 3.1

1. State that a thermometer requires some measurable physical property that changes with temperature.
2. Describe the operation of a liquid-in-glass thermometer.
3. Describe the main differences between a clinical and an ordinary thermometer.
4. Describe how body temperature is measured using a clinical thermometer.
5. Explain the significance of body temperature in diagnosis of illness.

Section 3.2

1. State that a solid, a liquid or a gas is required for the transmission of sound.
2. Explain the basic principles of a stethoscope as a 'hearing aid'.
3. Give one example of the use of ultrasound in medicine, e.g. images of an unborn baby.
4. State that high frequency vibrations beyond the range of human hearing are called ultrasounds.
5. Give two examples of noise pollution.
6. Give examples of sound levels in the range 0 dB–120 dB.
7. State that excessive noise can damage hearing.
8. Explain one use of ultrasound in medicine. `Credit`

Section 3.3

1. Describe the focusing of light on the retina of the eye.
2. State what is meant by refraction of light.
3. Draw diagrams to show the change of direction as light passes from air to glass and glass to air.
4. Describe the shapes of convex and concave lenses.
5. Describe the effect of various lens shapes on the rays of light.
6. State that the image formed on the retina of the eye is upside down and laterally inverted.
7. Explain using a ray diagram how an inverted image can be formed on the retina.
8. Describe a simple experiment to find the focal length of a spherical convex lens.
9. State the meaning of long and short sight.
10. State that long and short sight can be corrected using lenses.
11. State that fibre optics can be used as a transmission system for 'cold light'.
12. Use correctly in context the terms of incidence, angle of refraction and normal. `Credit`
13. Explain using a ray diagram how the lens of the eye forms, on the retina, an image of an object (a) some distance from the eye and (b) close to the eye. `Credit`
14. Carry out calculations on power/focal length to find either one, given the other. `Credit`
15. Explain the use of lenses to correct long and short sight. `Credit`
16. Explain the use of fibre optics in the endoscope (fibrescope). `Credit`

Section 3.4

1. Describe how the laser is used in one application of medicine.
2. Describe one use of X-rays in medicine.
3. State that photographic film can be used to detect X-rays.
4. Describe the use of ultraviolet and infrared in medicine.
5. State that excessive exposure to ultraviolet radiation may produce skin cancer.
6. Describe the advantage of computer tomography. `Credit`

learning outcomes

Section 3.5

1. State that radiation can kill living cells or change the nature of living cells.
2. Describe one medical use of radiation based on the fact that it can destroy cells (instrument sterilisation, treatment of cancer).
3. Describe one medical use of radiation based on the fact that radiation is easy to detect.
4. State the range and absorption of alpha, beta and gamma radiation.
5. State that radiation energy may be absorbed in the medium through which it passes.
6. Describe a simple model of the atom which includes protons, neutrons and electrons.
7. State that alpha rays produce much greater ionisation density than beta or gamma rays.
8. State one example of the effect of radiation on non-living things (e.g. ionisation, fogging of photographic film, scintillations).
9. State that the activity of a radioactive source is measured in bequerels.
10. State that the activity of a radioactive source decreases with time.
11. Describe the safety precautions necessary when dealing with radioactive substances.
12. State that the dose equivalent is measured in sieverts.
13. Explain the term ionisation. `Credit`
14. Describe how one of the effects of radiation is used in a detector of radiation (e.g. GM tube; film badges; scintillation counters). `Credit`
15. Describe a method of measuring the half-life of a radioactive element. `Credit`
16. State the meaning of the term 'half-life'. `Credit`
17. Carry out calculations to find the half-life of a radioactive element from appropriate data. `Credit`
18. State that for living materials, the biological effect of radiation depends on the absorbing tissue and the nature of the radiation. Understand that the dose equivalent measured in sieverts takes account of the type and energy of radiation. `Credit`

STUDY QUESTIONS

1 A pupil has her temperature measured and it is found to be 38.5°C.

(a) Describe how the construction of a clinical thermometer will allow this temperature to be taken.

(b) Discuss whether this temperature is too high or too low for the patient.

2 (a) State the noise level for normal conversation.

(b) Estimate the noise level for a jet engine.

3 (a) What is the advantage of using ultrasound for an examination compared to X-rays?

(b) The frequency of an ultrasound signal is 1.1 MHz. The speed of sound in tissue is 1100 m/s. Calculate the wavelength of the ultrasound.

(c) Describe one use of ultrasound in medicine.

4 Maureen can see distant objects clearly but near objects appear blurred.

(a) What is this type of eye defect called?

(b) What type of lens is needed to correct this problem?

5 (a) A lens has a power of 1.5 D. Calculate the focal length of the lens.

81

study questions

(b) State and explain whether the lens is convex or concave in shape.

6 (a) A laser can be used to correct eyesight defects by removing part of the cornea. At the edge of the eye the amount needed to be removed is 0.15 mm. The laser can remove 0.05 mm/s.

(i) Calculate the time required to do this operation.

(ii) The energy required for this operation is 96 J. Calculate the power of the laser.

(b) Describe one use of the laser other than that described in (a).

7 (a) X-rays are often used to detect injuries in sport. Why does a fracture in a bone appear as a black line in a photographic plate?

(b) Soft tissue such as the gullet cannot easily be seen using X-rays.

(i) Why does this happen?

(ii) What can be used to make this tissue be seen?

(c) What is the advantage of a CT scan compared to a normal X-ray photograph?

8 A patient is injected with a radioactive material called technetium-99m which can be detected by a gamma camera.

(a) Why is a gamma emitter used?

(b) The half life of this substance is six hours. If the activity of the source is 1.8 kBq when it is absorbed by the patient, what will the activity be after one day?

(c) The dose equivalent taken in by the patient depends on two factors.

(i) What are these factors?

(ii) What unit is used to measure the dose equivalent?

9 Different types of radiation can be used to treat patients.

(a) Alpha radiation can be easily absorbed by the skin but is dangerous if the radiation is absorbed inside the body. This is due to the large ionisation which is produced. Explain what is meant by ionisation.

(b) Describe a use of ionising radiation in medical treatment.

(c) Other radiations can be used but must be treated with care. Why must the exposure to ultraviolet radiation be limited?

10 An endoscope is used to examine the internal organs of patients.

(a) What is the advantage of using such an instrument?

(b) Draw a diagram to explain how the light travels down a fibre.

11 When a laser is used to send light down a fibre, the plate on the laser has the following information.

> Laser Class 1 serial number 21723, power output 20 W, wavelength 540 nm (1 nm = 10^{-9} m).

(a) Calculate the frequency of the radiation.

(b) Calculate the energy used in 5 s.

12 Radioactive materials can be used in a variety of ways.

(a) Give one use of radiation in medicine.

(b) If the activity of the source is 64 MBq and five weeks later the activity is 2 MBq, calculate the half-life of this material.

(c) Describe two precautions which must be taken in using radioactive material.

13 Read the following passage.

"Come in, Chris," said the doctor. "We are going to take a thermogram of your hand."

"What's a thermogram?" asked Chris.

"Your body gives out radiation, called infrared," explained the doctor. "This is similar to light but it has a longer wavelength. We have a special camera which makes use of this radiation to take a photograph of your hand. The photography is called a thermogram and is similar to the one shown in the diagram."

study questions

"What are the different patches in the photograph?" asked Chris.

"In a real thermogram," answered the doctor, "your hand will show up as patches of different colour. Each colour is due to a different temperature. The coldest parts are blue and the hottest parts are white. We can use the thermogram to detect unhealthy tissue since it is warmer than healthy tissue and so shows up as a different colour."

"Have you heard of any other type of radiation used in medicine?" asked the doctor. "Do you know how it is used?"

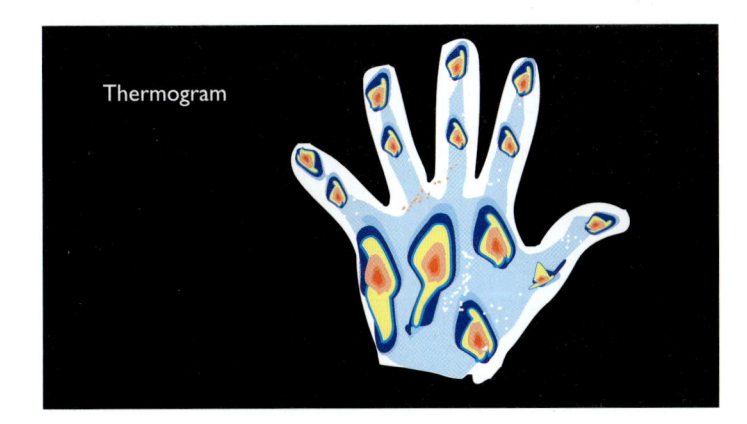

Thermogram

(a) Name the type of radiation given out by the human body.
GENERAL PS

(b) How does the wavelength of this radiation compare with that of light?
GENERAL PS

(c) If Chris did have unhealthy tissue in his hand, suggest how this would be detected on the thermogram.
GENERAL PS

(d) Answer the doctor's last question to Chris by naming another type of radiation used in medicine and stating its use.
SEB
GENERAL KU

14 The table below lists the upper and lower frequency limits which apply to the hearing range of different animals.

Animal	Frequency of lower limit of hearing (hertz)	Frequency of upper limit of hearing (hertz)
Elephant	20	10 000
Finch	100	15 000
Cat	30	45 000
Dog	20	30 000
Human	20	17 000
Whale	40	80 000

(a) What is the highest frequency which can be heard by a cat?
GENERAL PS

(b) A dog whistle emits sound which can be heard by a dog but not by a human. Using information from the table, state **one** possible frequency of the sound emitted by the dog whistle.
GENERAL PS

(c) Name **two** animals in the table, apart from humans, which will not respond to ultrasound.
GENERAL PS

(d) Choose the lowest frequency of sound which can be heard by a whale and calculate the wavelength of this sound in water. (Speed of sound in water = 1410 metres per second)
SEB
GENERAL PS

15 (a) The diagram below shows part of an optical fibre.

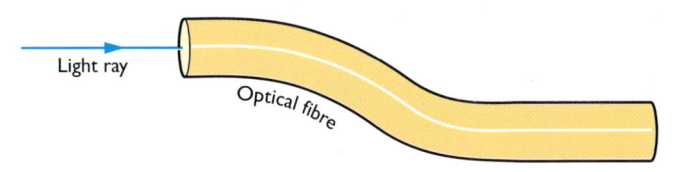

Light ray
Optical fibre

Copy the diagram and draw the path of the light ray through the fibre.
SEB
CREDIT KU

(b) Surgeons use optical fibres.

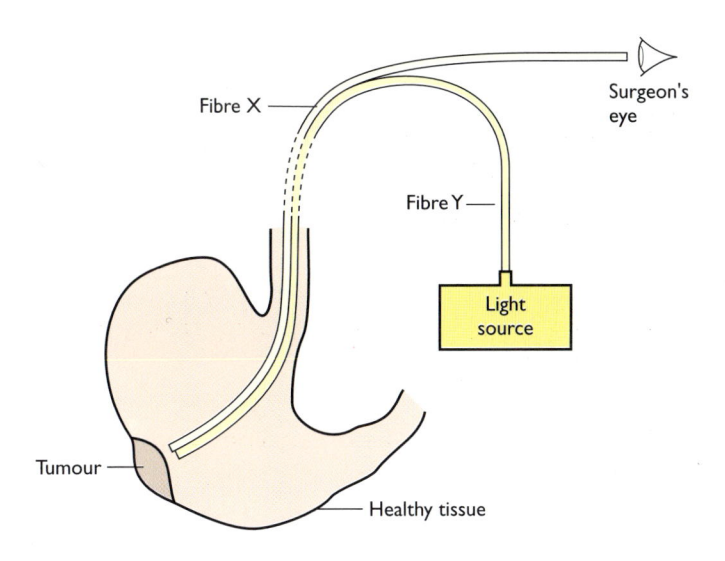

Fibre X
Surgeon's eye
Fibre Y
Light source
Tumour
Healthy tissue

(i) Explain how the fibres X and Y shown above allow a surgeon to see a tumour in a patient's stomach.
CREDIT KU

(ii) Describe how the surgeon would use a laser to destroy the tumour.
SEB
CREDIT PS

study questions

(c) While working with radioactive substances, the technician wears a film badge similar to that shown in the diagram below. A photographic film, protected from light, is placed behind the windows in the badge.

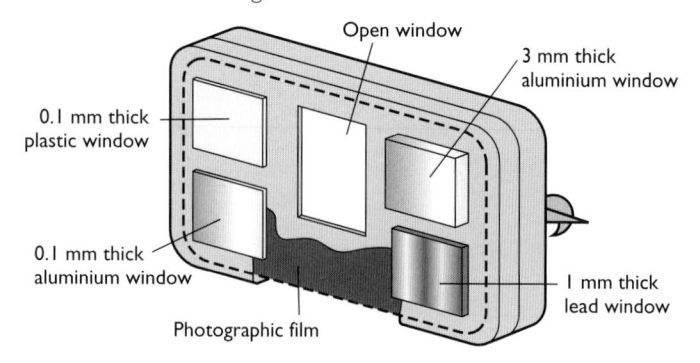

If the technician was exposed accidentally to too much beta radiation, which part or parts of the film would **not** be affected?
SEB
CREDIT PS

16 A sample of air containing a radioactive gas was collected from a house in Cornwall. The sample and a detector were put into a sealed lead container. A cutaway section of the container is shown below. The count rate for the sample was found at various times.

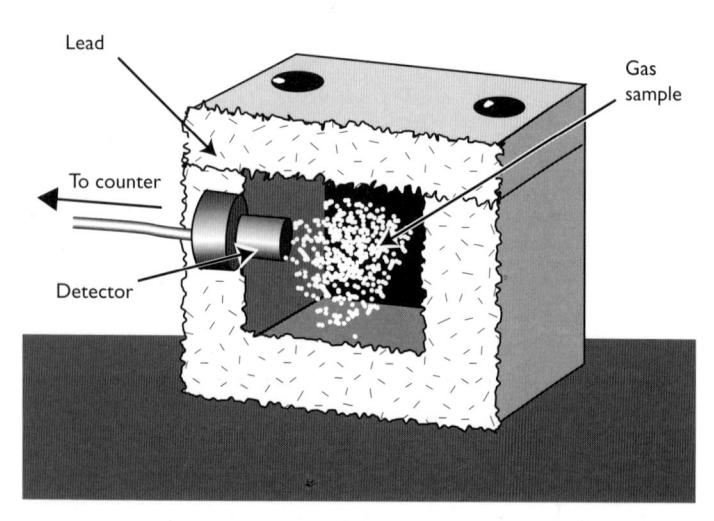

(a) (i) Why were the sample and detector enclosed in a thick lead container?
CREDIT PS

(ii) The measurements of count rate for the sample as time passed were as follows.

Time (h)	0	30	60	90	120	150	180
Count rate (counts min^{-1})	42.0	33.5	26.7	21.3	17.0	13.6	10.8

Use these figures to give an **estimate** of the half-life of the radioactive gas.
SEB
CREDIT PS

17 In some parts of North America, a daily ultraviolet index is published to give a guide to the amount of time that a person can sunbathe safely. The table shows such an index. The chart shows how the index changed during a week in May.

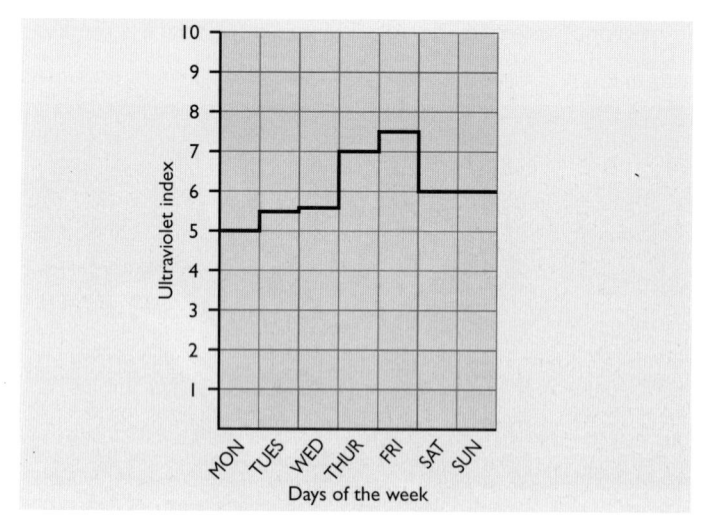

Ultraviolet index	Time to sunbathe (mins)
Greater than 9	15
7–8.9	20
4–6.9	30
0–3.9	60

(a) Use the chart and the table to estimate the maximum safe time allowed for sunbathing on Friday of that week.
GENERAL PS

(b) Why may it be dangerous for a person to be exposed to too much ultraviolet radiation?
SEB
GENERAL KU

84

Electronics

4.1 Overview

FIGURE 4.1 *The picture shows a person using a loudhailer. Why do you think he needs to use a loudhailer?*

Electronics is the science that deals with the control of electrons in an electrical circuit or electrical system. It usually involves the use of special electrical components such as 'transistors' or 'integrated circuits' (silicon chips).

An **electrical system** is a collection of electrical components connected together to perform a particular function, e.g. a loudhailer.

A simplified view of a loudhailer system would be:

- sound waves are changed into weak electrical signals;
- the weak electrical signals are then amplified (made bigger);
- the amplified electrical signals are then converted into sound.

Notice that it is convenient to break the loudhailer system into three parts:

1 the microphone which picks up the sound waves and converts them into weak electrical signals – known as the **input**;
2 the amplifier which boosts the weak electrical signals – known as the **process**;
3 the loudspeaker which converts the electrical signals to sound – known as the **output**.

In fact, all electronic systems can be broken into these three parts – input, process and output. The input section starts the system working, the process section alters the input so as to produce the required output, and the output section gives the desired result.

Since all electronic systems need to use electrical signals, devices are required to convert one form of energy (e.g. light, heat, sound, etc.) into electrical energy at the input stage and to do the opposite at the output stage.

Devices which convert input signals to electrical signals or electrical signals back to output signals are called **transducers**. Input transducers convert one form of energy into electrical energy, e.g. a microphone converts sound energy into electrical energy. Output transducers convert electrical energy into another form of energy, e.g. a loudspeaker converts electrical energy into sound energy.

An electronic system may be drawn as a **block diagram** (see figure 4.2). The arrows show how information is passed (electrically) from one block to another.

4 standard grade physics

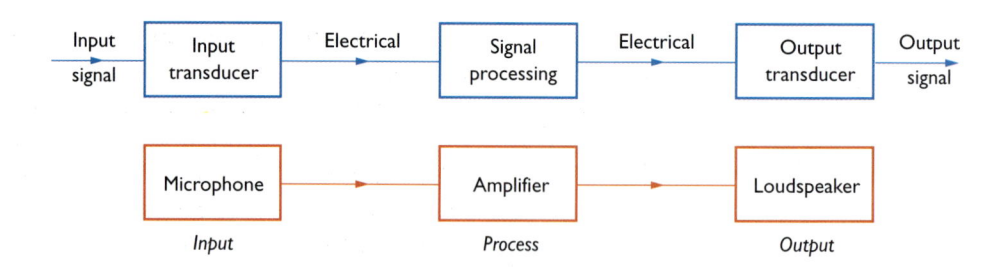

FIGURE 4.2 *Block diagram for a loudhailer*

Input signal → [Input transducer] → Electrical → [Signal processing] → Electrical → [Output transducer] → Output signal

[Microphone] → [Amplifier] → [Loudspeaker]
Input — Process — Output

Analogue signals and digital signals

The signals used by electronic systems are of two types: **analogue** or **digital**. The oscilloscope traces shown in figures 4.3 (a) and (b) show the differences between analogue and digital signals.

Figure 4.3 (a) shows a typical electrical signal from the microphone of a telephone when a person is speaking. The trace has a continuous range of values. This type of signal is called an analogue signal. Most input transducers produce analogue signals.

Figure 4.3 (b) shows a typical electrical signal from a compact disc player. The trace shows a series of electrical pulses each with the same amplitude. This type of signal is called a digital signal. In a digital signal the trace is either at a maximum value (called a **high** or **logic '1'**), or a minimum value (called **low** or **logic '0'**).

An analogue signal has a continuous range of values, while a digital signal can have only one of two possible values.

Many electrical systems consist of both digital and analogue signals. An analogue signal produced by an input transducer may be converted into a digital signal in the process unit. For example, many telephone systems change the human voice (an analogue signal) into a digital signal – which can be transmitted over long distances – then back into an analogue signal (sound) that can be heard.

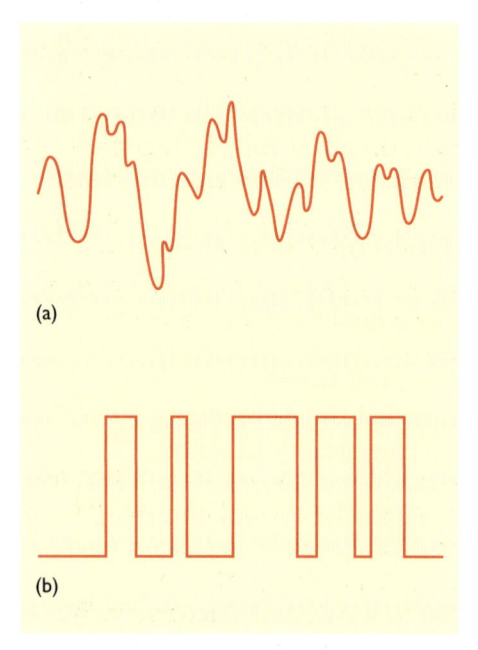

FIGURE 4.3 *(a) Analogue signal, (b) digital signal*

4.2 Output devices

There are a large number of output devices available for different applications.

The loudspeaker

Consider a signal generator connected to a loudspeaker. As the amplitude (energy of the electrical signal) from the signal generator is increased the sound from the loudspeaker gets louder. A loudspeaker is an analogue output device which changes electrical energy into sound energy. A radio and a television are examples of electronic systems that contain a loudspeaker.

The electric motor

Consider an electric motor connected to a variable voltage supply. An electric motor is an analogue output device which changes electrical

electronics 4

energy into kinetic (movement) energy. Its speed increases as the voltage is increased. The direction of rotation can be reversed by reversing the connections to the supply. Vacuum cleaners and washing machines contain mains-operated electric motors.

Note: an electric motor could become a digital output device by connecting it to a battery and a switch. The motor would then either be 'on' when the switch was closed, or 'off' when the switch was opened.

The relay

A **relay** is a switch operated by an electromagnet. A coil of wire, when carrying an electric current, provides the magnetic field required to close the switch contacts in the relay shown in figure 4.4. When switch S is closed a current passes through the coil surrounding the switch – the switch contacts close completing the lower electrical circuit, thus allowing the lamp to light. When S is opened, the switch contacts open and the lamp goes out. The advantage of a relay is that a small current in one circuit is able to control another circuit containing a device, such as a lamp, electric bell or motor, which requires a larger current. The relay is a digital output device which changes electrical energy into movement energy – the opening or closing of a switch.

The solenoid

A **solenoid** consists of a coil of wire surrounding a metal core. When no current passes through the coil, a spring pushes the metal core away from the coil. However, when a large enough current passes through the coil, the magnetic field produced attracts the metal core into the coil.

Figure 4.5 shows a solenoid connected to a switch and a battery. When the switch is closed, the metal core moves into the coil and is then held there. When the switch is opened, the metal core moves out of the coil and then stops. A solenoid is a digital output device which changes electrical energy into movement in a straight line. Solenoids are used in the central locking system of a car.

The filament lamp

A **filament lamp** consists of a thin tungsten wire (filament) in a glass container. When an electric current passes through the wire, electrical energy is changed into heat in the filament. Consider a lamp connected to a variable voltage supply. Increasing the voltage across the lamp, increases the current through it and so it gets brighter. No difference is observed when the connections from the supply to the lamp are reversed. The filament in the lamp requires a relatively large current to light properly and gets very hot in operation. Lamps can be used as analogue or digital output devices. They are analogue devices if used with a dimmer circuit (i.e. the brightness changes) and digital devices if they are switched on or off.

The light-emitting diode (LED)

Light-emitting diodes are made by joining two special materials together to produce a junction. When an electric current passes through the

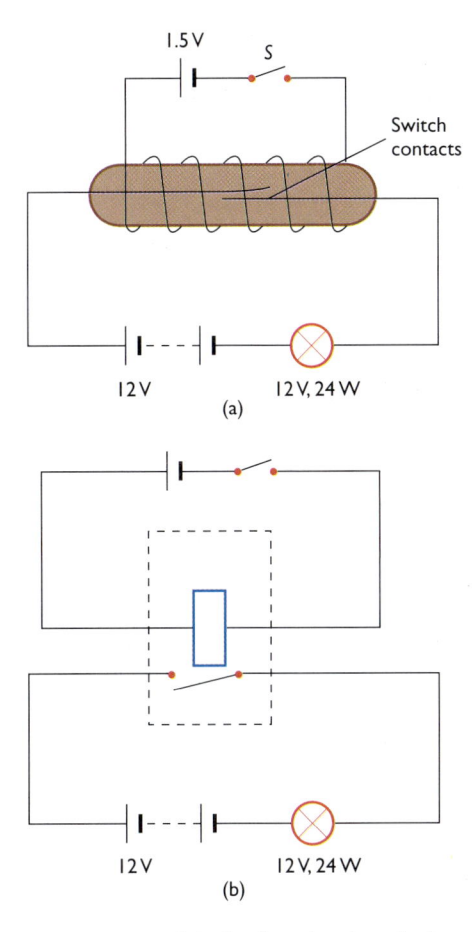

FIGURE 4.4 *(a) A relay circuit – closing switch S allows the lamp to light, (b) circuit diagram for relay*

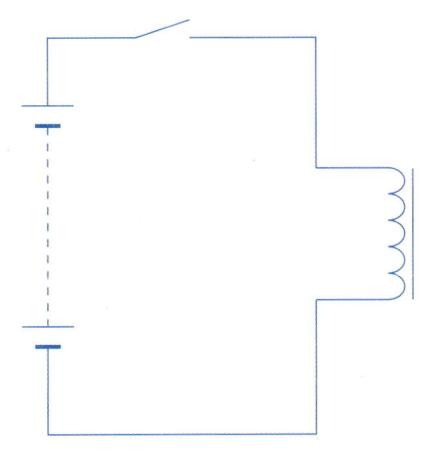

FIGURE 4.5 *A voltage supply connected to a switch and a solenoid*

87

4 standard grade physics

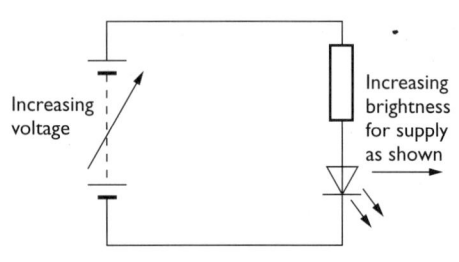

FIGURE 4.6 *A variable voltage supply connected to a resistor and an LED*

junction it emits light. LEDs are available in red, green, yellow and blue colours. A series resistor must be used to limit the current to about 15 mA or the junction will be destroyed. Figure 4.6 shows an LED connected to a variable voltage supply.

Increasing the voltage across the LED increases its brightness, but it does not light if the connections from the supply to it are reversed. The LED requires only a small current to operate properly and does not get hot in operation. LEDs are usually used as digital output devices, i.e. they are either 'on' or 'off'. LEDs can be used in hi-fi's and instrument panels.

Example: The maximum voltage allowed across an LED is 2 V and the current through it must not exceed 8 mA. If the LED is to be used with a 6 V supply, calculate the value of the resistor, R, connected in series with it.
Solution:

FIGURE 4.7 *Circuit diagram*

Since the LED and resistor are connected in series then $V_S = V_{LED} + V_R$ and the current through both components is the same (8 mA = 0.008 A). Therefore:
$$V_R = V_S - V_{LED} = 6 - 2 = 4 \text{ V}$$
$$V_R = IR$$
$$4 = 0.008 \times R$$
$$R = \frac{4}{0.008} = 500 \text{ } \Omega$$

The seven-segment display

A seven-segment display consists of 7 LEDs arranged in a rectangular package as shown in figure 4.8. Any number in the range 0 to 9 can be produced by lighting a number of the individual LEDs. For example, the number 1 is displayed by lighting LEDs connected to terminals b and c and number 3 is displayed by lighting the LEDs connected to a, b, c, d and g.

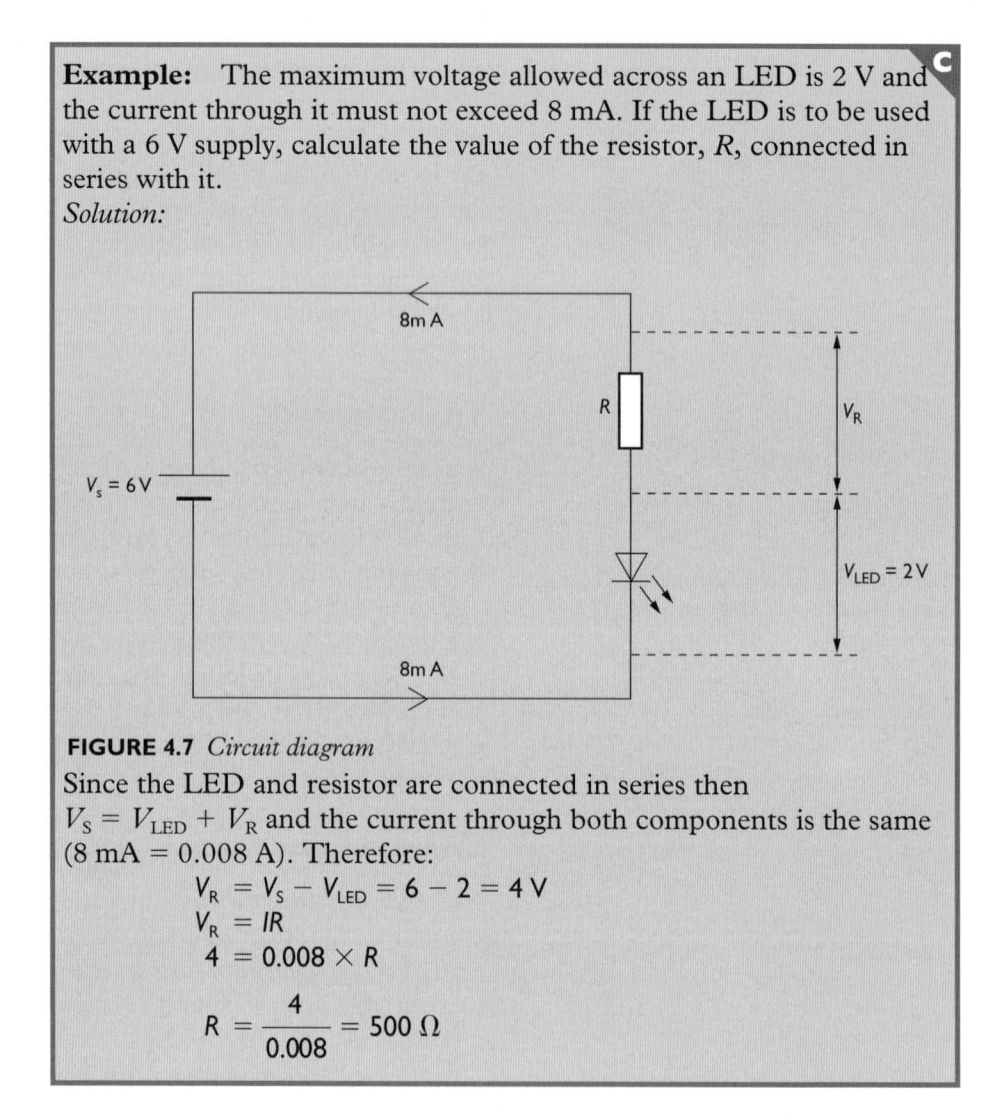

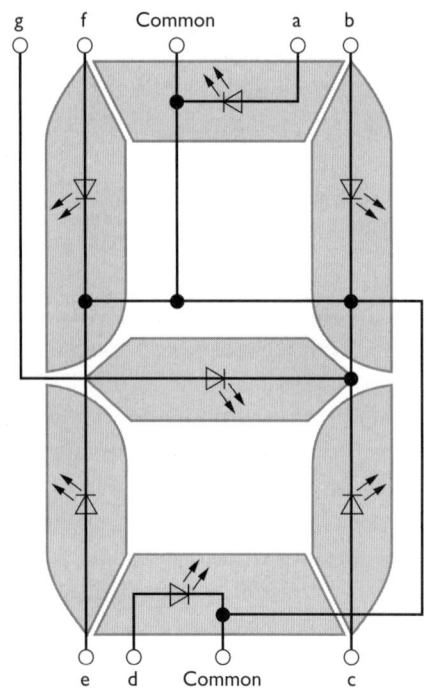

FIGURE 4.8 *Part of a seven-segment display showing each of the seven LEDs a to g*

Some calculators use seven-segment displays which are LED displays. Other calculators use liquid crystal displays (LCDs), again of the seven-segment display type.

The seven-segment display is a digital output device which changes electrical energy into light energy. Seven-segment displays are used in some televisions, hi-fi's, instrument panels and calculators.

Binary and decimal numbers

Decimal code
Normally we count on the scale of ten, or decimal system, using ten digits 0 to 9. When the count is greater than 9, we place a 1 in the second column to represent tens.

Binary code
Counting in electronic systems is done by digital circuits on the scale of two or binary system. The digits 0 and 1 are used and are represented by low and high voltages respectively. Many more columns are necessary since the number after 1 in binary is 10 (this is the number two in decimal).

Columns from the right in this case represent powers of 2:
$2^3 = 8 \quad 2^2 = 4 \quad 2^1 = 2 \quad 2^0 = 1$

Table 4.1 shows how the decimal numbers 0 to 9 are coded in the binary system:

TABLE 4.1

Decimal number	Binary code $2^3 = 8$	$2^2 = 4$	$2^1 = 2$	$2^0 = 1$
0	0	0	0	0
1	0	0	0	1
2	0	0	1	0
3	0	0	1	1
4	0	1	0	0
5	0	1	0	1
6	0	1	1	0
7	0	1	1	1
8	1	0	0	0
9	1	0	0	1

4.3 Input devices

There are a large number of input devices available for different applications.

The microphone

Consider a microphone connected to an oscilloscope. As louder notes are played into the microphone, the trace on the oscilloscope increases in amplitude.

A **microphone** is an input transducer which changes sound energy into electrical energy. The louder the sound, the greater the electrical energy produced.

The thermocouple

When the junction of the thermocouple, shown in figure 4.9, is placed in a Bunsen flame, the voltmeter reading increases.

A **thermocouple** is an input transducer which changes heat energy into electrical energy. The higher the temperature of the junction, the greater the electrical energy produced.

FIGURE 4.9 *A thermocouple connected to a voltmeter*

The solar cell

When the solar cell, shown in figure 4.10, is exposed to more light, the voltmeter reading increases.

A **solar cell** is an input transducer which changes light energy into electrical energy. The brighter the light shining on the solar cell, the greater the electrical energy produced.

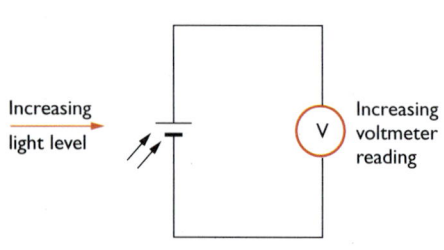

FIGURE 4.10 *A solar cell connected to a voltmeter*

The thermistor

When the thermistor, shown in figure 4.11, is heated the ohmmeter reading decreases.

A **thermistor** is an input device. The resistance of a thermistor decreases when its temperature increases.

Temperature ↑ – resistance of thermistor ↓

The only type of thermistor to be considered in this book will act as shown above, i.e. the resistance of the thermistor decreases as its temperature increases.

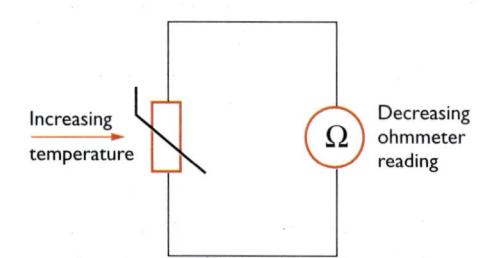

FIGURE 4.11 *A thermistor connected to an ohmmeter*

The light-dependent resistor (LDR)

When the light-dependent resistor, shown in figure 4.12, is exposed to more light, the ohmmeter reading decreases.

A **light-dependent resistor (LDR)** is an input device. As the light gets brighter (light intensity increases) the resistance of the LDR decreases.

Light intensity ↑ – resistance of LDR ↓

A capacitor

A **capacitor** consists of two metal plates separated by an insulator. The construction of a capacitor is shown in figure 4.13. It is a device which can store electric charge. The units of capacitance are **farads** (**F**). Most capacitors have very small values and so are measured in microfarads (μF), i.e. millionths of a farad.

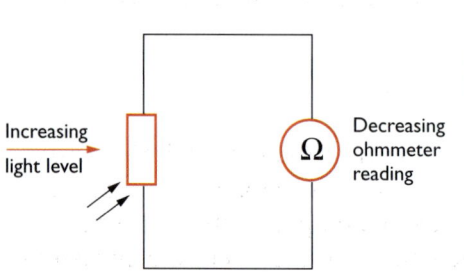

FIGURE 4.12 *A light dependent resistor (LDR) connected to an ohmmeter*

electronics 4

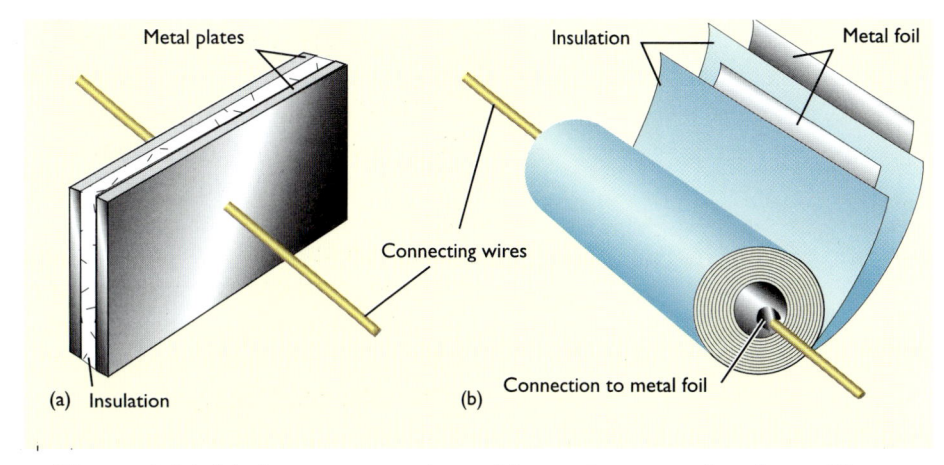

FIGURE 4.13 *(a) A capacitor consists of two metal plates separated by an insulator, (b) practical capacitors are constructed like a 'Swiss roll'. Why is this construction preferred to that shown in (a) for most capacitors?*

Figure 4.14 (a) shows a capacitor with no charge on its plates. Figure 4.14 (b) shows the capacitor when it is fully charged. This occurs when the voltage across its plates is equal to the supply voltage. Figure 4.14 (c) shows how a charged capacitor can be discharged by connecting the two plates together using a switch. When the switch is closed, the capacitor is discharged.

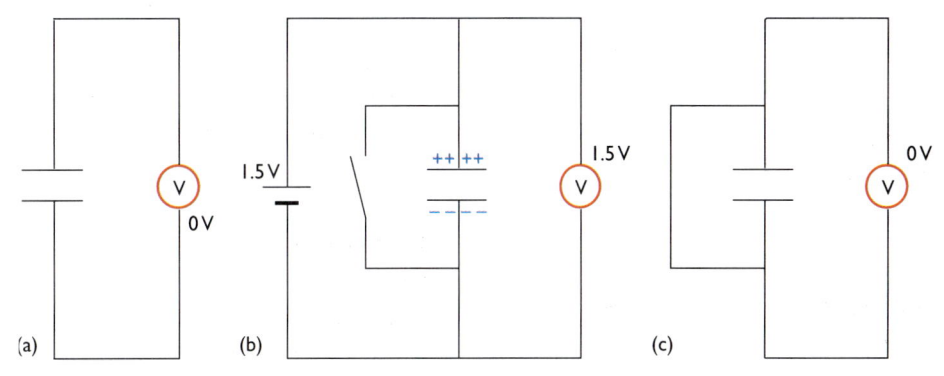

FIGURE 4.14 *(a) Uncharged capacitor, (b) fully charged capacitor, (c) discharged capacitor*

A capacitor can be used as an input device. A discharged capacitor has no voltage across its plates. When a capacitor is charging up, the voltage across the plates takes time to rise to the supply voltage. The voltage across a fully-charged capacitor is equal to the supply voltage.

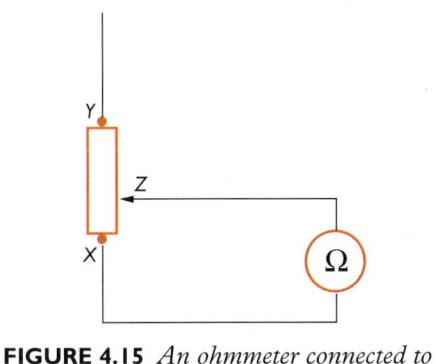

A potentiometer

Figure 4.15 shows an ohmmeter connected to the slider and one end of a potentiometer. As the slider Z of the potentiometer is moved from X to Y of the potentiometer, the ohmmeter reading increases.

A **potentiometer** can be used as an input device. As the slider Z is moved from X to Y, the resistance of XZ increases while the resistance of ZY decreases.

FIGURE 4.15 *An ohmmeter connected to the slider and one end of a potentiometer*

A switch

Consider an ohmmeter connected to a switch. When the switch is open, there is an air gap between the contacts of the switch and the ohmmeter reading is very, very high – the resistance of an open switch is infinite. When the switch is closed, the contacts touch and the ohmmeter reading is zero (or very close to zero).

A **switch** can be used as an input device.

91

Voltage dividers as input devices

You discovered in Unit 2 that for a series circuit the supply voltage was equal to the sum of the voltages across the individual resistors, i.e. $V_S = V_1 + V_2 + V_3$ (refer to figure 2.20 on page 36). This means that the supply voltage is split up into smaller bits and this is the basis for the input to an electronic system.

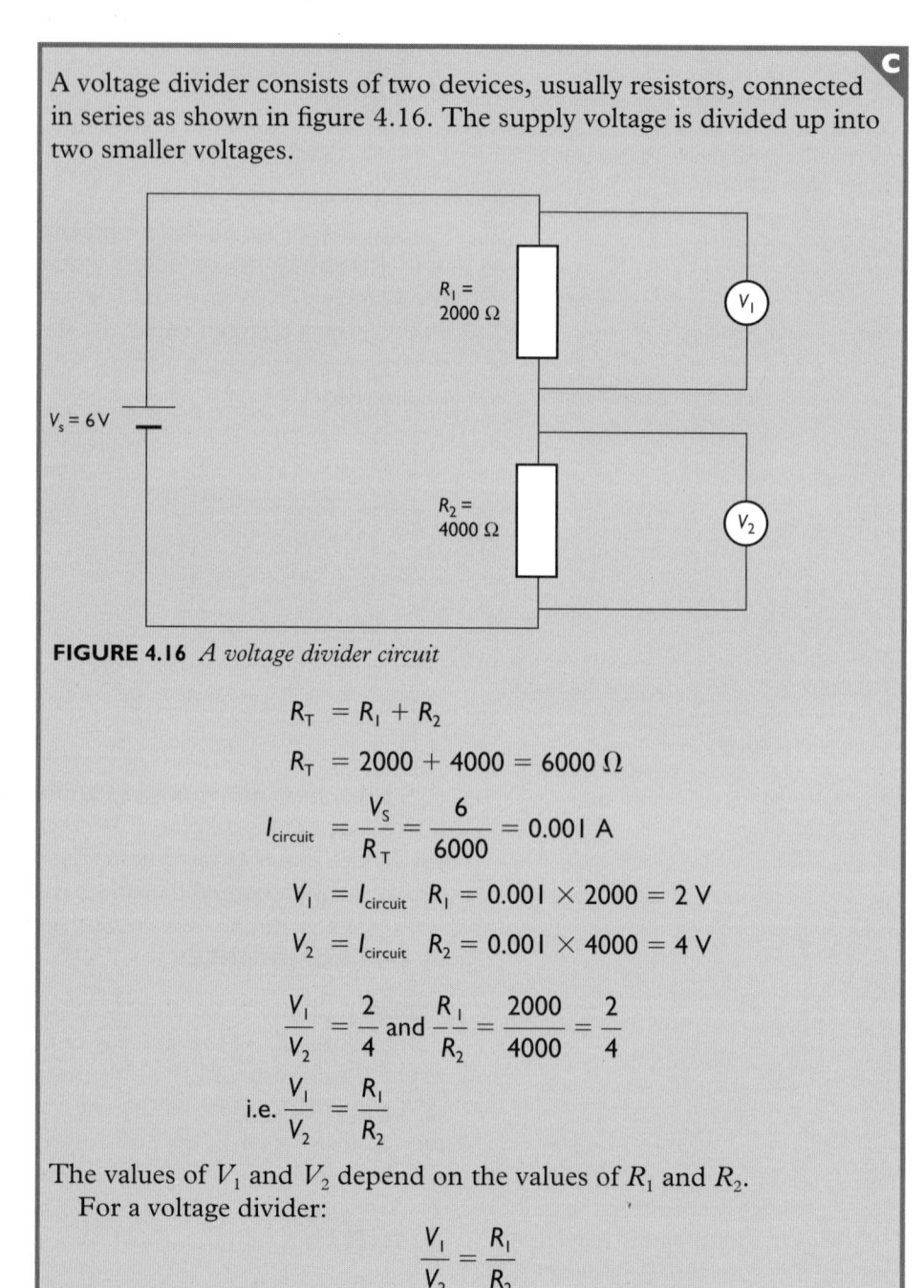

A voltage divider consists of two devices, usually resistors, connected in series as shown in figure 4.16. The supply voltage is divided up into two smaller voltages.

FIGURE 4.16 *A voltage divider circuit*

$$R_T = R_1 + R_2$$

$$R_T = 2000 + 4000 = 6000 \ \Omega$$

$$I_{circuit} = \frac{V_S}{R_T} = \frac{6}{6000} = 0.001 \ A$$

$$V_1 = I_{circuit} \ R_1 = 0.001 \times 2000 = 2 \ V$$

$$V_2 = I_{circuit} \ R_2 = 0.001 \times 4000 = 4 \ V$$

$$\frac{V_1}{V_2} = \frac{2}{4} \text{ and } \frac{R_1}{R_2} = \frac{2000}{4000} = \frac{2}{4}$$

i.e. $\dfrac{V_1}{V_2} = \dfrac{R_1}{R_2}$

The values of V_1 and V_2 depend on the values of R_1 and R_2.
 For a voltage divider:

$$\frac{V_1}{V_2} = \frac{R_1}{R_2}$$

Either voltage V_1 or V_2 could be used as the input voltage to an electronic system, but it is usual to use V_2 as the input voltage to an electronic process device. We shall be interested in what happens to this voltage when changes are made in a voltage divider circuit.

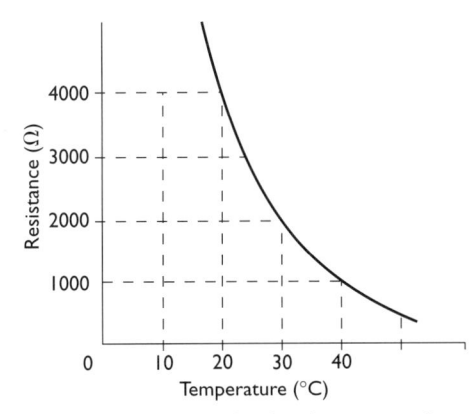

electronics 4

Voltage divider with a thermistor

A graph of resistance against temperature for a thermistor is given in figure 4.17.

Figure 4.18 shows the thermistor connected in series with a 10 kΩ resistor to form a voltage divider circuit. The voltages across the thermistor (V_1) and across the resistor (V_2) at different temperatures are shown in table 4.2. (You should check these values by calculation yourself.)

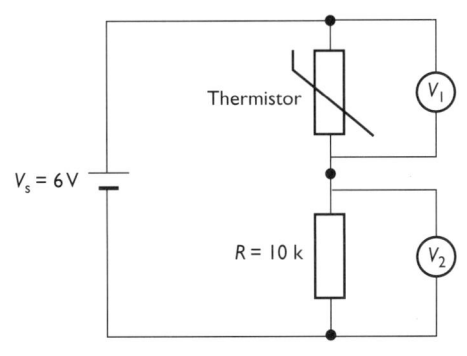

FIGURE 4.17 *Graph of resistance against temperature for a thermistor*

FIGURE 4.18 *Voltage divider circuit for the results shown in table 4.2*

Temperature of thermistor (°C)	$V_1 (= V_{th})$ (V)	$V_2 (= V_R)$ (V)	$V_S = V_1 + V_2$ (V)
20	1.7	4.3	6.0
30	1.0	5.0	6.0
40	0.5	5.5	6.0

TABLE 4.2

For this circuit, the resistance of thermistor decreases as its temperature increases and so the voltage across it (V_1) decreases and hence the voltage across the resistor R (V_2) increases even though the value of R has not been changed.

The circuit in figure 4.19 shows the same thermistor and resistor connected in series but with their positions interchanged.

Temperature of thermistor (°C)	$V_1 (= V_R)$ (V)	$V_2 (= V_{th})$ (V)	$V_S = V_1 + V_2$ (V)
20	4.3	1.7	6.0
30	5.0	1.0	6.0
40	5.5	0.5	6.0

TABLE 4.3

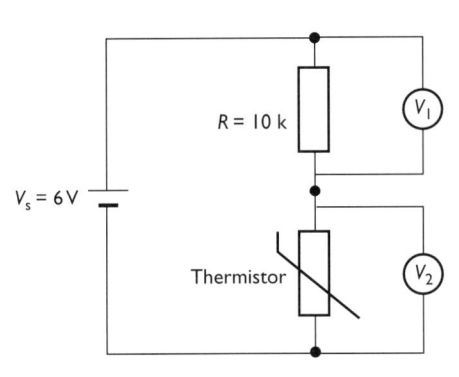

FIGURE 4.19 *Alternative voltage divider circuit. The results for this circuit are shown in table 4.3*

For this circuit, the resistance of the thermistor decreases as it is heated and so the voltage across it (V_2) decreases (and hence the voltage across the resistor increases).

4 standard grade physics

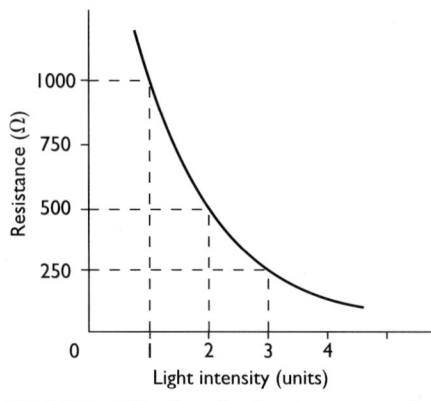

FIGURE 4.20 *Graph of resistance against light intensity for an LDR.*

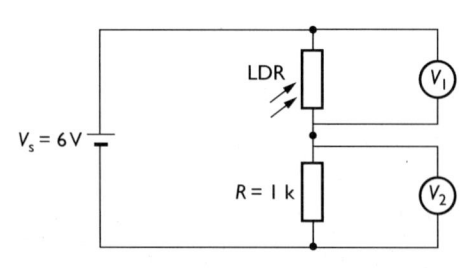

FIGURE 4.21 *Voltage divider circuit for the results shown in table 4.4*

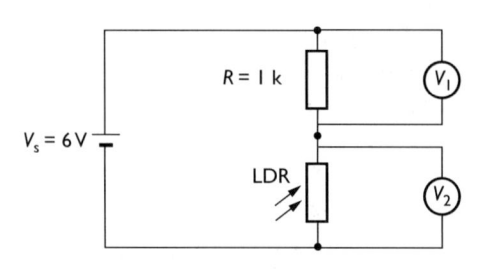

FIGURE 4.22 *Alternative voltage divider circuit. The results for this circuit are shown in table 4.5*

It should be noted that these two circuits, although containing the same components, give a voltage V_2 which changes in opposite directions – when the temperature increases in the first circuit, V_2 increases, while in the second, V_2 decreases.

Voltage divider with a light-dependent resistor

A graph of resistance for a light-dependent resistor (LDR) against light intensity is given in figure 4.20.

Figure 4.21 shows the LDR connected in series with a 1 kΩ resistor to form a voltage divider circuit. The voltages across the LDR (V_1) and across the resistor (V_2) at different light levels are shown in the table 4.4. (You should check these values by calculating them for yourself.)

Light intensity (units)	$V_1 (= V_{LDR})$ (V)	$V_2 (= V_R)$ (V)	$V_S = V_1 + V_2$ (V)
3	1.2	4.8	6.0
2	2.0	4.0	6.0
1	3.0	3.0	6.0

TABLE 4.4

For this circuit, the resistance of the LDR increases as less light falls on it and so the voltage across it (V_1) increases and so the voltage across the resistor R (V_2) decreases, even though the value of R has not been changed.

The circuit in figure 4.22 shows the same LDR and resistor connected in series but with their positions interchanged.

Light intensity (units)	$V_1 (= V_R)$ (V)	$V_2 (= V_{LDR})$ (V)	$V_S = V_1 + V_2$ (V)
3	4.8	1.2	6.0
2	4.0	2.0	6.0
1	3.0	3.0	6.0

TABLE 4.5

For this circuit, the resistance of the LDR increases as less light falls on it and so the voltage across it (V_2) increases (and so the voltage across the resistor R (V_1) decreases).

Voltage divider with a capacitor

The circuit shown in figure 4.23 was used to time how long it took a capacitor to charge up to 6 V. The results for different values of capacitor and resistor are shown in table 4.6.

The capacitor was discharged by closing switch S. As soon as the switch was opened, the capacitor began to charge up.

electronics 4

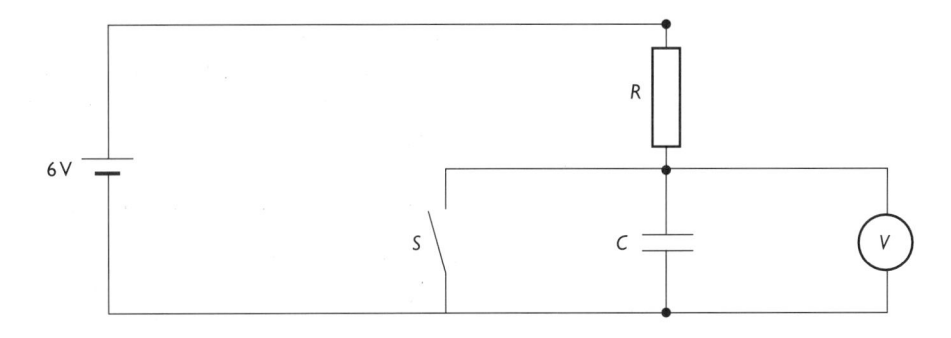

FIGURE 4.23 *Voltage divider circuit for a capacitor and a resistor*

Value of C (μF)	Value of R (kΩ)	Time taken for C to charge up to 6 V (seconds)
1000	10	70
1000	1	7
220	10	15

TABLE 4.6

> For the above circuit, the voltage across the capacitor (V) increases to the supply voltage, but the time taken is dependent on the values of C and R:
>
> - Increasing the value of the capacitor increases the time taken to charge it up, i.e. a larger capacitor is able to store more charge.
>
> $$\text{Capacitor} \uparrow - \text{time taken} \uparrow$$
>
> - Increasing the value of the series resistor decreases the charging current and so fewer charges flow on to the capacitor plates in one second. The capacitor therefore takes longer to become fully charged.
>
> $$\text{Resistance} \uparrow - \text{time taken} \uparrow$$

Capacitor charges up – voltage across it increases (to the supply voltage).
Capacitor discharges – voltage across it decreases (to zero).

Voltage divider with a potentiometer

Figure 4.24 shows a voltmeter connected to the slider and one end of a potentiometer. The voltmeter reading increases as the slider Z moves from X to Y of the potentiometer.

As the slider Z is moved from X to Y, the resistance of XZ increases, while the resistance of ZY decreases. The voltage across XZ therefore increases, i.e. the output voltage V (V_{XZ}) increases (while the voltage across ZY decreases).

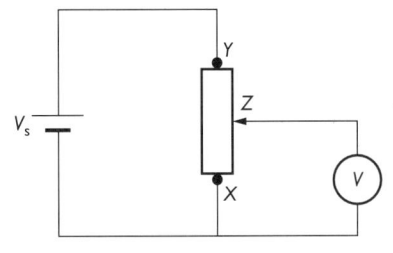

FIGURE 4.24 *Voltage divider circuit for a potentiometer*

Voltage divider with a switch

Figures 4.25 (a) and (b) show a switch connected in series with a resistor to form a voltage divider circuit.

4 standard grade physics

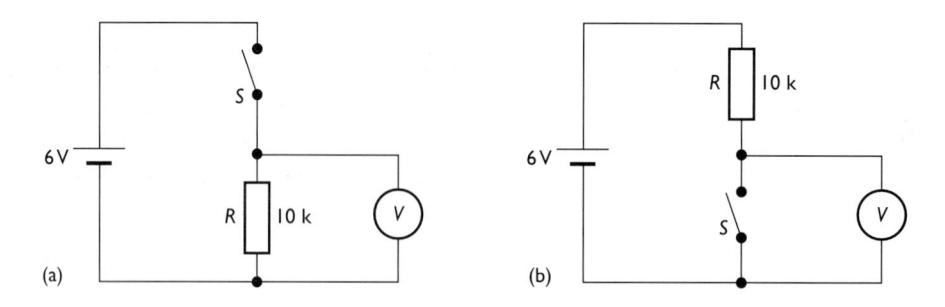

FIGURE 4.25 *Voltage divider circuits for a switch and a resistor*

In circuit (a), when the switch S is open $V = 0\,\text{V}$, and when S is closed $V = 6\,\text{V}$.

In circuit (b), when the switch S is open $V = 6\,\text{V}$, and when S is closed $V = 0\,\text{V}$.

The easiest way to understand these two circuits is to consider the switch when it is open, i.e. when there is no current. When the current through a resistor is zero, then the voltage across it is zero. Since the switch and the resistor form a voltage divider circuit and $V_S = V_1 + V_2$, then the voltage across the switch must equal V_S, i.e. 6 V.

4.4 Digital processes

A process device – the transistor

Now that we have looked at how signals may be passed into an electronic system by the input part of the system and how the desired output may be obtained, it is time to look at how the input signal is modified by the process part of the electronic system.

A transistor has three terminals called the **base**, the **emitter** and the **collector**. The symbol for an NPN transistor is shown in figure 4.26.

A transistor can be considered as an electronic switch with no moving parts. The switching is controlled by the voltage applied to the emitter-base. The transistor is off (non-conducting) when the emitter-base voltage is below a certain value, i.e. the electronic switch is open. For the type of transistor we are using this is about 0.7 V, although this voltage varies from one type of transistor to another. However, the transistor is on (conducting) when the emitter-base voltage is equal to or above this certain value ($\geq 0.7\,\text{V}$), i.e. the electronic switch is closed (figure 4.27).

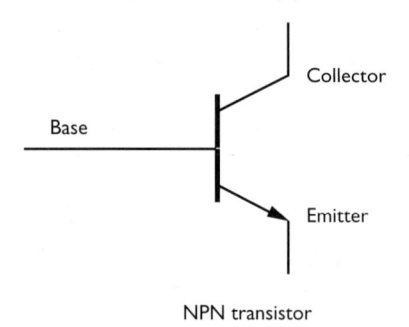

FIGURE 4.26 *Circuit symbol for a transistor*

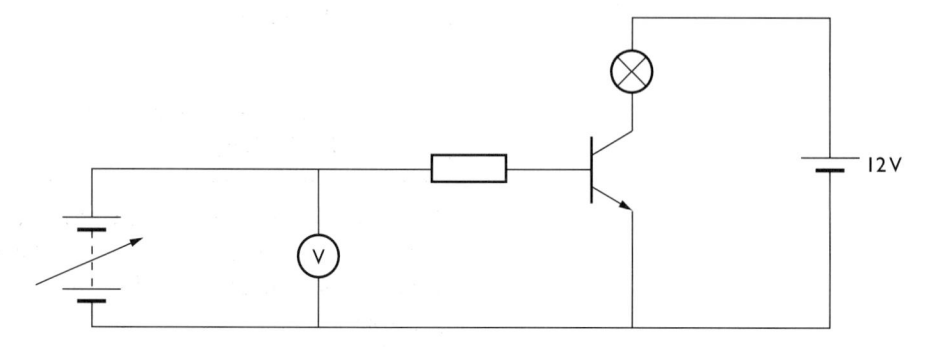

FIGURE 4.27 *The lamp lights when the voltmeter reading is greater than or equal to 0.7 V. When it is less than 0.7 V the lamp does not light*

electronics 4

Figure 4.28 shows an electronic system, i.e. an input (potentiometer), process (transistor) and an output (LED). The voltage across XZ (V_{XZ}) is the input voltage to the transistor. The voltage across XZ (V_{XZ}) has to reach a certain value (≥0.7 V) before the transistor will switch on and the output LED light.

FIGURE 4.28 *The LED only lights when the voltmeter reading is greater than or equal to 0.7 V*

A temperature-controlled circuit

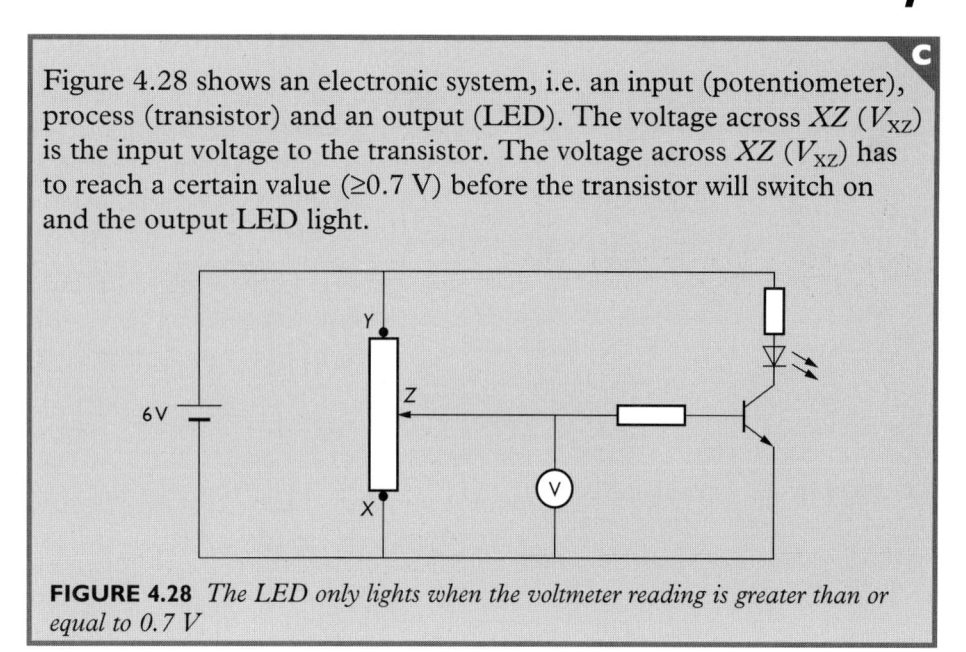

Figures 4.29 (a) and 4.29 (b) show two temperature-controlled circuits in an electronic system, i.e. an input (voltage divider with a thermistor), process (transistor) and an output (LED). The output device could be any of those discussed in section 4.2, depending on the output required.

The variable resistor is adjusted until (at room temperature) the LED is just off (see figures 4.29 (a) and (b)).

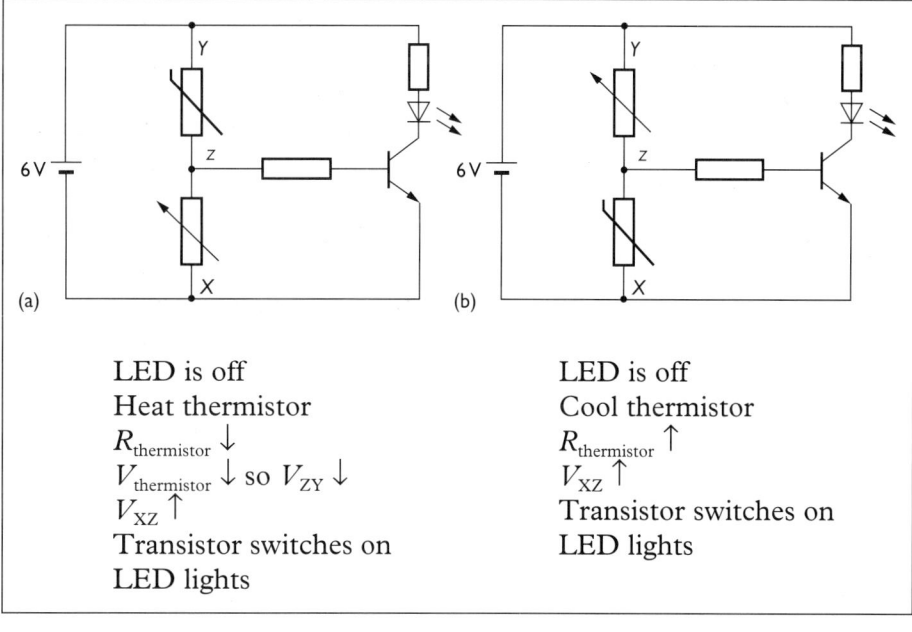

FIGURE 4.29 *(a) Temperature-controlled circuit, (b) alternative temperature-controlled circuit*

LED is off
Heat thermistor
$R_{thermistor}$ ↓
$V_{thermistor}$ ↓ so V_{ZY} ↓
V_{XZ} ↑
Transistor switches on
LED lights

LED is off
Cool thermistor
$R_{thermistor}$ ↑
V_{XZ} ↑
Transistor switches on
LED lights

Note: A variable resistor is used in this type of circuit instead of a fixed resistor. The variable resistor allows the circuit to be adjusted to different conditions (temperature in this case), before the output device comes on (or goes off).

A light-controlled circuit

Figures 4.30 (a) and (b) show two light-controlled circuits in an electronic system, i.e. an input (voltage divider with LDR), process (transistor) and an output (LED).

The variable resistor is adjusted until at normal light level the LED is just off (see figures 4.30 (a) and (b)).

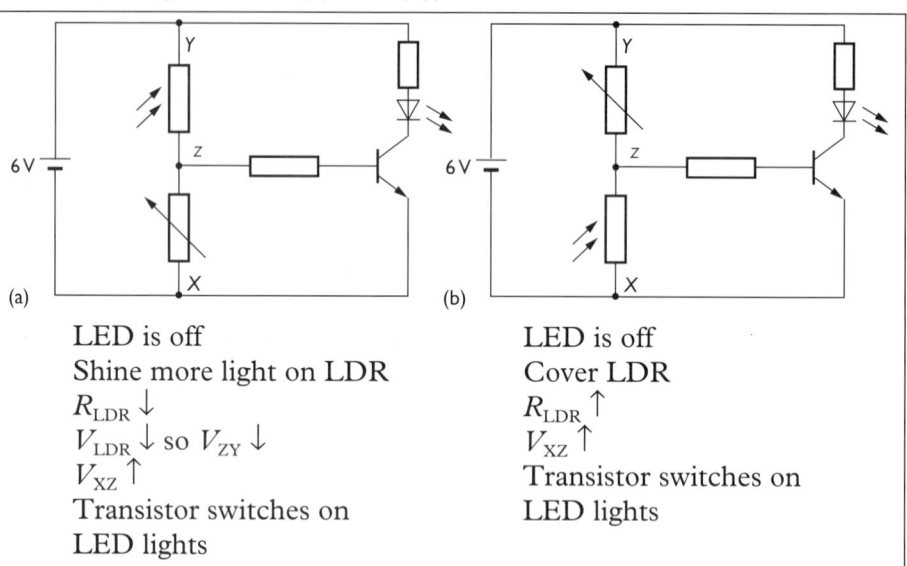

FIGURE 4.30 *(a) Light-controlled circuit, (b) alternative light-controlled circuit*

(a)
LED is off
Shine more light on LDR
$R_{LDR} \downarrow$
$V_{LDR} \downarrow$ so $V_{ZY} \downarrow$
$V_{XZ} \uparrow$
Transistor switches on
LED lights

(b)
LED is off
Cover LDR
$R_{LDR} \uparrow$
$V_{XZ} \uparrow$
Transistor switches on
LED lights

A time-controlled circuit

Figures 4.31 (a) and 4.31 (b) show two time-controlled circuits in an electronic system, i.e. an input (voltage divider with a capacitor), process (transistor) and an output (LED).

The switch S is closed to discharge the capacitor (voltage across capacitor, $V_C = 0$ V when discharged), then opened to allow the capacitor to start charging.

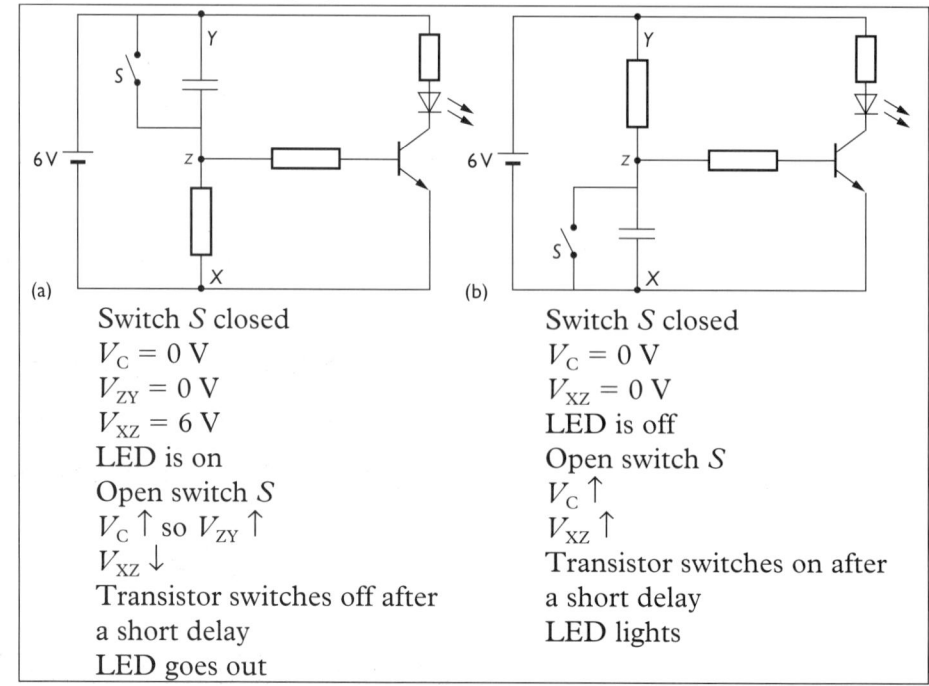

FIGURE 4.31 *(a) Time-controlled circuit, (b) alternative time-controlled circuit*

(a)
Switch S closed
$V_C = 0$ V
$V_{ZY} = 0$ V
$V_{XZ} = 6$ V
LED is on
Open switch S
$V_C \uparrow$ so $V_{ZY} \uparrow$
$V_{XZ} \downarrow$
Transistor switches off after a short delay
LED goes out

(b)
Switch S closed
$V_C = 0$ V
$V_{XZ} = 0$ V
LED is off
Open switch S
$V_C \uparrow$
$V_{XZ} \uparrow$
Transistor switches on after a short delay
LED lights

A switch-controlled circuit

Figures 4.32 (a) and 4.32 (b) show two switch-operated circuits in an electronic system, i.e. an input (voltage divider with a switch), process (transistor) and an output (LED).

When a switch is open in either circuit, no current passes through the resistor and so the voltage across the resistor, $V_{resistor}$, is zero and the voltage across the switch, V_{switch}, is 6 V.

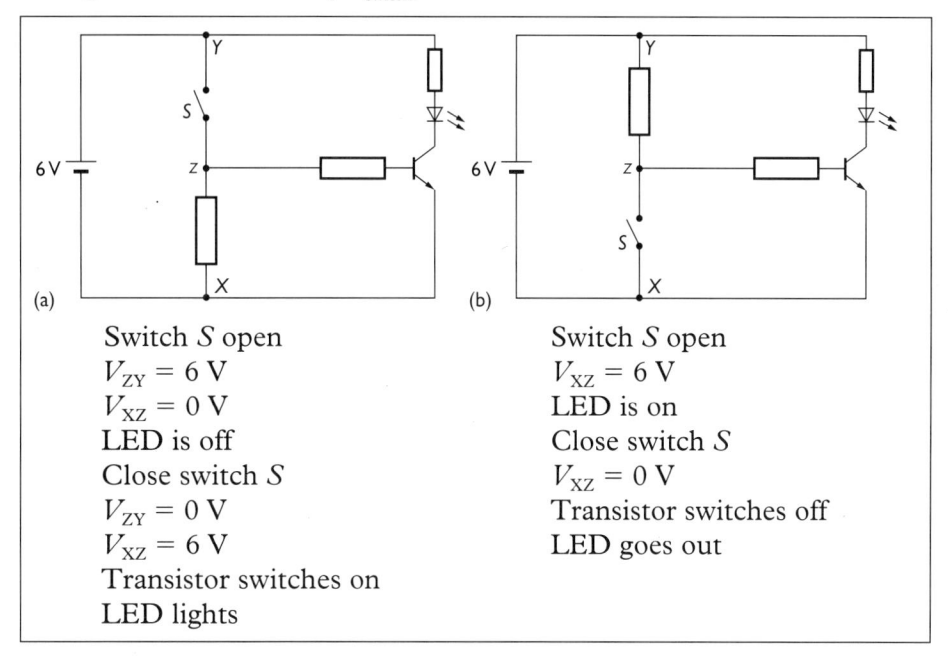

FIGURE 4.32 (a) Switch-controlled circuit, (b) alternative switch-controlled circuit

(a)
Switch S open
$V_{ZY} = 6$ V
$V_{XZ} = 0$ V
LED is off
Close switch S
$V_{ZY} = 0$ V
$V_{XZ} = 6$ V
Transistor switches on
LED lights

(b)
Switch S open
$V_{XZ} = 6$ V
LED is on
Close switch S
$V_{XZ} = 0$ V
Transistor switches off
LED goes out

Other process devices – logic gates

Logic gates

These are manufactured on a tiny, single chip called an **integrated circuit (IC)**.

Logic gates are digital devices which frequently obtain analogue signals as their inputs. These analogue inputs have to be converted into a digital form by the gate before it is able to carry out its task.

The physical inputs and outputs from a gate are voltages which may either be 'high' (close to the supply voltage) or 'low' (near to zero volts). These are referred to as logic '1' and logic '0'. A table known as a **truth table** shows how the output of the gate varies with the input or inputs. A truth table is a shorthand way to show the behaviour of an electronic system.

The NOT- (or inverter) gate

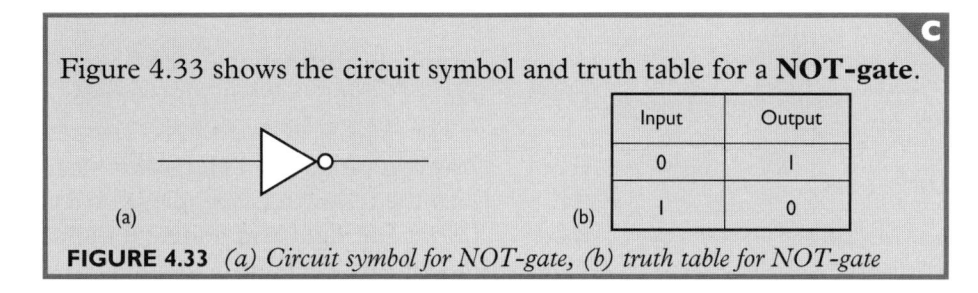

Figure 4.33 shows the circuit symbol and truth table for a **NOT-gate**.

Input	Output
0	1
1	0

FIGURE 4.33 (a) Circuit symbol for NOT-gate, (b) truth table for NOT-gate

From the truth table it can be seen that the output of a NOT-gate is 'not' (the same as) the input. A NOT-gate is also called an **inverter**.

The AND-gate

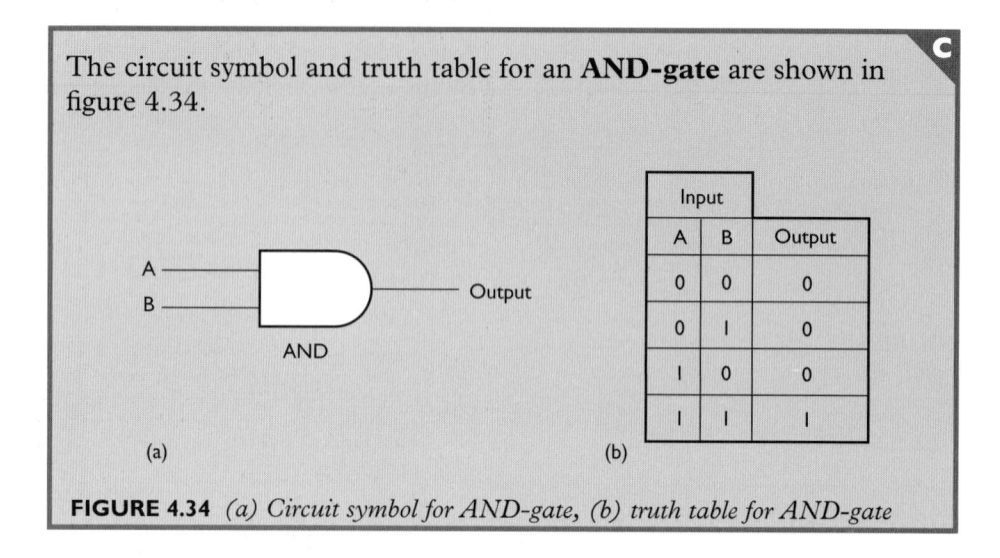

The circuit symbol and truth table for an **AND-gate** are shown in figure 4.34.

Input		Output
A	B	
0	0	0
0	1	0
1	0	0
1	1	1

(a) (b)

FIGURE 4.34 *(a) Circuit symbol for AND-gate, (b) truth table for AND-gate*

From the truth table, it can be seen that the output of an AND-gate will be logic '1' (high), only when inputs A and B are logic '1' (high).

The OR-gate

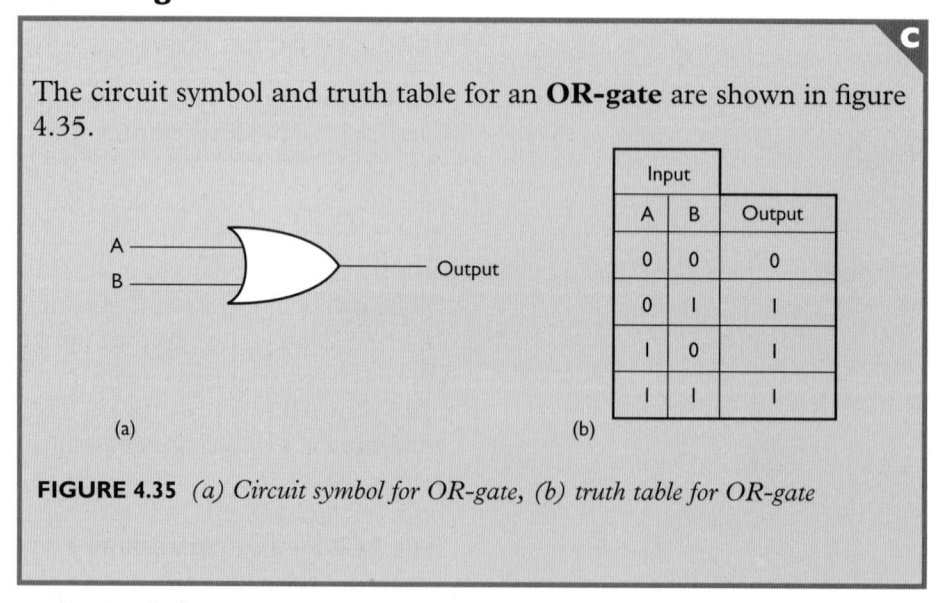

The circuit symbol and truth table for an **OR-gate** are shown in figure 4.35.

Input		Output
A	B	
0	0	0
0	1	1
1	0	1
1	1	1

(a) (b)

FIGURE 4.35 *(a) Circuit symbol for OR-gate, (b) truth table for OR-gate*

From the truth table, it can be seen that the output of an OR-gate will be logic '1' (high) when either of the inputs A or B are '1' (high).

The AND-, OR- and NOT-gates above may be combined together to form a sophisticated electronic system.

In the following examples you may assume that a light sensor gives out a logic 1 in light and a logic 0 in dark; and a temperature sensor gives out a logic 1 when warm and a logic 0 when cold.

Example 1: Draw a logic diagram and truth table for a warning LED to light when a car engine gets too hot. The lamp should only operate when the ignition of the car is switched on (logic 1).

Solution: Require LED to be on (1) when ignition is on (1) *and* engine is too hot (1).

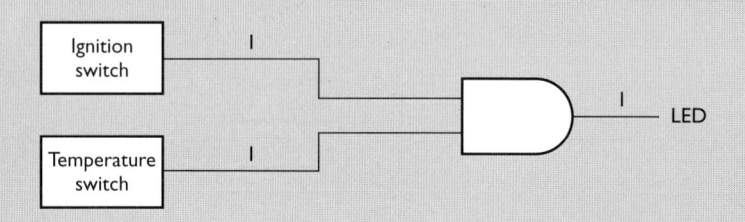

Temperature sensor	Ignition switch	LED
cold (0)	off (0)	off (0)
cold (0)	on (1)	off (0)
warm (1)	off (0)	off (0)
warm (1)	on (1)	on (1)

FIGURE 4.36 *Logic diagram and truth table for example 1*

Example 2: Draw a logic diagram and truth table which will switch on the pump of a central heating system when the house is cold and the central heating is switched on (logic 1).

Solution: Require pump on (1) when central heating is on (1) *and* temperature is cold (0) (*not* warm (1)).

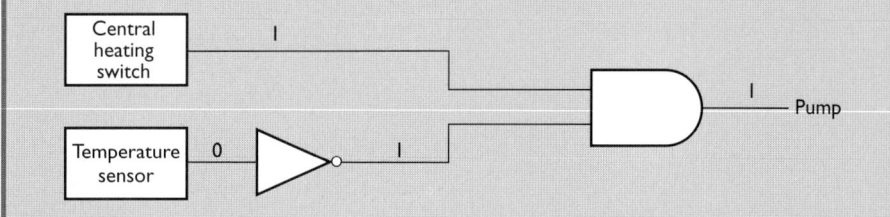

Temperature sensor	Central heating switch	Pump
cold (0)	off (0)	off (0)
cold (0)	on (1)	on (1)
warm (1)	off (0)	off (0)
warm (1)	on (1)	off (0)

FIGURE 4.37 *Logic diagram and truth table for example 2*

4 standard grade physics

Example 3: Draw a logic diagram and truth table which will turn on a heater in a greenhouse when it gets cold at night. The heater should be switched off (logic 0) during the day.

Solution: Require heater on (1) when it is cold (0) (*not* warm (1)) *and* dark (0) (*not* light (1)).

Light sensor	Temperature sensor	Heater
dark (0)	cold (0)	on (1)
dark (0)	warm (1)	off (0)
light (1)	cold (0)	off (0)
light (1)	warm (1)	off (0)

FIGURE 4.38 *Logic diagram and truth table for example 3*

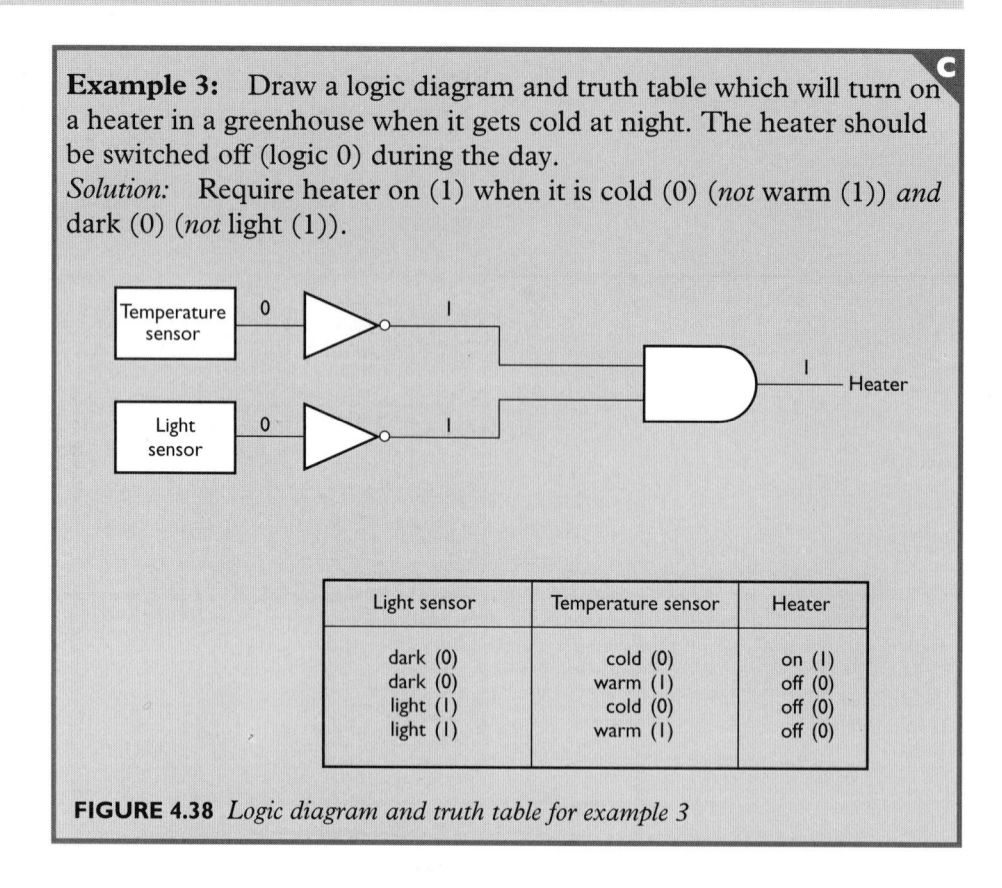

The clock-pulse generator

Clock pulses are pulses of voltage which occur regularly, like the ticking of a clock. The duration of the pulses and the rate at which pulses occur can be varied by altering the values of the capacitor or resistor to suit different applications. Clock pulses are mainly used in counting and timing signals, e.g. a traffic lights sequence.

The circuit shown in figure 4.39 can be used in counting and timing.

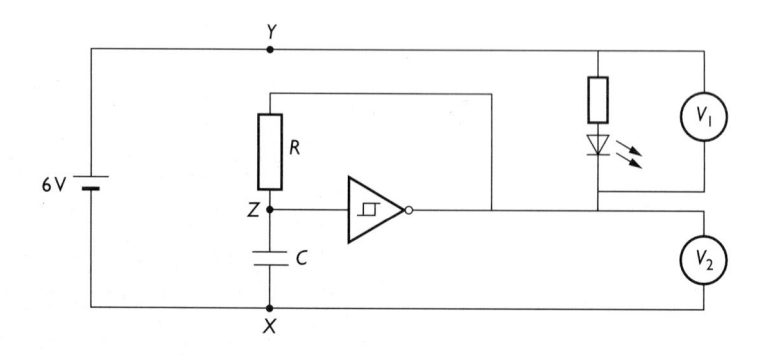

FIGURE 4.39 *A clock-pulse generator circuit*

Note:

- The input to the NOT-gate (inverter) is the voltage across the capacitor (V_{XZ}).

electronics 4

- The supply voltage of 6 V is equal to $V_1 + V_2$. When the output of the NOT-gate is logic 0, voltmeter $V_2 = 0\,\text{V}$ and so voltmeter $V_1 = 6\,\text{V}$. Since there is 6 V across the LED and resistor, the LED lights. When the output of the NOT-gate is logic 1, voltmeter $V_2 = 6\,\text{V}$ and so $V_1 = 0\,\text{V}$. Since there is no voltage across the LED and resistor, the LED does not light.

A simple explanation of how this circuit operates is shown in table 4.7.

Capacitor	Input to NOT-gate	Output from NOT-gate	V_2 (V)	V_1 (V)	LED
charged	1	0	0	6	lit
discharged	0	1	6	0	unlit
charged	1	0	0	6	lit
discharged	0	1	6	0	unlit

TABLE 4.7

The pattern in table 4.7 continues so that the generator produces pulses.

If the value of the capacitor is increased, it takes longer to charge and discharge, so there are fewer pulses per second, i.e. their frequency is lower. If the value of the resistor is increased, it takes longer for the capacitor to charge and discharge – fewer pulses per second – lower frequency. This means that the values of R and C control the frequency of the pulses.

Counting circuits

A counter is an electronic circuit which is able to count the electrical pulses of the clock-pulse generator. Figure 4.40 shows a counter connected to a timing circuit.

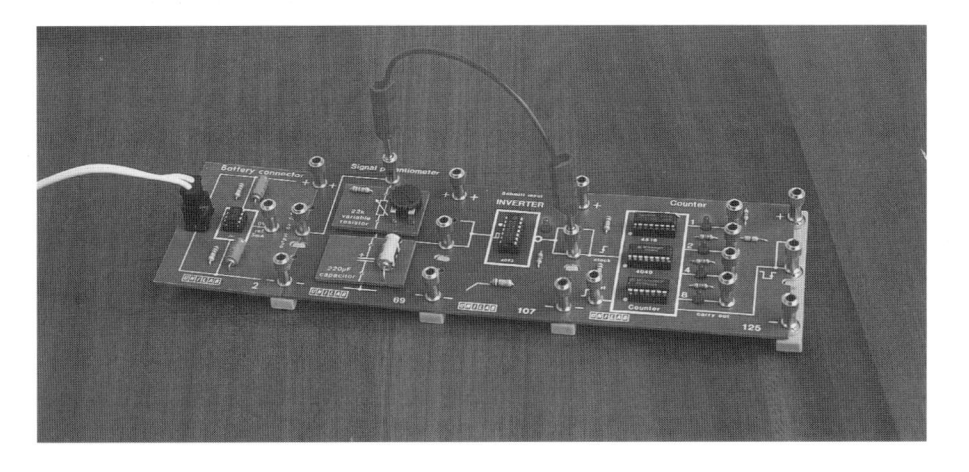

FIGURE 4.40 *An electronic counter circuit. The circuit counts in binary*

4 standard grade physics

Table 4.8 shows the number of pulses from the timing circuit and the display on the counter board (a logic 1 is equal to a lit LED).

Number of clock pulses	(8) D	(4) C	(2) B	(1) A
0	0	0	0	0
1	0	0	0	1
2	0	0	1	0
3	0	0	1	1
4	0	1	0	0
5	0	1	0	1
6	0	1	1	0
7	0	1	1	1
8	1	0	0	0
9	1	0	0	1

TABLE 4.8

The completed table shows the binary code for the decimal numbers from zero to nine. A circuit called a **binary-to-decimal decoder** together with a seven-segment display is used to convert the binary display on the counter to a decimal number on the seven-segment display.

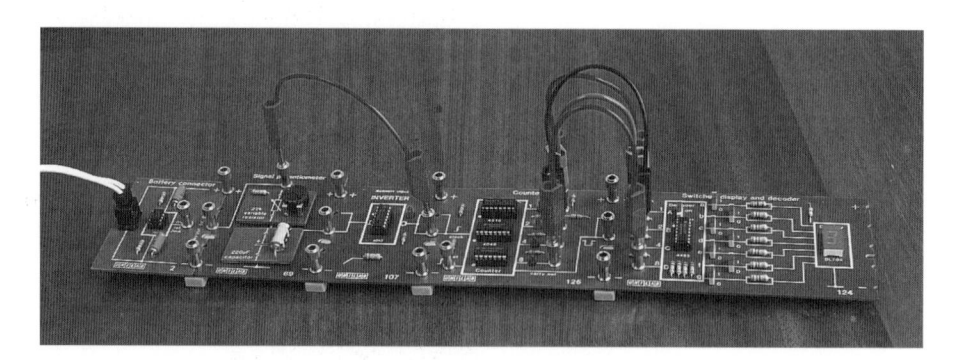

FIGURE 4.41 *An electronic counter circuit. The circuit counts in both binary and decimal*

4.5 Analogue processes

An amplifier is an analogue process device which is generally used to make electrical signals larger. For instance, a CD-player will give a signal of perhaps 10 mV (0.010 V). You would not be able to hear this tiny signal from the CD-player if it was directly connected to a loudspeaker. The amplitude of this signal has to be made bigger, i.e. amplified, before it can be connected to the loudspeaker.

electronics 4

Figure 4.42 (a) shows an amplifier being used to make the electrical signal from a signal generator larger. Both input and output signals from the amplifier are displayed on the screens of identical oscilloscopes as shown in figure 4.42 (b).

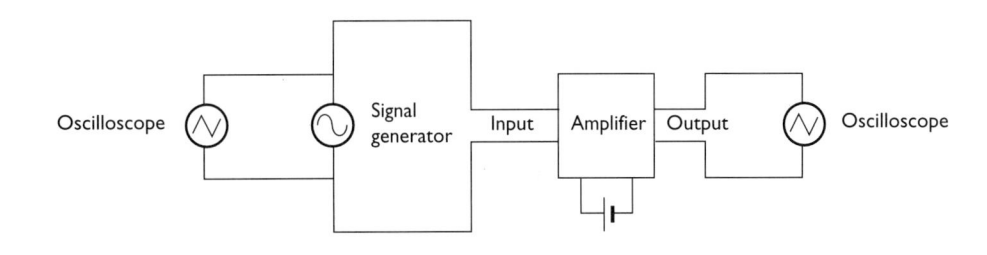

FIGURE 4.42a *This amplifier circuit makes the output voltage larger than the input voltage*

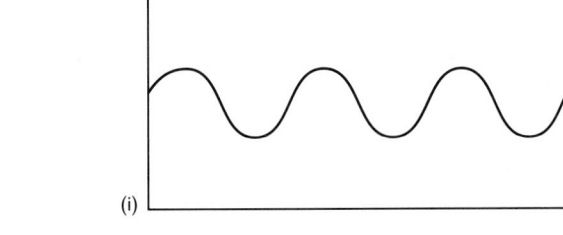

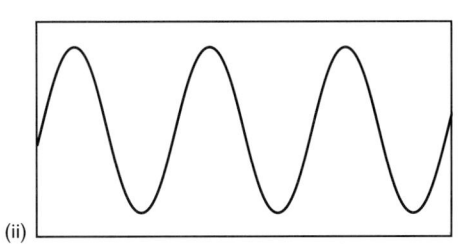

FIGURE 4.42b *(i) Input voltage, (ii) output voltage*

The amplitude of the output signal from an amplifier is larger than the amplitude of the input signal – the extra energy comes from the electrical supply to the amplifier. However, the output frequency from the amplifier is the same as the input frequency. In audio appliances the amplifier is generally the volume control.

Amplifiers

Amplifiers are to be found in many devices, e.g. radios, televisions, hi-fi's, intercoms and loudhailers. Two of these are shown in figure 4.43.

FIGURE 4.43 *(a) Intercom, (b) radio*

(a) *Input: small a.c. voltage from microphone. Output: larger a.c. voltage across loudspeaker.*

(b) *Input: small a.c. voltage from aerial. Output: larger a.c. voltage across loudspeaker.*

Voltage gain

If an amplifier has an input voltage of 0.5 V and an output voltage of 5.0 V, then the output voltage has increased by 10 times, i.e. the voltage gain is 10:

$$\text{voltage gain} = \frac{\text{output voltage}}{\text{input voltage}}$$

Note that voltage gain does not have a unit.

In most amplifiers, the voltage gain is produced from a series of transistors. The output from one is fed into the input of the next and so on. Usually the transistors form part of an integrated circuit (IC).

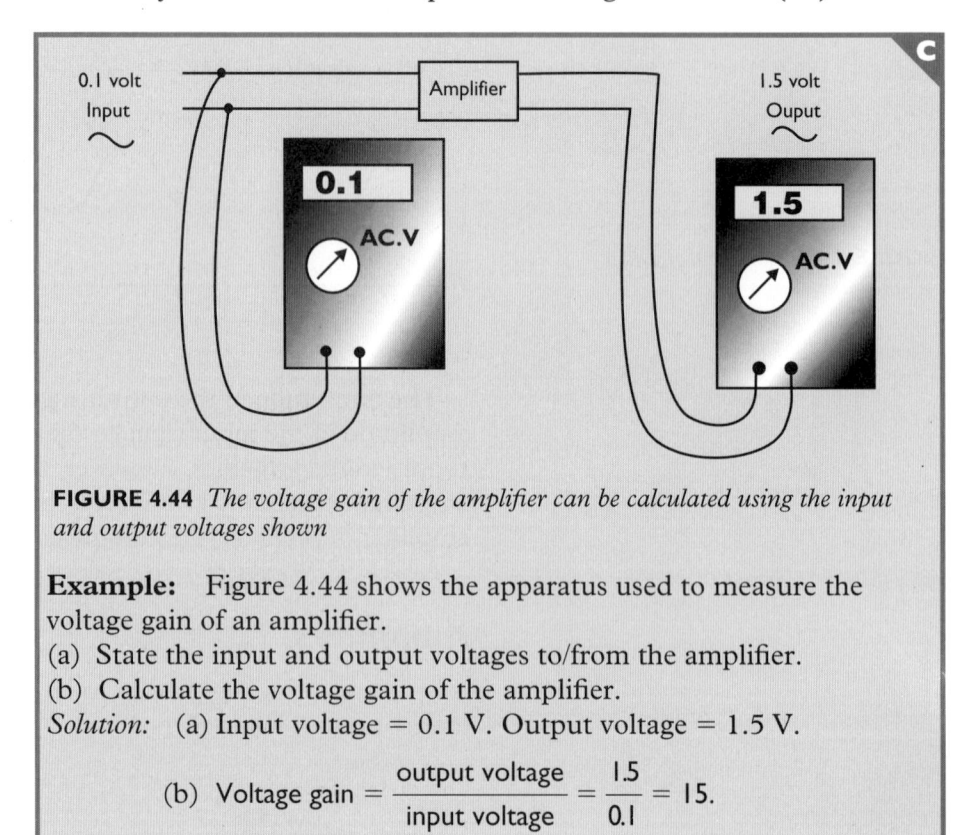

FIGURE 4.44 *The voltage gain of the amplifier can be calculated using the input and output voltages shown*

Example: Figure 4.44 shows the apparatus used to measure the voltage gain of an amplifier.
(a) State the input and output voltages to/from the amplifier.
(b) Calculate the voltage gain of the amplifier.
Solution: (a) Input voltage = 0.1 V. Output voltage = 1.5 V.

(b) $\text{Voltage gain} = \dfrac{\text{output voltage}}{\text{input voltage}} = \dfrac{1.5}{0.1} = 15.$

Power gain of amplifiers

The voltage gain is not particularly useful when comparing amplifiers, for example, in different hi-fi systems. It is better to consider the **power gain** of the amplifier:

$$\text{power gain} = \frac{\text{power output}}{\text{power input}}$$

Like voltage gain, power gain does not have a unit.

electronics 4

Power amplifiers have large power gains. Since most amplifiers have roughly the same power input, it is only necessary to give the maximum power output to be able to compare amplifiers.

> Power = current × voltage = IV but $V = IR$ (Ohm's law)
> $$\text{Power} = IV = I \times (IR) = I^2R$$
> $$\text{Power} = IV = V \times \frac{V}{R} = \frac{V^2}{R}, \text{ as } I = \frac{V}{R}$$
> i.e. Power = $IV = I^2R = \dfrac{V^2}{R}$
>
> Power = $\dfrac{V^2}{R}$ is a useful formula for finding either the input or output power of an amplifier.
>
> **Example:** A girl connects a set of headphones of resistance 16 Ω to her personal stereo. The amplifier in the stereo produces 0.04 W of power in the headphones.
> (a) What is the voltage applied to the headphones?
> (b) Calculate the input power to the stereo amplifier when the power gain is 20.
>
> *Solution:*
> (a) $P = \dfrac{V^2}{R}$
>
> $0.04 = \dfrac{V^2}{16}$
>
> $V^2 = 0.04 \times 16 = 0.64$
> $V = 0.8$ V
>
> (b) Power gain = $\dfrac{\text{output voltage}}{\text{input voltage}}$
>
> $20 = \dfrac{0.04}{\text{input power}}$
>
> input power = $\dfrac{0.04}{20} = 0.002$ W = 2 mW

LEARNING OUTCOMES

After studying this chapter you should be able to:

Section 4.1

1. State that an electronic system consists of three parts: input, process and output.
2. Distinguish between digital and analogue outputs.
3. Identify analogue and digital signals from waveforms viewed on an oscilloscope.

Section 4.2

1. Give examples of output devices and the energy conversions involved.
2. Give examples of digital output devices and of analogue output devices.
3. Draw and identify the symbol for an LED.
4. State that an LED will light only if connected one way round.
5. Explain the need for a series resistor with an LED.
6. State that different numbers can be produced by lighting appropriate segments of a seven-segment display.
7. Identify appropriate output devices for a given application. **Credit**
8. Describe by means of a diagram a circuit which will allow an LED to light. **Credit**
9. Calculate the value of the series resistor for an LED. **Credit**
10. Calculate the decimal equivalent of a binary number in the range 0000–1001. **Credit**

Section 4.3

1. Describe the energy transformations involved in the following devices: microphone, thermocouple, solar cell.
2. State that the resistance of a thermistor changes with temperature and the resistance of an LDR decreases with increasing light intensity.
3. Carry out calculations using $V = IR$ for the thermistor and LDR.
4. State that during charging, the voltage across a capacitor increases with time.
5. Identify from a list an appropriate input device for a given application.
6. Carry out calculations involving voltages and resistances in a voltage divider. **Credit**
7. State that the time it takes to charge a capacitor depends on the values of the capacitance and the series resistance. **Credit**
8. Identify appropriate input devices for a given application. **Credit**

Section 4.4

1. State that a transistor can be used as a switch.
2. State that a transistor may be conducting or non-conducting, i.e. ON or OFF.
3. Draw and identify the circuit symbol for an NPN transistor.
4. Identify from a circuit diagram the purpose of a simple transistor switching circuit.
5. Draw and identify the symbols for two input AND- and OR-gates, and a NOT-gate.
6. State that logic gates may have one or more inputs and that a truth table shows the output for all possible input combinations.
7. State that high voltage = logic '1'; low voltage = logic '0'.
8. Draw the truth tables for two input AND- and OR-gates, and a NOT-gate.
9. Explain how to use combinations of digital logic gates for control in simple situations.
10. State that a digital circuit can produce a series of clock pulses.
11. Give an example of a device containing a counter circuit.
12. State that there are circuits which can count digital pulses.
13. State that the output of the counter circuit is in binary.

learning outcomes

14 State that the output of a binary counter can be converted to decimal.

15 Explain the operation of a simple transistor switching circuit. `Credit`

16 Identify the following gates from truth tables: two-input AND-; two-input OR-; NOT- (inverter). `Credit`

17 Complete a truth table for a simple combinational logic circuit. `Credit`

18 Explain how a simple oscillator built from a resistor, capacitor and inverter operates. `Credit`

19 Describe how to change the frequency of the clock. `Credit`

Section 4.5

1 Identify from a list devices in which amplifiers play an important part.

2 State the function of the amplifier in devices such as radios, intercoms and music centres.

3 State that the output signal of an audio amplifier has the same frequency as, but a larger amplitude than, the input signal.

4 Carry out calculations involving input voltage, output voltage and voltage gain of an amplifier.

5 Describe how to measure the voltage gain of an amplifier. `Credit`

6 State that power may be calculated from V^2/R, where V is the voltage and R the resistance (impedance) of the circuit. `Credit`

7 State that the power gain of an amplifier is the ratio of power output to power input. `Credit`

8 Carry out calculations involving the power gain of an amplifier. `Credit`

STUDY QUESTIONS

1 State which of the signals shown below are digital and which are analogue.

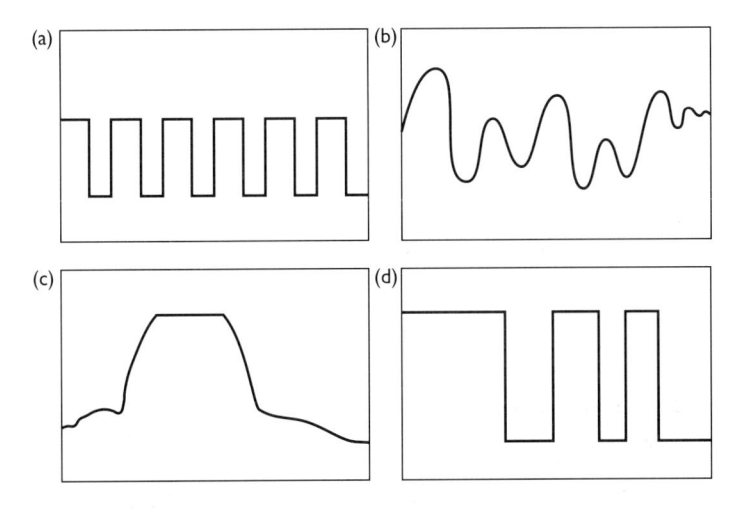

(a) (b) (c) (d)

2 List the following devices as analogue or digital: radio; television; mercury thermometer; electronic thermometer; CD-player; computer; cassette recorder.

3 (a) Draw the circuit symbol for a light emitting diode (LED).

(b) The data sheet accompanying a green LED gives the following information: $V_{max} = 1.5$ V and $I_{max} = 10$ mA.

  (i) Draw a circuit diagram which will allow the LED to light from a 9 V battery and explain why a resistor is required.
  (ii) Calculate the value of the series resistor.

4 The current through the lit LED shown below is 10 mA.

(a) Calculate the voltage across the resistor, R.

(b) Calculate the voltage across the LED.

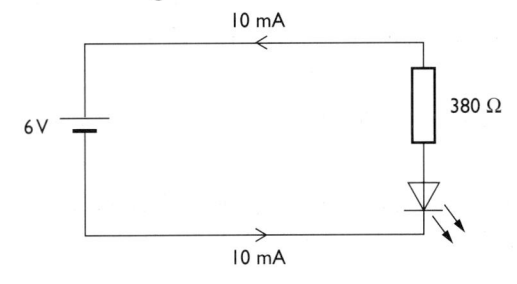

(6 V supply, 380 Ω resistor, 10 mA)

109

study questions

5 The maximum voltage allowed across an LED is 1.8 V and the current through it must not exceed 10 mA. If the LED is to be used with a 5 V supply, calculate the value of the resistor, R, connected in series with it.

6 What LEDs in figure 4.8 on page 88 are required to be lit in order to make the numbers:

(a) 5

(b) 7

(c) 9?

7 (a) What binary number represents the decimal number:

(i) 2

(ii) 5

(iii) 7

(iv) 9?

(b) What is the decimal number represented by the binary numbers:

(i) 0 0 0 1

(ii) 0 1 0 0

(iii) 0 1 1 0

(iv) 1 0 1 0?

8 (a) Draw the circuit symbol for the following devices:

(i) capacitor

(ii) thermistor

(iii) LDR.

(b) What is the energy change which occurs with:

(i) a solar cell

(ii) a thermocouple

(iii) a microphone?

9 In each circuit shown below calculate the voltmeter readings or reading.

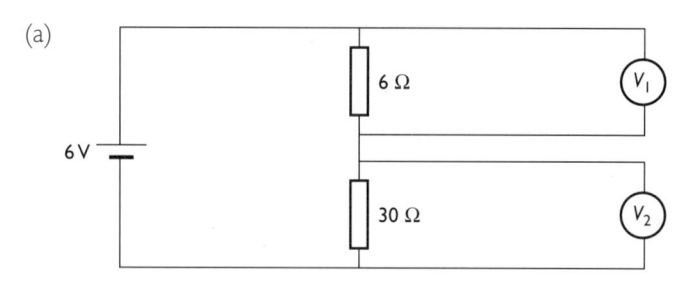

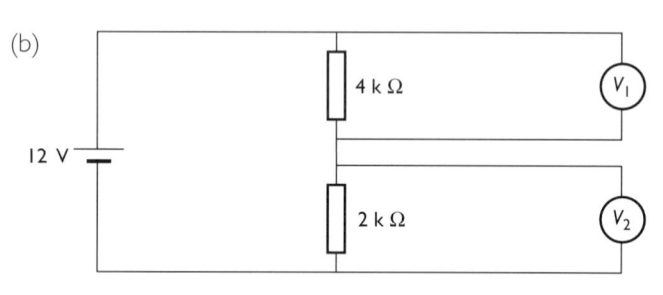

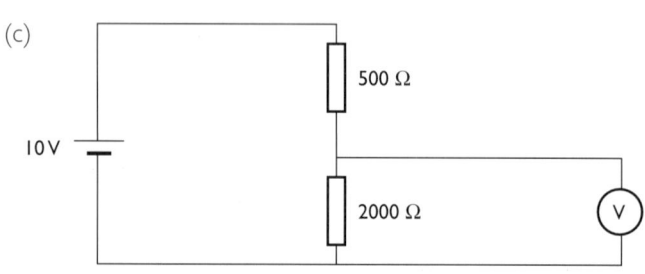

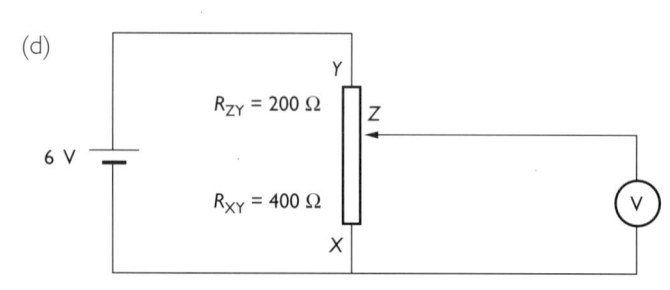

(a)

(b)

(c)

(d)

10 Name an input device which could be used:

(a) to measure the intensity of noise at an airport

(b) as a time control circuit for a pedestrian crossing

(c) to control the light level in a room

(d) as a high temperature warning for a car engine.

study questions

11 At a certain light level, the voltage across the LDR shown below is 5 V.

(a) What is the voltage across the resistor?

(b) Calculate the current in the circuit.

(c) Calculate the resistance of the LDR.

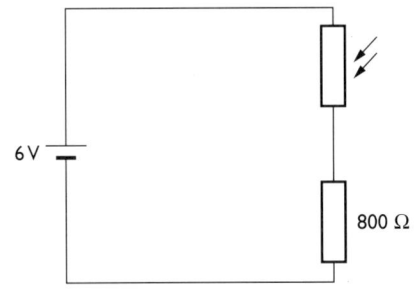

12 Describe what happens to the voltage across the resistor when the thermistor is cooled in the figure below.

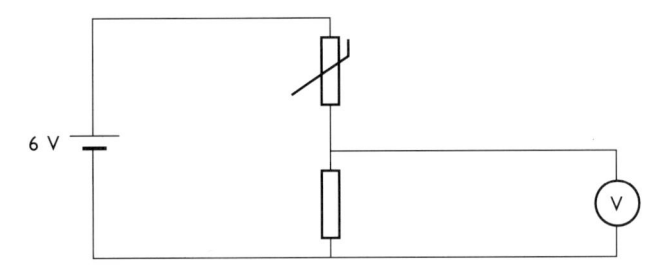

13 A pupil sets up the circuit shown below and adjusts the variable resistor so that the LED is just off when the temperature is 20°C.

(a) Name the components X, Y and Z.

(b) Describe how the circuit works when the temperature rises above 20°C.

(c) Suggest a possible use for this circuit.

(d) The pupil decides that this circuit could be altered to warn a gardener of frosty conditions. Draw a circuit diagram that would allow the LED to light when the temperature fell below 0°C.

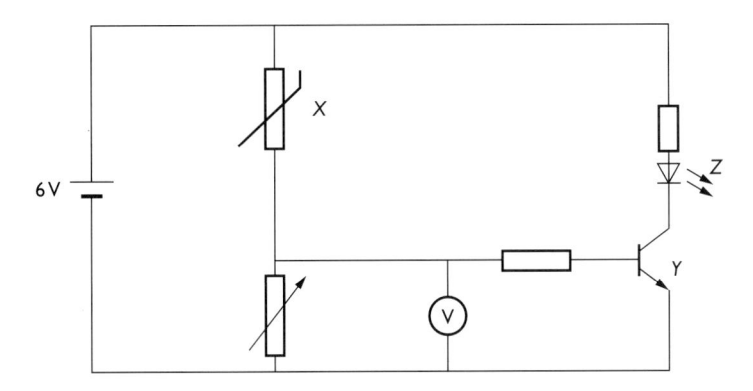

14 Draw the circuit symbol and truth table for the following logic gates:

(a) NOT

(b) AND

(c) OR.

15 An audio amplifier amplifies a 2 mV (0.002 V) signal to 1.6 V. What is its voltage gain?

16 The input voltage from a CD-player to an amplifier is 15 mV (0.015 V). The input resistance of the amplifier is 20 kΩ.

(a) Calculate the power input to the amplifier.

(b) The power output of the amplifier is 25 W. What is its power gain?

17 A gardener sees the following circuit in an electronics book. He thinks he could use it.

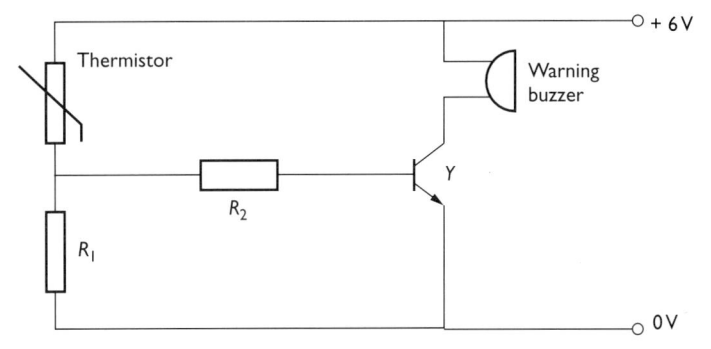

(a) What name is given to component Y?

GENERAL KU

(b) What is the purpose of component Y?

GENERAL KU

(c) What happens to the resistance of the thermistor as the temperature rises?

GENERAL KU

(d) State **one** practical use for this circuit.
SEB

GENERAL KU

111

5 Transport

On the move

After a long day at work, George was driving home. It was a wet day and he was tired. Suddenly the lorry in front put on its brakes. George noticed the lorry's brake lights come on and he slammed on his brakes. He noticed that he took longer to stop than usual. He had been accelerating at that time and he was travelling at almost the speed limit. He would need to be more careful in future. Indeed, he started to wonder about how speed and acceleration were measured. What was meant by speed and acceleration? He would ask his daughter Monica who was studying physics. She could explain these ideas to him!

This chapter looks at the ideas of speed and acceleration and how we measure them, and uses these quantities to calculate other useful aspects such as forces, which are dealt with later in the chapter.

5.1 Speed

Speed is the distance travelled by a body in a certain time:

$$\text{Speed} = \frac{\text{distance travelled}}{\text{time taken}}$$

If you cycled a distance of 600 m from A to B in 100 s, your average speed would be six metres per second (6 m/s). However, your speed will vary throughout the journey, particularly if you divided the journey at X, e.g. slower than 6 m/s from A to X, faster than 6 m/s from X to B.

$$\text{Average speed} = \frac{\text{total distance travelled}}{\text{total time taken}} = \frac{d}{t}$$

Speed and average speed have the same units of m/s (sometimes written as m s^{-1}).

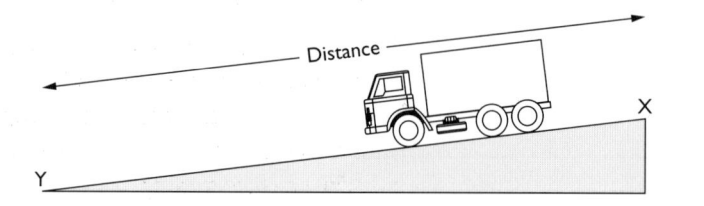

FIGURE 5.1 *Measuring speed*

112

Measuring average speed using a stopclock, trolley and measuring tape

The distance is measured between two points X and Y which are a few metres apart. The time for the journey is measured by starting a stopwatch when the trolley reaches X and stopping the watch when it reaches Y (figure 5.1).

Instantaneous speed and average speed

If we could measure very small time intervals, for example hundredths or even thousandths of a second, then we could measure the speed of any object just at that moment in time.

- Instantaneous speed is the speed of a body at a particular time (instant).
- Average speed is the steady speed a body has to cover the distance in the time allowed.

$$\text{Average speed} = \frac{\text{total distance travelled}}{\text{total time taken}} = \frac{d}{t}$$

When the time taken (t) is very small, the closer the average speed is to the instantaneous (actual) speed.

Example: A body moves between A and B, a distance of 100 m in a time of 20 s.

$$\text{Average speed between A and B} = \frac{100}{20} = 5 \text{ m/s}$$

The time interval between A and B is too large to give a reasonable estimate of the instantaneous speed at X. But the time interval between C and D is much smaller, so gives a much better estimate of the (actual) speed at X. This is shown in figure 5.2.

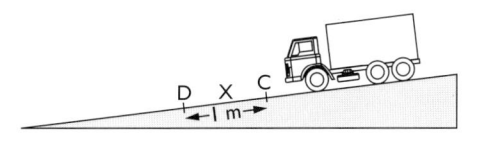

FIGURE 5.2

$$\text{Distance CD} = 1 \text{ m}$$

$$\text{Time to travel from C to D} = 0.25 \text{ s}$$

$$\text{Average speed between C and D} = \frac{1}{0.25} = 4 \text{ m/s}$$

This is closer to the instantaneous speed at X as the time interval involved is very small.
This means that

Instantaneous speed = Average speed of a body

provided the time used is very small.

Measuring instantaneous speed using a computer

The computer uses an internal clock which allows very small time intervals to be measured. The computer starts timing when the light beam is cut by the card, and stops when the light beam is restored. The time taken for the card to pass through the beam is recorded in the computer (figure 5.3).

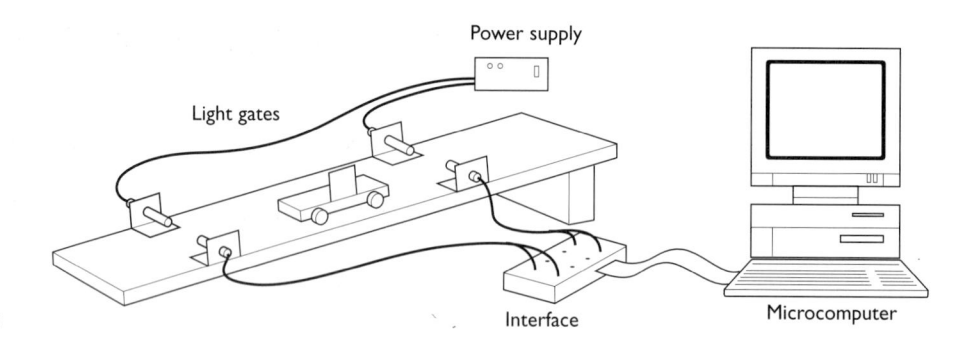

FIGURE 5.3

The computer, already pre-programmed with the length of the card, calculates the speed of the vehicle using:

$$\text{Speed} = \frac{\text{length of card}}{\text{time on computer}}$$

Typical results might be:

$$\text{Length of card} = 5 \text{ cm} = 0.05 \text{ m}$$
$$\text{Time measured by computer} = 0.02 \text{ s}$$
$$\text{Speed} = \frac{0.05}{0.02}$$
$$= 2.5 \text{ m/s}$$

Acceleration

Acceleration (a) is the change in speed of a body over a certain time:

$$\text{Acceleration} = \frac{\text{change in speed}}{\text{time for change}} = \frac{\text{final speed} - \text{initial speed}}{\text{time for change}}$$

$$a = \frac{v - u}{t}$$

where v = final speed, u = initial speed and t = time for change in speed to occur.

Acceleration is usually calculated in metres per second per second (or metres per second squared), i.e. m/s^2 or m s^{-2}.

A car has an acceleration of 5 m/s^2. This means that the speed of the car increases by 5 m/s in every second. If the car starts from rest then:

after 1 s, speed = 5 m/s
after 2 s, speed = 10 m/s
after 3 s, speed = 15 m/s
after 4 s, speed = 20 m/s.

Example: A motorbike starting from rest can reach a speed of 5 m/s in 4 s. What is the acceleration?

Solution: $u = 0$; $v = 5$ m/s; $a = ?$; $t = 4$ s.

$$\text{Acceleration} = \frac{\text{change in speed}}{\text{time taken}} = \frac{v - u}{t} = \frac{5 - 0}{4} = \frac{5}{4} = 1.25 \text{ m/s}^2$$

When an object is slowing down, it will have a negative value for its acceleration – this is called deceleration, i.e. minus acceleration =

deceleration. The minus sign only indicates that there is a reduction in speed over time.

Example: A pupil on a bicycle slows down from 9 m/s to 3 m/s in 2 s. Calculate her deceleration.
Solution: $u = 9$ m/s; $v = 3$ m/s; $a = ?$; $t = 2$ s.

$$\text{Acceleration} = \frac{\text{change in speed}}{\text{time taken}} = \frac{v - u}{t} = \frac{3 - 9}{2} = \frac{-6}{2} = -3 \text{ m/s}^2$$

Deceleration = 3 m/s²

Speed–time graphs

If we measure the speed of an object at different times, we can draw graphs from the results. These graphs allow us to see the motion of an object more clearly than just looking at a table of results. It also allows us to make calculations from the graph to give additional information.

Three types of motion are shown in figure 5.4.

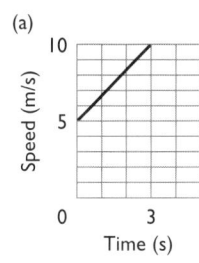

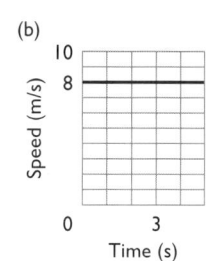

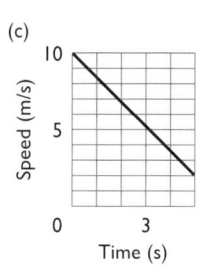

FIGURE 5.4 *Speed–time graphs*

(a) Constant acceleration.
    This is a straight line at an angle to the horizontal.
(b) Constant speed.
    This is a straight line parallel to the time axis.
(c) Constant deceleration.
    This is a straight line heading down towards the time axis.

> **Key points**
> - The area under any part of a speed–time graph is the distance travelled by the body.
> - To calculate the average speed of a body when more than one type of motion is involved, draw a speed–time graph. Find the area under the graph, i.e. distance travelled.
>
> $$\text{Average speed} = \frac{\text{total distance travelled}}{\text{total time taken}}$$
>
> - For a body moving only with constant acceleration or constant deceleration:
>
> $$\text{Average speed} = \frac{\text{initial speed} + \text{final speed}}{2}$$

5 standard grade physics

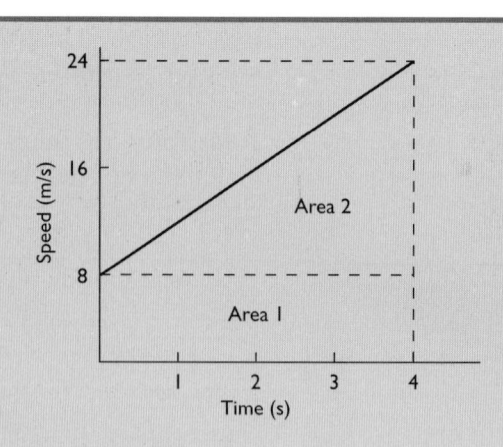

FIGURE 5.5

Example: The graph in figure 5.5 shows the motion of a car travelling along a road.

(a) Calculate the acceleration.

(b) What is the distance travelled?

Solution: (a) The acceleration is given as

$$a = \frac{v - u}{t}$$

where $u = 8$ m/s, $v = 24$ m/s and $t = 4$ s.

$$a = \frac{24 - 8}{4} = \frac{16}{4} = 4 \text{ m/s}^2$$

(b) Distance = Area under v–t graph
= Area 1 + Area 2
= $8 \times 4 + \frac{1}{2} \times (24 - 8) \times 4$
= $8 \times 4 + \frac{1}{2} \times 16 \times 4$
= $32 + 32$
= 64 m

5.2 May the force be with you

The effects of forces

When an object is pushed or pulled, a force is exerted on it.

- A force can make a stationary object move.
- A force can change the speed of an object.
- A force can change the direction of travel of a moving object.
- A force can change the shape of an object (deform it).

These effects depend on the size of the force applied to the object.

Measuring force

Springs can be used to measure force:

- A spring stretches evenly – each time an identical mass is added to the carrier, the spring stretches by the same amount.
- A spring returns to its original length when the force is removed. (If the force is too great, the spring will not return to its original length when the force is removed.)

We use a Newton balance to measure force (figure 5.6).

FIGURE 5.6

Frictional forces

Moving objects such as cars can slow down due to forces acting on them. These forces can act through the road surface, the tyres or the brakes. The force that tries to oppose motion is called the **force of friction**. A frictional force always acts when particles are sliding across one another and can oppose any motion.

Car brakes

Car brakes operate to slow down the car. When the brake pedal is pressed, it causes the expander to push the brake shoes against the drum. Some cars are fitted with an anti-lock braking system, called **ABS**, which has sensors located at each wheel to detect when it is about to lock during braking. If the brakes lock it will be very difficult to steer. ABS prevents this by rapidly releasing and re-applying the brake, so preventing skidding (figure 5.7).

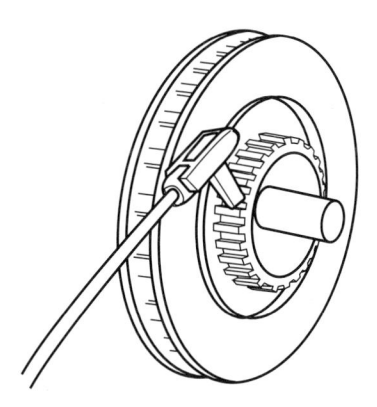

When the sensor detects that there is wheel lock, it reduces brake pressure and then reapplies the brakes.

FIGURE 5.7

Reducing friction

Lubrication

The frictional force between two surfaces moving against each other can be reduced by lubricating the surfaces. This generally means that oil can be placed in between two metal surfaces. This happens in car engines and reduces wear on the engine, since the metal parts are not actually meeting each other but have a thin layer of oil between.

Streamlining

Modern cars are designed to offer as little resistance (drag) to the air as possible. This is the friction of the air on the car. To reduce this friction, the designers try to streamline the vehicle in a variety of ways. This streamlining is measured by a number called the **drag coefficient**, C_d.

standard grade physics

The larger the C_d number, the greater the resistance to air flow. The calculation of C_d is difficult and involves the vehicle being placed in wind tunnels and smoke flowing over it as shown in figure 5.8. Most C_d values range from 0.3 to 0.4.

The drag on the car can be reduced in a number of ways:

- reducing the front area of the car
- not carrying a roof rack
- using door mirrors instead of wing mirrors
- using a smooth round body shape
- using aerials made as part of the car windows.

FIGURE 5.8

Balanced and unbalanced forces

When two or more forces act on a body, the combined effect depends on their size and direction.

Balanced forces acting on a body are equal in size, but act in opposite directions. They cancel each other out and are the same as zero force acting on the body (figure 5.9). An unbalanced force acting on a body causes it to speed up or slow down.

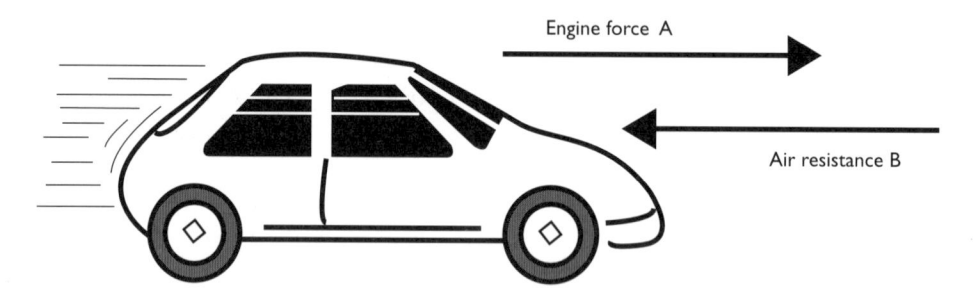

FIGURE 5.9 *Balanced forces*

In figure 5.9, when *A* and *B* are both the same size, the same force is applied to each side of the vehicle, i.e. the forces are balanced. If the vehicle is at rest, it will stay at rest. If it is moving, it will keep moving at a constant speed in a straight line.

When the engine force *A* is greater than the air resistance force *B*, the car will accelerate to the right since the forces are now unbalanced.

Newton's First Law

Sir Isaac Newton is regarded as one of the greatest scientists (figure 5.10). He was born in 1642 in Grantham and studied at home and school and later went on to study at the University of Cambridge. At the age of 24 he was appointed Lucasian Professor of Mathematics and worked on mathematics and astronomy. He proposed three laws of motion.

This is his First Law:

A body will remain at rest or move at constant speed in a straight line unless acted on by an unbalanced force.

FIGURE 5.10 *Sir Isaac Newton*

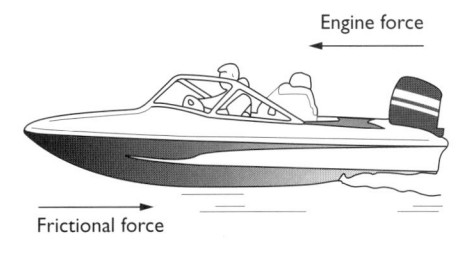

FIGURE 5.11

Using Newton's First Law, we can explain the following motions:

- A speed boat travelling at a steady speed through the water (figure 5.11). The resistive force offered by the water will balance out the force exerted by the engine.
- A car is moving at a constant speed along a level road. No matter how hard the driver tries to accelerate, the car will not increase its speed. This is because the resistive forces have balanced out the force produced by the engine.

Newton's Second Law

If a mass m is acted on by an unbalanced force (F), then an acceleration is produced. If the unbalanced force is doubled, then the acceleration is doubled.

If you keep the force constant and double the mass, then you will halve the acceleration. This can be written as Newton's Second Law, namely:

When a body is acted on by a constant unbalanced force, the body moves with constant acceleration in the direction of the unbalanced force.

$$\text{Unbalanced force} = \text{mass} \times \text{acceleration}$$
$$F = ma$$

where F is in newtons (N), m is in kilograms (kg) and a is in metres per second squared (m/s^2).

Example: A force of 5 N acts on a mass of 10 kg. Calculate the acceleration.
Solution: $F = 5$ N $m = 10$ kg $a = ?$

$$F = ma \quad a = \frac{F}{m} = \frac{5}{10} = 0.5 \text{ m/s}^2$$

Example: A car on a fun ride is being pulled by a force of 500 N and accelerates at 25 m/s^2. What is the mass of the car?
Solution:
$$F = 500 \text{ N} \quad a = 25 \text{ m/s}^2$$
$$F = ma$$
$$500 = m \times 25$$
$$m = \frac{500}{25} = 20 \text{ kg}$$

Example: A toy car is being pulled by a force of 20 N. The car has a mass of 2 kg. There is a frictional force of 4 N acting on the car. Calculate the acceleration of the car (figure 5.12).

FIGURE 5.12

› *Solution:* The unbalanced force acting on the car is:
$$F = 20 - 4 = 16 \text{ N}$$
$$a = \frac{F}{m} = \frac{16}{2} = 8 \text{ m/s}^2$$

Mass and weight

People often talk about the weight of a person being 70 kg. A physicist would say the mass of the person is 70 kg. The distinction may not be obvious, but first let's talk about mass.

Mass

Mass is the quantity of matter forming a body. Mass depends on the number and type of atoms making it up, so the mass of a body remains constant. If you go to different parts of the Earth or even to the Moon, you have the same mass (since hopefully you do not lose an arm or a leg on the journey!).

Force of gravity

Force of gravity is the downward pull of the Earth on a body:

Force of gravity = pull of Earth on a body
         = gravitational force on a body
         = weight of body

Weight

The weight of a body depends on: (a) mass, and (b) where it is.
   Being a force, weight is measured in newtons (N).

› $$\frac{\text{weight of body}}{\text{mass of body}} = \frac{W}{m} = \text{constant}$$

This constant is called the gravitational field strength (g). The units of g are N/kg or m/s².

The gravitational field strength varies depending on where you are. For instance, on Earth $g = 10$ N/kg but on the Moon $g = 1.6$ N/kg and on Jupiter $g = 26.4$ N/kg. This information is shown on the data page.
   So:

$$\text{Weight} = \text{mass} \times \text{gravitational field strength}$$
$$W = mg$$

Example: What is the weight of a 4 kg mass on the Earth?
Solution:
$$W = mg$$
$$= 4 \times 10$$
$$= 40 \text{ N}$$

transport 5

Acceleration due to gravity

The force of gravity causes all bodies to accelerate as they fall back to Earth, since the Earth is so massive and exerts a very strong force on these small objects. This gravitational force is the one force that we cannot switch off.

$$\text{Gravitational field strength} = \frac{\text{force of gravity on a body}}{\text{mass of body}}$$

$$g = \frac{\text{weight}}{\text{mass}}$$

$$= \frac{W}{m}$$

$$= \text{acceleration due to gravity}$$

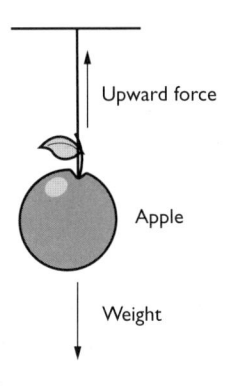

FIGURE 5.13

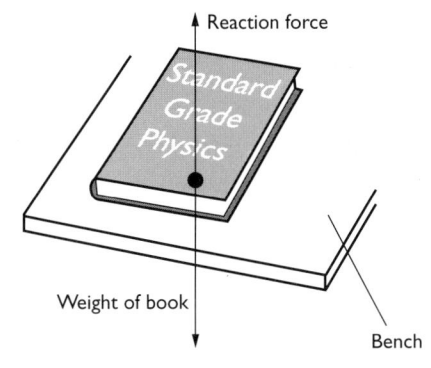

FIGURE 5.14

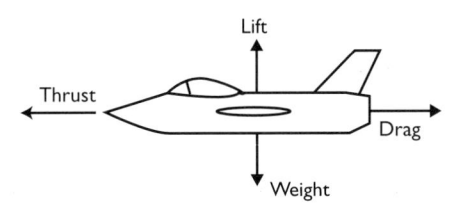

FIGURE 5.15

FIGURE 5.16

Forces and supported bodies

We know from Newton's First Law that if a body remains stationary or moves at constant speed, then the forces acting on the body are balanced.

Example 1: A stationary mass m is hanging from a string. The weight of the object is mg (N) and acts downwards, but this is balanced by a force of the same size acting upwards due to the tension in the string (figure 5.13).

Example 2: A book rests on a shelf. This gives an upward force equal in size to the weight; therefore the forces are balanced (figure 5.14).

We can also see examples of balanced forces in action in different situations.

Aircraft

The engines provide a forward force or **thrust** which accelerates the aircraft forward. However, as it moves faster, the air resistance, or drag, increases until the forces (horizontally) are balanced. The aircraft would move at constant speed (Newton's First Law). When in level flight at constant speed the lift force upwards will equal the weight downwards, giving balanced forces (figure 5.15). Horizontally, the thrust equals the drag force but acts in the opposite direction and so produces balanced forces.

Powerboats

Air offers less resistance to motion than water. A powerboat uses most of its power to push its hull through the water. This is because the force of friction due to the water is large.

Hovercraft

A hovercraft is supported by a cushion of air. The hovercraft floats just above the surface and overcomes the greater resistance of water or ground. It has the advantage of being able to travel across both land and sea (figure 5.16).

5 standard grade physics

Inertia

All bodies are unwilling (or reluctant) to change their motion. This means that a steady force is required to change the motion of a body. This reluctance to change its motion is called its **inertial mass** or mass or inertia. Inertia depends on mass. The larger the mass, the larger the inertia and the more unwilling the body is to change its motion. It is easier to stop a lighter object than a heavier one, if both are travelling at the same speed.

Seat belts: why you should belt up!

When a car brakes suddenly, any unrestrained object will continue to move at the car's speed before braking (Newton's First Law). It will probably collide with some part of the interior, causing damage or injury.

When we wear a seatbelt and the car brakes suddenly, the seatbelt applies a force which opposes our motion. This causes us to decelerate rapidly. The webbing straps are designed to have a certain amount of 'give' so that the sudden force applied to the person does not cause injury (figure 5.17). Air bags fitted behind the steering wheel produce a similar effect and the large area of the bag, when it inflates, prevents chest injuries.

Adult seat belts are not suitable for young children. Children tend to slip down in the seat. This effect is called 'submarining' and can be prevented by using a special design for children.

FIGURE 5.17

Frictional forces in a fluid

A fluid is a liquid or gas. In a fluid, the frictional force on a body travelling through it increases as the speed of the body increases. This can be shown by dropping metal spheres into tubes of a thick oily liquid or water.

In both cases, the spheres accelerate and then move with constant speed (**terminal velocity**). When the sphere is accelerating, there is an unbalanced force acting on it. When the terminal velocity is reached, the forces are balanced. This is reached sooner in the thick liquid than in water, showing that the frictional force in a liquid depends on the type of liquid.

The motion of a body falling through any fluid can be divided into three parts (figure 5.18).

1. Initially, an unbalanced force acts on the body due to its weight and the body falls with a constant acceleration of 10 m/s² (which is the acceleration due to gravity).
2. After a short time, the frictional force begins to act and opposes the motion. This force will be increasing as the speed of the body increases. There is a smaller unbalanced force ($F_{un} = W - F_R$) and the acceleration is therefore less than 10 m/s². This acceleration will continue to decrease as the frictional force increases.

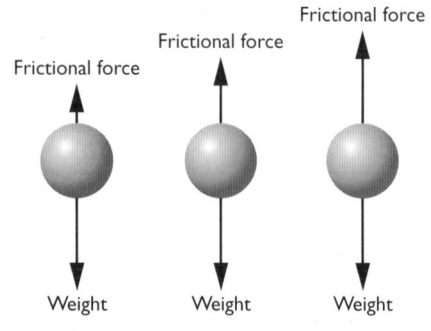

FIGURE 5.18

3 Finally, the frictional force balances the weight. We now have balanced forces. The body now falls at a constant speed in a straight line. The body has reached its greatest speed, the terminal speed or terminal velocity.

Free-falling parachutist

The graph shows speed against time (figure 5.19b) for a parachutist falling in free-fall out of an aircraft and then opening the rip cord some time later. Each part of the graph is explained below:

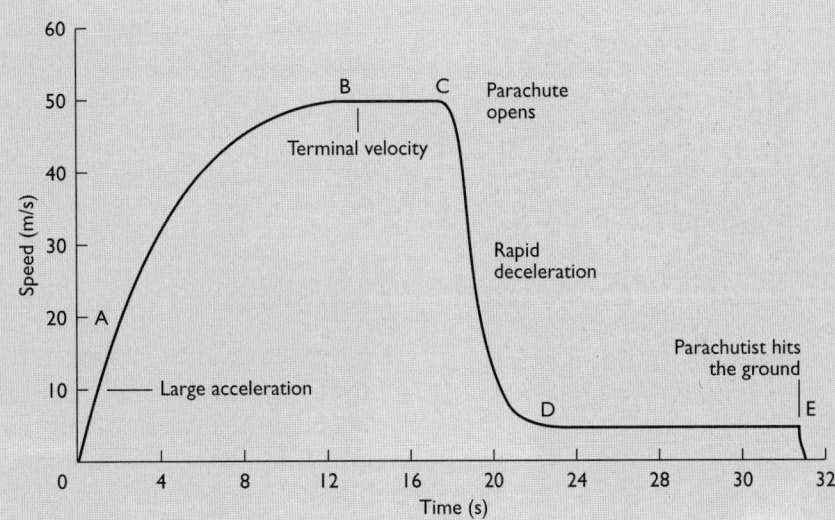

FIGURE 5.19a *The sky diver has reached her terminal velocity.*

FIGURE 5.19b

0A = constant acceleration due to gravity.
AB = decreasing acceleration as frictional force acts.

Unbalanced force = weight − frictional force

BC = constant speed as frictional force upwards = weight downwards.
CD = non-uniform deceleration due to parachute opening and increasing frictional force.
DE = constant speed as frictional force upwards = weight downwards.
EF = parachutist hits the ground safely.

5.3 *Movement means energy*

Work and energy

Energy is a very useful quantity. Simply, energy allows objects to move and lets you do things – it is called **work**.

Although it has many different forms, there are ways of measuring the different types of energy. When work is done, energy is transferred to a body or changed into another form.

Energy transferred = work done
= force × distance moved by the force

Thus

$$\text{Work done} = F \times d$$

where F = force in newtons and d = distance in metres.

The unit of energy and work done is the joule (J), thus:

$$1 \text{ joule} = 1 \text{ newton metre}$$
$$1 \text{ J} = 1 \text{ N m}$$

Example: A boy finds he has to exert a force of 50 N to lift a box 2 m onto a shelf. What is the work done?

Solution:
$$\begin{aligned}\text{Work done} &= F \times d \\ &= 50 \times 2 \\ &= 100 \text{ J}\end{aligned}$$

Conservation of energy

Energy cannot be created or destroyed but can be changed from one form to another when work is done. For example, the kinetic energy of movement in a car is mainly changed into heat when the brakes are applied. If a system gains energy, then another system loses the same amount. This is called the conservation of energy.

Gravitational potential energy (E_p)

Water in a mountain loch has stored energy (gravitational potential energy) which can be transferred into electrical energy in a hydroelectric scheme. It is available since the water is above the generating station and can be transferred by allowing it to fall.

We can derive an equation to allow us to calculate the change in gravitational potential energy for a mass being lifted. A mass, m, is lifted at constant speed through a vertical height, h (figure 5.20).

The work done in lifting it is calculated as

$$\text{Work done} = F \times d$$

In this case, the force applied must balance the weight of the box.

$$\begin{aligned}\text{Applied force upwards} &= \text{weight downwards} \\ &= mg \\ \text{Work done} &= mg \times h \\ &= mgh \\ &= \text{gain in gravitational potential energy } (E_p)\end{aligned}$$

$E_p = mgh$ where E_p = change in gravitational E_p (J)
m = mass (kg)
g = gravitational field strength (N/kg)
h = vertical height (m)

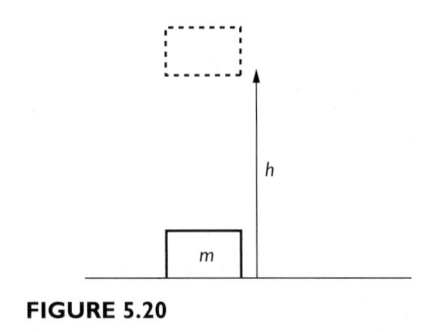

FIGURE 5.20

Kinetic energy (E_k)

This is the energy possessed by moving bodies. We can also derive an equation for this type of energy.

Consider a mass, m, starting from rest, which is accelerated by a force, F, to a final speed, v, in a time, t (figure 5.21).

FIGURE 5.21

Work done on body $= F \times d$

$\qquad \qquad \qquad \quad = ma \times$ area under speed–time graph (figure 5.22)

and $a = \dfrac{v - u}{t} = \dfrac{v - 0}{t} = \dfrac{v}{t}$

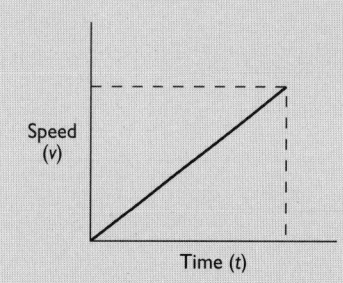

FIGURE 5.22

Area under the graph $= \frac{1}{2} \times t \times v = \frac{1}{2} vt$

Work done on body $= \dfrac{mv}{t} \times \frac{1}{2} vt$

$\qquad \qquad \qquad \quad = \frac{1}{2} mv^2$

Work done on body $=$ gain in E_k

$E_k = \frac{1}{2} mv^2$

Note that E_k depends on v^2. This means that

- if the speed doubles, then the kinetic energy increases by four
- if the speed trebles, then the kinetic energy increases by nine.

standard grade physics

Power

When we say that an appliance is more powerful than another one, then we mean that it uses up energy at a faster rate.

Power = energy transferred in 1 s = work done in 1 s

$$\text{Power} = \frac{\text{energy transferred}}{\text{time taken}} = \frac{\text{work done}}{\text{time}}$$

Power is measured in watts (W). A power of one watt means that one joule of energy is transferred in one second.

Example: A 3 kg box is raised through 20 m in 4 s.

(a) Calculate the gain in gravitational E_p of the box.

(b) Calculate the power used to lift the box.

(c) Why would more power be needed than the value calculated in (b)?

Solution:

(a) $E_p = mgh$
$= 3 \times 10 \times 20$
$= 600 \text{ J}$

(b) $P = \dfrac{E}{t} = \dfrac{600}{4} = 150 \text{ W}$

(c) Some power supplied is changed into heat during the lifting.

Example: A 50 kg girl on a 15 kg bicycle is moving at a uniform speed of 5 m/s when she applies the brakes and comes to rest in 2 s.

(a) What is the kinetic energy of the girl and her bicycle before she brakes?

(b) What becomes of this kinetic energy during the braking?

(c) Calculate the power of the brakes.

Solution:

(a) $E_k = \tfrac{1}{2} mv^2$
$= \tfrac{1}{2} \times 65 \times (5)^2$
$= 813 \text{ J}$

(b) The kinetic energy changes into heat.

(c) Change in $E_k = 813 \text{ J} =$ energy transferred

$P = \dfrac{E}{t} = \dfrac{813}{2} = 407 \text{ W}$

FIGURE 5.23

Estimating your own power

In going up stairs, you will gain in gravitational potential energy. An applied force equal to your weight (force of gravity) acts vertically upwards and so the distance moved by the applied force is the vertical height of the stairs.

You can measure your mass by standing on bathroom scales. To calculate your power you also need to find time taken for you to go up the stairs (figure 5.23).

Run up the stairs and time how long it takes you to run up a measured vertical height. Typical results for an adult are:

$$\text{Height of stairs} = 3 \text{ m}$$
$$\text{Time taken to go up stairs} = 3.5 \text{ s}$$
$$\text{Mass} = 70 \text{ kg}$$

$$\begin{aligned} \text{Work done going up stairs} &= \text{energy transferred} \\ &= \text{gain in gravitational potential energy} \\ &= mgh \\ &= 700 \times 3 \\ &= 2100 \text{ J} \end{aligned}$$

$$\text{Power} = \frac{\text{energy transferred}}{\text{time taken}} = \frac{mgh}{t} = \frac{2100}{3.5} = 600 \text{ W}.$$

The power of a horse is about 750 W and an Olympic runner can produce up to 3000 W. However, we cannot sustain this power for any length of time. Only about half of this is used to propel the athlete forward; the rest is given out as heat energy.

Safety and design in moving vehicles

Every year there are many people killed or injured as a result of motor accidents. Some of these accidents can be prevented by better driving, particularly in bad weather conditions. However, accidents will occur. In attempting to avoid an accident, there are only two things a driver can do – change the car's speed and/or its direction.

In an accident, the design of the car and of the roadside environment can greatly determine the amount of damage and injury which might occur. If there were no protective devices or designs in a car, then you would continue to move at the same speed as the car if the car is struck or suddenly comes to a halt. This would result in you going through the windscreen or being injured by the sides of the door being crushed against you. Some car designs have a safety cage passenger compartment which will not collapse and this, combined with crumple zones to the front and rear, absorbs and transfers the energy of the impact to the roof and floor. Most new cars now have side impact bars to prevent the doors crumpling and causing damage to the driver and passengers. Look at some recent adverts for cars and see if you can detect any other features (figure 5.24). Safety costs money, and companies have to balance the additional costs of safety against the overall cost of a car.

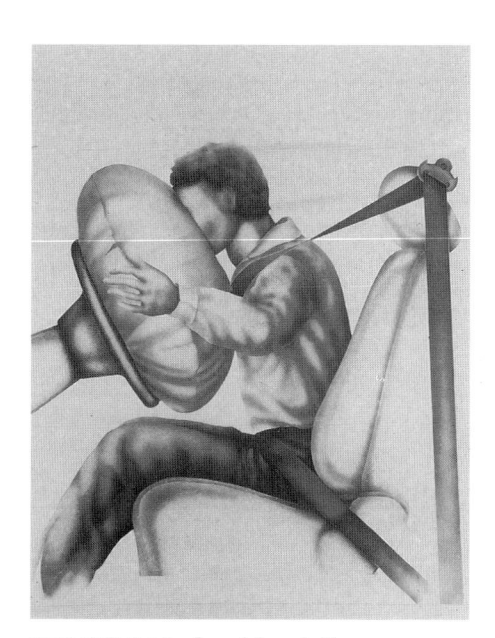

FIGURE 5.24 *An airbag inflates to prevent injury to the driver*

The roadside environment

Twenty-five per cent of road accidents are with roadside objects, so safety rails and posts are now designed to deform on impact and absorb most of the energy of a vehicle, reducing the effects of an accident. Roadside barriers are made of metal sheets which absorb some of a vehicle's energy when struck. More energy is absorbed by the posts, which 'give' since they are not buried deep in the ground.

Many road accidents are caused by speed. Doubling the speed of the car gives it four times the kinetic energy. This kinetic energy has to be used up in an accident. Lower speeds can dramatically reduce the damage to a car involved in a road accident. This reduction in speed can reduce fuel consumption and should also help reduce damage and injury in accidents.

Thinking and braking

- Reaction time is the time between seeing and reacting to an event.
- Reaction time varies from person to person. An average driver has a reaction time of about 0.6 s when this is measured under normal conditions of driving.
- Reaction time is likely to be much longer if drugs or alcohol have been taken. Even a small amount of alcohol can greatly increase reaction time.
- Thinking distance is the distance travelled during this reaction time.

Thinking distance = speed × reaction time

- Braking distance is the distance travelled from the time the brakes were applied to the vehicle becoming stationary.
- Stopping distance consists of two parts: the thinking distance and the braking distance, which are added together. The stopping distance for a car travelling at 30 mph in good road conditions is 23 m, and at 60 mph it is 72 m. The table below shows the shortest stopping distances for various speeds.

Speed (mph)	Thinking distance (m)	Braking distance (m)	Overall stopping distance (m)
20	6	6	12
30	9	14	23
40	12	24	36
50	15	38	53
60	18	54	72
70	21	75	96

Since thinking distance is speed × time and the reaction time remains constant, the thinking distance increases by the same amount when the speed increases. What will happen to these distances when the road conditions change, for example on wet roads?

Energy conservation – gravitational E_p to E_k

During any energy transformation, the total amount of energy is always conserved. That is, it stays the same, but may be changed into less useful forms.

Energy transfer or energy changes

When work is done on a system, energy is transferred to or from that system.

- If the speed of a body changes, then, from the conservation of energy:

$$\text{Work done} = \text{change in } E_k$$
$$\text{Force applied} \times \text{distance moved by force} = E_k \text{ (large)} - E_k \text{ (small)}$$

- If the height of a body changes, then, from the conservation of energy:

$$\text{Work done} = \text{change in gravitational } E_p$$
$$\text{Force applied} \times \text{distance moved by force} = mgh$$

Examples of energy transfer

The pendulum

Figure 5.25 shows a pendulum bob moving from B to A. As it moves, work is done and energy transferred to the bob.

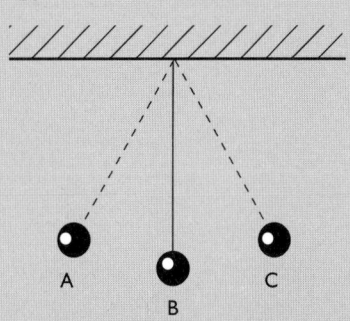

FIGURE 5.25

$$\text{Work done on bob} = \text{energy transferred to bob}$$
$$= \text{gain in gravitational } E_p$$
$$= mgh$$

When the bob swings from A to B, it 'loses' gravitational potential energy, E_p, but gains kinetic energy, E_k. At B it has maximum speed and hence maximum E_k.

If no energy is transferred with the surroundings then:

$$\text{Loss in gravitational } E_p = \text{gain in } E_k$$
$$mgh = \tfrac{1}{2}mv^2 - 0$$
$$mgh = \tfrac{1}{2}mv^2$$

If friction is present, the bob still loses the same amount of gravitational E_p. This is now transferred into E_k and work is done against friction. The work done against friction may be in the form of heat and sound energies, which are 'lost' or dissipated from the system:

i.e. loss in gravitational E_p = gain in E_k + work done against friction.

Ball on a slope

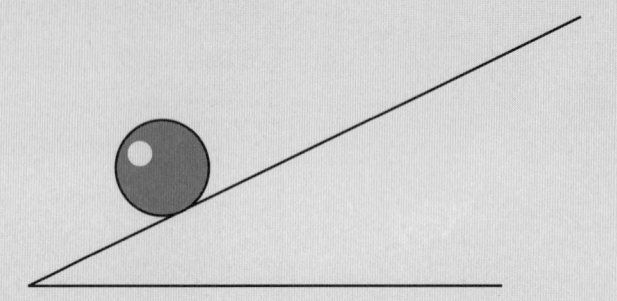

FIGURE 5.26

If a ball is **projected up the slope**, it gets slower and slower and so is losing E_k, but gaining gravitational E_p.

If no energy is transferred with the surroundings, then:

$$\text{Loss in } E_k = \text{gain in } E_p$$

$$\tfrac{1}{2}mv^2 - 0 = mgh$$

If frictional force (F) is present on the incline, then work will be done against friction:

$$\text{Loss in } E_k = \text{gain in gravitational } E_p + \text{work done against friction}$$

$$\tfrac{1}{2}mv^2 - 0 = mgh + F \times d$$

$$\tfrac{1}{2}mv^2 = mgh + F \times d$$

The falling body: sky-diving without the parachute

As a body falls, it 'loses' gravitational E_p but gains E_k. Just before impact with the ground, it has 'lost' all its gravitational E_p and has only E_k (figure 5.27).

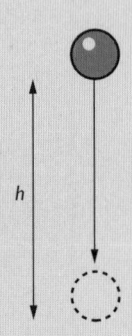

FIGURE 5.27

If no energy is transferred with the surroundings, then:

$$\text{Gain in } E_k = \text{loss in gravitational } E_p$$
$$\tfrac{1}{2}mv^2 - 0 = mgh$$
$$\tfrac{1}{2}mv^2 = mgh$$

If the body is **projected vertically upwards**, for example the human 'cannonball' at a circus, then it slows down and so loses E_k and in gaining height has gained gravitational E_p. If no energy is transferred with the surroundings, then:

$$\text{Loss in } E_k = \text{gain in gravitational } E_p$$
$$\tfrac{1}{2}mv^2 - 0 = mgh$$
$$\tfrac{1}{2}mv^2 = mgh$$

Example: A pendulum swings as shown in figure 5.25. Points A and C are the extremities of the swing. The mass of the bob is 0.5 kg. The maximum vertical height reached is 0.1 m. Find for the bob:

(a) The maximum potential energy.

(b) The maximum kinetic energy.

(c) The top speed.

Solution: (a) $E_p = mgh$
$$= 0.5 \times 10 \times 0.1$$
$$= 0.5 \text{ J}$$

(b) Since we assume that all the potential energy changes into kinetic energy,
$$E_k = E_p = 0.5 \text{ J}$$

(c) $\tfrac{1}{2}mv^2 = 0.5$

$\tfrac{1}{2}(0.5)v^2 = 0.5$

$v^2 = 2$
$v = 1.44 \text{ m/s}$

Example: When Galileo dropped metal spheres of different mass from the Leaning Tower of Pisa he found that they hit the ground at the same time. How can his discovery be explained in terms of the conservation of energy?

Solution: If the change in gravitational potential energy equals the change in kinetic energy, then:

$$mgh = \tfrac{1}{2}mv^2 - 0$$

Then the masses will cancel on both sides of the equation, giving:

$gh = \frac{1}{2}v^2$

Since the height and speed are connected but are independent of mass, then any mass will fall and hit the ground at the same time as any other mass.

Galileo did this experiment, but the initial ideas on gravity were put forward by Sir Isaac Newton.

LEARNING OUTCOMES

After studying this chapter you should be able to:

Section 5.1

1. Describe how to measure an average speed.
2. Carry out calculations involving the relationship between distance, time and average speed.
3. Describe how to measure instantaneous speeds.
4. Explain the terms speed and acceleration.
5. Calculate acceleration from change of speed per unit time (miles per hour per second or metres per second per second).
6. Draw speed–time graphs showing steady speed, slowing down and speeding up.
7. Describe the motions represented by a speed–time graph.
8. Calculate acceleration, from speed–time graphs, for motion with a single constant acceleration.
9. Identify situations where average and instantaneous speeds are different. **Credit**
10. Explain how the method used to measure the time of travel can have an effect on the measured value of the instantaneous speed. **Credit**
11. Calculate distance covered and acceleration from speed–time graphs for motion involving more than one constant acceleration. **Credit**
12. Carry out calculations involving the relationship between initial speed, final speed, time and uniform acceleration. **Credit**

Section 5.2

1. Describe the effects of forces in terms of their ability to change the shape, speed and direction of travel of an object.
2. Describe the use of a newton balance to measure force.
3. State that weight is a force and is the Earth's pull on the object.
4. Use the approximate value of 10 N/kg to calculate weight.
5. State that the force of friction can oppose the motion of a body.
6. Describe and explain situations in which attempts are made to increase or decrease the force of friction.

learning outcomes

7 State that equal forces acting in opposite directions on an object are called balanced forces and are equivalent to no force at all.

8 State that when balanced forces or no forces act on an object, its speed remains the same.

9 Explain, in terms of the forces required, why seat belts are used in cars.

10 Describe the qualitative effects of change of mass or of force on the acceleration of an object.

11 Carry out calculations involving the relationship between a, F and m.

12 Distinguish between mass and weight. **Credit**

13 State that the weight per unit mass is called the gravitational field strength. **Credit**

14 Explain the movement of objects in terms of Newton's First Law. **Credit**

15 Carry out calculations using the relationship between a, F and m and involving more than one force, but in one dimension only. **Credit**

Section 5.3

1 Describe the main energy transformations as a vehicle accelerates, moves at constant speed, brakes and goes up or down a slope.

2 State that work done is a measure of the energy transferred.

3 Carry out calculations involving the relationship between work done, force and distance.

4 Carry out calculations involving the relationship between power, work and time.

5 State that the change in gravitational potential energy is the work done against/by gravity.

6 State that the greater the mass and/or the speed of a moving object, the greater is its kinetic energy.

7 Carry out calculations involving the relationship between kinetic energy, mass and speed. **Credit**

8 Carry out calculations involving energy, work, power and the principle of conservation of energy. **Credit**

STUDY QUESTIONS

1 (a) What is the average speed of a car which travels 1600 m in 80 s?

(b) How long does a cyclist take to travel 500 m when travelling at an average speed of 2 m/s?

(c) A train is travelling at a constant speed of 50 m/s. What distance does the train cover in one minute?

2 What is meant by an acceleration of:
(a) 2 m/s^2
(b) 10 m/s^2
(c) 0.5 m/s^2
(d) -3 m/s^2?

3 (a) A speedboat, starting from rest, reaches a speed of 14 m/s in 28 s. What is its acceleration?

(b) A bus accelerates from 3 m/s to 9 m/s in 5 s. What is its acceleration?

(c) A motor cycle initially travelling at 8 m/s accelerates at 5 m/s^2. What is its speed after 3 s?

4 (a) A plane, when preparing to land, reduces its speed from 80 m/s to 60 m/s in a time of 40 s. What is the deceleration of the plane?

(b) A car decelerates at 2 m/s^2 to rest in a time of 12 s. What was the initial speed of the car?

133

study questions

5 The diagrams below show the speed–time graphs for four different objects. Find, for each of the objects:

(a) the acceleration

(b) the distance travelled

(c) the average speed.

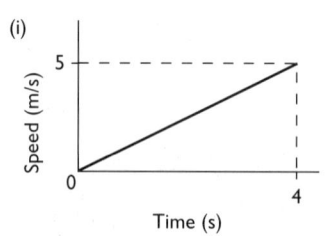

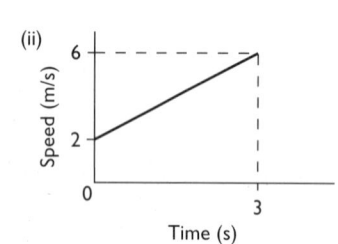

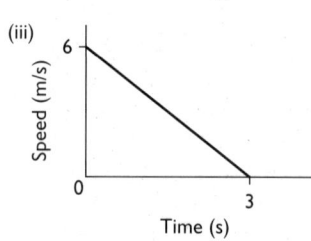

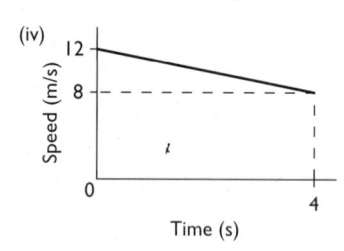

(i) Speed (m/s) graph from 0 to 5 m/s over 4 s

(ii) Speed (m/s) graph from 2 to 6 m/s over 3 s

(iii) Speed (m/s) graph from 6 to 0 m/s over 3 s

(iv) Speed (m/s) graph from 12 to 8 m/s over 4 s

6 The diagram below shows the speed–time graph for a car.

(a) What is the motion of the car between (i) O and A; (ii) A and B; (iii) B and C?

(b) Calculate the deceleration of the car between B and C.

(c) Find the total distance travelled by the car.

(d) Calculate the average speed of the car during the journey.

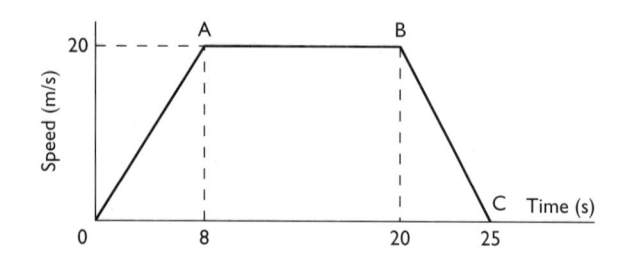

Graph: Speed (m/s), 0 to 20 m/s, A at 8 s, B at 20 s, C at 25 s.

7 What is the size of the unbalanced force acting on the bodies shown below?

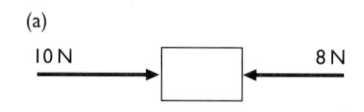

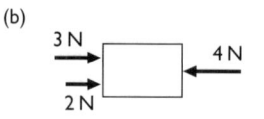

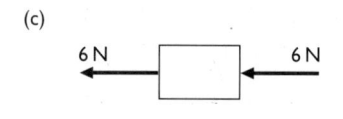

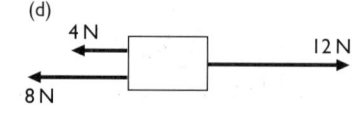

(a) 10 N → □ ← 8 N

(b) 3 N →, 2 N → □ ← 4 N

(c) 6 N ← □ ← 6 N

(d) 4 N ←, 8 N ← □ ← 12 N

8 Describe the motion of the objects shown below.

(a) □ → 5 N, Initially at rest

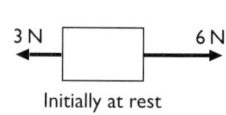

(b) 3 N ← □ ← 6 N, Initially at rest

(c) 4 N ← □ ← 4 N, Initially at rest

(d) 10 N → □ ← 15 N, □ ← 5 N, Initially travelling at 2 m/s to the left

9 (a) What force is required to accelerate a 3 kg mass at 2 m/s²?

(b) What is the acceleration of a 5 kg mass when a force of 50 N is acting on it?

(c) A trolley accelerates at 2 m/s² when acted upon by an unbalanced force of 6 N. What is the mass of the trolley?

10 A force of 1000 N acts on a body of mass 200 kg. The body has a uniform acceleration of 3 m/s². Calculate:

(a) the unbalanced force acting on the vehicle

(b) the force of friction.

11 A car with a mass of 1200 kg, accelerates from 8 m/s to 26 m/s in 9 s.

(a) Calculate the acceleration of the car

(b) What is the unbalanced force required to produce this acceleration?

(c) Explain why the force from the engine has to be greater than this.

12 (a) What is the weight of the following masses on the Earth:
(i) 1 kg; (ii) 5 kg; (iii) 3.4 kg; (iv) 0.4 kg; (v) 300 g; (vi) 50 g?

(b) What masses would have the following weights on the Earth:
(i) 30 N; (ii) 150 N; (iii) 5 N; (iv) 0.4 N; (v) 2 kN?

13 A pupil pulls a 2 kg mass vertically up with a force of 25 N.

(a) What is the unbalanced force acting on the 2 kg mass?

(b) What is the acceleration of the 2 kg mass?

14 (a) A girl pulls a sledge with a force of 12 N for a distance of 200 m on level snow. How much work did she do?

(b) A boy used up 50 J of energy when he pushed a trolley 5 m along a bench. Calculate the constant force he exerted on the trolley.

(c) A man pushes a vehicle with a force of 80 N. How far does he have to push it to use up 480 J of energy?

15 A 25 kg wheel barrow is pushed 30 m using a 35 N force for a time of 60 s. Calculate:

(a) the work done

(b) the power developed in pushing the wheel barrow.

16 (a) How much potential energy does a 3 kg mass gain when it is lifted 1.5 m vertically?

(b) How high must a 5 kg mass have been raised before it gained 400 J of energy?

(c) A pump raises 90 kg of water through a vertical height of 2 m in one minute. What is the minimum power rating of the pump?

17 (a) Calculate the kinetic energy of a 1.5 kg ball travelling at 5 m/s.

(b) A 800 kg car is travelling at 13 m/s. How much kinetic energy does it have?

(c) A girl runs at a constant speed of 4 m/s and has 400 J of kinetic energy. What is her mass?

(d) A 55 kg skier slides to a halt in a distance of 45 m against a frictional force of 5 N. How much kinetic energy did the skier lose?

18 A 0.05 kg stone is thrown vertically upwards with a speed of 12 m/s.

(a) What is the initial kinetic energy of the stone?

(b) How high will the stone go?

19 A car, travelling at 20 metres per second, accelerates to 30 metres per second along a straight section of motorway in a time of five seconds.

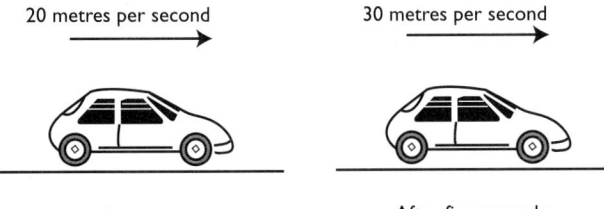

20 metres per second   30 metres per second

At start   After five seconds

(a) Calculate the acceleration of the car.
GENERAL KU

(b) The mass of the car and passengers is 1200 kilograms. What size of force is required to give the acceleration?
GENERAL KU

(c) The Highway Code suggests that a car travelling at 30 metres per second needs a distance of 70 metres to stop from the instant the brakes are applied. Why will a distance greater than this be required when the driver of a car, travelling at 30 metres per second, has to make an emergency stop?
SEB
GENERAL PS

20 (a) Gwen is a passenger in a car travelling along a motorway. She notices a road sign which gives the distances to the next two service stations.

SERVICE STATIONS ON M6

4 KILOMETRES 2½ MILES
80 KILOMETRES 50 MILES

She uses her watch to find the time taken to reach the **first** service station. It takes 160 seconds. Calculate the average speed of the car in metres per second.
GENERAL PS

(b) During another part of the journey, the car travels at a steady speed through road works for a distance of 2400 metres. The frictional force on the car is 500 newtons. How much work is done against friction during this part of the journey?
SEB
GENERAL KU

21 A boy pushes a bale of straw of mass 45 kilograms up a ramp on to a trailer by applying a force of 250 newtons as shown. The length of the ramp is five metres and the height of the trailer above the ground is 1.2 metres.

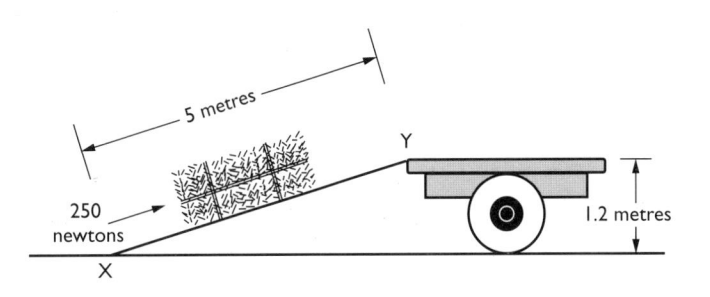

135

study questions

(a) How much work does the boy do pushing the bale up the ramp from X to Y?
GENERAL KU

(b) What is the weight of the bale of straw?
GENERAL KU

(c) How much work does a man do in lifting an identical bale vertically from the ground on to the trailer?
GENERAL PS

(d) Why does it take more work to push the bale up the ramp than to lift the bale vertically on to the trailer?
SEB
GENERAL PS

22 The driver of a car, travelling along a motorway, sees a speed limit of 20 m/s (45 mph) flashing on an overhead gantry in front of him and decides to brake. The graph shows the speed of the car from the instant the driver sees the sign.

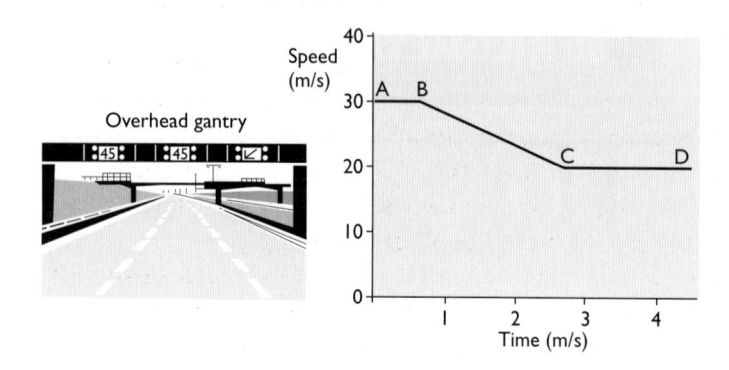

(a) How long did it take the driver to react by applying the brakes of his car after seeing the sign?
CREDIT PS

(b) Describe the motion of the car between:
 (i) B and C
 (ii) C and D.
CREDIT KU

(c) The driver was 100 m from the gantry when he saw the sign. Was the car travelling at the required speed when it passed the gantry? You **must** clearly show your working which leads you to your answer.
SEB
CREDIT PS

23 (a) A car of mass 1200 kg is being towed at a constant speed of 5 m/s by a breakdown lorry. The force of friction on the car at this speed is 400 N.

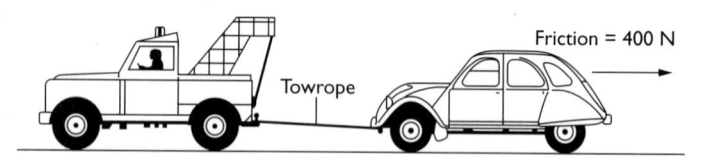

What size of force is exerted by the towrope on the car?
CREDIT KU

(b) The force exerted by the towrope on the car is increased to 2000 N. Assuming that the force of friction on the car remains constant at 400 N, find the acceleration of the car.
SEB
CREDIT KU

Energy matters

6.1 Supply and demand

Industrialised countries, like Britain, use large quantities of energy for heating, transport and industry. This energy comes largely from the **fossil fuels**: coal, oil and gas. They are called fossil fuels because they are the remains of plants and animals which lived many millions of years ago. Once they have been used up, they cannot be replaced, i.e. they are finite. Coal is mainly used to produce electrical energy at power stations. Britain has sufficient coal reserves to last about 300 years.

Oil is used mainly for transport. World supplies of oil are expected to last about 60 years. Gas is largely used for space heating (heating homes) and more recently for generating electricity. Britain's North Sea oil and gas supplies will run out by about the year 2020. Burning fossil fuels produces large quantities of poisonous gases, such as sulphur dioxide, and carbon dioxide (one of the causes of global warming).

Because fossil fuels will run out, cause pollution and are expensive, it is important to use them efficiently. In addition, alternative sources of energy are slowly being developed to take the place of fossil fuels.

Energy conservation (Save it!)

Government agencies and the gas and electricity companies all produce literature which explains how we can save energy (and therefore money) in our homes. Some examples are fitting a hot-water tank jacket, reducing draughts through windows and doors, loft insulation and the replacement of filament lamps with energy-efficient lamps.

There are a number of ways that energy can be saved in our everyday lives. In transport: by sharing a car, using public transport instead of a car, walking or cycling. In industry: by using energy-efficient lighting, heating only the parts of a factory that are being used, and installing energy-efficient machinery.

Power stations

In a conventional power station, coal, oil or gas is burnt in a furnace and the heat produced changes water into steam in a boiler. The steam produced in the boiler is at high pressure. It drives the **turbine** at high speed and this drives the **generator** which produces electrical energy. Steam leaving the turbine enters the **condenser** which turns it back into water. The water is then pumped back to the boiler under pressure.

Cooling towers are required to cool the large quantities of water needed by the condenser. Only about 35 per cent of the fuel's energy (the energy input to the power station) is converted into electrical energy, the remaining 65 per cent is 'lost' as waste heat. A large proportion of this waste heat is transferred to the atmosphere by the cooling towers.

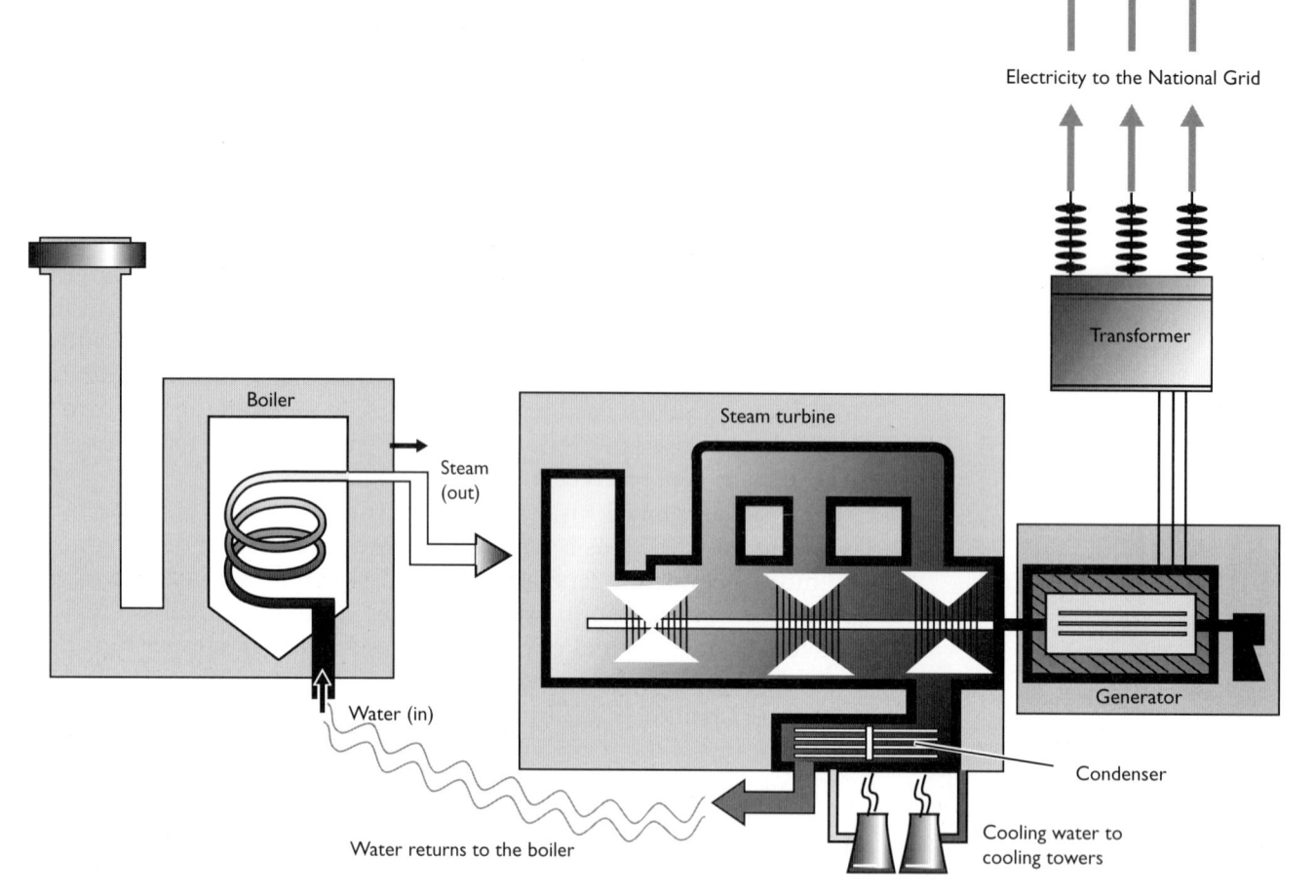

FIGURE 6.1 *A conventional power station*

A **combined heat and power** (CHP) station not only generates electricity but also supplies hot water to heat buildings in district heating schemes. The hot water is piped to local houses and other buildings, passed through radiators and returned, cooler, to the power station for re-heating. About 25 per cent of the energy input to the power station is converted into electrical energy and 50 per cent is usefully used to heat homes and offices, leaving about 25 per cent as waste heat.

Renewable energy sources

- The Sun provides our planet with the energy required to drive the weather systems of the world and to allow plants to grow.
- The tides are a consequence of the gravitational pull of the Sun and the Moon.
- The Earth has a very hot interior which in some parts of the world comes close to the surface.

All of these offer alternative ways of obtaining the energy that we need. Scientists and engineers are slowly developing technologies to extract useful amounts of energy from them.

energy matters 6

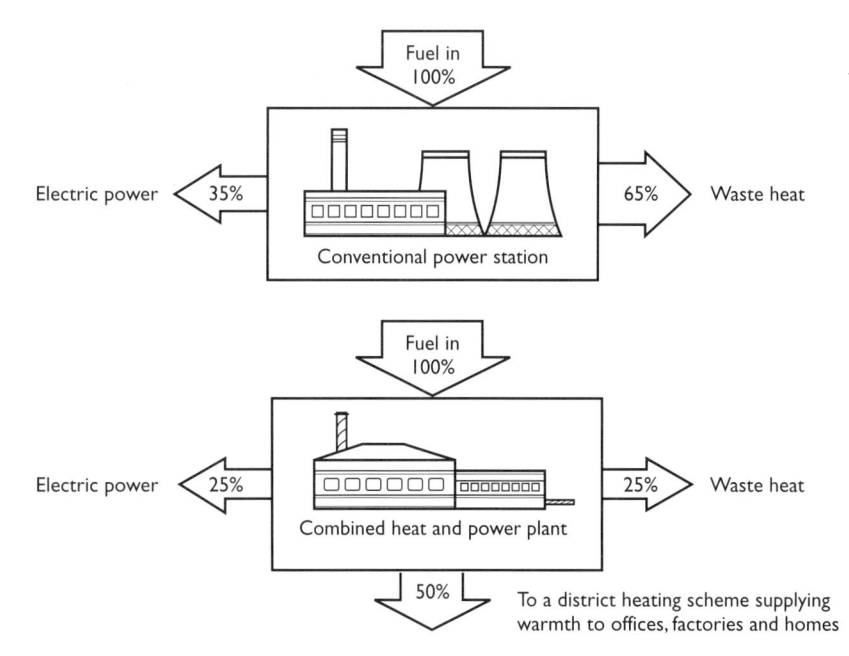

FIGURE 6.2 *Efficiencies of conventional and combined heat and power stations*

FIGURE 6.3 *A house fitted with solar-powered heating panels*

FIGURE 6.4 *Wind turbines grouped to form a wind farm*

Solar energy

The heat in sunlight (even on a dull Scottish day) is sufficient to heat water in panels on the roofs of houses and so provide heating for the house. Sunlight can also be used to generate electricity directly using **photocells** similar to those found in solar-powered calculators.

Solar energy is a renewable and clean source of energy. It is, however, difficult and expensive to convert large amounts into useful forms such as electrical energy, and this can only take place during daylight hours.

Wind energy

The kinetic energy of the wind can be used to generate electricity using modern wind turbines. These turbines are normally situated in a windy location, such as a hilltop, in what are called **wind farms**. There are several commercial wind farms in Britain.

The wind is a renewable and clean source of energy. Conditions for wind energy in Britain are favourable since the prevailing winds are strong, especially in winter when energy demand is at its greatest. However, the wind cannot always be relied on to blow and so it is difficult to maintain a constant supply of electricity. In addition, wind generators can be unsightly and noisy, and since the best locations are generally in areas of great natural beauty, there have been environmental objections.

standard grade physics

FIGURE 6.5 *A hydroelectric power station*

Hydroelectric power

The gravitational potential energy of water is used to generate electrical energy. It is widely used in the hilly parts of Scotland where there is ample rainfall.

Hydroelectric power is a renewable, reliable and clean source of energy. However, there are environmental objections to the building of dams as they flood large areas of land and there is a risk (minimal) of a dam bursting.

Wave energy

Winds cause waves to form on the sea. The energy in the waves can be extracted using a number of devices. Wave energy is more reliable than the wind, since the waves continue long after the wind which produced them has died away. However, there are major difficulties in the construction, maintenance and energy conversion of these devices and it will be some years before large-scale wave energy devices are available.

Tidal energy

Some estuaries, such as that of the River Severn, provide suitable locations for tidal barrages. The principle is generally similar to hydroelectric power. Large gates are opened during the incoming tide allowing water to pass until high tide, when they are closed. On the outgoing tide the potential energy of the trapped water drives turbines, allowing electricity to be generated. There are significant environmental objections to such schemes.

Biomass (plants)

The most common way of extracting energy from the Sun from biomass is to burn wood. Properly looked after forests provide a sustainable source of energy. Alcohol distilled from plants is used in some countries to fuel cars (instead of petrol). Biomass is a renewable source of energy, but growth is too slow to provide large amounts as a fuel.

energy matters 6

Renewable energy sources	Non-renewable (finite) energy sources
solar	coal
wind	oil
water	gas
biomass (plants)	

TABLE 6.1

Geothermal energy and uranium

The heat inside the Earth can be extracted when water is pumped into a bore hole. When the water boils, the steam formed can be used to drive turbines and generate electricity. Geothermal energy is a clean source of energy. However, it is dependent on suitable sites and the extraction of geothermal energy can present considerable technical difficulties.

Even in small quantities, uranium can produce large amounts of electrical energy. Known reserves will last a very long time, but the radioactive waste produced can be extremely dangerous and needs very careful handling and storage.

Geothermal energy and uranium may be considered as either renewable or non-renewable sources of energy. The heat that can be extracted from an area inside the Earth will decrease over a number of years. However, the heat will be renewed slowly if extraction is stopped. Uranium is a material which is finite. However, since it is used in relatively small quantities and will last a very long time, it is sometimes considered to be renewable.

Energy units

Different industries use different energy units, e.g. the electrical industry uses kilowatt hours and the food industry uses kilojoules. The unit used in physics for energy is the **joule (J)**.

Unit	Abbreviation	Number of joules	
1 kilojoule	1 kJ	10^3 J	= 1 000 J
1 megajoule	1 MJ	10^6 J	= 1 000 000 J
1 gigajoule	1 GJ	10^9 J	= 1 000 000 000 J
1 terajoule	1 TJ	10^{12} J	= 1 000 000 000 000 J
1 kilowatt hour	1 kWh	3.6×10^6 J	= 3 600 000 J

TABLE 6.2

6.2 Generation of electricity

Fossil-fuelled and nuclear power stations

Most of Britain's electricity is generated in large power stations using coal, oil, gas or nuclear fuel. Figure 6.6 shows a conventional (fossil-fuelled) power station. The chemical energy of the coal, oil or natural gas is changed into heat when the fuel is burned.

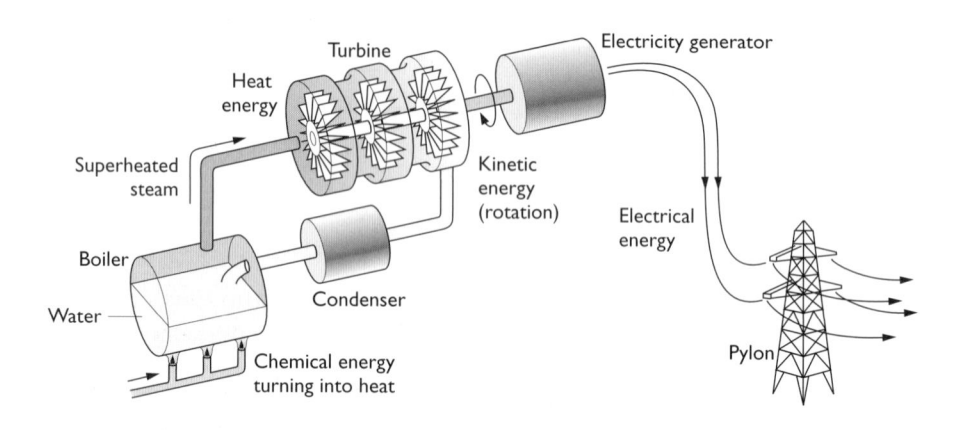

FIGURE 6.6 *Layout of a fossil-fuelled power station*

The fuel of a nuclear power station is the uranium-235 nucleus. To obtain energy from these nuclei, they are bombarded with neutrons. **Neutrons** are uncharged particles found in the nucleus of an atom. When a neutron strikes a uranium-235 nucleus, the nucleus becomes unstable and splits into two pieces. The splitting of a uranium-235 nucleus is called **nuclear fission** and the pieces produced are called **fission fragments** (figure 6.7(a)). A large amount of (heat) energy is released during the fission of a uranium-235 nucleus together with two further neutrons. These neutrons can cause other fissions of uranium-235 nuclei and these, in turn, release further neutrons which can cause further fissions. When a continuous reaction of fissions occurs like this, it is called a **chain reaction** (figure 6.7(b)).

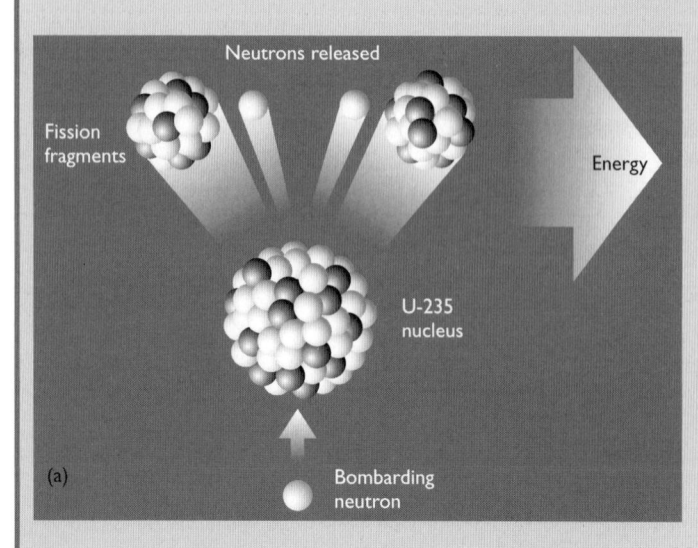

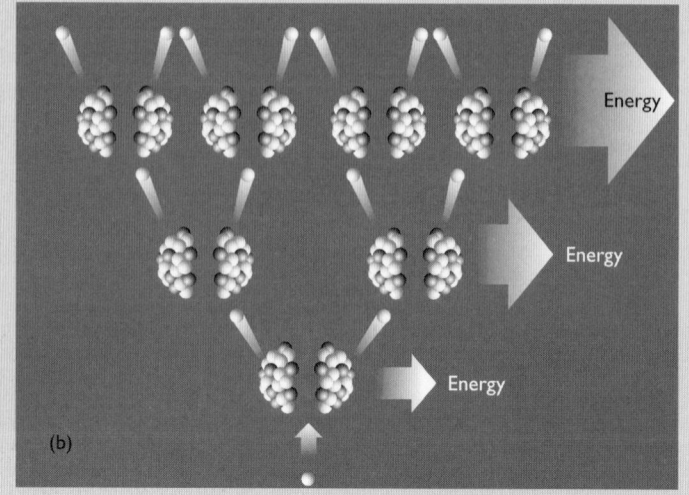

FIGURE 6.7 *(a) Nuclear fission, (b) a chain reaction*

142

In a nuclear power station, a reactor replaces the boiler used in a conventional power station. The chemical energy of the uranium-235 fuel is changed to heat during the fission process. Carbon dioxide gas then carries heat produced by the fission of uranium-235 nuclei in the reactor to a heat exchanger. The heat exchanger transfers heat from the carbon dioxide to water, which turns into steam. The steam is used to turn turbines, just as it would in a conventional power station. Figure 6.8 shows part of a nuclear power station.

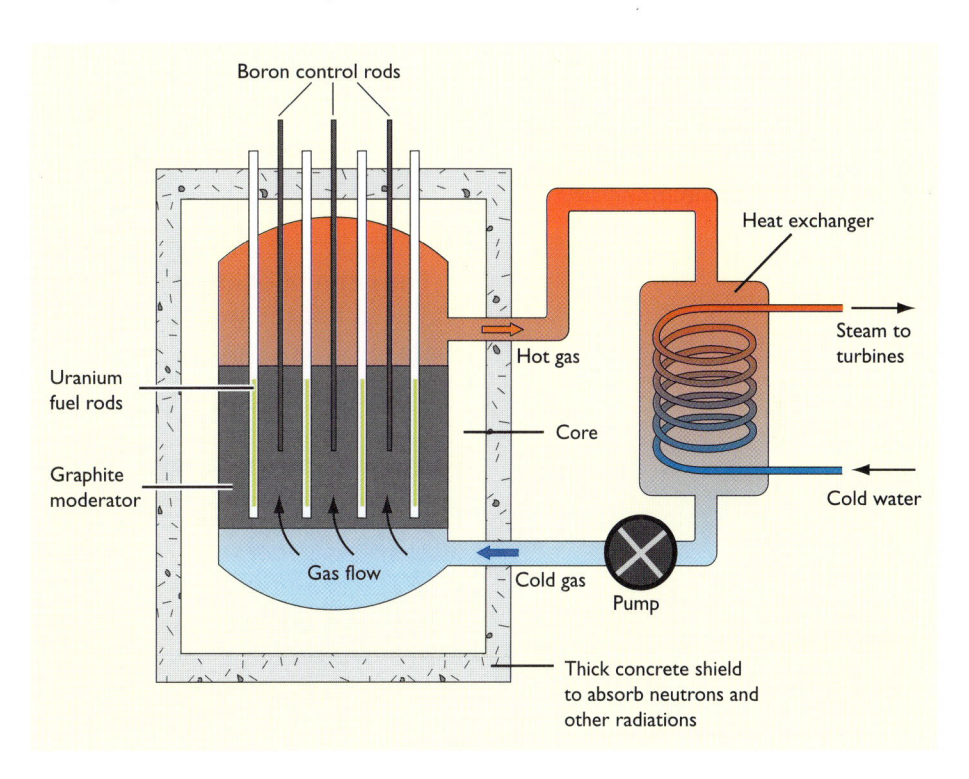

FIGURE 6.8 *Part of a nuclear power station*

A nuclear power station requires much less fuel than the equivalent coal-fired power station.

> This is because 1 kg of coal produces about 30 MJ of energy when burnt, but 1 kg of uranium fuel produces 5 000 000 MJ of energy during the fission process.

Nuclear power stations do, however, produce radioactive waste which can be very dangerous to us and the environment. This waste has to be safely stored for many years.

Hydroelectric power stations

About two per cent of Britain's electricity is obtained from hydroelectric power stations. Hydroelectric power generation uses the gravitational potential energy of water in a high-level dam or reservoir. The water is allowed to flow in pipes down a steep hill, to turn turbines which drive generators to produce electricity. Figure 6.9 shows a diagram of a hydroelectric power station.

6 standard grade physics

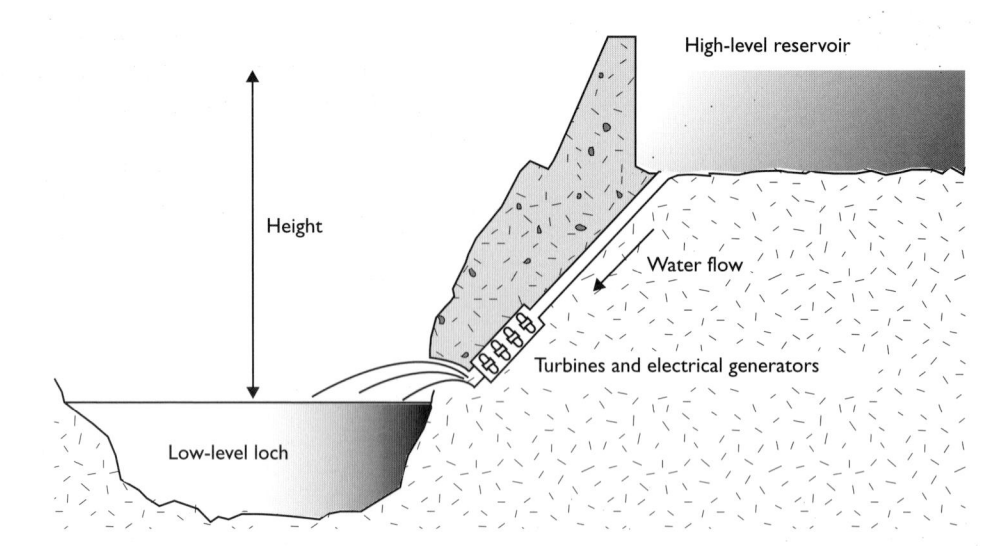

FIGURE 6.9 *A hydroelectric power station*

The amount of electrical energy produced is dependent on the mass and height of the water, i.e. the water's change in gravitational potential energy.

Change in gravitational potential energy, $E_p = mgh$

Pumped hydroelectric power stations

Electrical energy in large quantities cannot be stored and so it must be used as it is generated. However, demand for electricity changes with the time of day and the season of the year. Figure 6.10 shows how the demand for electrical energy changes on a typical winter day.

In a hydroelectric station with pumped storage, electricity generated at 'off-peak' periods of the day or night is used to pump water back up from a low-level reservoir to a high-level reservoir. At 'peak' periods of the day, the potential energy of the water in the high-level reservoir is converted back into electrical energy for the National Grid. Although only three kWh (kilowatt hours) of electricity are recovered for every four supplied, i.e. the system is 75 per cent efficient, pumped-storage schemes are an economical way of meeting peak demand, and they help to increase the overall efficiency of the electrical supply system.

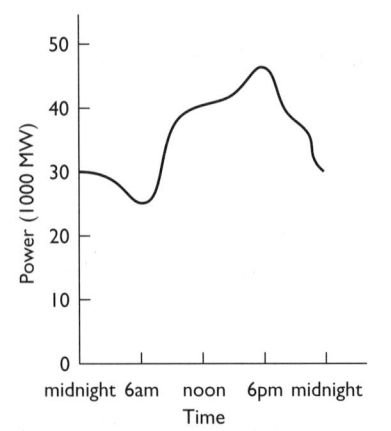

FIGURE 6.10 *Electricity demand varies during a day*

Efficiency

The efficiency of a power station (or any other machine) is given by:

$$\text{efficiency} = \frac{\text{useful energy output}}{\text{total energy input}} \times 100\%$$

As the energy output from a power station or any other machine is always less than the energy input, the efficiency is always less than 100 per cent. The useful energy we get from a machine is never as great as the energy we put in, because some of the energy is transferred into other forms such as heat and perhaps sound. We say that some of the energy put into the machine has been 'lost'. However, the total amount of all the energies remains the same, i.e. the total energy is **conserved**. Sometimes it is easier to look at the energy being used every second (the power). In this case 'power' replaces 'energy' in the equation.

144

Example: A hydroelectric power station has an efficiency of 75 per cent. When operating, the power station produces 3 MJ of energy every second.
(a) What is the power output of the station?
(b) What is the energy input to the station every second?
(c) The water falls through a vertical height of 100 m. What mass of water per second is required to produce this energy input every second?
(d) The efficiency of the power station is 75 per cent. What happened to the other 25 per cent?

Solution: (a) $P = \dfrac{E}{t} = \dfrac{3 \times 10^6}{1} = 3 \times 10^6 = 3 \text{ MW}$

(b) Efficiency $= \dfrac{\text{useful energy output}}{\text{total energy input}} \times 100\%$

$75\% = \dfrac{3 \times 10^6}{E_{input}} \times 100\%$

$E_{input} = \dfrac{3 \times 10^6}{75\%} \times 100\% = 4 \times 10^6 = 4 \text{ MJ}$

i.e. energy input per second is 4 MJ.
(c) In 1 s the total energy input equals the change in gravitational energy of the falling water.
$E_p = mgh$
$4 \times 10^6 = m \times 10 \times 100$
$m = 4000 \text{ kg}$
i.e. mass of water per second is 4000 kg.
(d) Twenty-five per cent of the energy input was changed into heat and sound in the power station.

Useful and useless energy

Energy cannot be created or destroyed, it is simply changed from one form to another. There is always the same amount of energy, although it may be in a number of different forms after the energy change has taken place. However, less of the energy after the change is 'useful' – the rest being in a form or forms that cannot easily be used. Energies, such as heat, light and sound, which cannot easily be used again are said to be **degraded**. The following example provides an illustration of degraded energy.

One joule of electrical energy can produce one joule of heat in a resistor, but this heat cannot reproduce one joule of electrical energy. The electrical energy produced would be less than one joule, as some heat would be 'lost' to the atmosphere and could not be recovered.

6.3 Source to consumer

Generating electricity

In Unit 2 you saw how movement (or a force) was produced when a current-carrying wire was placed in a magnetic field (see page 46). However, the opposite effect is possible. Figure 6.11 shows a coil of wire connected to an oscilloscope being moved through a magnetic field. When the coil is moved up or down through the magnetic field we find that a voltage is produced across the ends of the coil.

The size of this voltage is dependent on:

- The number of turns of wire on the coil – the greater the number of turns the greater the voltage produced.
- The strength of the magnetic field – the stronger the magnetic field, the greater the voltage produced.
- The speed of movement – the faster the coil is moved up or down through the magnetic field, the greater the voltage produced.

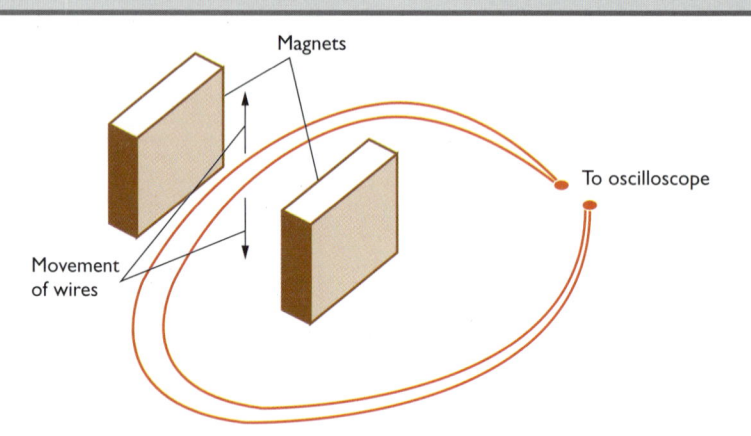

FIGURE 6.11 *Generating electricity by moving a wire through a magnetic field*

A simple generator

In Unit 2 you looked at how an electric motor changed electrical energy into kinetic energy. The motor, however, can be made to work in reverse, i.e. to change kinetic energy into electrical energy. When the motor is used in this way it is acting as a **dynamo**. Figure 6.12 shows an 'electric motor' being used to generate electricity.

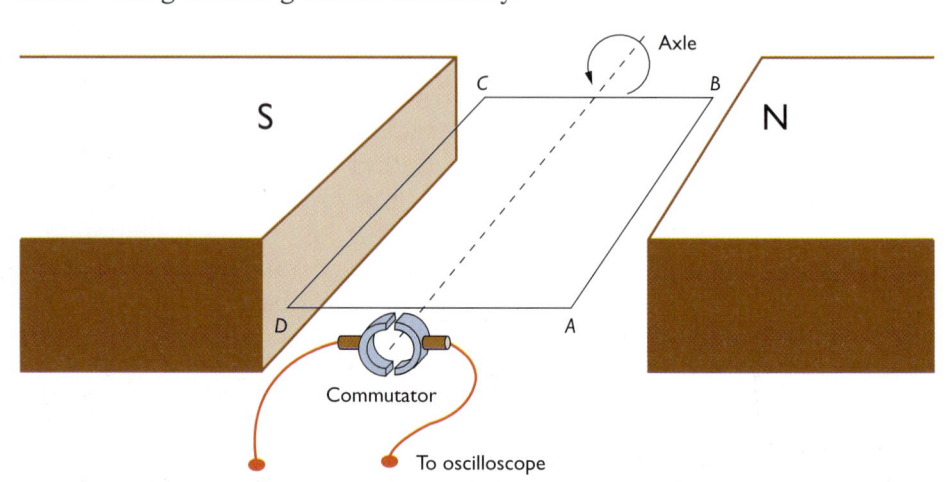

FIGURE 6.12 *A dynamo is an electric motor in 'reverse'*

energy matters 6

Generation of a.c.

Alternating current (a.c.) can be produced by using slip rings which rotate with the coil, as shown in figure 6.13 (a). The slip rings ensure one brush is always connected to one side of the coil whether it is moving up or down through the magnetic field. Figure 6.13 (b) shows the output from the generator and figure 6.13 (c) shows the coil at various positions as it makes one revolution. As the coil rotates, the right-hand side, AB, and the left-hand side, CD, of the coil move through the magnetic field. The magnetic field through the coil changes and a voltage is produced. When the coil is in the vertical position, there is no change in the magnetic field through the coil and so there is no voltage. When the coil moves through the vertical position, the voltage across the coil is now in the opposite direction as the direction of motion has changed, since AB is now moving down and CD is moving up. The direction of the voltage changes each time the coil rotates through half a revolution, i.e. alternating current is produced. This type of generator is often called an **alternator**.

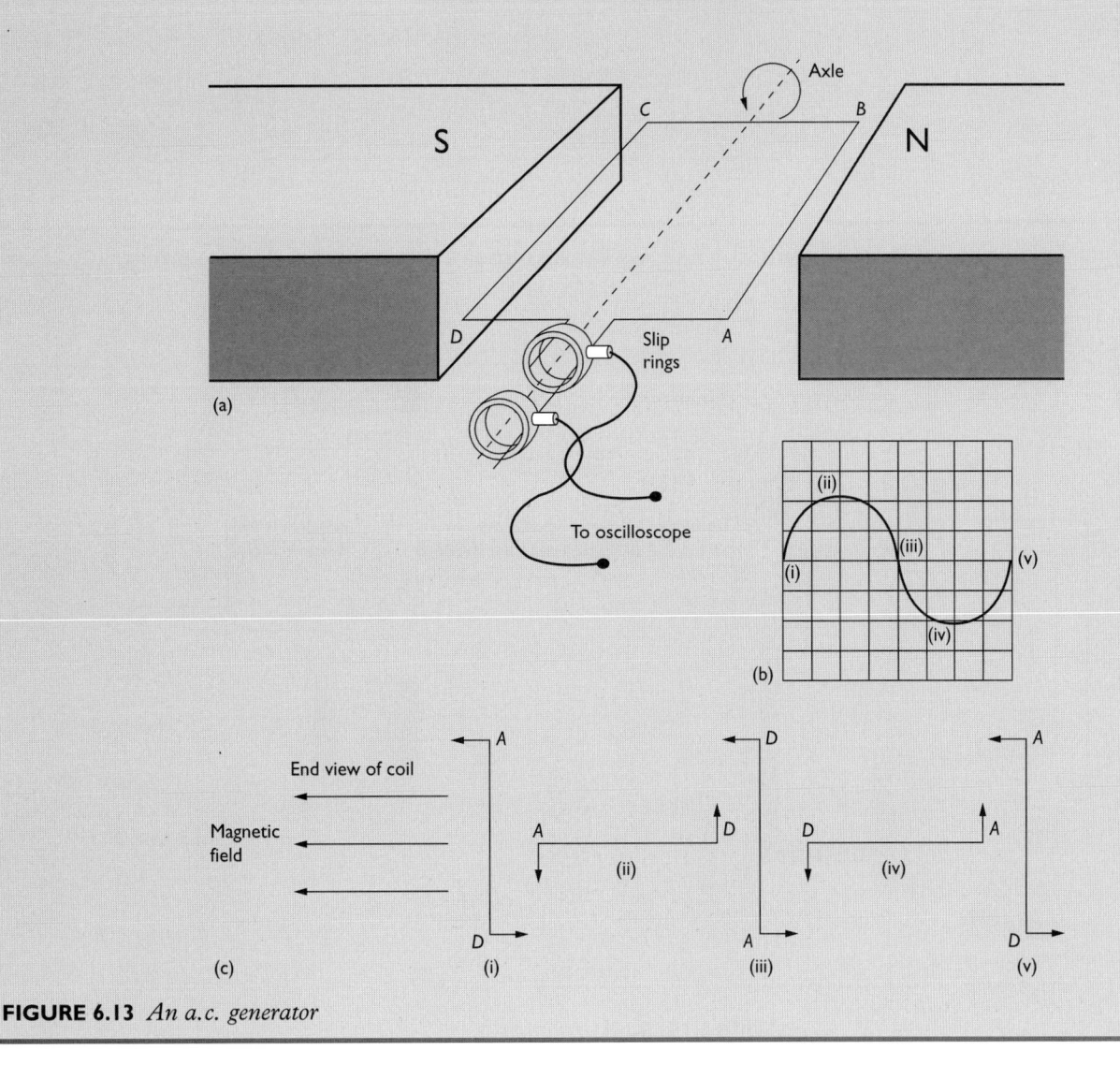

FIGURE 6.13 *An a.c. generator*

147

standard grade physics

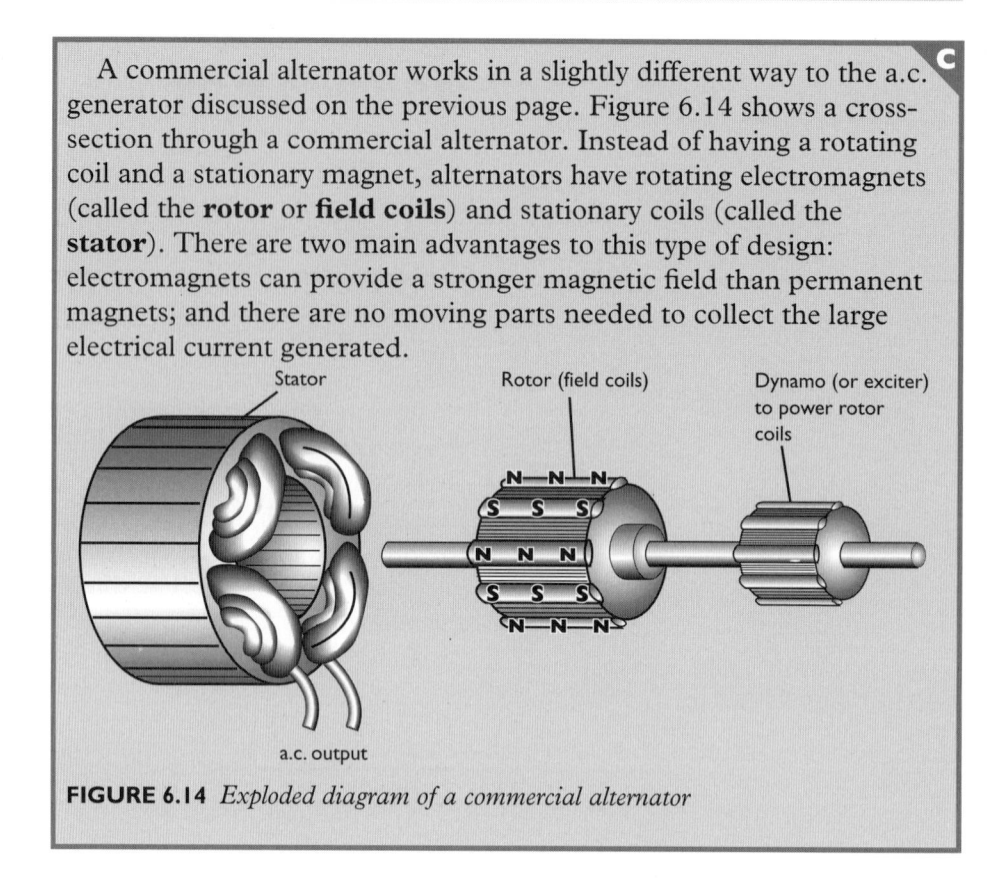

A commercial alternator works in a slightly different way to the a.c. generator discussed on the previous page. Figure 6.14 shows a cross-section through a commercial alternator. Instead of having a rotating coil and a stationary magnet, alternators have rotating electromagnets (called the **rotor** or **field coils**) and stationary coils (called the **stator**). There are two main advantages to this type of design: electromagnets can provide a stronger magnetic field than permanent magnets; and there are no moving parts needed to collect the large electrical current generated.

FIGURE 6.14 *Exploded diagram of a commercial alternator*

Figure 6.15 shows the layout of a conventional power station.

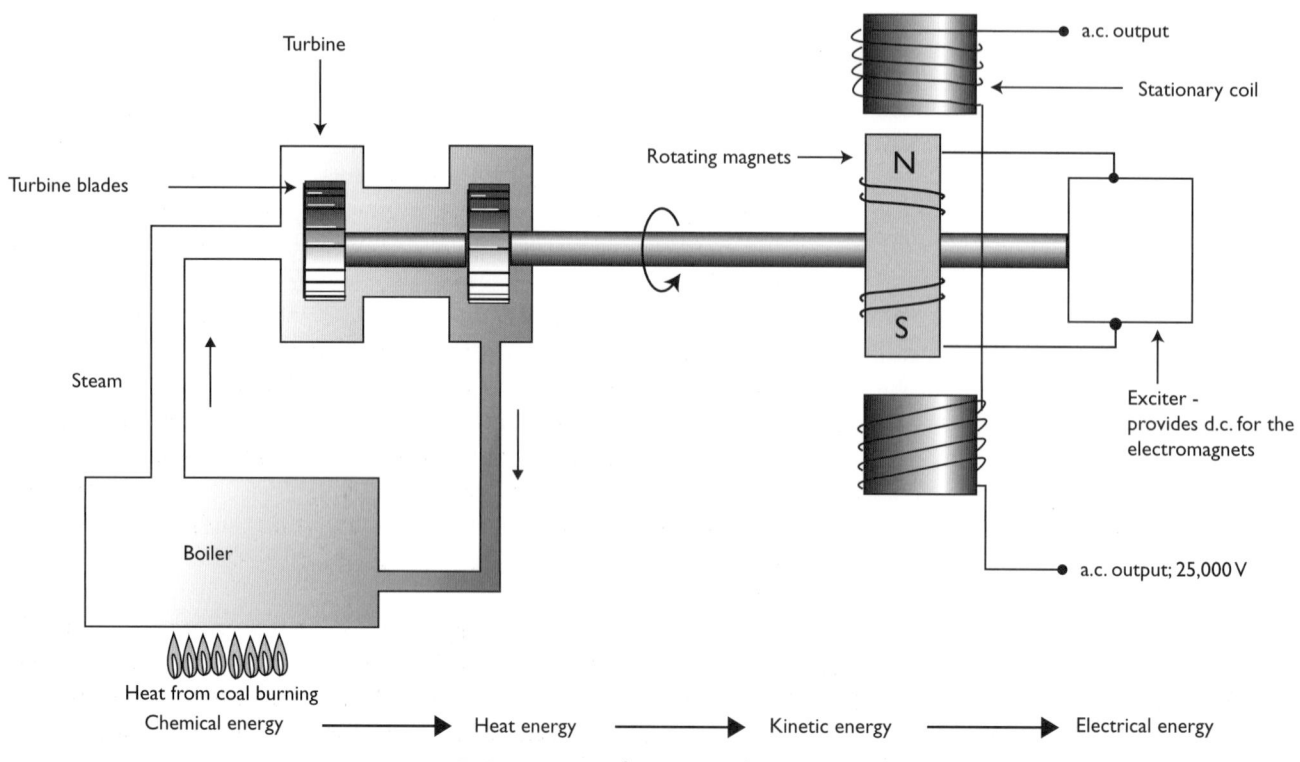

Chemical energy ⟶ Heat energy ⟶ Kinetic energy ⟶ Electrical energy

FIGURE 6.15 *A power station*

energy matters 6

Transmitting electrical energy

Figure 6.16 shows how electricity, generated at a power station, is distributed through the National Grid transmission system to our homes.

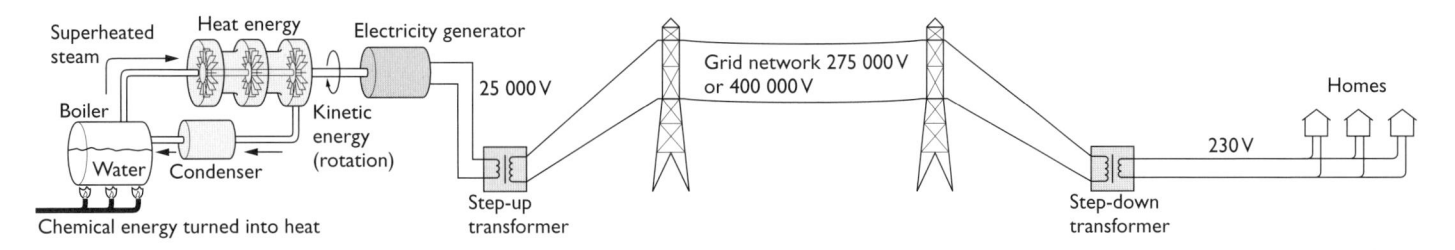

FIGURE 6.16 *Power transmission and distribution*

The generator at the power station produces electricity at 25 000 volts, but for efficient transmission over long distances this is increased by a (step-up) transformer to 275 000 volts (or 400 000 volts for the National Grid system). At the end of the transmission lines a (step-down) transformer reduces it for distribution to consumers.

Model power line

Figure 6.17 shows an experiment to demonstrate why transformers are required in the transmission of electricity.

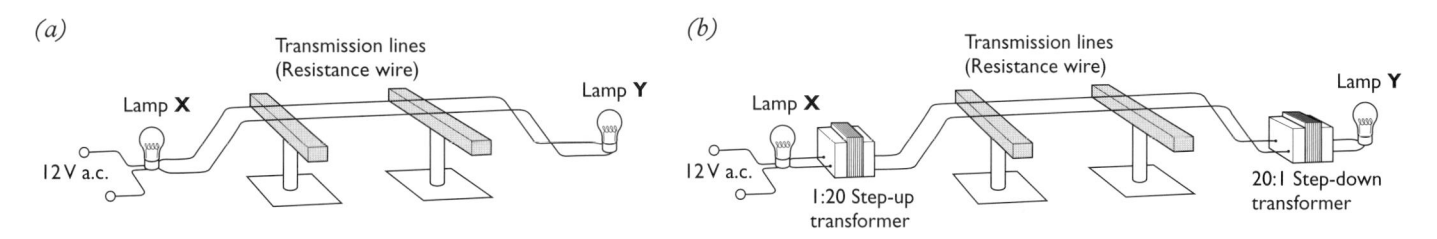

FIGURE 6.17 *Figures (a) and (b) show power transmitted without and with transformers*

In figure 6.17 (a) power is transmitted directly along the transmission lines. Lamp Y is less brightly lit than lamp X. This is due to some of the electrical energy being changed to heat in the transmission lines. The amount of energy changed to heat every second (the power loss) is given by $P = I^2R$ where I is the current through the transmission line and R is the total resistance of the transmission lines.

In figure 6.17 (b) the voltage is increased (stepped up) before transmission, and reduced (stepped down) at the far end of the transmission lines. In this case, lamp Y is much brighter, indicating that much less heat energy has been produced in the transmission lines.

When electrical power is passed along transmission lines, it is important to keep the power loss as low as possible. Since the power loss from the transmission lines = I^2R, the current through the transmission lines, and the resistance of the transmission lines, should both be as low as possible.

In practice there is a limit to how low the resistance of the transmission lines can be economically made. However, transformers make it possible to reduce the size of the current through the transmission lines by increasing the voltage. Transformers are therefore essential when electricity is to be passed over large distances.

6 standard grade physics

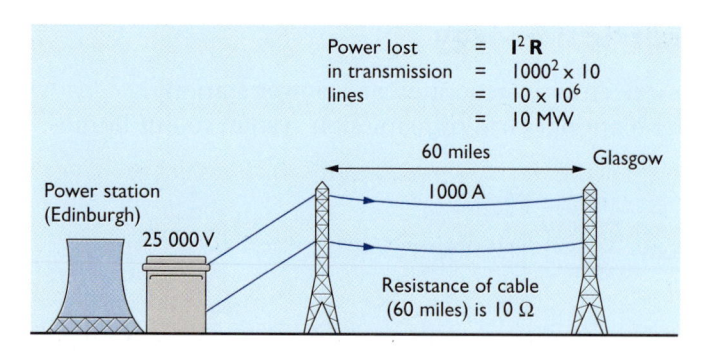

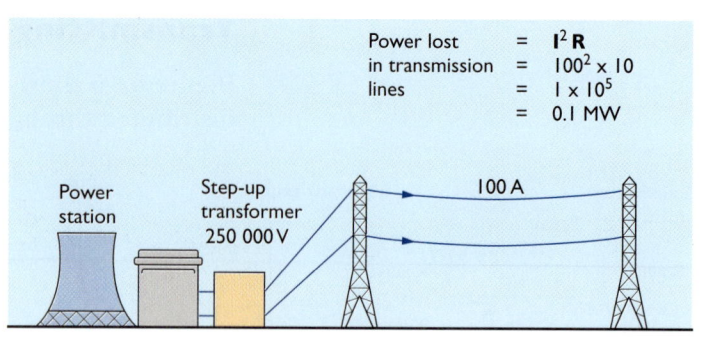

FIGURE 6.18 *Power loss in transmission lines can be greatly reduced by the use of transformers*

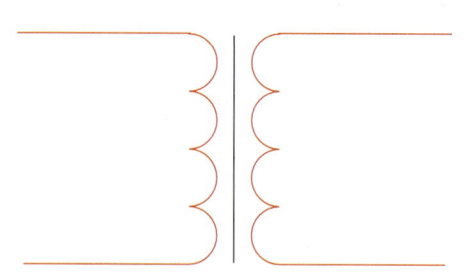

FIGURE 6.19 *Circuit symbol for a transformer*

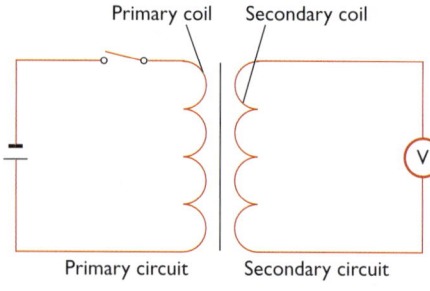

FIGURE 6.20 *A transformer circuit*

The transformer

A transformer consists of two separate coils of wire wound on the same iron core. The circuit symbol for a transformer is shown in figure 6.19. The straight line between the coils is the iron core.

Figure 6.20 shows a transformer connected to a switch and a battery. When the switch is closed, a current passes through the primary coil. This results in a magnetic field in the primary coil which rapidly builds up through both sets of coils, since they are joined by the iron core. This gives a changing magnetic field in the secondary coil and so a voltage is produced.

When the current in the primary circuit is steady, there is no change in the magnetic field and no voltage is produced in the secondary circuit. However, when the switch is opened, the primary current is switched off and the magnetic field around both the primary and secondary coils rapidly collapses (disappears). This changing magnetic field through the secondary circuit results in a voltage being produced but in the opposite direction. Removing the iron core through the coils decreases the effect, since the iron core concentrates the magnetic field through the coils. With a d.c. supply connected to the primary coil, a changing magnetic field can only be obtained by opening and closing the switch. However, a more practical way of obtaining a changing magnetic field is to connect the primary coil to an a.c. supply, since the current is always changing in size and direction. Transformers, therefore, only work on a.c.

A transformer is used to investigate the relationship between the alternating voltages at the primary and secondary coils and the number of turns on the primary and secondary coils.

Primary turns (Np)	Secondary turns (Ns)	$\frac{N_s}{N_p}$	Primary voltage in volts (Vp)	Secondary voltage in volts (Vs)	$\frac{V_s}{V_p}$
125	500	4	2	8	4
500	125	0.25	2	0.5	0.25
125	625	5	2	10	5
500	500	1	2	2	1
625	125	0.2	2	0.4	0.2

TABLE 6.3

From the results in table 6.3 we see that:

$$\frac{N_s}{N_p} = \frac{V_s}{V_p}$$

In a step-up transformer: secondary turns are more than the primary turns, i.e. $N_s > N_p$ thus $V_s > V_p$.

In a step-down transformer: secondary turns are less than the primary turns, i.e. $N_s < N_p$ thus $V_s < V_p$.

In real transformers, there are some energy losses. These are due to:

- The heating effect of the current in the coils. The primary and secondary coils of a transformer are made up of a long length of wire. Although the wire is made of a good conductor, the coils still have a resistance. This means that when a current passes through the coils, some of the electrical energy is changed into heat.
- The iron core is continually being magnetised and demagnetised, and this results in heat being produced.
- The transformer vibrates as a result of the magnetising and demagnetising of the iron core and so sound is produced.
- Some of the magnetic field produced by the primary coil 'leaks' from the iron core and so does not pass through the secondary coil. This results in a smaller voltage being produced at the secondary coil.

Since the energy losses in transformers are normally very small (about 5 per cent to heat, sound and leakage) it is convenient when doing problems to consider the transformer is 100 per cent efficient, i.e. an ideal transformer.

For an **ideal** transformer, all the power at the primary is transferred to the secondary.

Therefore:

$$\text{input power} = \text{output power}$$

$$I_p \times V_p = I_s \times V_s$$

$$\text{i.e. } \frac{V_s}{V_p} = \frac{I_p}{I_s}$$

Hence:

$$\frac{V_s}{V_p} = \frac{N_s}{N_p} = \frac{I_p}{I_s}$$

Example: An ideal transformer steps up the voltage from 6 V a.c. to 12 V a.c. If the secondary coil has 100 turns, how many turns has the primary?

Solution:

$$\frac{N_p}{N_s} = \frac{V_p}{V_s}$$

$$\frac{N_p}{100} = \frac{6}{12}$$

$$N_p = 0.5 \times 100 = 50 \text{ turns}$$

Example: An ideal transformer has 400 primary turns and 10 secondary turns. If the current in the primary coil is 10 mA, what will the current in the secondary coil be?
Solution:

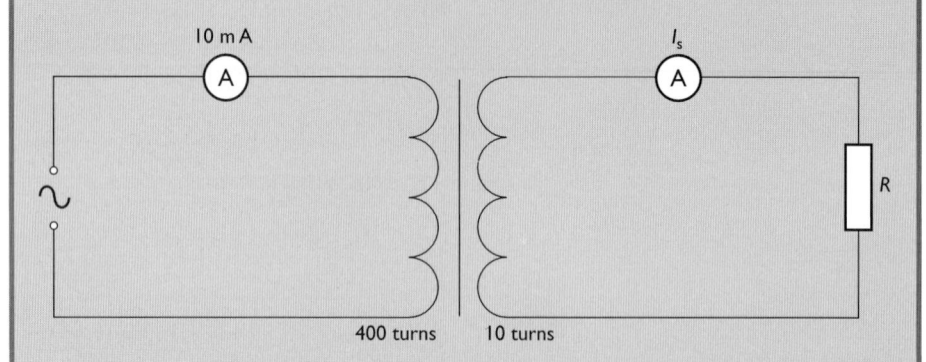

FIGURE 6.21 *Circuit diagram*

$$\frac{N_s}{N_p} = \frac{I_p}{I_s}$$

$$\frac{10}{400} = \frac{0.01}{I_s}$$

$$\frac{1}{40} = \frac{0.01}{I_s}$$

$$I_s = 0.01 \times 40$$
$$I_s = 0.4 \text{ A}$$

Example: A 230 V mains transformer is 95 per cent efficient for the figures shown in figure 6.22. The current in the primary coil is 0.1 A and the transformer gives an output voltage of 12 V.

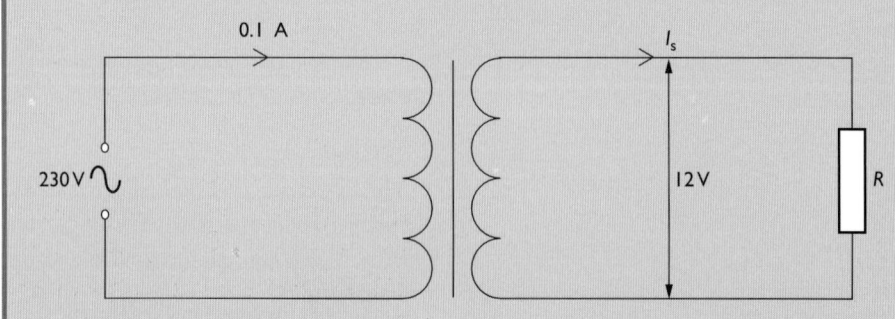

FIGURE 6.22 *Circuit diagram*

For the transformer, calculate the:
(a) power input
(b) power output
(c) current through the resistor.

energy matters 6

> *Solution:* (a) Power input to transformer $= IV = 230 \times 0.1 = 23$ W
>
> (b) Efficiency $= \dfrac{\text{useful power output}}{\text{total power input}} \times 100\%$
>
> $95\% = \dfrac{\text{power output}}{23} \times 100\%$
>
> power output $= \dfrac{95\%}{100\%} \times 23 = 21.85$ W
>
> (c) Power output $= IV$
> $21.85 = 12 \times I$
> $I = \dfrac{21.85}{12} = 1.8$ A

6.4 *Heat in the home*

Heat and temperature

The terms heat and temperature are very often confused. Heat, just like light and sound, is a form of energy and is measured in joules (J). Temperature is a measure of how hot a substance is, and is measured in degrees Celsius (°C). The discussion below illustrates the difference between them.

Two pupils, Jack and Jean, each heat water in identical kettles. Jack heats 0.3 kg of water for one minute, while Jean heats 0.6 kg of water for one minute. During this time the kettles both supplied the same amount of heat to the water, but the temperature of Jack's water was higher than that of Jean's.

Heat transfer

Heat always moves from a hot substance to the cooler surroundings. There are three possible ways in which it can move: **conduction**, **convection** and **radiation**.

Conduction
- Heat is transferred through a solid material by conduction. The particles making up the solid cannot change their position, but pass the heat from particle to particle.
- Heat moves from a high temperature to a low temperature.
- Materials which allow heat to move easily through them are called **conductors** while materials which do not allow heat to move through them easily are called **insulators**. Metals are the best conductors while liquids and gases are good insulators (poor conductors).

Convection
- Convection occurs in liquids and gases. Heat is transferred by the movement of the heated particles making up the liquid or gas. The

153

heated fluid (liquid or gas) becomes less dense and rises, so cold fluid falls to take its place, i.e. convection currents are set up.
- Convection cannot take place in a solid.
- Many heat insulators contain trapped air, e.g. cotton wool, felt, woollen clothes. Convection cannot take place because the air is trapped and cannot move. Also, air is a non-metal, so it is a poor conductor of heat.

Radiation
- Radiation travels in straight lines until absorbed by an object. It can travel through a vacuum (the Earth is heated by radiation from the Sun).
- All hot materials radiate heat energy.

Heat loss and temperature difference

David and Mary decided to investigate how heat loss depended on the temperature of the surroundings. They heated two identical metal blocks to 100°C. One block was placed into cold water and the other into warm water. The temperature of each block was measured every minute for ten minutes. The results were plotted on graph paper, as shown in figure 6.23.

From their investigation they concluded that the metal block in the cold water lost more heat energy than the block in the warm water.

The amount of heat energy lost every second depends on the difference in temperature between an object and its surroundings. The greater the difference in temperature, the greater the loss of heat energy in one second. The smaller the difference in temperature, the smaller the loss of heat energy in one second.

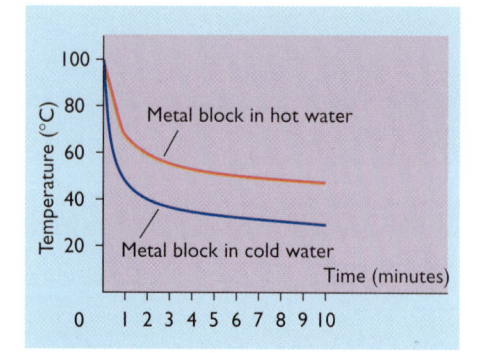

FIGURE 6.23 *Graphs of temperature against time for both metal blocks*

Heat loss from houses

FIGURE 6.24 *Main heat losses from a house*

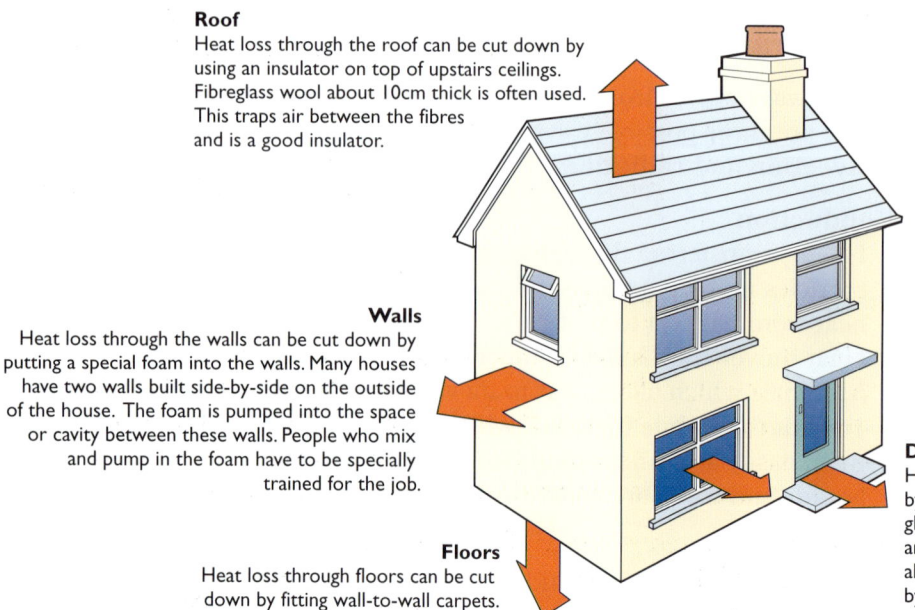

Figure 6.24 shows the main heat losses from a house. Such heat losses can be reduced by insulation.

Roof
Heat loss through the roof can be cut down by using an insulator on top of upstairs ceilings. Fibreglass wool about 10cm thick is often used. This traps air between the fibres and is a good insulator.

Walls
Heat loss through the walls can be cut down by putting a special foam into the walls. Many houses have two walls built side-by-side on the outside of the house. The foam is pumped into the space or cavity between these walls. People who mix and pump in the foam have to be specially trained for the job.

Floors
Heat loss through floors can be cut down by fitting wall-to-wall carpets.

Doors and windows
Heat loss through the windows can be cut down by fitting an extra pane of glass. This is called double glazing. The two panes are a few millimetres apart and trap a thin layer of air. Curtains (when closed) also help to cut heat loss. Draughts can be stopped by sealing doors and windows.

energy matters 6

In most houses, hot water is stored in a large copper tank. If the tank is not insulated, a great deal of heat will be lost by convection. This is because the temperature of the hot water is usually about 60°C, while the temperature of the surrounding air is about 18°C.

Draughts are a very obvious and uncomfortable sign of a badly insulated house. Wherever you can feel cold air coming in, warm air is rushing out.

More heat energy is lost through the walls of an average uninsulated house than by any other route. However, effective wall insulation can reduce this heat loss by up to two-thirds. The floors of your house can also be insulated and the windows double- or triple-glazed, while insulating the loft of your house can cut as much as 20 per cent off your energy bill.

Changing temperature

When you want to make a hot drink, you put some water in the kettle and switch it on. The water will get hot as a result of the heat energy supplied by the kettle. However, the amount of heat energy required to warm the water depends on:

- the temperature rise – more energy is needed for a larger temperature rise;
- the mass of the water – more energy is needed for a greater mass of water.

Example: It requires 20 900 J of energy to increase the temperature of 0.5 kg of water by 10°C.

(a) How much energy is required to increase the temperature of 0.5 kg of water by 20°C?

(b) How much energy is required to increase the temperature of 1 kg of water by 40°C?

Solution: (a) It takes 20 900 J to heat up 0.5 kg of water by 10°C, so it will take twice as much energy to heat 0.5 kg by 20°C. Therefore, it takes 41 800 J to heat up 0.5 kg of water by 20°C.

(b) It takes 20 900 J to heat up 0.5 kg of water by 10°C. So it takes 41 800 J to heat up 1 kg of water by 10°C. Therefore, it takes 167 200 J to heat up 1 kg of water by 40°C.

Specific heat capacity

So far we have only considered heating the same substance, namely water. However, if you were to heat equal masses of water and copper with the same quantity of heat energy, then you would find that the copper would have a much higher rise in temperature. The heat energy needed to change the temperature of a substance depends on:

- the change in temperature of the material (ΔT);
- the mass of the material (m);
- the type of material (specific heat capacity of the material).

standard grade physics

The **specific heat capacity** of a substance is the amount of energy required to change the temperature of 1 kg of the substance by 1°C. The units of specific heat capacity are joules per kilogram per degree Celsius (J/kg°C).

Water has a specific heat capacity of 4180 joules per kilogram per degree celsius (4180 J/kg°C). This means that it takes 4180 joules of heat energy to change the temperature of 1 kg of water by 1°C.

It would take 4180 J to heat up 1 kg of water by 1°C, so it would take 16 720 J to heat up 4 kg of water by 1°C and 83 600 J to heat up 4 kg of water by 5°C.

This can be put in the form of an equation:

$$E_h = c \times m \times \Delta T$$

where E_h = energy required to change the temperature of the substance (J)
c = specific heat capacity of substance (J/kg°C)
m = mass of substance (kg)
ΔT = change in temperature of substance (°C)

Table 6.4 shows the specific heat capacities of some substances.

Material	Specific heat capacity (J/kg°C)	Material	Specific heat capacity (J/kg°C)
Water	4180	Sea water	3900
Lead	128	Ice	2100
Aluminium	902	Concrete	800
Alcohol	2350	Glass	500
Steel	500	Copper	386

TABLE 6.4

Example: How much energy is required to heat 0.2 kg of water from 20°C to 50°C?
Solution:
$E_h = cm\Delta T$
$E_h = 4180 \times 0.2 \times (50 - 20)$
$E_h = 4180 \times 0.2 \times 30$
$E_h = 25\ 080$ J

Example: A night-storage heater contains 70 kg of concrete bricks. How much heat energy is released by the bricks when they cool from 70°C to 20°C?
Solution:
$E_h = cm\Delta T$
$E_h = 800 \times 70 \times (70 - 20)$
$E_h = 800 \times 70 \times 50$
$E_h = 2\ 800\ 000$ J

energy matters 6

Heat problems

Although energy can be changed from one form to another, the total amount remains unchanged. This is the **principle of conservation of energy** – an electric heater converts electrical energy into an equal amount of heat energy.

Due to conduction, convection and radiation, some of the heat energy supplied will be transferred ('lost') to the surroundings. This means that a substance being heated will absorb (take in) less energy than was supplied by the heater.

Energy supplied = energy absorbed + energy transferred to the surroundings

In most heat problems it is assumed that no energy is transferred to the surroundings, so:

Energy supplied (by heater) = energy absorbed (by the material)

Example: An immersion heater is used to heat 0.4 kg of water from 16°C to 34°C in a well-insulated cup. If the time taken to do this is ten minutes, calculate the power rating of the heater.
Solution:
$$E_h = cm\Delta T = 4180 \times 0.4 \times (34 - 16)$$
$$E_h = 4180 \times 0.4 \times 18$$
$$E_h = 30\,096\text{ J}$$
$$P = \frac{E}{t} = \frac{30\,096}{600} = 50.2\text{ W}$$

Example: A deep-fat fryer is used to heat 800 g of cooking oil of specific heat capacity 3000 J/kg°C from 20°C to 140°C, in a time of 180 s.
(a) Calculate the power rating of the deep-fat fryer.
(b) Find the current in the element of the deep-fat fryer, if it operates from 230 V mains.
Solution:
(a) $E_h = cm\Delta T = 3000 \times 0.8 \times (140 - 20)$
$E_h = 3000 \times 0.8 \times 120 = 288\,000\text{ J}$
$$P = \frac{E}{t} = \frac{288\,000}{180} = 1600\text{ W}$$

(b) $P = IV$
$1600 = I \times 230$
$$I = \frac{1600}{230} = 6.96\text{ A}$$

Specific latent heat

When cold water in a kettle is heated, its temperature rises until the water starts to boil at 100°C. Further heating of the water no longer produces a rise in the temperature of the water, but steam at 100°C is produced (i.e. the heat energy supplied by the kettle is now being used to change water

157

at 100°C into steam at 100°C). The energy required to change 1 kg of a liquid at its boiling point into 1 kg of vapour is called the **specific latent heat of vaporisation**. The word **latent** means 'hidden' and refers to the fact that the temperature does not rise, while the heat energy supplied to it seems to have disappeared.

When ice at its melting point of 0°C is heated, it turns into water at 0°C. Heat energy is required to change the ice to water at a constant temperature. The energy required to change 1 kg of a solid at its melting point into 1 kg of liquid is called the **specific latent heat of fusion**.

The three **states** of matter are solid, liquid and gas. Whenever a substance changes state, latent heat energy is required.

When a substance changes from a solid to a liquid, or a liquid to a gas, energy is needed to break down the force (or bond) holding the particles together and to push the particles further apart.

Specific latent heat of fusion
The energy required to change 1 kg from solid at its melting point to liquid without a change in temperature.

Specific latent heat of vaporisation
The energy required to change 1 kg from liquid at its boiling point to gas without a change in temperature.

When a substance changes state from solid to liquid or liquid to gas, latent heat is absorbed (taken in). When a substance changes state from gas to liquid or liquid to solid, latent heat is released (given out).

> The symbol for specific latent heat is l, and it is measured in J/kg. The specific latent heat of vaporisation is the heat energy required to change 1 kg of liquid to vapour without temperature change.

For a material with a specific latent heat of vaporisation l:

- to change 1 kg of liquid to gas at constant temperature requires l J
- to change m kg of liquid to gas at constant temperature requires $m \times l$ J, i.e. $E_h = ml$.

The specific latent heat of fusion is the heat energy required to change 1 kg of solid to 1 kg of liquid without temperature change, i.e. $E_h = ml$.

> Energy required to change state = mass × specific latent heat
> $E_h = ml$

where E_h = energy required to change state (J), m = mass which changed state (kg), l = specific latent heat (J/kg).

> **Example:** A 36 W electric heater is used to bring 0.5 kg of a liquid to its boiling point. The heater is left on for a further 300 s. If the specific latent heat of vaporisation of the liquid is 200 000 J/kg, what is the mass of liquid boiled off?

Solution:

$$P = \frac{E}{t} \qquad 36 = \frac{E}{300} \qquad E = 36 \times 300 = 10\,800\,J$$

$$E_h = ml$$

$$10\,800 = m \times 200\,000$$

$$m = \frac{10\,800}{200\,000} = 0.054\,kg$$

Mass of liquid boiled off is 0.054 kg.

Specific latent heat of vaporisation of water

The specific latent heat of vaporisation of water can be measured using the apparatus shown in figure 6.25. The lid of the kettle is left off so that the automatic cut-out does not work.

Mass of water changed to steam = 0.1 kg
Power rating of kettle = 2000 W
Time of supply = 116 s

$$\text{Energy supplied by heater} = P \times t = 2000 \times 116 = 232\,000\,J$$

$$\text{Using } E_h = ml$$

$$232\,000 = 0.1 l$$

$$l = 2\,320\,000\,J/kg$$

In practice, energy is lost to the surroundings, and so the above result is only an estimate. The accepted value for the specific latent heat of vaporisation of water is 2 260 000 J/kg. The difference between the experimental result and the accepted value can be explained as:

- Not all of the energy supplied by the heater element is absorbed by the water. Some of it is 'lost' in heating up the air around the kettle, which means that more energy is supplied to produce 0.1 kg of steam and so the value for l is too large.

- Some of the steam condensed on the cooler parts of the kettle and fell back in to be reheated – this results in more energy being supplied to produce 0.1 kg of steam and this makes the value for l too large.

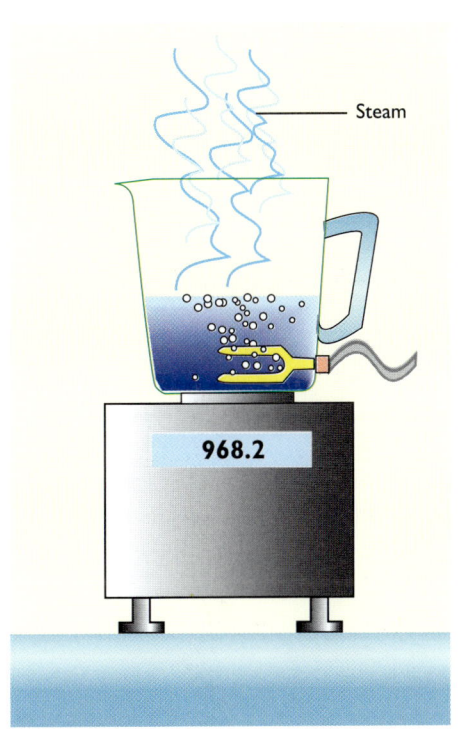

FIGURE 6.25 *An experiment to obtain a value for the specific latent heat of vaporisation of water*

Cooling by evaporation

Lindsey went to the swimming pool. While standing out of the water just after swimming, she felt cold, even though before entering the water she was quite warm.

We have all experienced this effect – when you are dry you feel quite warm, but if you are wet in the same location, you quickly feel cold. This is due to the water evaporating off your body. For the water to evaporate, it requires energy which it takes from your skin and so you feel cold.

6 standard grade physics

Refrigerator

The cooling effect of an evaporating liquid is used by a refrigerator. The cooling liquid is called **freon**, which boils at a very low temperature (about −30°C). When liquid freon reaches the freezer box, it expands rapidly through a small valve and evaporates. To evaporate, the liquid freon takes in heat energy from the freezer compartment. The freezer compartment, having lost heat, becomes cold. The warmed freon gas enters the compressor which compresses it and pumps it to the back of the refrigerator, where it cools and turns back into a liquid. During the cooling stage, the freon releases heat energy into the room from the large black fins at the back of the refrigerator which help the freon to cool to room temperature. The freon is then allowed to expand and its temperature falls. The freon is now ready to pass through the ice box to start the cooling cycle again.

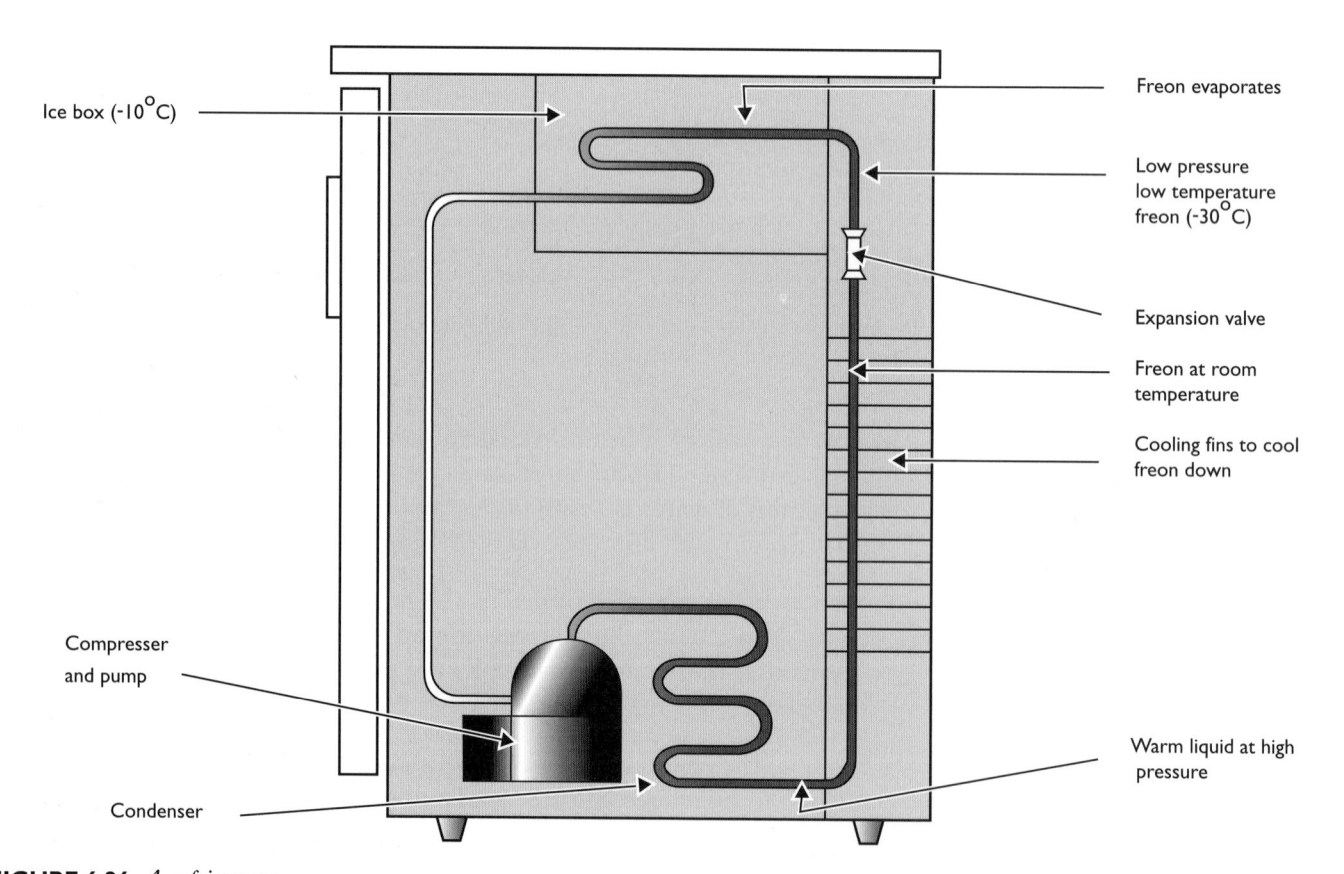

FIGURE 6.26 *A refrigerator*

LEARNING OUTCOMES

After studying this chapter you should be able to:

Section 6.1

1. State that fossil fuels are at present the main sources of energy.

2. State that the reserves of fossil fuels are finite.

3. Explain one means of conserving energy related to the use of energy in industry, in the home and in transport.

4. Carry out calculations relating to energy supply and demand.

5. Classify renewable and non-renewable sources of energy.

6. Explain the advantages and disadvantages associated with at least three renewable energy sources. **Credit**

Section 6.2

1. Identify from a diagram the energy transformation at each stage of a thermal power station; a hydroelectric power station; a nuclear power station.

2. State that radioactive waste is produced by nuclear reactors.

3. Carry out calculations on energy transformation to include gravitational potential energy.

4. Describe the principle, and give the advantages of, a pumped hydroelectric scheme.

5. Compare the energy output from equal masses of coal and nuclear fuel. **Credit**

6. Carry out calculations involving efficiency of energy transformation. **Credit**

7. State that energy is degraded in energy transformation. **Credit**

8. Explain in simple terms a chain reaction. **Credit**

Section 6.3

1. Identify circumstances in which a voltage will be induced in a conductor.

2. Identify on a given diagram the main parts of an a.c. generator.

3. State that transformers are used to change the magnitude of an a.c. voltage.

4. Describe the structure of a transformer.

5. Carry out calculations involving the relationship between V_s, V_p, N_s and N_p.

6. State that high voltages are used in the transmission of electricity to reduce power loss.

7. Describe qualitatively the transmission of electrical energy by the National Grid system.

8. Explain from a diagram how an a.c. generator works. **Credit**

9. State the main differences between a full-size generator and a simple working model. **Credit**

10. State the factors which affect the size of the induced voltage, i.e. field strength, number of turns on the coil, relative speed of magnet and coil. **Credit**

11. Explain why a transformer is not 100 per cent efficient. **Credit**

12. Carry out calculations on transformers involving input and output voltages; turns ratio; primary and secondary currents and efficiency. **Credit**

13. Carry out calculations involving power loss in transmission lines. **Credit**

Section 6.4

1. Use the following terms correctly in context: temperature; heat; Celsius.

2. Describe two ways of reducing heat loss in the home due to conduction; convection; radiation.

3. State that heat loss in a given time depends upon the temperature difference between the inside and the outside of the house.

4. State that the same mass of different materials require different quantities of energy to raise their temperature of unit mass by one degree.

5. Carry out calculations based on practical applications involving heat, mass, specific heat capacity and temperature change.

6. Give examples of applications which involve a change of state, e.g. refrigerator or picnic box cooler.

learning outcomes

7 Use the following terms correctly in context: specific heat capacity; change of state; latent heat of fusion; latent heat of vaporisation.

8 State that a change of state does not involve a change of temperature.

9 State that energy is gained or lost by a substance when its state is changed.

10 Use the principle of conservation of energy to carry out calculations on energy transformations which involve temperature change, e.g. $IVt = E_h = cm\Delta T$. **Credit**

11 Carry out calculations involving specific latent heat. **Credit**

STUDY QUESTIONS

1 Name the fossil fuels. Why are they called 'fossil fuels'?

2 (a) List the following sources of energy under the headings 'renewable' and 'non-renewable': solar; coal; gas; wind; oil; water; biomass.

(b) Explain the difference between renewable and non-renewable energy sources.

3 Give one advantage and one disadvantage of the following sources of energy: wind; solar; water; nuclear.

4 What is the energy change which takes place in:
(a) a coal-fired power station

(b) a hydro electric power station

(c) a nuclear power station?

5 An electric motor is used to lift a mass from the floor. During the lifting, the mass gains 12 J of potential energy. The electrical energy supplied to the motor during the lifting process was 36 J. Calculate the efficiency of the system during the lifting operation.

6 The figure below shows a loop of wire connected to a sensitive voltmeter.

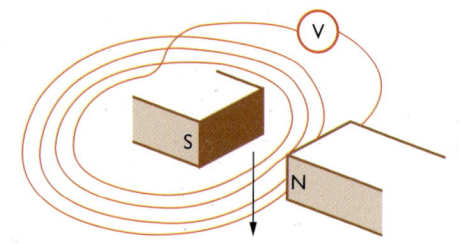

When the loop of wire is moved between the poles of the magnet, as shown, a reading is detected on the voltmeter. What changes could be made to increase the reading on the voltmeter?

7 The following circuit diagram shows an a.c. source connected to the primary coil of a transformer. A lamp is connected to the secondary coil of the transformer.

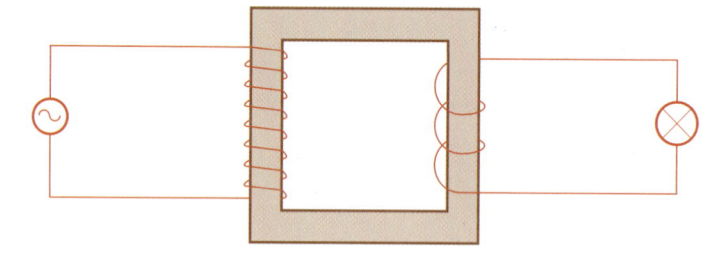

A changing current in the primary circuit produces a changing magnetic field in the primary coil.

(a) The lamp is brightly lit. Is the current in the secondary coil a.c. or d.c.?

(b) The a.c. source is replaced with a d.c. source. Explain the effect this will have on the lamp.

8 Calculate the unknown quantity or quantities for the ideal transformers shown below:

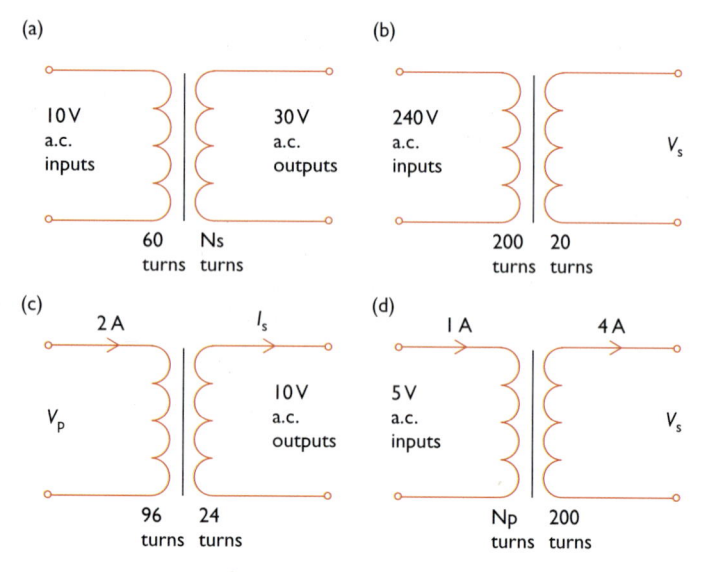

(a)
10 V a.c. inputs
60 turns
N_s turns
30 V a.c. outputs

(b)
240 V a.c. inputs
200 turns
20 turns
V_s

(c)
2 A
V_p
96 turns
I_s
24 turns
10 V a.c. outputs

(d)
1 A
5 V a.c. inputs
N_p turns
4 A
200 turns
V_s

9 A 230 V a.c. supply is connected to the primary circuit of an ideal transformer as shown opposite above. A 115 W lamp is connected across the secondary coil.

162

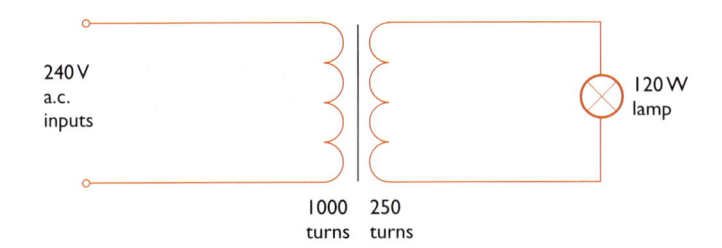

study questions

(a) What is the voltage across the lamp?

(b) Calculate the current passing through the lamp if it is working at its correct power rating.

(c) Calculate the current in the primary circuit.

10 A real transformer is not 100 per cent efficient, but wastes some energy. Suggest some of the causes of this waste of energy.

11 If 5000 J of energy raise the temperature of 2 kg of a liquid by 1°C, how much energy will be required to raise the temperature of:

(a) 4 kg of the liquid by 1°C

(b) 6 kg of the liquid by 1°C

(c) 4 kg of the liquid by 2°C

(d) 8 kg of the liquid by 5°C.

12 How much heat energy is required to increase the temperature of a 0.40 kg aluminium pan from 15°C to 85°C? (The specific heat capacity of aluminium is 902 J/kg°C.)

13 A kettle with a 2000 W element contains 1.2 kg of water. The initial temperature of the water is 20°C. Assuming all the energy is absorbed by the water, find how long it will take to boil the water.

14 A heater operating from a 230 V supply draws a current of 2 A. The heater is used to heat a 3 kg block of aluminium. The heater is switched on for three minutes. (The specific heat capacity of aluminium is 902 J/kg°C.)

(a) How much heat energy was produced in this time?

(b) Calculate the maximum possible rise in the temperature of the aluminium block.

15 (a) How much energy is required to change 2 kg of ice at 0°C into water at the same temperature? (The specific latent heat of fusion of ice is 334 000 J/kg.)

(b) How much energy is required to change 2 kg of steam at 100°C into water at the same temperature? (The specific latent heat of vaporisation of water is 2 260 000 J/kg.)

16 A 50 W heater is used to bring 0.8 kg of water to its boiling point. Calculate the mass of water boiled off if the heater is left on for a further 100 s. (The specific latent heat of vaporisation of water is 2 260 000 J/kg.)

17 (a) The compartment of a refrigerator is kept cool by removing heat. Which of the following changes of state could be used to remove this heat?
A Liquid to gas
B Gas to liquid
C Liquid to solid.

GENERAL KU

(b) Explain why the door and sides of a refrigerator are filled with insulating foam.

GENERAL PS

(c) A jug containing 0.5 kilograms of milk at 20°C is cooled in a refrigerator to 4°C. How much energy is removed from the milk? (Specific heat capacity of milk = 4000 joules per kilogram per degree celsius.)
SEB

GENERAL KU

18 The diagram below shows the percentage of heat lost through various parts of a house. All the remaining heat lost from the house is due to draughts. What percentage of heat is lost due to draughts?
SEB

GENERAL PS

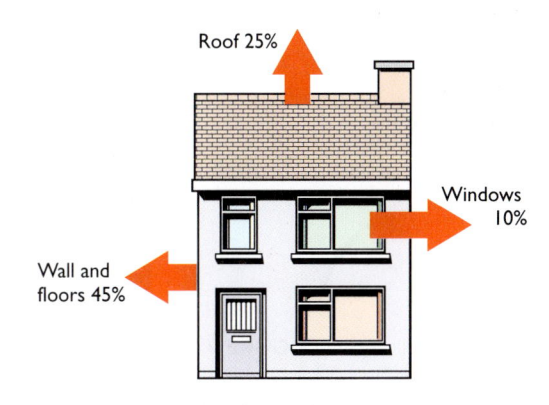

Roof 25%
Windows 10%
Wall and floors 45%

163

7 Space physics

7.1 Space: the final frontier

To boldly go where no one has gone before.
Star Trek opening credits

Neil Armstrong: Houston, Tranquility Base here. The Eagle has landed.

Mission Control: Roger, Tranquility, we copy you on the ground. We're breathing again. Thanks a lot.
Apollo 11 Lunar Mission (1969)

Houston, we have a problem.
Jim Lovell, Commander Apollo 13

FIGURE 7.1

FIGURE 7.2

Since the beginning of time, people have dreamed of going into space and of travelling to different planets. Since 1969 it has been possible to reach the Moon and it is possible that one day people will travel to Mars. But we can observe signals from space without travelling there since we can use telescopes and other instruments to make both measurements and observations.

space physics 7

Seeing afar

Terms used to talk about space have a special meaning:

- A **planet** is an object that orbits a star. It reflects light and produces no energy.
- A **moon** is an object that orbits a planet. It reflects light.
- A **star** is a ball of gases which produces heat and light.
- A **galaxy** is a system of stars and dust that is both spinning and travelling (figure 7.3).
- The **Universe** is the whole of space which can be detected.

We live on a planet called Earth. The Earth is the third of nine planets which orbit around the Sun. The Sun is a star which glows, giving off both heat and light energies.

The nine planets circling around the Sun form the Solar System (figure 7.4). The Solar System is a very small part of thousands of millions of stars which form part of a galaxy called the Milky Way. In turn there are millions of further galaxies which together form the Universe.

FIGURE 7.3

The light years

A light year is the distance travelled by a beam of light in one year. Light years are used to measure distances in space as these are too large to measure in the usual units of distance (e.g. metres or miles).

$$
\begin{aligned}
\text{Speed of light in space} &= 3 \times 10^8 \text{ m/s} \\
\text{Distance travelled by light in one second} &= 3 \times 10^8 \text{ m} \\
\text{Number of seconds in one hour} &= 3600 \\
\text{Number of seconds in one day} &= 3600 \times 24 \\
\text{Number of seconds in one year} &= 3600 \times 24 \times 365 \\
\text{Distance travelled by light in one year} &= 3600 \times 24 \times 365 \times 3 \times 10^8 \text{ m} \\
&= 9.5 \times 10^{15} \text{ m} \\
\text{One light year} &= 9.5 \times 10^{15} \text{ m}
\end{aligned}
$$

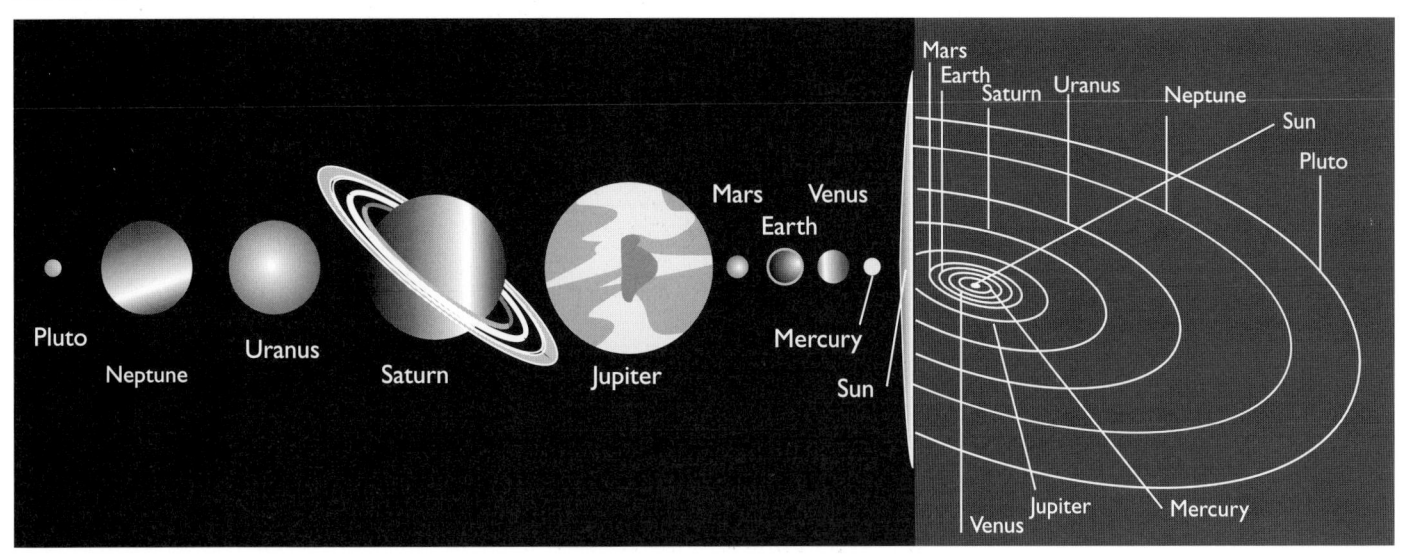

FIGURE 7.4

This distance is far too large for us to understand, so you can see that it is far easier to use the term light year to help us appreciate these large distances.

The table below shows the time for light to travel to us from various points in space, and the distance and light years it covers in that time.

Source	Time taken for light to reach Earth	Distance travelled	Number of light years
Moon	1.2 seconds	3.6×10^8 m	3.8×10^{-8}
Sun	8 minutes	1.4×10^{11} m	1.5×10^{-5}
Nearest star (after the Sun): Proxima Centauri	4.3 years	4.1×10^{16} m	4.3
Other side of our galaxy	100 000 years	9.5×10^{20} m	100 000
Andromeda galaxy (our nearest galaxy)	2 200 000 years	2.1×10^{22} m	2 200 000

Light and its components

In Chapter 3, the different parts of the electromagnetic spectrum were used in health physics. The use of light from lasers was mentioned. It is possible to show that white light consists of a number of different colours. This can be done by passing white light through a glass triangular prism. The white light splits into a **spectrum** of colours. Each colour has a different frequency and wavelength. At one end of the spectrum, as shown in figure 7.5, there is red. It has the longest wavelength. The colours below red are orange, yellow, green, blue and indigo. At the other end there is violet, which has the shortest wavelength. Blue light is refracted more than red. All the colours travel at the same speed, which is the speed of light.

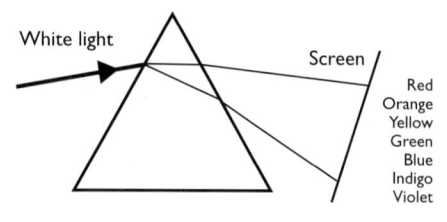

FIGURE 7.5

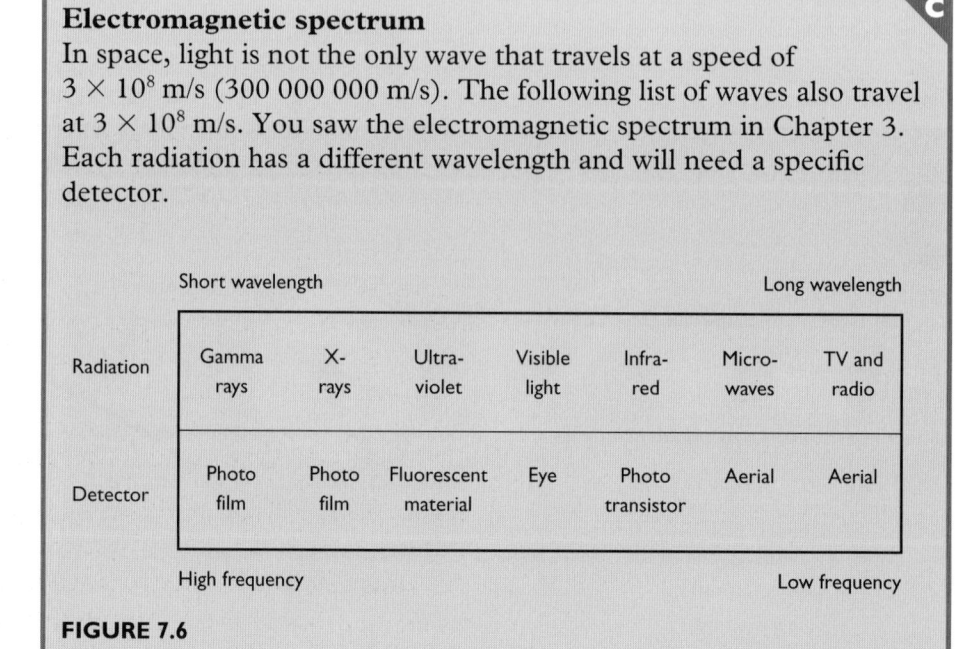

Electromagnetic spectrum

In space, light is not the only wave that travels at a speed of 3×10^8 m/s (300 000 000 m/s). The following list of waves also travel at 3×10^8 m/s. You saw the electromagnetic spectrum in Chapter 3. Each radiation has a different wavelength and will need a specific detector.

Short wavelength → Long wavelength

Radiation	Gamma rays	X-rays	Ultra-violet	Visible light	Infra-red	Micro-waves	TV and radio
Detector	Photo film	Photo film	Fluorescent material	Eye	Photo transistor	Aerial	Aerial

High frequency → Low frequency

FIGURE 7.6

space physics 7

Radiation	Detector
Gamma rays (from radioactive substances such as cobalt-60 or certain rocks or power stations)	Photographic film or Geiger counter
X-rays (from X-ray tubes)	Photographic film
Ultraviolet (Sun or certain lamps)	Fluorescent material
Visible light (Sun)	Eye or photographic film
Infrared (lamps or very hot objects)	Photo transistor
Microwaves (cookers)	Aerial
TV and radio (transmitters)	Aerial

All the information and facts that we know about space have been discovered by detecting signals given out by stars throughout the Universe. These signals have different wavelengths (and frequencies) and so are different members of the electromagnetic spectrum (since they all have a speed of 3×10^8 m/s in air). To pick up some of these different types of signals, different kinds of telescopes are used.

Detecting the signals from space

Radio telescopes
Large unpolished metal dishes, often formed of mesh wire, collect and direct the weak radio waves on to an aerial, which feeds the signals to an amplifier. Radio waves have a large wavelength (0.001 m to 1000 m) and so the collecting surface does not need to be accurately shaped (figure 7.7).

To see fine detail, the opening of a telescope should be as large as possible. Sufficiently large openings cannot be achieved in a single-dish radio telescope. Several small dishes in a line are used. The results are computerised, and openings of up to 5 km diameter can be simulated.

Microwaves
Astronomers can detect radiation from space travelling at the speed of light and having a wavelength of several millimetres. This is called microwave radiation. (The wavelength used in a microwave oven at home is about 12 cm.) This radiation can give astronomers information about the temperature of stars, and also indicates the age of the stars.

Infrared radiation
Infrared radiation arrives at the Earth from objects in space and provides astronomers with another source of information: infrared radiation has a longer wavelength (lower frequency) than visible light and shows up as heat. This is discussed on page 65.

Optical refracting telescopes (light telescopes)

Stars are so far from the Earth that we need to have telescopes to view them. A basic telescope consists of a long tube with a lens at either end. You might like to revise your knowledge of lenses from Chapter 3. The lens you look through is the eyepiece and the other lens is called the objective (figure 7.8).

FIGURE 7.7

167

7 standard grade physics

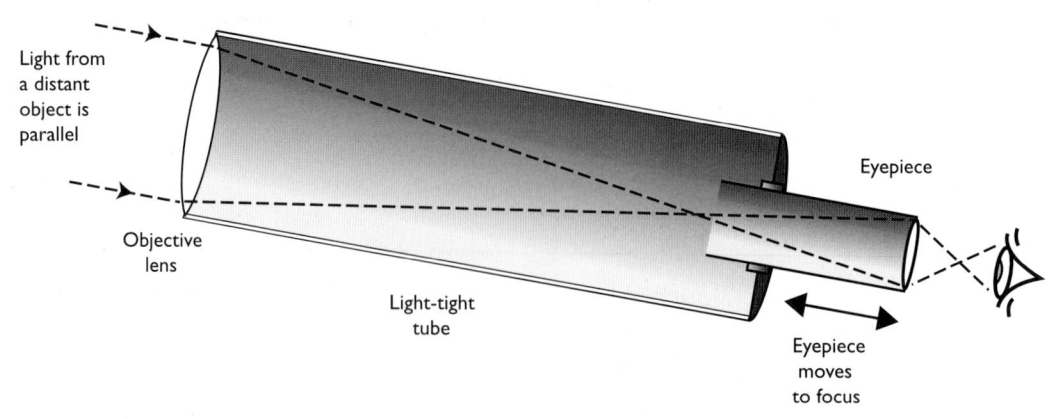

FIGURE 7.8

- The objective lens has a long focal length and the light from a distant star is brought to a focus part way down the tube.
- This image is then magnified by the eyepiece lens. The final image is upside down.

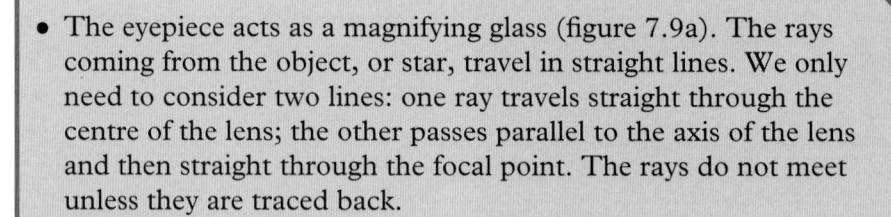

- The eyepiece acts as a magnifying glass (figure 7.9a). The rays coming from the object, or star, travel in straight lines. We only need to consider two lines: one ray travels straight through the centre of the lens; the other passes parallel to the axis of the lens and then straight through the focal point. The rays do not meet unless they are traced back.

The image from the eyepiece is called a virtual image since it cannot be displayed on a screen.

Magnification
The magnification of an image can be found by measuring the height of the image from the eyepiece lens and dividing by the height of image from the objective lens.

$$\text{Magnification} = \frac{\text{height of image from eyepiece lens}}{\text{height of image from objective lens}}$$

If the magnification of the final image is three, the height of the image is three times that of the object.

Image brightness
How clear the final picture of the star is also depends on its brightness. The brightness of the star decreases as its diameter decreases. The broader the star, the brighter it is and so the easier it is to view with an optical telescope.

To get as bright an image as possible, the diameter of the objective lens should be as big as possible, so that as much light as possible can be collected (figure 7.9 b).

(a)

(b)

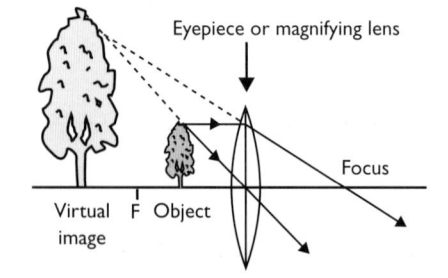

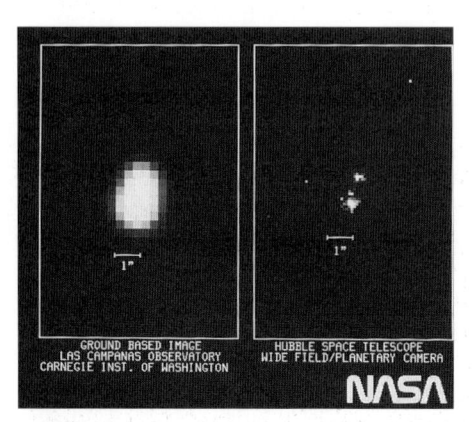

FIGURE 7.9

168

space physics 7

FIGURE 7.10

Temperature of stars

Colour and temperature

When substances are strongly heated, a whole range of wavelengths are usually given out to form a continuous spectrum. The amount of light of each colour depends on the temperature of the substance. If you heat a piece of metal in a very hot flame, then it changes from red hot to white heat to blue heat; that is a change of temperature is shown as a change of colour. As the temperature increases, the wavelength of light emitted becomes smaller.

Astronomers can judge the temperature of the surface of stars by noting the colour of light which the stars give out (figure 7.10). The colour of a star depends on its surface temperature.

Some familiar stars can be placed in order of increasing temperature: Bernard's Star – red; Betelgeuse – orange-red; the Sun – yellow; Rigel – bluish-white.

Type of stars

Astronomers can identify the elements that are present in stars by carefully examining the spectrum produced when the light from a star is viewed through a prism. The spectrum from a star is a line spectrum made up from the spectra (colours) of all the elements present.

Line spectra

When an electric current passes through a gas, it transfers energy to the gas. This energy is then emitted as light of several definite wavelengths (colours). This is called a **line emission spectrum**. Each element has its own particular spectrum by which it may be identified. This enables astronomers to identify elements present in distant stars. Sodium, for example, has two distinct yellow lines which are unique to it. Typical spectra for hydrogen and helium are shown below the spectrum of sodium.

Spectrum

You can identify elements which are present in several simplified stellar spectra as follows:

- The lines from the spectra of some of the known elements should match against some of the lines from the star's spectrum (figure 7.11).
- By examining the spectrum of the unknown star, it is seen to contain hydrogen and helium, since the lines in these spectra coincide with the star's spectrum.

FIGURE 7.11

169

7.2 Jets and rockets

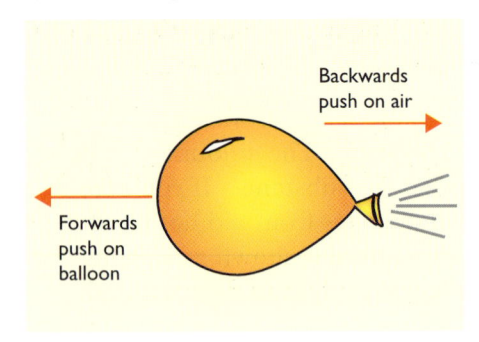

FIGURE 7.12

Jets

Jet engines in aircraft work using physics that we experience in our everyday life. The following are examples of the ideas behind their operation.

- If you push against a wall, the wall pushes you backwards.
- To stand up, you push down.
- In walking, you push your foot backwards but the floor pushes you forwards.
- In swimming, you push the water backwards but you are pushed forward.
- If you release a blown up balloon with its neck open, the air is pushed out the back but the balloon is pushed forward (figure 7.12).

Newton's Third Law

These are all examples of Newton's Third Law of motion which states that

to every action, there is an equal but opposite reaction

Put simply this means that when A pushes B, B pushes A back with the same size of force.

In the example above, the balloon pushes the air to the right, so the air pushes the balloon to the left.

Action: *balloon* pushes *air* to *right*
Reaction: *air* pushes *balloon* to *left*

Newton's Third Law is the principle behind how rockets and jet engines are able to produce motion. In both cases, a high-speed stream of hot gases (produced by burning fuel) is pushed backwards from the vehicle with a large force (figure 7.13) and a force of the same size pushes the rocket forwards.

Action: *vehicle* pushes *hot gases backwards* (downwards)
Reaction: *hot gases* push *vehicle forwards* (upwards)

For the fuel to burn and produce hot gas (exhaust gas), a supply of oxygen is needed. Space rockets carry their own oxygen supply but jet engines use the oxygen in the surrounding air. This means that rockets can fly in space, despite the vacuum (no oxygen), but jet aircraft cannot.

FIGURE 7.13 *An Atlas rocket. The burnt fuel is driven away from the rocket with great force. In turn, the fuel gives an equal and opposite force to the rocket, which drives it into space*

Rockets

In 1926, Robert Goddard, an American physicist, developed a liquid propellant rocket which burned petrol and liquid oxygen. During the Second World War, a great deal of rocket development took place. After the war, the development of rockets concentrated on putting objects into space. Initially the objects were satellites, but eventually humans could be put into space. Modern rockets use liquid hydrogen as the fuel. To support the tremendous rate of fuel-burn required, a large supply of oxygen is needed. This is carried in the form of liquid oxygen.

space physics 7

A simple rocket is shown in figure 7.14. The two liquids mix and burn in the combustion chamber, where the hot gases produced expand rapidly and are forced through the nozzle. These hot gases are pushed downwards and exert an upwards force on the rocket (Newton's Third Law). As long as the force is greater than the weight of the rocket, lift-off can take place.

FIGURE 7.14 *A simple design for a rocket. The rocket carries with it fuel, such as kerosene, and liquid oxygen. These are mixed and burnt in the combustion chamber*

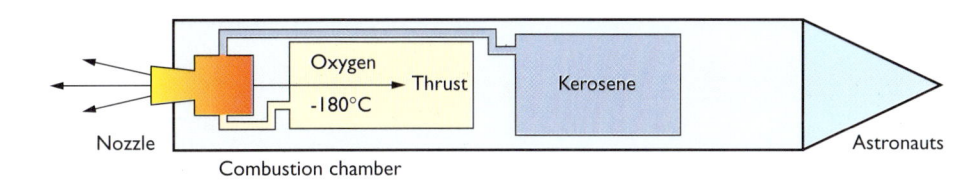

Ditching

When a space rocket is launched, the force that the exhaust gas exerts on the rocket causes the rocket to accelerate upwards. The Earth's gravitational pull will prevent the rocket from escaping from the Earth, unless the rocket is travelling fast enough. For a rocket to escape the Earth's gravitational pull, it must reach a speed of more than 11 000 m/s. To reduce the amount of fuel required, a clever trick is used. When a rocket reaches a certain speed, its mass is reduced. This is usually done by releasing empty fuel tanks or the lower stage of the rocket. The rocket motor now exerts a force on a smaller mass and therefore its acceleration will increase.

Taking off

Close to the Earth's surface, the gravitational pull (force of gravity or weight of the rocket) on the rocket is very large. This means that a large force (or thrust) must be exerted by the rocket engines (figure 7.15).

Unbalanced force (F_{un}) = engine thrust − weight of rocket

Acceleration of rocket (a) = $\dfrac{\text{unbalanced force}}{\text{mass of rocket}}$

The Saturn V rocket which launched the Apollo missions to the Moon had a total mass at lift-off of 3×10^6 kg. The rocket motors could exert a thrust of 3.3×10^7 N.

$$\begin{aligned}\text{Weight of rocket} &= mg \\ &= 3\,000\,000 \times 10 \\ &= 30\,000\,000 \text{ N}\end{aligned}$$

$$\begin{aligned}F_{un} &= \text{engine thrust} - \text{weight of rocket} \\ &= 33\,000\,000 - 30\,000\,000 \\ &= 3\,000\,000 \text{ N}\end{aligned}$$

$$a = \frac{F_{un}}{m} = \frac{3\,000\,000}{3\,000\,000} = 1 \text{ m/s}^2$$

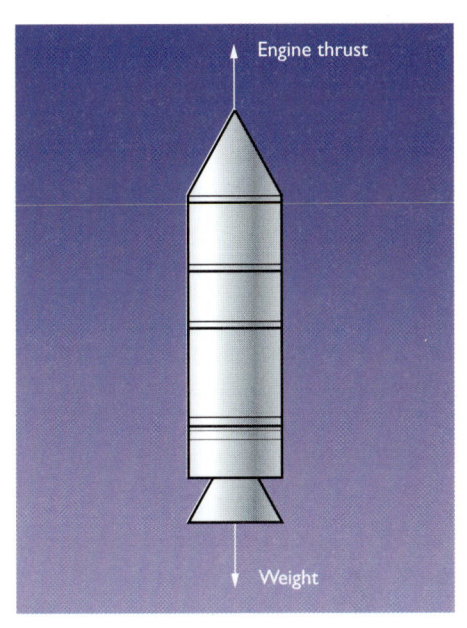

FIGURE 7.15

171

In outer space, where the gravitational field strength is zero, the weight of the rocket is zero. In this case:

Unbalanced force on rocket = engine thrust

You should note that the effect did not occur with the Apollo spacecraft, since there was never a chance that it could travel to deep space.

A Space Shuttle rocket engine can produce a thrust of 10 000 N when fired to reposition the Shuttle in space. The Shuttle has a total mass of 75 000 kg.

$$\text{Acceleration of Shuttle} = \frac{\text{unbalanced force}}{\text{mass}}$$

$$= \frac{\text{engine thrust}}{\text{mass}}$$

$$= \frac{10\,000}{75\,000}$$

$$= 0.13 \text{ m/s}^2$$

Acceleration due to gravity

An object falling near the surface of the Earth accelerates (if the effects of air resistance are negligible). This acceleration is called the acceleration due to gravity (g).

Consider two bodies of mass 2 kg and 7 kg, falling near the surface of the Earth. We are assuming that there is no friction present.

Weight = force of gravity	Weight = force of gravity
= mg	= mg
= 2 × 10	= 7 × 10
= 20 N	= 70 N

Since we are assuming no friction is present:

Unbalanced force = F_{un} = weight	Unbalanced force = F_{un} = weight
= 20 N	= 70 N
$a = \dfrac{F_{un}}{m} = \dfrac{20}{2}$	$a = \dfrac{F_{un}}{m} = \dfrac{70}{7}$
= 10 m/s²	= 10 m/s²

This shows clearly that the acceleration due to gravity in the absence of friction (air resistance) is the same for **all** bodies no matter what their mass is.

The acceleration due to gravity on a planet has the same value as the gravitational field strength on the planet. For example:

- On any planet: acceleration due to gravity = gravitational field strength
- On Jupiter: gravitational field strength = 25 N/kg
  acceleration due to gravity = 25 m/s²

7 space physics

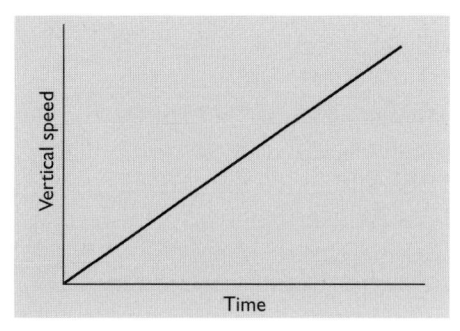

FIGURE 7.16

Measuring the acceleration due to gravity
Using a light gate, computer and a piece of card cut as a mask, we can calculate the acceleration due to gravity. The card is dropped through the light gate, from different heights, and the acceleration measured in each case.

Height (m)	Acceleration (m/s²)
0.5	10.2
1.0	9.8
1.5	9.9

The height the body is released from does not affect the acceleration. For the Earth, the acceleration due to gravity, $g = 10$ m/s².

A graph of speed against time for a body dropped vertically, from rest, near the Earth's surface (ignoring air resistance) is shown in figure 7.16.

Weight on the Earth and other planets
The weight of an object near the surface of a planet such as the Earth is the pull of the planet on the object. Like all forces, the weight is measured in newtons.

The pull of gravity on a falling object (the weight) can be calculated using the equation:

$$W = mg$$
$$\text{Weight} = \text{mass} \times \text{gravitational field strength}$$

The value of g on the Earth = 10 N/kg.

The pull of gravity per kilogram mass on a planet is called its gravitational field strength. Gravitational field strength is measured in newtons per kilogram (N/kg or N kg⁻¹). The table on the left shows the weight of objects on the Earth.

The table below shows the weight of a 1 kg mass on different planets and the Moon.

Weight (N)	Mass (kg)
10	1
300	30
4	0.4
1	0.1
500	50
0.3	0.03

Planet	Weight of 1 kg (N)	Gravitational field strength (N/kg)
Mercury	4	4
Venus	9	9
Earth	10	10
Mars	4	4
Jupiter	25	25
Saturn	10	10
Uranus	10	10
Neptune	12	12
Moon	1.6	1.6

7 standard grade physics

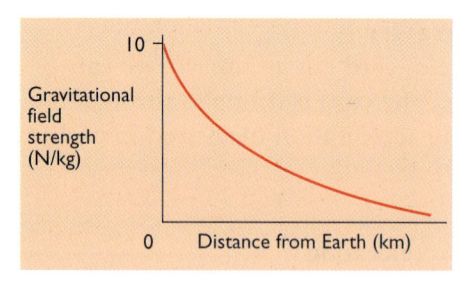

FIGURE 7.17 *Change in gravitational field strength*

Effect of distance on gravitational field strength

As a spacecraft rises from the surface of the Earth, the pull of the Earth's gravity on it gets smaller and smaller. Figure 7.17 shows a graph of gravitational field strength, *g*, against distance. Astronauts in orbit around the Earth (usually about 200 km above the surface) appear to be weightless. True weightlessness can happen only where the pull of gravity is zero.

The Space Shuttle

The Space Shuttle (figure 7.18) is a reusable craft that can carry payloads and crews to and from space. On the launch pad, it is joined to two solid fuel rocket boosters and a large external fuel tank. The boosters help lift the craft away from the Earth's gravitational pull and then they fall away into the ocean where they can be retrieved for further use. The external tank is not reused and holds a total of over 700 000 kg of fuel. The fuel from this tank is used to position the shuttle to a point just short of its final orbit. The tank then separates and falls back into the ocean. The Shuttle then coasts for a few seconds and fires its two orbital engines to put it into the correct position for its orbit. At launch, you would hear the immense roar of the engines. You would experience an acceleration of about three times that of the pull of gravity. (This is about the same level of discomfort as if you turn a corner much too fast in a car.) This happens for a short time near the two-minute mark, just before the two solid fuel boosters burn out and drop off. About five minutes later the liquid tank empties and separates and re-enters the atmosphere. This happens about 185 km from the Earth (figure 7.19).

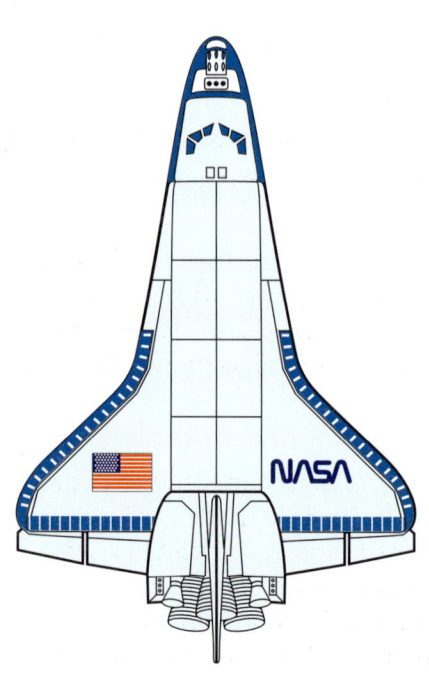

FIGURE 7.18

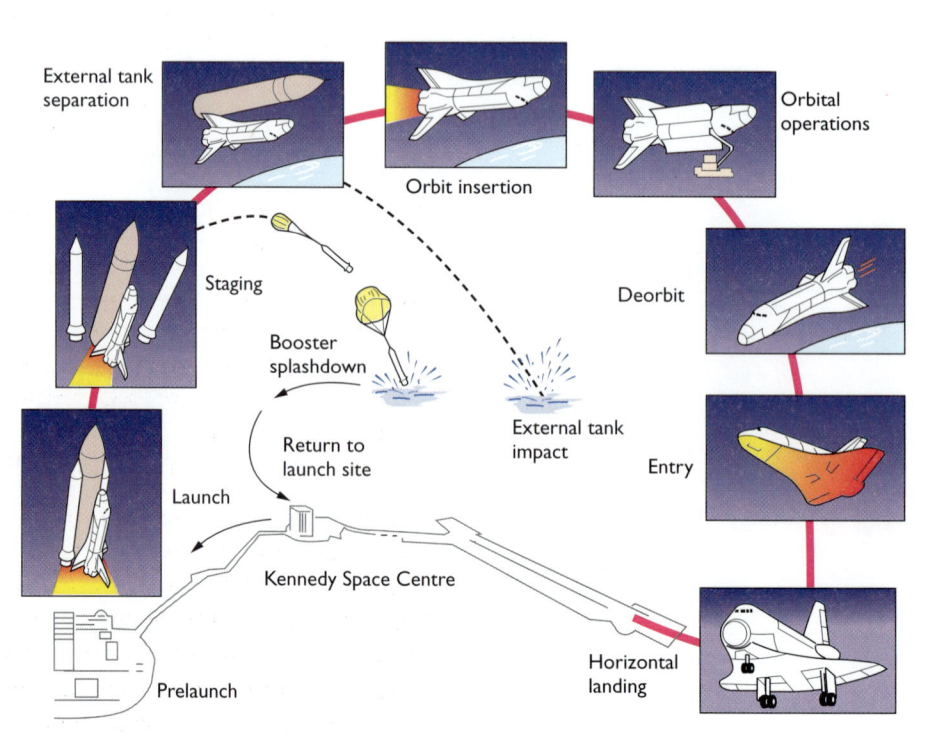

FIGURE 7.19 *Space Shuttle typical mission profile*

174

space physics 7

The Space Shuttle, or the Space Transportation System (STS), is launched vertically. At launch, it has a total mass of 2.05×10^6 kg and the thrust developed by the engines is 2.1×10^7 N. Once in orbit, the cargo doors open to allow experiments to take place, satellites to be launched and observations to be made. The duration of the flight depends on the nature of the experiments to be carried out. In orbit, the Orbital Manoeuvring System engines can be used to alter the orbit of the Shuttle orbiter. When all experiments are complete, the cargo doors are closed and the crew prepare for re-entry into the Earth's atmosphere. The Shuttle is about the same length and weight as a commercial aircraft. Its appearance, however, is very different. The absence of the triangular wings and a large cargo bay where passengers would be gives the Shuttle a different look.

Re-entry

Before re-entry, each astronaut puts on a special suit which is really an inflatable pair of pants. This prevents the blood from pooling into the lower part of the body and causing blackout. One hour before landing, the speed of the Shuttle is reduced by turning it backwards. The two small engines ignite and the burn takes it out of its orbit. The Shuttle begins to drop. While it falls, the pilot turns it round again and pulls its nose up. After 30 minutes, the shuttle has entered the Earth's atmosphere at a height of 120 km. It will then be programmed by the computers to cover a distance of 6400 km and drop 120 km in the next 30 minutes. When it re-enters the atmosphere, there is a communications blackout. On re-entry, the intense heat produced by friction will cause the temperature to reach about 1650°C on the surface of the nose and the leading edges of the wings. As the craft slows down, it will reach a height of 23 km and, travelling at 550 m/s, it will be lined up with the flight path.

The approach will start at 4000 m and there will be no noise, since the Shuttle will land like a glider. Its speed will now be about 150 m/s and its angle of descent will be about seven times that of an ordinary aircraft. At a height of 500 m it levels off. The landing wheels come down at a height of 90 m and the speed on touch-down will be about 90 m/s (figure 7.20).

FIGURE 7.20

Satellites

We have learned to make use of space in many ways, but most of the benefits affecting people on Earth are brought about by unmanned satellites.

Communication satellites

A number of satellites called Intelsat are in orbit. They are nearly always in geostationary orbits. They have the capacity to cope with a number of television channels and a large number of telephone calls. An Intelsat satellite is about the size of a house. Other communication satellites can handle up to 24 000 telephone calls each.

Astronomy and solar satellites

One of the problems of observing the Sun, planets and distant galaxies from Earth is the absorption and bending of light and other radiations by the atmosphere. The answer is to put a telescope in a satellite in orbit above the atmosphere, and to send the information gathered back to Earth. Astronomy and solar satellites are greatly improving our knowledge of the Universe. The picture on the front cover shows the Hubble telescope being repaired in space.

Navigation satellites

Most aeroplanes and ships can receive signals from navigation satellites. There are 24 navigation satellites orbiting the Earth, positioned in such a way that six are always visible to the user. The user has a receiver-computer which locks on to signals from the satellites and uses the information from the satellites to calculate his position and speed. It is possible to work out one's position to within a few metres using satellite navigation.

Weather satellites

Some weather satellites such as Meteosat are in geostationary orbits, while others such as NOAA9 are in polar orbits. Scanners on the satellites build up visible light and infrared pictures of the Earth, which are then transmitted back to weather stations. This information helps meteorologists to make more accurate short-term weather forecasts. These satellites tend to be in lower orbits than the communication satellites, since they orbit more times during the day.

Earth resource satellites

It is possible, by looking at the radiation from a crop, to tell the crop type and even whether there is any disease present. Satellites such as Landsat are used to work out how much of the various crops are being grown and whether they are healthy. Other uses include looking for pollution, forest fires or even locating natural resources such as oil.

Projectile motion

There is a wide variety of objects in orbit around the Earth, ranging in size from satellites the size of a house to an astronaut's glove. To understand how it is possible for these objects to stay in orbit, we study objects moving horizontally and vertically at the same time. These are called projectiles.

If a body is projected horizontally at 16 m/s, then its inertia (unwillingness to change its motion) should tend to keep it moving at 16 m/s horizontally (in a straight line). Due to the force of gravity (the body's weight) this is not possible and the body experiences a force pulling it downwards, while it tries to move horizontally at constant speed. To overcome this conflict between its inertia and its weight, the body follows a curved path (figure 7.21). This is called **projectile motion**. The motion of the projectile is therefore made up of two separate motions.

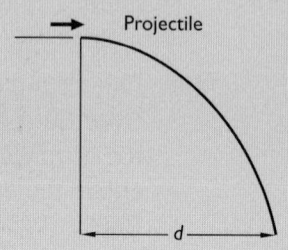

FIGURE 7.21 *Projectile motion*

space physics 7

1 A vertical motion under the influence of the force of gravity.
2 A horizontal motion under the influence of its inertia.

Look at the photo of a ball being projected, and a ball being dropped vertically at the same time.

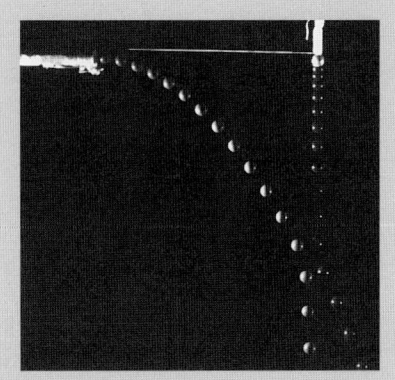

FIGURE 7.22

The vertical motion of the projectile and the free-falling body are in step all the way down. This means that the vertical motion of the projectile is the same as a free-falling body, that is, both are accelerating with a downward acceleration of 10 m/s². This is the acceleration due to gravity which was discussed earlier.

The horizontal spacing between the images of the projectile are all equal. This means that the horizontal motion of the projectile is at a constant speed and is equal to the speed of projection.

The motion of a projectile can be treated as two independent motions.

1 Constant speed in the horizontal direction.
2 Constant acceleration in the vertical direction due to the force of gravity.

These two motions are shown in figure 7.23.

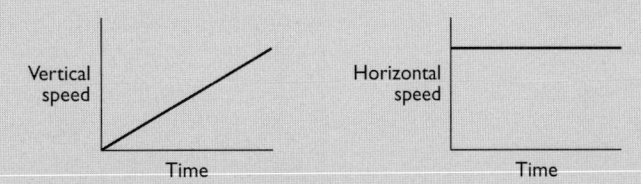

FIGURE 7.23 *Horizontal and vertical motions*

When solving problems, we can treat the motion in the horizontal direction **separately** from the motion in the vertical direction.

Example: A flare is fired out to sea from a cliff top at a horizontal speed of 40 m/s. The flare takes 3 s to reach the sea.

(a) What is its horizontal speed after 3 s?

(b) Calculate its vertical speed after 3 s.

(c) Draw a graph of vertical speed against time and use it to calculate the height of the cliff top.

177

7 standard grade physics

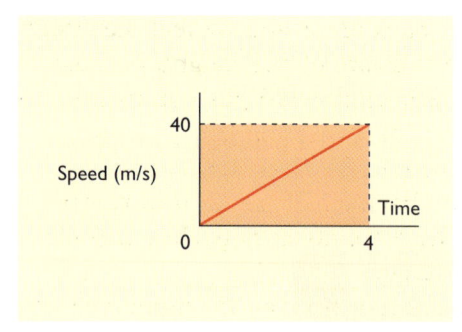

FIGURE 7.24

Solution:

(a) Horizontal speed remains at 40 m/s.
(b) Using $v - u = at$ for the vertical motion, where $u = 0$, $a = g = 10$ m/s^2 and $t = 3$ s.
$$v - 0 = 3 \times 10$$
$$= 30 \text{ m/s}$$
(c) The graph is shown in figure 7.24. The height of the cliff is the area under the graph.
$$\text{Distance} = \tfrac{1}{2} \times \text{base} \times \text{height}$$
$$= 0.5 \times 3 \times 30$$
$$= 45 \text{ m}$$

Newton's satellite

Newton, in considering the motion of the Moon around the Earth carried out the following 'thought experiment': Suppose a bullet is fired horizontally from a gun situated on top of a high mountain. The bullet will have two motions which occur simultaneously.

1 A horizontal motion at uniform speed (if air resistance is negligible).
2 A vertical motion with an acceleration of 10 m/s^2 towards the Earth under the action of the gravitational attraction between the bullet and the Earth.

As a result, the bullet will follow a curved path and will hit the ground no matter how fast it was fired, as long as the Earth is flat. However, the approximation of the 'flat' Earth is only valid over a limited range. For a 'round' Earth, it becomes important to take the curvature of the Earth into account for projectiles of long range (figure 7.25).

If there was no force of gravity, the bullet would follow the path AB because if no forces act on it, it must travel with a uniform speed in a straight line. Due to the gravitational field of the Earth, the bullet falls continuously below this line. If the bullet falls below the line AB faster than the Earth's surface curves away under it, the bullet will still hit the Earth, e.g. at the point C or D according to the bullet's speed.

If the bullet were fired at such a speed that it fell vertically at the same rate as the Earth's surface curved away under it, then it would always be at the same height above the surface. The bullet would then never reach the surface, but would circle it at a constant altitude. This was the first theory of the artificial satellite. Remember Newton 'thought' about this experiment long before we had rockets or satellites.

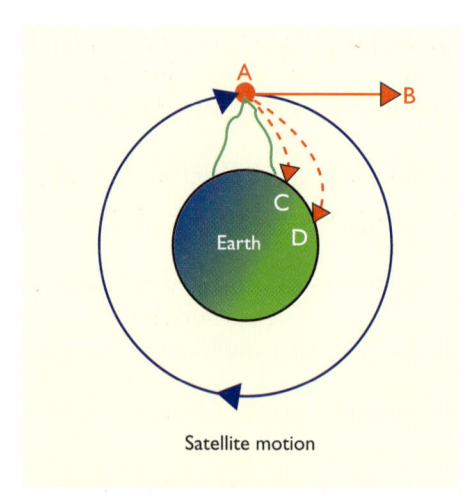

FIGURE 7.25 *Newton's thought experiment. When an object is projected at the correct speed it never reaches the ground because the earth is curved, so it remains in orbit in free-fall*

Weightlessness

When astronauts are floating around a space vehicle, we say that they are weightless (figure 7.26).

Weight is a force which pulls us down towards the ground. This causes us to exert a force on the ground. Using Newton's Third Law, the

space physics 7

FIGURE 7.26

ground must exert the same size of force back on us and we feel the effect of the ground supporting us. We are made aware of our weight, because the ground (or whatever supports us) exerts an upward push on us as a result of the downward push our feet exert on the ground.

When you stand in a lift, you push down on the floor. Using our knowledge of forces, the floor pushes you back up. If the lift is at rest or moving up or down at constant speed, there are no extra pushes or pulls on you, so you will appear to weigh the same.

If the lift accelerates upwards, the floor will push you up with a greater force. The reaction is that you will push down with a larger force and you will appear to weigh more.

If the lift accelerates downwards, the floor will push you up with a smaller force. Again you will push down with a smaller force and you will appear to weigh less. If our feet were unsupported we would experience 'weightlessness'. Passengers in a lift with a continual downward acceleration of 10 m/s^2 would get no support from the floor, since they, too, would be falling with the same acceleration. There is no upward push on them and so no sensation of weight is felt. This is experienced briefly when we jump off a wall or dive into a swimming pool. You do still have weight. You just do not experience it.

If an astronaut is in space at a height of 1000 km above the surface of the Earth, the Earth's gravitational field strength (about 7.3 N/kg) is still strong enough to exert a force and pull the astronaut towards the floor of the spaceship. However, at the same time there is a force acting on the spaceship accelerating it downwards, so the floor of the spaceship tends to fall away from the astronaut. If the floor of the spaceship falls away from the astronaut **at the same rate as the astronaut is falling**, the floor will not be in contact with the astronaut. The floor exerts no force on the astronaut so that weightlessness is felt.

The astronaut and the spaceship are two projectiles in a continual state of free-fall, **both accelerating towards the Earth with the same acceleration**. This state is called weightlessness.

True weightlessness can only be experienced by a spaceship in an area where the gravitational field strength is equal to zero. This is deep in space.

Re-entry and friction

When a spacecraft re-enters the Earth's atmosphere, it is travelling at about 11 100 m/s. It collides with the air particles of the atmosphere, causing a large force of friction on the spacecraft, which is slowed down. The work done by friction reduces the kinetic energy of the spacecraft. This kinetic energy is changed into heat energy. Some of the heat energy is 'lost' to the surroundings. However, some of the heat energy produced is absorbed by the spacecraft and is enough to raise the temperature to around 1300°C.

The Space Shuttle makes an unpowered glide through the atmosphere and lands on a runway using its wheels, just like an ordinary aircraft. Since it has no power, it can only attempt this in one try. Other returning spacecraft use parachutes to slow the spacecraft down and make a gentle 'splashdown' in the sea or on the land.

7 standard grade physics

Spacecraft design

Apollo

The heat shield on the Apollo craft was made from a honeycomb of stainless steel to which an epoxy resin coating was bonded. Apollo hit the atmosphere at an angle and this allowed the thickness of the heat shield to be varied to cut down on the overall weight of the craft. Pitch control rockets rotated the craft to ensure that the thickest part of the shield hit the atmosphere first, as the intense heat could have burned through the thinner sections of the shield. Some lift was also obtained from the shape of the capsule, to enable the re-entry corridor to be selected. Vaporising metal from the shield carried away most of the heat, reducing its thickness to less than a centimetre (figure 7.27).

FIGURE 7.27

Shuttle

The Shuttle is made from aluminium alloy covered in special tiles to protect it from the intense heat. Each Shuttle orbiter will require almost 34 000 thermal protection tiles in different sizes, shapes and thicknesses. The material of the tiles must be able to withstand repeated heating and cooling plus extreme noise and vibrations for up to 100 flights without replacement. The material is a high-purity silica compound which sheds heat so quickly that a piece of material can be held in an ungloved hand only seconds after removal from an extremely hot oven (although the interior of the tile glows red hot!). Tiles for the underside of the Shuttle and other areas exposed to high temperatures up to 1300°C receive a black glass coating. For lower temperature use (up to 700°C), a white silica compound is used with shiny alumina oxide added to reflect the Sun's rays and keep the Shuttle cool while in orbit. The tiles are also treated to protect them from absorbing extra water and adding weight to the craft (figure 7.28).

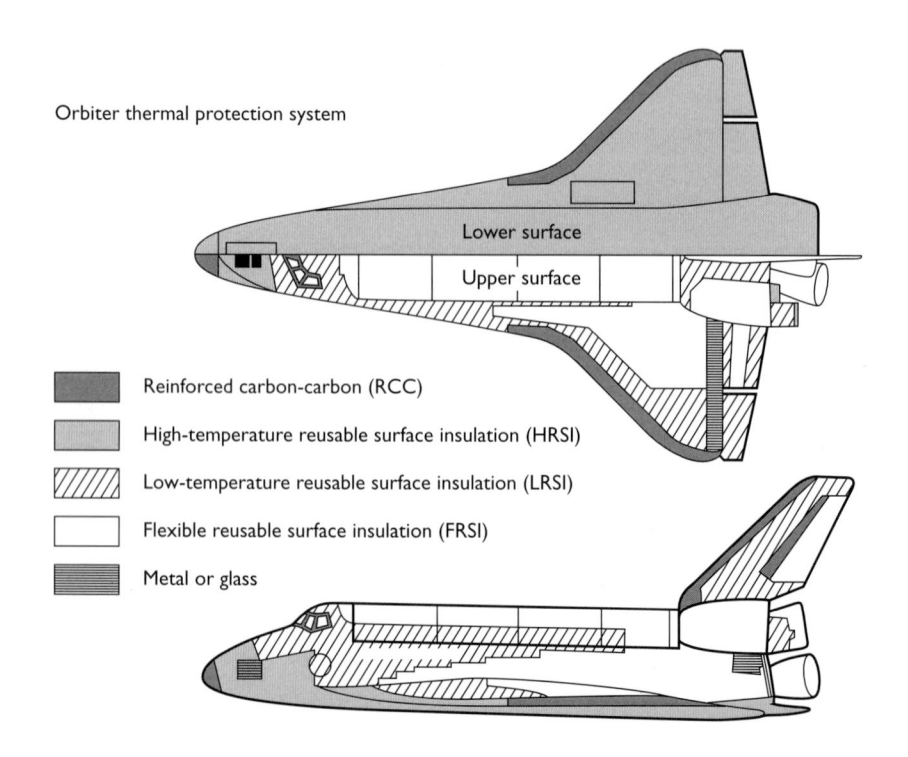

FIGURE 7.28

space physics

> **Example:** A heat shield on a spacecraft has a mass of 50 kg. The spacecraft is travelling at 1000 m/s. On re-entry into the Earth's atmosphere, the speed is reduced to 200 m/s.
>
> (a) Calculate the change in kinetic energy of the heat shield.
>
> (b) If all of this loss in kinetic energy is changed into heat in the shield, calculate the change in temperature (ΔT) of the shield (specific heat capacity of the heat shield is 1050 J/kg°C).
>
> *Solution:* (a) E_k initially $= \frac{1}{2}mu^2$
> $= \frac{1}{2} \, 50 \, (1000)^2$
> $= 2.5 \times 10^7$ J
> $= 25\,000\,000$ J
> E_k finally $= \frac{1}{2}mv^2$
> $= \frac{1}{2} \times 50 \times (200)^2$
> $= 1 \times 10^6$ J
> $= 1\,000\,000$ J
> Difference in kinetic energy $= 24\,000\,000$ J $= 2.4 \times 10^7$ J
> (b) $E_h = mc\Delta T$
> $2.4 \times 10^7 = mc\Delta T$
> $2.4 \times 10^7 = 50 \times 1050 \times \Delta T$
> $\Delta T = 460$°C

Space forms both a beginning of an adventure for humankind and the end of this book. Let us end on a note of hope:

> It is difficult to say what is impossible, for the dream of yesterday is the hope of today and the reality of tomorrow.
>
> *Robert Goddard, space pioneer*

LEARNING OUTCOMES

After studying this chapter you should be able to:

Section 7.1

1. Use correctly in context the following terms: Moon, planet, Sun, Star, Solar System, galaxy, Universe.

2. State approximate values for the distance from the Earth to the Sun, to the next nearest star, and to the edge of our galaxy in terms of the time for light to cover these distances.

3. Draw a diagram showing the main features of a refracting telescope (objective, eyepiece, light-tight tube).

4. State that the objective lens produces an image which is magnified by the eyepiece.

5. State that different colours of light correspond to different wavelengths.

6. List the following colours in order of wavelength: red, green, blue.

7. State that white light can be split into different colours using a prism.

8. State that the line spectrum produced by a source provides information about the atoms within the source.

9. State that there exists a large family of waves with a wide range of wavelengths which all travel at the speed of light.

10. State that telescopes can be designed to detect radio waves.

11. Use correctly in context the term 'light year'. [Credit]

12. Draw a ray diagram to show the formation of an image by a magnifying glass. [Credit]

13. Explain why the brightness of an image depends on the diameter of the objective. [Credit]

14. Classify as members of the electromagnetic spectrum the following radiations: gamma rays, X-rays, ultraviolet, visible light, infrared, microwaves, TV and radio. [Credit]

15. List the above radiations in order of wavelength (and frequency). [Credit]

16. Give an example of a detector for each of the above radiations. [Credit]

17. Explain why different kinds of telescope are used to detect signals from space. [Credit]

Section 7.2

1. State that a rocket is pushed forward because the 'propellant' is pushed back.

2. Explain simple situations involving the rule: A pushes B, B pushes A back.

3. Carry out calculations involving thrust, mass and acceleration.

4. Explain why a rocket motor need not be kept on during interplanetary flight.

5. State that the force of gravity near the Earth's surface gives all objects the same acceleration (if the effects of air resistance are negligible).

6. State that the weight of an object on the Moon or on different planets is different from its weight on Earth.

7. State that objects in free-fall appear weightless.

8. Explain the curved path of a projectile in terms of force of gravity.

9. State that an effect of friction is the transformation of E_k into heat.

10. State that Newton's Third Law is: 'If A exerts a force on B, B exerts an equal but opposite force on A'. [Credit]

11. Identify 'Newton pairs' in situations involving several forces. [Credit]

12. Explain the equivalence of acceleration due to gravity and the gravitational field strength. [Credit]

13. Carry out calculations involving the relationship between: weight, mass, acceleration due to gravity and/or gravitational field strength (including situations where g is not equal to 10 N/kg). [Credit]

14. Use correctly in context the following terms: mass, weight, inertia, gravitational field strength, acceleration due to gravity. [Credit]

15. State that the weight of a body decreases as its distance from the Earth increases. [Credit]

learning outcomes

16 Explain how projectile motion can be treated as two independent motions and solve numerical problems using this method. **Credit**

17 Explain satellite motion as an extension of projectile motion. **Credit**

18 Carry out calculations involving the relationships:
$E_h = cm\Delta T$, work done = Fd and $E_k = \frac{1}{2}mv^2$. **Credit**

STUDY QUESTIONS

1 (a) State the time taken for the light to reach us from the nearest star excluding the sun.

(b) A telescope can be used to view distant stars.

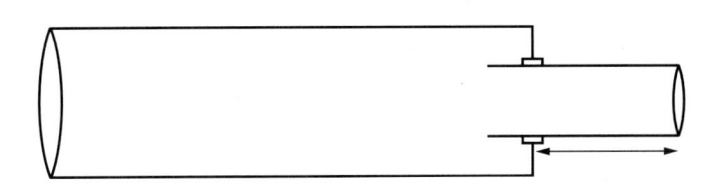

(i) Copy and label the diagram shown above to show the two different lenses of the telescope.

(ii) Some distant stars are very faint. How could the brightness of the image from the telescope be increased?

(c) In 1990, the Hubble telescope was launched from the Space Shuttle. This telescope produces images from above the Earth's atmosphere. Suggest why such a telescope can provide better images than one based on Earth.

2 The table below shows information about some members of the electromagnetic spectrum with decreasing wavelength.

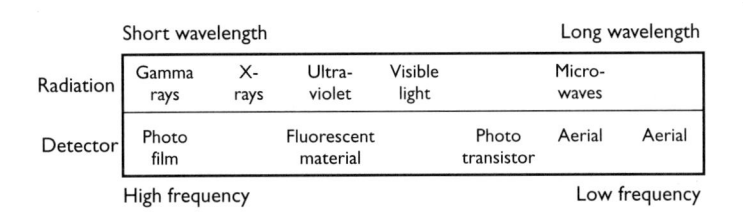

	Short wavelength				Long wavelength	
Radiation	Gamma rays	X-rays	Ultra-violet	Visible light		Micro-waves
Detector	Photo film		Fluorescent material		Photo transistor	Aerial	Aerial
	High frequency				Low frequency	

(a) What is the speed at which all the radiations travel?

(b) Copy and complete the table to show the two missing radiations and the detectors.

3 An object is placed as shown in front of a converging lens.

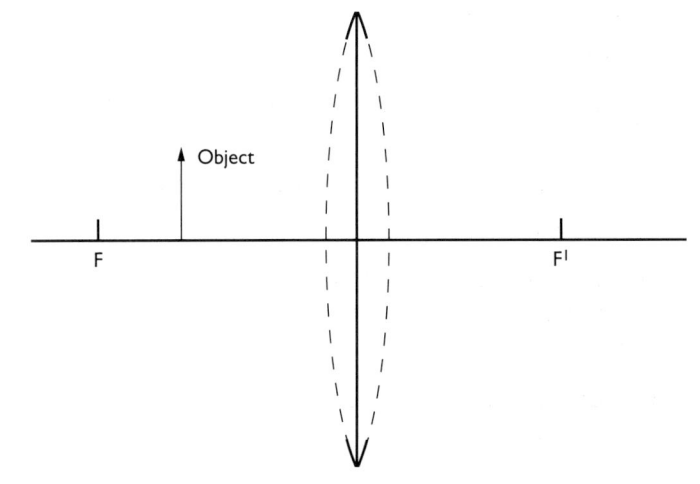

(a) Copy and complete the diagram to show how the final image is formed.

(b) This is part of an optical telescope. What other type of telescope can be used to detect radiations from stars?

4 The Galileo space probe was used to explore the atmosphere on Jupiter.

(a) Part of the probe had a mass of 80 kg. If this could have reached the surface of Jupiter, what would it weigh?

(b) Name a detector which could be carried by the probe so that the amount of gamma radiation could be measured.

(c) The probe was launched from the mother ship, which continued in orbit around Jupiter. Explain why the mother ship does not fall into the atmosphere of Jupiter.

183

study questions

5 During a space flight with the Shuttle, one of the astronauts was weightless, yet gravity was still acting on the spacecraft.

(a) Explain how this happens.

(b) At one point on the journey to the Moon, the rockets on the spacecraft exert a force of 12 500 N on the craft (which has a mass of 4000 kg). Calculate the acceleration of the craft.

(c) Explain why the action of the gases being forced out of the craft pushes the craft forward.

6 A spacecraft of mass of 750 kg is travelling at 350 m/s.

(a) Calculate the kinetic energy of the spacecraft.

(b) As the spacecraft passes through the atmosphere, its speed is reduced from 350 m/s to 200 m/s. Calculate the heat energy produced.

(c) The heat shield on the spacecraft has a mass of 60 kg and a specific heat capacity of 1100 J/kg/°C. Assuming that all the heat energy produced is absorbed by the shield, calculate the change in temperature of the shield.

7 Radio telescopes and optical telescopes are used to observe stars.

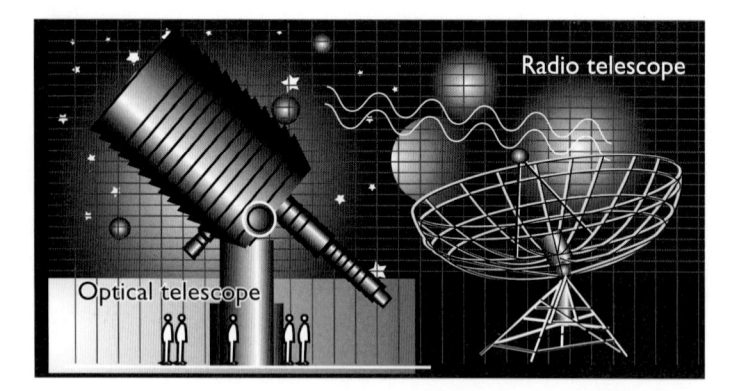

(a) The waves detected by the radio and optical telescopes have different wavelengths. How does the speed of the waves detected by the radio telescope compare with the speed of the waves detected by the optical telescope?
SEB   **GENERAL** KU

(b) Why is a **large** curved reflector necessary on a radio telescope which detects radio waves from a distant star?
SEB   **GENERAL** PS

(c) Light, collected by an optical telescope from a star, can be used to produce a line spectrum of the star. An example of the star's spectrum is shown below.

(i) What use is made of such a spectrum by astronomers studying the star?
GENERAL KU

(ii) What would you use to split a beam of white light into different colours?
SEB   **GENERAL** KU

8 (a) The navigation satellite shown in the figure below moves in a circular orbit above the Earth's atmosphere.

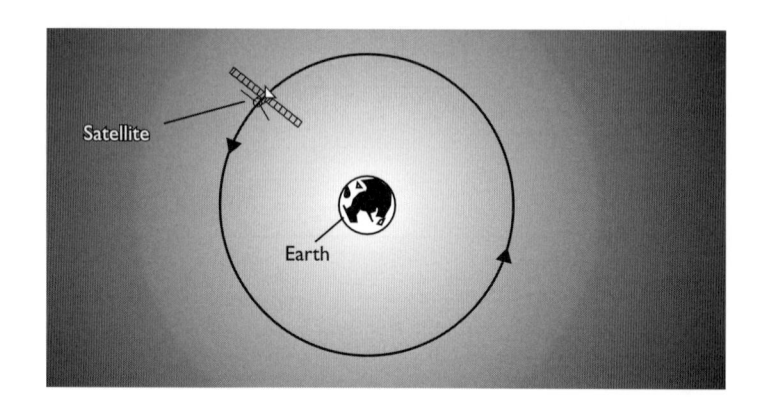

Explain why:

(i) the satellite does not move in a straight line into space;

(ii) the satellite does not fall straight down to Earth.
SEB   **GENERAL** KU

(b) The diagram below shows the flight plan for the journey to the Moon. At X the rocket motors are switched off and remain off until Z.

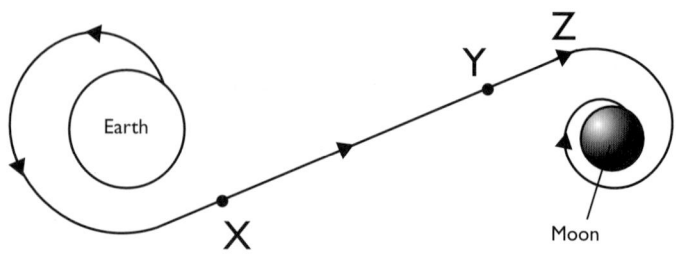

Explain why the rocket slowed down between X and Y and then speeded up between Y and Z.
SEB   **GENERAL** PS

184

study questions

9 A satellite of mass 80 kg orbits the Earth at a speed of 4000 m/s. The satellite is constructed mainly from a metal alloy of specific heat capacity 320 J/kg°C.

(a) Calculate the kinetic energy of the satellite when in orbit.
CREDIT KU

(b) Calculate the change in the temperature of the satellite which might be expected if all its kinetic energy is rapidly converted to heat energy as the satellite comes back to Earth.
CREDIT KU

(c) Suggest why, in practice, the change in temperature you have calculated in part (ii) will not be obtained.
SEB
CREDIT PS

10 The table below gives some information about our solar system.

	Mass (Earth masses)	Distance from Sun (million kilometres)	Weight of 1 kilogram at surface (newtons)
Sun	333 000	–	270
Mercury	0.06	58	4
Venus	0.82	110	9
Earth	1	150	10
Moon	0.013	150	1.6
Mars	0.11	228	4
Jupiter	318	780	26
Saturn	95	1430	11

(a) Which **planet** in the table has the greatest mass?
GENERAL PS

(b) Which object in the table is a star?
GENERAL PS

(c) On which two planets would you have the same weight?
GENERAL PS

(d) Which planet is nearest to Earth?
SEB
GENERAL PS

11 When a feather and a hammer are dropped together from the same height on the Moon, they hit the surface together. If the experiment is repeated on Earth, the hammer will land first. Explain why the same experiment gives two different results.
SEB
GENERAL PS

12 The distance from Earth to the nearest star, Proxima Centauri, is 4.3 light years. **Estimate** the month and year in which light radiated on May 15th 1991 from Proxima Centauri will be seen on Earth.
SEB
CREDIT PS

13 During space missions, crews experience the effect known as 'weightlessness'. 'Weightlessness' can be demonstrated on Earth. The diagram (a) below shows a person holding a newton balance from which a 2 kilogram mass is suspended. Diagram (b) shows the person shortly after stepping off a diving board.

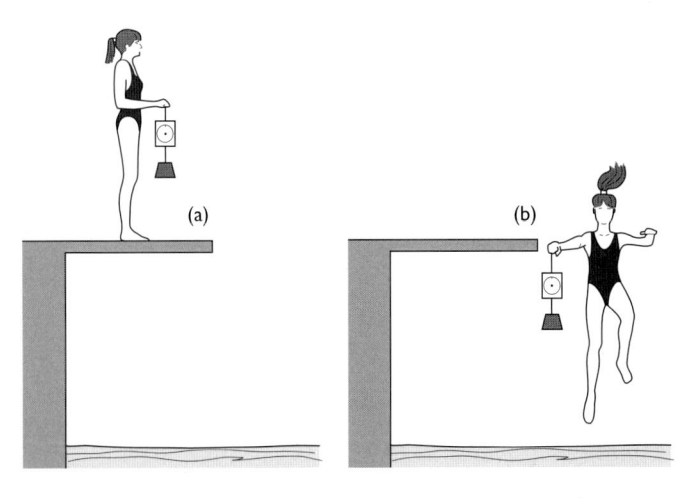

(a) What is the reading on the newton balance while the person is standing still on the board, as shown above?
GENERAL KU

(b) What happens to the reading on the newton balance as the person is falling towards the water?
SEB
GENERAL PS

14 A party of astronauts has carried out a scientific survey on the planet Mars. They are preparing to return to Earth in their spaceship. The on-board computer provides them with the following information about their lift-off.

> Constant thrust exerted by rocket motors = 160 000 N
> Mass of spaceship = 25 000 kg

(a) What is the weight of the spaceship on Mars? (The data you require will be found in the Data sheet on page 186.)
CREDIT KU

(b) (i) Draw a diagram showing the forces acting on the spaceship just as it lifts off.
CREDIT PS

(ii) Assuming that the mass of the spaceship remains constant, what is the acceleration during lift-off?
CREDIT KU

(c) If the same values for thrust and mass had been provided by the on-board computer on Earth, explain why the spaceship would not be able to lift off.
SEB
CREDIT PS

Data sheet

Speed of light in materials

Material	Speed in m/s
Air	3.0×10^8
Carbon dioxide	3.0×10^8
Diamond	1.2×10^8
Glass	3.0×10^8
Glycerol	2.1×10^8
Water	2.3×10^8

Gravitational field strengths

	Gravitational field strength on the surface (N/kg)
Earth	10
Jupiter	26
Mars	4
Mercury	4
Moon	1.6
Neptune	12
Saturn	11
Sun	270
Venus	9

Specific latent heat of fusion of materials

Material	Specific latent heat of fusion (J/kg)
Alcohol	0.99×10^5
Aluminium	3.95×10^5
Carbon dioxide	1.80×10^5
Copper	2.05×10^5
Glycerol	1.81×10^5
Lead	0.25×10^5
Water	3.34×10^5

Specific latent heat of vaporisation of materials

Material	Specific latent heat of vaporisation (J/kg)
Alcohol	11.2×10^5
Carbon dioxide	3.77×10^5
Glycerol	8.30×10^5
Turpentine	2.90×10^5
Water	22.6×10^5

Speed of sound in materials

Material	Speed (m/s)
Aluminium	5200
Air	340
Bone	3000
Carbon dioxide	270
Glycerol	1900
Muscle	1600
Steel	5200
Tissue	1500
Water	1500

Specific heat capacity of materials

Material	Specific heat capacity (J/kg°C)
Alcohol	2350
Aluminium	902
Copper	386
Diamond	530
Glass	500
Glycerol	2400
Ice	2100
Lead	128
Water	4180

Melting and boiling points of materials

Material	Melting point (°C)	Boiling point (°C)
Alcohol	−98	65
Aluminium	660	2470
Copper	1077	2567
Glycerol	18	290
Lead	328	1737
Turpentine	−10	156

SI prefixes and multiplication factors

Prefix	Symbol	Factor	
mega	M	1 000 000	$= 10^6$
kilo	k	1000	$= 10^3$
milli	m	0.001	$= 10^{-3}$
micro	µ	0.000 001	$= 10^{-6}$

Electrical and electronic graphical symbols

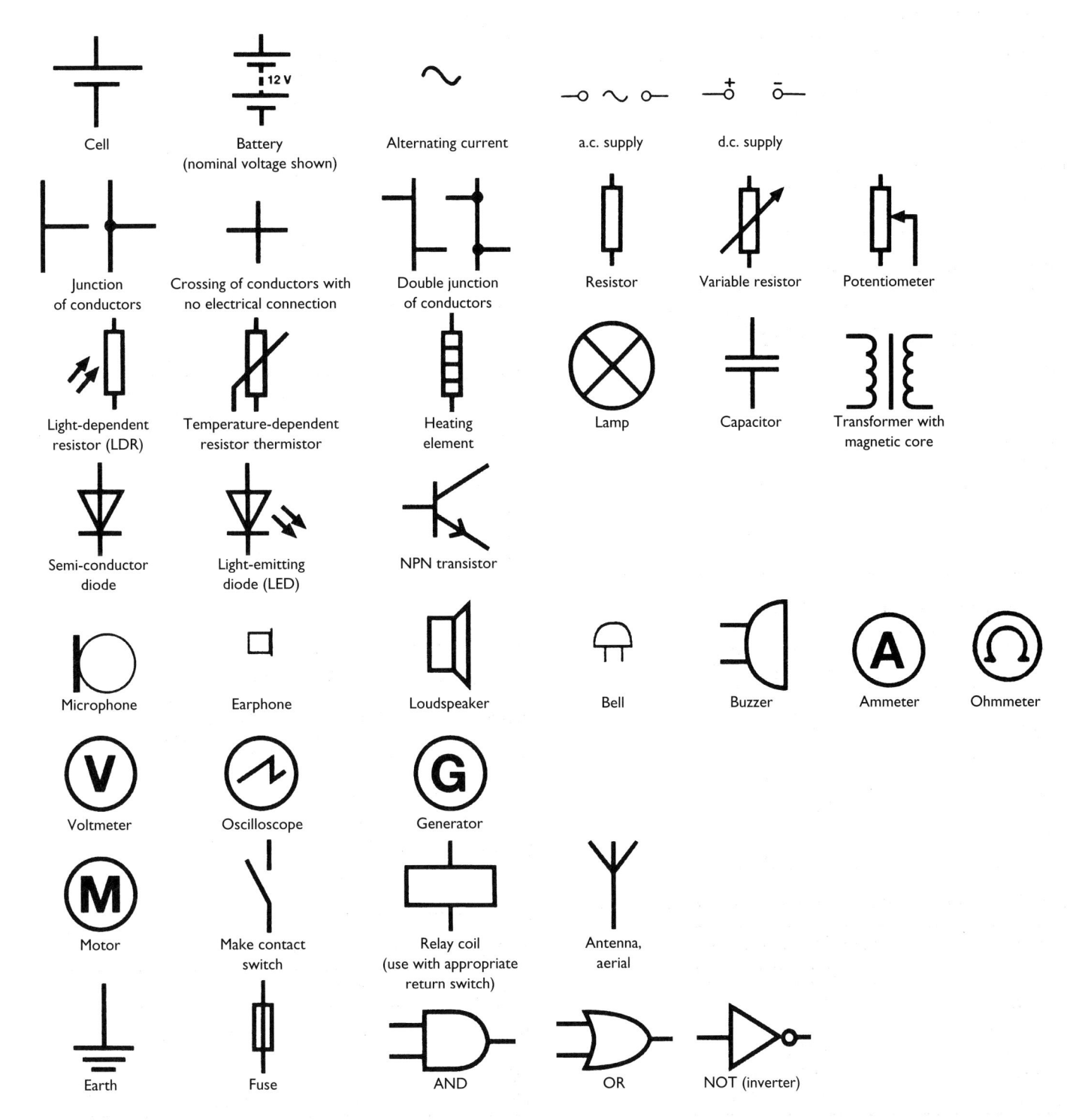

Symbol	Name
	Cell
	Battery (nominal voltage shown)
	Alternating current
	a.c. supply
	d.c. supply
	Junction of conductors
	Crossing of conductors with no electrical connection
	Double junction of conductors
	Resistor
	Variable resistor
	Potentiometer
	Light-dependent resistor (LDR)
	Temperature-dependent resistor thermistor
	Heating element
	Lamp
	Capacitor
	Transformer with magnetic core
	Semi-conductor diode
	Light-emitting diode (LED)
	NPN transistor
	Microphone
	Earphone
	Loudspeaker
	Bell
	Buzzer
	Ammeter
	Ohmmeter
	Voltmeter
	Oscilloscope
	Generator
	Motor
	Make contact switch
	Relay coil (use with appropriate return switch)
	Antenna, aerial
	Earth
	Fuse
	AND
	OR
	NOT (inverter)

Index

acceleration 114, 119
  due to gravity 121, 172, 173
activity, radioactive 73
aerials 8, 10, 17, 105
alternating current (a.c.) 29, 30
alternator 147, 148
analogue signal 86, 104
ampere 30
amplitude 5, 9, 104, 105
ammeter connection 30
amplifier 8–10, 105–107
AND-gate 100
analogue 86, 104
Apollo 164, 180
atom 28, 142
average speed 112, 113, 115

balanced forces 118, 121, 123
becquerel 73
binary code 89
biomass 140
body temperature 52–55
braking distance 128
brushes 47

cable television 20
capacitor 90, 91, 94, 95, 102, 113
car wiring 39
chain reaction 142
charge 28
circuit
  breaker 42, 43
  symbols 187
  tester 40
clinical thermometer 53
clock pulse generator 102, 103
coal 137, 141, 143
colour, mixing of 12
combined heat and power 53
communication with wires 4
commutator 47
conduction
  of heat 153
  of electricity 29
conductor, body as 28
convection 153, 154

cornea 61
coulomb 28, 29
counting circuits 103
crest 5
CT scan 69, 70

Data sheet 186
deceleration 114
decibel 57, 58
decoder 8, 10
diffraction 12, 13
digital signal 86
dioptres 62, 63
direct current (d.c.) 29, 30
dish aerials 17
dose equivalent 75
double insulation 26, 28
drag coefficient 117, 118
dynamo 146

efficiency 144, 145
electric
  bell 45
  charge 28, 29, 86, 87
  motor 46, 47
electromagnet 45
electromagnetic spectrum 64, 166, 167
electrons 28, 29
endoscope 66
energy conservation 124, 129, 137
eye 61
eyepiece 167, 168

fault finding 39
filament 32–34, 87
flexes 25, 27
fluorescent lamp 33, 34
focal length 62, 63
focus 62
force of gravity 120
forces 116–121
fossil fuels 137
frequency 5, 30
free-fall 123
friction 117, 130
fuses 26, 42

galaxy 165
gamma camera 78, 79
gas 137, 141
gas discharge 33
geostationary orbit 19, 175
gravitational
  field strength 120, 121, 124, 172–174
  potential energy 124

half life 73, 74
hearing loss 59
heat loss 154, 155
heat shield 180
hertz 5, 30
house wiring 41
Hubble 175, cover
hypothermia 54

image
  formation 168
  retention 11
inertia 122
infrared 65, 167
input 85
input devices 90–92
instantaneous speed 113, 114
insulators 29
Internet 20
inverter 99
ionisation 71
iris 61

jets 170

kilowatt hour 43
kinetic energy 125

lasers 67, 68
lenses 62–64, 167, 168
light-dependent resistor (LDR) 90, 94, 98
light-emitting diode (LED) 87
light year 165
lighting circuit 41, 42
logic gates 99
long sight 63
loudspeaker 5, 9, 10, 86, 105

188

index

magnetic field 44–47
mains voltage 30
mass 120
microphone 5, 90, 105
microwaves 17–19, 167
mirrors, plane 14
mobile phones 13, 14
modulation 8, 10
Moon 165, 178
Morse code 2

neutrons 28, 142
Newton 118
Newton's First Law 118
   satellite 178
   Second Law 119
   Third Law 170
normal 14, 59
NOT-gate 99, 102, 103
nuclear
   fission 142, 143
   power 142, 143
nucleus 28

objective lens 167, 168
octave 6
oil 137, 141
ohm 31
open circuit 39, 40
optical fibre 14–16, 66
OR-gate 100
output 85
   devices 86–89

parallel circuit 34, 36–39
period 19
pitch 6
picture build-up 11
planet 165
potentiometer 91
potential energy 124
power 32, 34, 125, 126
   gain 106
   hydroelectric 140, 143, 144
   of a lens 62, 63
   rating 25, 26
   station 137, 138, 142–148
   transmission 149
principal focus 62
prism 60, 166
process 85
   devices 96, 99, 104

projectile 176, 177
protons 28
pumped storage 144
pupil 61

radiation
   alpha 71, 72
   background 73–76
   beta 71, 72
   biological effect of 74
   gamma 71, 72
   heat 154
   ionising 71
radio 7–10
radioactive
   decay 73
   symbol 77
radiotherapy 77
rays, light 59, 60
reaction time 3, 128
reflection of light 14
refraction 59, 60
refrigerator 160
relay 46, 87
renewable energy sources 138–141
resistance, factors affecting 31
resistors
   in parallel 37–39
   in series 35, 36, 39
retina 61
ring circuit 41, 42
rockets 171
rotor 148

safety
   cars 127
   electrical 27, 28
   radiation 77
satellites 17, 19, 175, 176, 178
seat belts 122
series circuit 34–36, 39
seven-segment display 88, 89
short circuit 39, 40
short sight 64
Shuttle, Space 174, 175, 180
sievert 75
solar cell 90
solenoid 87
sound levels 57, 58
specific heat capacity 155, 156
specific latent heat 157–159

spectrum 166, 169
speed 3, 112–115
   of sound 4, 187
   of light 13, 165, 187
   of radio wave 7
   of telephone signal 6
   of television signal 7
   instantaneous 112, 113
speed–time graphs 115
star 165, 169
state, change of 158
stator 148
stethoscope 55
stopping distance 128

telephone 5, 20
telescope 167, 168
television 10–12
tidal energy 140
thermistor 90, 93, 97
thermocouple 90
thermometers 52, 53
thinking distance 128
total internal reflection 14
transformer 150, 151, 152
transducers 85
transistor switch 96–99
transmitter 5–7
trough 5
truth tables 99, 100
tuner 8, 10

ultrasound 56, 57
ultraviolet 65
Universe 165
unbalanced force 119

voltage 29
   divider 92, 93
   gain 106
voltmeter connections 30

wave energy 140
wavelength 5
weight 120, 173
weightlessness 178, 179
wiring, house 49
wiring a plug 27
work 123–126

X-rays 68, 69

Acknowledgements

The publishers would like to thank the following artists who drew the illustrations:
Phil Ford, Garry Nevin Associates, Tom Cross Illustration and Mike Feeney of Red Herring Design and Illustration.

We are grateful to the following companies, institutions and individuals who have given permission to reproduce photographs in this book. Every effort has been made to trace and acknowledge ownership of copyright. The publishers will be glad to make arrangements with any copyright holders whom it has not been possible to contact.

Agema Infrared Systems Ltd / SEPASU (65 bottom); J. Allan Cash (122); A. Baillie (31, 35, 36, 40, 43, 103, 104); Alex Bartel / Science Photo Library (45, 123); John Bayosi / Science Photo Library (67 bottom); Martin Bond / Science Photo Library (139 top and bottom, 140); British Telecommunications Plc (15, 16); Bruel and Kjaer (57 bottom); Dr Ray Clarke and Mervyn Goff / Science Photo Library (65 top); Clinical Radiology Department, Salisbury District Hospital / Science Photo Library (68 bottom, 69 bottom); CNRI / Science Photo Library (69 top, 70); Chris Davies (2); Martin Dohrn / Science Photo Library (121); Tim Fisher / Life File (2, 26, 50 left and right, 105 right); Vaughn Fleming / Science Photo Library (55); G-I Associates / Custom Medical Stock Photo / Science Photo Library (66); John Hadfield / Science Photo Library (59); Hodder & Stoughton (28, 46, 64); Bruce Iverson / Science Photo Library (44); Seth Joel / Science Photo Library (53); Kairos, Latin Stock / Science Photo Library (127); Kodansha, Japan (177); Mehau Kulyk / Science Photo Library (57 top); John Mead / Science Photo Library (167); Matt Meadows / Science Photo Library (78 bottom); NASA / Science Photo Library (164 left, 165, 170, 175, 179); Novosti, London (74); NTH / Custom Medical Stock Photo / Science Photo Library (67 top); David Parker / Science Photo Library (78 top, 118 bottom); Mark Paternostro / Science Photo Library (164 right); Philip Harris Instruments (117); Chris Priest and Mark Clarke / Science Photo Library (54); Roger Ressmeyer / Science Photo Library (34); Rimmer Brothers (57 middle); Science Museum / Science and Society Picture Library (180); Science Photo Library (85); Siemens Medical Engineering (69 middle, 77, 79); Space Telescope Science Institute / NASA / Science Photo Library (168); Heini Sschneebeli / Science Photo Library (56); Takeshi Takahara / Science Photo Library (118 top); Alexander Tsiaras / Science Photo Library (68 top); Andrew Ward / Life File (105 left); Frank Zullo / Science Photo Library (169).